Integrated Assurance

Building and sustaining cybersecurity in the enterprise isn't just a technical challenge; it is an organizational imperative. In a world where most guidance is geared toward mid-sized environments, *Integrated Assurance* fills a critical gap by addressing the realities of large, complex enterprises where traditional security practices break down.

This book introduces a strategic, business-aligned model for integrating cybersecurity and IT operations that acknowledges the friction between legacy systems and modern demands, global operations and local control, and innovation and compliance. It reframes security as an embedded operational function, not an isolated overlay.

With practical insights and a disciplined methodology, *Integrated Assurance* helps leaders navigate organizational silos, align teams around shared goals, and manage risk across fractured environments. It's a guide for those ready to move beyond checklists and fire drills and toward building systems that are resilient, secure by design, and aligned with business growth.

Ideal for CISOs, CIOs, enterprise architects, risk officers, and transformation leaders, this book is for anyone who lives at the intersection of complexity and accountability and who is ready to bridge the divide between security and operations.

Security, Audit and Leadership Series

Series Editor: Dan Swanson, Dan Swanson and Associates, Ltd., Winnipeg, Manitoba, Canada.

The scope and mandate for internal audit continues to evolve each year, as does the complexity of the business environment and speed of the changing risk landscape in which it must operate. The fundamental goal of this exciting series is to produce leading-edge books on critical subjects facing security and audit executives and practitioners. Key topics addressed include Leadership, Cybersecurity, Security Leadership, Privacy, Strategic Risk Management, Auditing IT, Audit Management and Leadership, and Operational Auditing.

Next-Generation Enterprise Security and Governance
Edited By Mohiuddin Ahmed, Nour Moustafa, Abu Barkat, Paul Haskell-Dowland

Auditing Information and Cyber Security Governance: A Controls-Based Approach
By Robert E. Davis

Evidence-Based Cybersecurity: Foundations, Research, and Practice
By Pierre-Luc Pomerleau, David Maimon

Operational Auditing: Principles and Techniques for a Changing World
By Hernan Murdock

The Security Leader's Communication Playbook: Bridging the Gap between Security and the Business
By Jeffrey W. Brown

The CISO 3.0: A Guide to Next-Generation Cybersecurity Leadership
By Walt Powell

Securing Talent: Building and Retaining High-Performance Cybersecurity Teams
By Kevin Lynn McLaughlin

Digitalization and Women's Rights: Volume 1
By Muharrem Kılıç and Sezer Bozkus Kahyaoglu

Analysis of Threat Perceptions: NATO and Türkiye's Cyber Terrorism Policies
By Mehmet Emin Erendor

Members, Methods, and Measures: Unlocking the Secrets of IT Leadership
By Thomas E. Armstrong

Philosophy.exe: The Techno-Philosophical Toolkit for Modern Minds
By Matthias Muhlert

Guardians of the Digital Age: Securing the Future
By ***Elçin Biren***

Ironwill 360° Leadership: A Blueprint for Level 5 Unicorn Leadership
By Douglas P. Pflug

Behavioral Insights in Cybersecurity: A Guide to Digital Human Factors
By Dustin S. Sachs

Integrated Assurance: Unified Risk Strategy
By Patrick Hayes

For more information about this series please visit: https://www.routledge.com/Security-Audit-and-Leadership-Series/book-series/CRCINTAUDITA?

Integrated Assurance

Unified Risk Strategy

Patrick Hayes

CRC Press
Taylor & Francis Group
Boca Raton London New York

CRC Press is an imprint of the
Taylor & Francis Group, an **informa** business

Designed cover image: Shutterstock Image ID 2553420179

First edition published 2026
by CRC Press
2385 NW Executive Center Drive, Suite 320, Boca Raton FL 33431

and by CRC Press
4 Park Square, Milton Park, Abingdon, Oxon, OX14 4RN

CRC Press is an imprint of Taylor & Francis Group, LLC

ISBN: 978-1-032-91073-4 (hbk)
ISBN: 978-1-032-91253-0 (pbk)
ISBN: 978-1-003-56215-3 (ebk)

DOI: 10.1201/9781003562153

Typeset in Times
by Newgen Publishing UK

To my wife, Yvonne. Your love has been my anchor, your strength my steady guide. Across countries, time zones, and countless journeys, you stood beside me with grace and courage. Every move we made and every challenge we faced, you met with unwavering support and quiet determination. This book, like so much of my life, exists because of you.

To my children, Olivia, Tadeus, and Adam. You are my reason and my hope. Growing up across countries and states, you have shown resilience, openness, and joy in the face of change. I hope you carry forward the spirit of adventure and the values of kindness, curiosity, and courage wherever life leads you.

Contents

Foreword

In recent years, businesses have been transformed by an accelerating wave of digital change. What used to be well-defined enterprise perimeters have dissolved into complex, hybrid infrastructures shaped by cloud platforms, connected devices, edge computing, AI workloads, and expanding third-party ecosystems. In this environment, risk is a central, strategic concern and no longer something managed on the periphery. Cybersecurity can no longer be a "bolt-on" siloed function, regardless of how well run it may be. It must contribute directly to strategic priorities, resilience planning, and competitive differentiation. The function must now be a real partner integrated into the enterprise architecture and a major participant in how business manages risk.

For years, the fragmentation between IT, cybersecurity, and risk was an outgrowth of conflicting goals. Governing frameworks have not been coordinated as part of an overall enterprise architecture that is centered around business outcomes. IT focuses on uptime and minimizing disruption, using frameworks like ITIL, COBIT, or ISO/IEC 2000 as a guide, while security teams follow NIST, CIS, or ISO 27001 to protect IT systems and data, and risk managers leverage ESRM, SABSA, and enterprise governance tools. Each group has performed as well as possible in isolation, but the world has changed. APIs now link systems across departments and vendors, cloud assets are spun up in minutes, and SaaS platforms store critical data. Integrating these operational functions with shared goals and measurements has become urgent because this isolation puts organizations at risk.

The risks our enterprises are faced with aren't just technical anymore, nor are they always in our control. There are growing challenges from misconfigured third-party applications, BYOD and IoT devices, and vulnerabilities from integration points. A partner's breach can quickly and easily become our own breach. Data sovereignty, localization, and compliance evidence readiness also require well-designed and coordinated efforts across departments. These are fundamental business risks, and without a cross-functional structure and continuous risk intelligence, these risks stay hidden until they trigger a crisis.

Today's CISOs are required to be more than cybersecurity experts. They are expected to be the translator of risk. They need to be able to explain exposure, cost, and impact in clear business terms. They have to provide options and articulate the business value of risk mitigation strategies, not in abstract technical controls but the impact on revenue, customer trust, and resilience. CISOs are the custodians of enterprise risk, entrusted with navigating the chaotic landscape of cyberattacks, insider threats, leaks of intellectual property, and managing breach disclosures.

This is where Integrated Assurance fits in.

Not just another framework or compliance checklist, Integrated Assurance is the strategic unification of IT, cybersecurity, and risk. Unlike many other texts that consider these as adjacent or complementary disciplines, this book argues they must coevolve through a unified strategy. Most frameworks treat integration as optional; Integrated Assurance treats it as foundational.

Offering strategic insights on issues like global operations, third-party risk, compensating controls, and architectural integration at scale, this book lays out how Integrated Assurance works, not as a theory but as a practical guide. Identifying existing organizational maturity and creating an extensible enterprise architecture that incorporates risk management across the organization, the book examines the frameworks currently governing organizations today and how they can intersect, creating a flexible structure and ensuring continuous improvement. The book outlines technologies that underpin modern business, from enterprise platforms to hybrid infrastructure and the security and operational controls required to protect them. The Integrated Assurance Maturity Model walks through an approach that unifies these silos and manages the change along the way.

- For the **executive**, this book provides a strategic model for aligning technical and business priorities, embedding assurance into organizational culture and decision-making.
- For the **CISO**, this book offers a collaborative blueprint for aligning security efforts across the enterprise with the language and priorities of your executive team.
- For the **enterprise architect**, the book offers a pattern for embedding risk controls into infrastructure and design, not as afterthoughts but as core requirements to support business objectives.
- For the **practitioner**, this book helps synthesize multiple established frameworks with clear mappings and apply them in a business-aligned manner.

This book offers a way to lead together with clarity, accountability, and shared direction.

Integrated Assurance isn't just about doing security better. It's about helping the organization make better decisions together, faster, with more confidence, and with full visibility into risk. This isn't just what the board expects. It's what long-term, sustainable business performance requires.

Devin Jones, CEO
Gordius Systems

Acknowledgments

I am deeply grateful for the support, feedback, and encouragement.

- **Devin Jones**—we have certainly experienced the pain that has inspired this story over our intertwined careers, and your wisdom in editing this book has been invaluable.
- **Crystal Jones**—we have been working in the trenches on this messaging for so many years, and your insights throughout this journey have been incredibly helpful.

I also want to acknowledge those who shaped my path:

- To my colleagues from **Seccuris**, especially **Michael Legary** and **Geoff Besko**—your collaboration was essential in deepening my expertise in Enterprise Security Architecture.
- To my longtime friend **Rick Holod**—our work together over the years has been instrumental in developing Integrated Assurance and shaping me as a practitioner.
- A special thanks to **Dan Swanson**, whose enthusiasm and belief in the vision helped bring *Integrated Assurance* from concept to print.
- To all my current and past clients, without whom I would have not had the opportunity to develop and refine my skills as an enterprise security architect. This book was born from all these great experiences.

About the Author

Patrick Hayes is a recognized strategy and operations leader, certified enterprise security architect, and technology executive with over two decades of experience driving innovation, growth, and resilience in the IT and cybersecurity sectors. Throughout his career, he has founded or scaled multiple startups and has spearheaded global expansion strategies across North America, Latin America, and Europe.

Patrick has served in senior executive roles including Chief Strategy Officer, Chief Product Officer, and Chief Information Security Officer, where he architected and launched award-winning SaaS platforms in risk management and security operations. As a certified enterprise security architect, he has led several large-scale security transformation programs for Fortune 500 companies, delivering trusted results in complex and highly regulated environments.

A trusted advisor to emerging tech companies and an active contributor to the cybersecurity community, Patrick blends technical depth with strategic insight. He is a frequent speaker and published author in business and security journals and holds multiple industry certifications.

Patrick is the creator of the **Integrated Assurance: Unified Risk Strategy** and the **Integrated Assurance Maturity Model (IAMM)**, frameworks that have helped modernize cybersecurity, governance, and operational assurance across global enterprises. He is also the registered trademark holder of **Integrated Assurance®**, reinforcing his leadership and thought ownership in this evolving field.

Abbreviations

ABAC	Attribute-Based Access Control
ADM	Architecture Development Method
AI	Artificial Intelligence
AI/ML	Artificial Intelligence/Machine Learning
AIOps	Artificial Intelligence for IT Operations
API	Application Programming Interface
APM	Application Performance Management
APT	Advanced Persistent Threat
AWS	Amazon Web Services
BAP	Business Attributes Profile
BC/DR	Business Continuity/Disaster Recovery
BCP	Business Continuity Plan
BEC	Business Email Compromise
BIA	Business Impact Analysis
BPO	Business Process Outsourcing
BYOD	Bring Your Own Device
CAB	Change Advisory Board
CASB	Cloud Access Security Broker
CCM	Cloud Controls Matrix
CCPA	California Consumer Privacy Act
CD	Continuous Delivery/Continuous Deployment
CEO	Chief Executive Officer
CFO	Chief Financial Officer
CI	Continuous Integration
CI/CD	Continuous Integration/Continuous Delivery
CIA	Confidentiality, Integrity, Availability
CIO	Chief Information Officer
CIS	Center for Internet Security
CISO	Chief Information Security Officer
CJIS	Criminal Justice Information Services
CMDB	Configuration Management Database
CMMC	Cybersecurity Maturity Model Certification
CMMI	Capability Maturity Model Integration
COBIT	Control Objectives for Information and Related Technologies
COO	Chief Operating Officer
COSO ERM	Committee of Sponsoring Organizations of the Treadway Commission–Enterprise Risk Management
CPRA	California Privacy Rights Act
CPS	Cyber-Physical Systems
CRM	Customer Relationship Management
CRO	Chief Risk Officer
CSA CCM	Cloud Security Alliance Cloud Controls Matrix
CSF	Cybersecurity Framework
CSP	Cloud Service Provider
CSPM	Cloud Security Posture Management
CTF	Capture The Flag (cybersecurity competition)

CVE	Common Vulnerabilities and Exposures
DAST	Dynamic Application Security Testing
DCS	Distributed Control System
DDoS	Distributed Denial-of-Service
DevOps	Development and Operations (collaborative approach to software delivery)
DevSecOps	Development, Security, and Operations
DLP	Data Loss Prevention
DLT	Distributed Ledger Technology
DR	Disaster Recovery
DSPM	Data Security Posture Management
EA	Enterprise Architecture
eBPF	Extended Berkeley Packet Filter
EDR	Endpoint Detection and Response
ERP	Enterprise Resource Planning
ESA	Enterprise Security Architecture
ESG	Environmental, Social, and Governance
ESRM	Enterprise Security Risk Management
ETL	Extract, Transform, Load
FedRAMP	Federal Risk and Authorization Management Program
FIM	File Integrity Monitoring
FISMA	Federal Information Security Management Act
GDPR	General Data Protection Regulation
GRC	Governance, Risk, and Compliance
HIPAA	Health Insurance Portability and Accountability Act
HR	Human Resources
IaaS	Infrastructure as a Service
IaC	Infrastructure as Code
IAM	Identity and Access Management
IAMM	Integrated Assurance Maturity Model
IDE	Integrated Development Environment
IDS	Intrusion Detection System
IEC	International Electrotechnical Commission
IG	Implementation Group (CIS controls)
IIoT	Industrial Internet of Things
IoT	Internet of Things
IPS	Intrusion Prevention System
IR	Incident Response
IRP	Incident Response Plan
ISACA	Information Systems Audit and Control Association
ISMS	Information Security Management System
ISO	International Organization for Standardization
ISO 27001	ISO Standard for Information Security Management
ISO/IEC	International Organization for Standardization/International Electrotechnical Commission
ISO/IEC 27001	ISO/IEC Information Security Management Standard
IT	Information Technology
ITIL	Information Technology Infrastructure Library
ITOM	IT Operations Management
ITSM	IT Service Management
KPI	Key Performance Indicator

KRI	Key Risk Indicator
LLM	Large Language Model
LME	Large and Medium-Sized Enterprise (contextual)
M&A	Mergers and Acquisitions
MDR	Managed Detection and Response
MES	Manufacturing Execution System
MFA	Multi-Factor Authentication
ML	Machine Learning
MSSP	Managed Security Service Provider
MTTD	Mean Time to Detect
MTTR	Mean Time to Resolution
NERC CIP	North American Electric Reliability Corporation Critical Infrastructure Protection
NFT	Nonfungible Token
NIST	National Institute of Standards and Technology
NIST CSF	National Institute of Standards and Technology Cybersecurity Framework
NLP	Natural Language Processing
OPA	Open Policy Agent
OT	Operational Technology
PaaS	Platform as a Service
PAM	Privileged Access Management
PCI DSS	Payment Card Industry Data Security Standard
PII	Personally Identifiable Information
QaaS	Quantum as a Service
R&D	Research and Development
RACI	Responsible, Accountable, Consulted, Informed
RBAC	Role-Based Access Control
RMF	Risk Management Framework
ROI	Return on Investment
RPA	Robotic Process Automation
RPO	Recovery Point Objective
RTO	Recovery Time Objective
SaaS	Software as a Service
SABSA	Sherwood Applied Business Security Architecture
SaC	Security as Code
SASE	Secure Access Service Edge
SAST	Static Application Security Testing
SBOM	Software Bill of Materials
SCA	Software Composition Analysis
SCADA	Supervisory Control and Data Acquisition
SDLC	Software Development Lifecycle
SDN	Software-Defined Networking
SEC	Securities and Exchange Commission
SIEM	Security Information and Event Management
SLA	Service Level Agreement
SLO	Service Level Objective
SME	Small and Medium-Sized Enterprise
SoA	Statement of Applicability
SOAR	Security Orchestration, Automation, and Response
SOC	Security Operations Center
SOCaaS	Security Operations Center-as-a-Service

SOP	Standard Operating Procedure
SOX	Sarbanes–Oxley Act
SRE	Site Reliability Engineering
SSI	Self-Sovereign Identity
SSO	Single Sign-On
SSOA	Security Services-Oriented Architecture
TCO	Total Cost of Ownership
TOGAF	The Open Group Architecture Framework
TPRM	Third-Party Risk Management
TTPs	Tactics, Techniques, and Procedures
UEBA	User and Entity Behavior Analytics
VPN	Virtual Private Network
XDR	Extended Detection and Response
XSS	Cross-Site Scripting

Part I

IT Operations Management and Cybersecurity Landscape

1 Introduction to IT Operations Management and Cybersecurity

LEARNING OBJECTIVES

- Define the context behind the challenges faced by enterprises
- Understand the differences between small/medium enterprise and large enterprise
- Review the common IT and cybersecurity challenges of an enterprise
- Discuss potential strategies to address challenges

As organizations evolve and expand, their complexity increases, leading to operational silos. A prominent divide often emerges between IT and cybersecurity teams due to conflicting objectives, poor communication, increasingly isolated, and competing practices. IT operations teams prioritize smooth system functioning, uptime, and business continuity. Meanwhile, cybersecurity teams focus on safeguarding assets, monitoring threats, and responding to incidents. Though operating within similar infrastructures, their differing perspectives can create friction that compromises organizational assurance and resiliency.

A major obstacle is the conflicting objectives between groups. IT operations may prioritize system efficiency over security to prevent interruptions. Cybersecurity teams might be seen as imposing unnecessary limitations and interruptions. Without proper coordination, this misalignment can lead to tension, communication gaps, and overlooked vulnerabilities as teams make assumptions about each other's responsibilities.

The lack of collaboration between IT and cybersecurity exacerbates challenges. Operating in isolation can delay sharing critical information during outages or incidents, resulting in slower responses and missed mitigation opportunities. Poor coordination may also lead to lost evidence needed for root cause analysis, breach reporting, and potential litigation.

Fostering teamwork and cooperation helps close departmental gaps and ensure successful collaboration. Integrated tools enable seamless interaction and information sharing. Regular joint meetings improve collaboration by allowing teams to exchange ideas and understand each other's priorities. Open communication channels promote real-time information sharing and reduce misunderstandings. Aligning objectives allows IT operations and cybersecurity teams to jointly identify vulnerabilities and implement safeguards. Prioritizing collaboration significantly enhances an organization's cybersecurity posture and risk mitigation.

Cybersecurity incidents threaten business operations globally with potentially severe consequences. The sophisticated and evolving threat landscape has led to increased critical infrastructure compromise. It is fundamental to have the right information, processes, and technology to address this evolving capability to inflict harm. Enterprise risk management has become complex, requiring a multifaceted approach across disciplines. Businesses cannot operate at full potential

DOI: 10.1201/9781003562153-2

without seamlessly integrated IT. These risks exist as interconnected threats, creating a convergence of IT and cybersecurity risk that is inevitable in the digital era.

Recognizing the interconnected nature of cybersecurity and IT operations is important. Addressing cybersecurity risk requires balancing likelihood and impact. Many standards provide information security guidelines, while others propose broader information management systems. However, effectiveness may be compromised by inability to associate IT with business operations. Development of integrated operational cybersecurity, business continuity, and crisis management remains nascent despite existing guidance frameworks.

The nature of information risk and limitations of current standards suggest a need for a more integrated, comprehensive risk management approach considering today's complex, interconnected digital landscape. Cybersecurity should be addressed as an integral part of IT operations, not in isolation. Industry frameworks can help identify the need to seamlessly integrate cybersecurity with IT operations management. Embracing defense strategies allows organizations to develop practical, efficient, proactive solutions safeguarding against potential threats in the evolving cyberspace.

LARGE ENTERPRISE VS. SMALL/MID-SIZED ENTERPRISE

There is a common misunderstanding that IT and cybersecurity requirements are uniform across organizations. Examining the needs of small/mid-sized enterprises (SME) versus large enterprises requires establishing their distinct characteristics. SMEs typically have fewer resources, less complex operational structures, and simpler IT environments compared to large enterprises.

Large enterprises and SMEs differ significantly in several ways. A key distinction is operational scale. Large enterprises often employ thousands, generating substantial revenue exceeding $1 billion. They operate nationally or internationally, serving vast customer bases across regions. Organizationally, large enterprises are more complex, with intricate hierarchies and specialized roles contrasting SMEs' simpler structures. Large firm management is typically professional and segmented, overseeing various business aspects, while employees have more specialized roles than SME generalists.

Large enterprises access greater resources, capabilities, and often custom solutions unique to their environments. They can raise significant capital through stocks and bonds, investing in advanced technology and extensive research and development. They often dominate industries, influencing trends and establishing strong brand recognition. Their financial strength allows hiring highly skilled professionals across fields, providing a substantial expertise edge.

Large enterprises and SMEs approach innovation and risk differently. Large firms invest heavily in research and development but tend to be risk-averse due to stakeholder expectations. Their standardized processes can lead to slower decision-making due to bureaucracy. SMEs often excel in niche innovations and are generally more willing to take risks, making them nimbler in implementing new ideas.

Category	Large Enterprise	SME
Operational scale	Thousands of employees, national or international presence, revenue exceeding $1 billion.	Fewer employees, localized operations, revenue under $1 billion.
Organizational structure	Complex, hierarchical structures with specialized roles and segmented management.	Simpler structures with fewer management layers; employees often wear multiple hats.
Resources and capabilities	Substantial financial resources; capable of raising capital through stocks and bonds, investing in research and development, and utilizing advanced technology.	Limited financial resources; must prioritize cost-effective solutions.

Category	Large Enterprise	SME
Innovation and risk	Invest heavily in R&D but risk-averse due to bureaucracy and stakeholder expectations.	More agile and willing to take risks; excels in niche innovations.
Cybersecurity focus	Advanced security programs with multilayered defenses; targeted by APTs and state actors.	Focus on essential cybersecurity needs such as phishing, ransomware, and endpoint protection.
IT complexity	Global presence with complex IT systems, hybrid cloud environments, and legacy system integrations.	Simpler IT environments; primarily cloud-based with fewer legacy system challenges.
Regulatory compliance	Strict regulatory adherence across multiple regions and industries; requires dedicated compliance teams.	Fewer regulatory requirements but must still comply with industry-specific standards.
Incident response	Established incident response teams and protocols; may still struggle with response speed due to scale.	Limited incident response capabilities; relies on external cybersecurity services or managed providers.
Security investment	High budgets for cybersecurity, able to afford top-tier security tools and regular audits.	Budget constraints make it harder to invest in advanced security tools; prioritizes affordable solutions.
Talent and expertise	Large talent pool but struggles with high demand and retention of cybersecurity professionals.	Struggles to hire and retain cybersecurity talent due to salary competition with larger firms.
Infrastructure	Vast IT infrastructure with complex integrations across multiple business units and global networks.	Less complex IT infrastructure; relies on managed services for maintenance and security.
Scalability and flexibility	Requires scalable solutions to accommodate international growth; must balance security with performance.	Needs cost-effective and scalable solutions to support business growth without overextending resources.

IT AND CYBERSECURITY IN SME AND LARGE ENTERPRISE

SMEs' IT and cybersecurity needs differ considerably from large enterprises. With fewer employees and localized operations, their cybersecurity needs are typically simpler, focusing on protecting essential assets like customer data, communications, and critical business systems. Their approach emphasizes simplicity and effectiveness.

Cost-effectiveness is a major SME consideration. They seek easily implemented and maintained solutions given limited resources. Scalability is important to support business growth. They prioritize network uptime and defense against common threats like phishing, ransomware, and unauthorized access, guiding their cybersecurity strategies.

Large enterprises face more complex challenges. Greater financial and human resources allow investment in advanced cybersecurity measures. They can afford specialized talent and sophisticated security programs. Regular audits and advanced threat detection are feasible. Larger IT teams help manage these demands effectively.

Enterprises are known for extensive global presence and intricate technological infrastructure spanning continents, involving vast networks and data management processes. This scale introduces unique challenges in handling enormous data volumes and ensuring consistent performance across regions. Unlike SMEs, large organizations must maintain robust systems supporting international operations.

Their infrastructure complexity means large enterprises face more sophisticated threats, from advanced persistent threats to ransomware. Their valuable data makes them prime cybercriminal targets. Consequently, their cybersecurity measures must be far more advanced than smaller firms. Protecting extensive networks and sensitive information requires a multilayered security approach.

Regulatory compliance adds complexity. Finance, healthcare, and energy enterprises must adhere to myriad regulations varying by country and industry. Specialized teams handle these requirements alongside cybersecurity professionals to ensure security measures meet legal standards, preventing potential fines and legal issues. Large enterprises implement sophisticated IT processes to address these challenges. Multilayered security frameworks protect different infrastructure layers, from network security to data encryption. This approach ensures critical asset protection even if one layer is compromised. Aligning frameworks with organizational needs balances security and operational efficiency.

Performance and security must be carefully balanced. Overly secure but difficult-to-use systems can hinder operations. Large enterprises must optimize IT systems to remain secure and efficient, requiring ongoing monitoring and adjustments. The goal is maintaining high security without impacting performance or accessibility.

Managing enterprise cybersecurity involves more than technology. Compliance and cybersecurity teams must collaborate closely, especially in regulated industries where minor lapses can have serious consequences. This teamwork develops security measures protecting the enterprise and ensuring regulatory compliance. Adapting to changes is a constant challenge as threats and regulations evolve. Large enterprises must stay ahead by regularly updating strategies and technologies. Continuous cybersecurity investment is essential to address new threats and comply with emerging regulations.

Large enterprises must customize cybersecurity strategies due to size and complexity. They face sophisticated threats and stringent regulatory obligations. Managing diverse IT environments spanning multiple locations and borders adds complexity. Their cybersecurity measures need robustness and adaptability.

SMEs must focus on manageable strategies revolving around fundamental security practices. Though not facing the same threat sophistication, they remain vulnerable to common attacks. Budget-friendly, off-the-shelf solutions help maintain security without excessive spending.

An organization's scale and scope influence its cybersecurity approach. SMEs need practical solutions tailored to their size and resources. Large enterprises, with extensive operations and higher stakes, require comprehensive, customizable strategies. Each organization type must align cybersecurity measures with specific needs and challenges.

Understanding these differences is key to ensuring effective, proportionate cybersecurity efforts aligned with organizational scale. Recognizing varying needs helps organizations protect against threats fitting their unique circumstances.

COMMON MISCONCEPTIONS OF ENTERPRISE NEEDS

Enterprise IT and cybersecurity requirements are often misunderstood, especially given that the majority of the IT and cybersecurity solutions providers seem to be overly focused on the needs of SMEs. This leads to misrepresenting that both organization types face identical problems. Many believe large organizations can invest in cutting-edge technologies due to financial resources, while SMEs use basic, less efficient solutions. However, the idea that only the most expensive technologies provide adequate solutions is flawed. Effective IT and cybersecurity programs rely on implementing best practices, training employees, and fostering communication and collaboration, not just technology.

Another misconception is that large companies maintain strong environmental control due to size and resources. While large companies have more resources, this doesn't necessarily mean better resiliency. In reality, large company complexity, with extensive networks, legacy systems, multiple device types, and hybrid environments of on-premises, cloud and operational technologies, can challenge maintaining consistent, effective assurance. Companies, large and small, also face challenges like shadow IT, insider threats, and difficulty enforcing security policies across a global workforce.

Assuming cybersecurity is mainly an IT problem the IT department can handle alone, regardless of organization size, is another common misunderstanding. This ignores cybersecurity's complexity impacting all organizational parts, from operations and finance to legal and human resources. In large companies, cybersecurity requires coordination across multiple departments and regions, necessitating a well-organized, integrated approach. For example, the IT operations team may simply reimage and redeploy end user devices when they are not functioning properly, as a common solution to the issue. However, if the issue is a malware infection due to an advanced persistent threat, these machines will keep reinfecting and IT operations will be losing valuable evidence of the root cause.

The assumption that large enterprises can better handle cybersecurity incidents due to resources and established response protocols is also false. More resources and extensive incident response teams don't necessarily mean better preparation. Effective response depends on how well an organization has planned and practiced incident response procedures. An organization's ability to recover from cyber incidents often depends on resilience, including technical recovery, communication, legal, and reputational management.

ENTERPRISE IT AND CYBERSECURITY CHALLENGES

Understanding enterprise IT and cybersecurity team pressures requires comprehending the complexity they face. Large enterprises face various challenges managing IT and cybersecurity, starting with budgetary limitations. Despite significant resources, they often make difficult decisions about fund allocation. IT departments need to invest in latest technologies, cybersecurity tools, and infrastructure upgrades, but competing priorities can stretch budgets thin. They must justify spending to executives who may not fully understand investment urgency, particularly when immediate return is hard to demonstrate.

Regulatory compliance and legal considerations add complexity. Enterprises operating across regions must adhere to various local, national, and international regulations. Noncompliance can lead to severe fines or legal actions, but staying compliant requires constant monitoring of changing laws and regulations. The legal framework intersects with privacy issues, further complicating data management and cybersecurity strategies.

IT operations are burdened by managing massive, often global infrastructure complexity. Many enterprises have outdated systems difficult to integrate with newer technologies, leading to inefficiencies and increased security risks. These operations are strained by data volume, from customer information to internal processes. Large datasets can slow systems, making it difficult to ensure all data is secure and accessible while meeting scalability and flexibility demands.

Cybersecurity challenges are constant. Large enterprises are prime cyberattack targets, and keeping systems secure requires more than firewalls or antivirus software. With IT and cybersecurity field staff shortages, companies struggle to maintain adequate coverage across operations. Their global nature means securing not only local operations but also international business units with different cybersecurity needs and vulnerabilities. Balancing these priorities while ensuring scalability and adaptability in a fast-evolving digital landscape is a major challenge.

BUDGETARY LIMITATIONS

Budgetary limitations significantly impact enterprise cybersecurity strategy implementation effectiveness. Many organizations struggle with tough financial resource allocation decisions. They often focus on protecting critical assets, leaving less vulnerable areas less fortified. This critical asset focus can create security gaps, making other organizational parts vulnerable to cyber threats and attacks. Budget constraints also mean updates and security patches, essential for protection maintenance, might be delayed. Such delays can increase data breach risk as vulnerabilities remain unaddressed longer. The urgency to manage immediate threats with available funds often pushes necessary updates down the priority list, leaving the organization exposed.

In some cases, organizations may have no choice but to rely on outdated or inadequate security measures due to financial pressures. This reliance on insufficient defenses can increase vulnerability to growing cyber landscape threats. Consequently, enterprises face higher cyberattack victimization risk, further compounding budgetary constraint challenges.

Regulatory Compliance

Regulatory compliance is foundational to large enterprise IT and cybersecurity strategies. These entities often face complex regulation and standards designed to protect sensitive data, ensure privacy, and maintain operational integrity. Compliance is not just a legal requirement but key to maintaining customer, partner, and stakeholder trust. Regulatory frameworks and industry-specific standards impose stringent data handling, storage, and protection requirements. Widely adopted regulatory frameworks include Federal Risk and Authorization Management Program (FedRAMP) and Cybersecurity Maturity Model Certification (CMMC) for US Government IT work participation, General Data Protection Regulation (GDPR) and California Consumer Privacy Act (CCPA) for privacy, Health Insurance Portability and Accountability Act (HIPAA) for healthcare data, and Payment Card Industry Data Security Standard (PCI DSS) for payment card data. Noncompliance can lead to severe penalties, including hefty fines, legal action, and reputational damage. These frameworks will be defined in further detail in further chapters.

Legal Considerations

Beyond global and industry-specific regulations, large companies must navigate national and local laws that can vary greatly. For multinationals, this means simultaneously following multiple regulation sets, a challenging task. To manage this complexity, large enterprises usually have dedicated teams ensuring geographical legal obligation understanding. Working with IT and cybersecurity teams, legal and risk departments identify, implement and track required controls. These teams regularly check policy and procedure currency and that company IT and cybersecurity measures meet latest legal requirements. Ensuring legal alignment is essential to avoid legal problems and adapt quickly to regulatory changes.

Legal cybersecurity responsibilities also include incident reporting and breach notification requirements. Several regulations require companies to report data breaches to regulatory authorities and affected individuals within specific timeframes. Failure can result in serious legal consequences like fines and sanctions. Additionally, data breach legal ramifications can be extensive, potentially resulting in lawsuits, regulatory probes, and lasting reputational and financial harm. Large companies must have thorough incident response plans handling not only breach technical aspects but also ensuring prompt, accurate legal obligation satisfaction.

Ultimately, rule and law adherence and meeting legal obligations are fundamental in shaping large business cybersecurity approaches. Ensuring compliance centrality in cybersecurity plans allows companies to take proactive risk management approaches. This means constant monitoring, employee training, and legal and regulatory concern integration into all cybersecurity operation aspects. The goal is not just meeting legal minimums but exceeding them to lower breach chances and strengthen overall company security. In an era of constantly evolving cyber threats, regulatory compliance proactivity isn't just legally necessary but can provide strategic advantages in protecting critical resources: data and reputation.

IT Operations Challenges

Large enterprise IT operations face many productivity-affecting obstacles. A key challenge is managing competing priorities as IT teams navigate various tasks, from current system upkeep to new project launches, all with limited resources. This often demands thorough planning and prioritizing to address critical issues promptly while tending to other essential areas.

Large organizations often manage multiple IT priorities due to operational complexity and balancing various competing demands. A key reason is ensuring IT project alignment with overall business strategy. Organizations must guarantee IT endeavors help achieve strategic aims, whether improving operations, enhancing customer satisfaction, or fostering innovation. As business and technology evolve, priorities can change, requiring adaptable IT management. This alignment often necessitates existing project rethinking, resource reallocation, and initiative postponement or acceleration based on strategic importance.

IT priority management isn't just about addressing different organizational department needs and demands. External pressures like regulatory changes and competition add prioritization process complexity. For instance, new data protection regulation compliance may require immediate attention and resources, potentially shifting focus from other critical projects. Balancing these priorities necessitates effective communication and collaboration among all involved parties, along with adaptable project management approaches.

Many large companies use formal approaches and methods to effectively handle IT priorities. Frameworks like Information Technology Infrastructure Library (ITIL) or project management methodologies like Agile and Scrum offer structured IT project prioritization and management methods. These methods help organizations systematically assess project proposals, monitor progress, and adjust priorities when necessary. Utilizing these frameworks ensures IT priority alignment with overall objectives, efficient resource allocation, and organized adaptation to changing circumstances.

The Human Element

Big companies often struggle to spread their IT resources around. They only have so much money and not enough experts. When new tech shows up or business needs change, they have to figure out which projects are worth doing. This means making tough choices about what to fund, what to put off, and what to cancel. To do this well, they need to really get what each project could do for them and what risks it might have.

People can be a big headache for keeping big businesses safe online. Workers, temps, and partners who can use company systems might mess things up by accident or on purpose. Scammers love to use fake emails to trick people into letting them into company systems. It's important to teach workers about staying safe online, but getting everyone to follow the rules all the time is unrealistic. There's also the worry about insiders causing trouble, whether it's an angry worker or just someone making a mistake. As companies get bigger, it's even more important to make sure everyone cares about security and to set up good ways to control who can access what.

There aren't enough people who know how to protect companies online. This makes it hard for big businesses to keep their sensitive info safe. As online threats get trickier, companies really need skilled security experts. But there just aren't enough people with the right skills and experience. This leaves companies open to attacks because they can't find enough people who can spot and stop complex threats. It's especially tough for big companies, which need experts in lots of different areas of online security.

One big reason for this shortage is that online threats are changing faster than schools can teach new security experts. What students learn in school might already be out of date by the time they graduate. Also, cybersecurity jobs often need very specific skills, so even experienced IT workers might not know exactly what's needed to fight today's threats. Big companies, which often face more and tougher risks because they're so big and spread out, really feel the pinch from this lack of skilled workers.

Not having enough security experts also costs companies a lot of money. Since there aren't enough experts to go around, companies have to offer big salaries to attract and keep good workers. This makes their costs go up. Often, companies have to hire outside firms to handle some of their security work, which can be expensive and risky. Using these outside firms brings its own problems, like making sure they're doing things the right way and keeping an eye on their work. Also, it takes longer to find and hire good security experts, which leaves important jobs empty for a long time and makes companies more vulnerable to attacks.

Another problem caused by not having enough security experts is that the people who do work in security at big companies are often overworked. In many big organizations, security teams don't have enough people and have too much to do. This leads to burnout and people quitting their jobs. The constant pressure to stay ahead of new threats and manage complicated security systems can make people unhappy with their jobs. This makes the shortage even worse, as experienced workers leave for easier jobs or quit altogether. When these experienced people leave, the company loses their knowledge and skills, which makes it even harder to defend against attacks.

On top of all this, big companies now have to deal with more people working from home and using cloud technology. The Covid-19 pandemic made more people work from home, which meant workers were using company networks from all sorts of places and devices. This brought new security challenges, like keeping remote connections safe, protecting sensitive info on personal devices, and making sure cloud-based systems are secure.

Infrastructure Complexity

Enterprises must also grapple with the growing complexity of their IT infrastructure. As organizations expand and diversify their operations, their networks become more intricate, incorporating multiple branches and subsidiaries, as well as cloud-based systems. Each addition to the IT ecosystem creates potential vulnerabilities that cybercriminals can exploit. Therefore, companies must not only defend against external threats but also ensure robust internal security protocols and employee awareness programs to mitigate the risk of insider threats.

Volume of Data

One major issue is the sheer volume of data that needs to be monitored and protected. Large organizations generate and store enormous amounts of data daily, from customer information to intellectual property. This data needs to be continuously monitored, analyzed, and protected against threats, requiring substantial investment in cybersecurity technologies, infrastructure, and personnel. Even with significant budgets, allocating sufficient resources to cover all potential vulnerabilities is challenging, especially when cybersecurity is just one of many priorities competing for attention and funding.

Outdated Systems

Managing obsolete systems poses a major obstacle as well. Numerous big companies function with outdated systems that could be ineffective, expensive to upkeep, and not compatible with current technologies. Upgrading or substituting these systems can be a formidable undertaking, often involving significant financial commitments and meticulous strategizing to limit interruption while moving to more sophisticated solutions.

Large organizations face a significant challenge when it comes to dealing with antiquated and outmoded IT systems. These systems, which are frequently vital to core business operations, can present considerable risks such as security weaknesses, inefficiencies, and compatibility problems. In order to tackle this issue, businesses typically employ strategic planning, risk assessment, and technology enhancements.

Initially, businesses perform thorough evaluations of their current IT framework to pinpoint obsolete systems. This undertaking encompasses the evaluation of hardware, software, and applications to establish which parts are approaching or have already reached obsolescence. The assessment also considers the impact of these systems on business activities, including their efficiency, dependability, and protection. This stage is vital in determining which systems require urgent attention and in shaping the implementation of a phased strategy for substitution or enhancement.

After conducting an audit, companies create a strategic plan to deal with their outdated systems. This plan involves clearly defining the goals of the upgrade or replacement, which may include increasing efficiency, strengthening security, enabling new features, or to use a version that provides technical support. The plan also lays out the timeline, budget, and resources needed and typically involves getting input from stakeholders to ensure it aligns with business objectives. Additionally, the strategy may include a risk management plan to minimize any potential disruptions during the transition phase.

The next step includes the selection and integration of new technologies. Companies usually conduct a comprehensive assessment to determine the most appropriate replacements, taking into account compatibility with current systems, ability to grow, and support from vendors. This may involve testing new solutions in a controlled setting to evaluate their effectiveness before fully implementing them. The implementation process also involves training employees on new systems and procedures to guarantee a seamless transition.

In order to reduce interruptions, businesses frequently employ a step-by-step method for upgrading obsolete systems. This method consists of slowly shifting from outdated to modern systems while guaranteeing that essential business activities carry on without any interruptions. Throughout this process, businesses operate both the old and new systems simultaneously, enabling them to address any issues and make adjustments to the new technology before completely phasing out the old systems.

Ongoing assistance and upkeep are critical to the success of the new IT systems. Businesses implement regular monitoring and maintenance procedures to deal with any arising issues and enhance system performance. This also involves strategizing for future upgrades and replacements to avoid outdated technology problems from reoccurring. By adopting a proactive approach to IT management, businesses can effectively adapt to technological advancements and uphold operational efficiency.

Scalability and Flexibility

It is important to consider scalability and flexibility in IT infrastructure. As businesses expand and change, their IT systems need to be able to adapt to support increased workloads and evolving needs. It is a constant challenge to ensure that IT systems can accommodate rapid growth or changing business priorities without sacrificing performance or security. This requires forward-thinking strategies and strong infrastructure planning. Scalability and flexibility are extremely important for large businesses, as they allow for the ability to adjust to changing demands and evolving business requirements. Scalability specifically refers to an IT system's ability to handle a growing workload or to be expanded to accommodate growth. This can be done through scaling up by improving existing systems or scaling out by adding more systems to share the workload. For enterprises, scalability ensures that as the number of users, amount of data, or volume of transactions increases, the IT infrastructure can efficiently handle these changes without sacrificing performance or reliability.

Flexibility refers to an IT system's capacity to adjust to changes and incorporate new technologies or processes effectively. In a fast-changing business environment, companies need to be able to adapt swiftly to market changes, technological progress, or new regulatory demands. Flexible IT systems are built to accommodate a range of applications, workflows, and platforms, enabling smooth updates and modifications. This adaptability assists organizations in remaining competitive and innovative while minimizing disruptions to their daily operations.

Scalability and flexibility are important components of a strong IT strategy. An IT infrastructure that is scalable and flexible allows businesses to make the most of their resources, adapt to new opportunities, and minimize the risks that come with changes in technology or the market. By investing in scalable and flexible solutions, companies can ensure that their IT environments are well equipped to handle both current needs and future growth.

International Business Units

Operating international branches introduces an added level of difficulty. Corporations with a worldwide footprint must manage their IT operations across various regions, each with its own unique regulations, technological requirements, and cultural nuances. This can make it challenging to implement uniform IT strategies and solutions, necessitating strong coordination and communication to ensure smooth operations across the different locations. A key challenge is ensuring compatibility and integration of IT systems across different locations, often requiring standardized technology infrastructure, such as network protocols, software platforms, and data management systems. Successful integration improves operational efficiency, communication, and data consistency, which are essential for supporting decision-making and overall business performance.

Aside from technical integration, overseeing IT for global branches involves dealing with different regulatory and compliance matters. Each country has its own laws and regulations regarding data privacy, data sovereignty, cybersecurity, and technology usage. For instance, the GDPR enforces strict rules on data management in Europe, while other geographic regions may have their own standards. IT managers must keep up with these regulations and guarantee that all branches adhere to local laws to prevent legal complications and penalties. This includes establishing localized policies and controls and frequently collaborating with legal and compliance teams to address regional issues.

An important factor to consider is the support and upkeep of IT infrastructure across various time zones and languages. International offices might encounter difficulties with system downtime, availability of support, and user training. To tackle these challenges, IT departments should create strong support systems, such as around-the-clock help desks, teams that can provide support in multiple languages, and tools for remote diagnostics. Additionally, investing in dependable communication channels and documentation in various languages can improve the user experience and reduce interruptions. It is also beneficial to ensure that IT staff are well trained and familiar with the cultural and operational differences in different regions, which can enhance support and collaboration.

Ultimately, overseeing IT for international branches requires finding the right balance between centralization and decentralization. While central control can offer consistency and cost savings, local branches may need some degree of independence to meet their unique needs. A combination of the two approaches can be beneficial, with standardized core IT functions and policies but the flexibility for local branches to adjust certain elements to better suit their operations. This helps maintain a unified IT strategy while meeting the diverse needs of different geographic units, ultimately contributing to the overall success of the international business.

Cybersecurity Landscape

Over the past two decades, the frequency and sophistication of cyberattacks have surged at an alarming rate. This trend is particularly concerning for critical infrastructure sectors such as telecommunications, healthcare, transportation, and financial institutions. A successful attack against these systems isn't just a technological disruption, it can have severe economic consequences, endanger public safety, and even undermine national security.

Governments and private organizations are increasingly aware of this growing threat, leading to heightened regulatory efforts and security investments. However, reactive defenses are no longer sufficient. The cybersecurity industry must shift toward a more proactive approach, identifying and neutralizing threats before they escalate.

A common misconception is that most cyberattacks originate from independent hackers seeking financial gain or notoriety. While cybercriminals remain a significant threat, the landscape has evolved. Today's adversaries include sophisticated cybercrime syndicates and nation-state actors. These groups deploy advanced persistent threats designed to evade detection, infiltrate networks for extended periods, and extract valuable data or disrupt operations. Traditional security solutions, such as signature-based antivirus programs, are often ineffective against such advanced tactics.

To counter these evolving threats, organizations are turning to artificial intelligence and machine learning to enhance their cybersecurity posture. These technologies provide predictive analytics, anomaly detection, user behavior analysis, and automated threat response capabilities. However, implementing such solutions comes with challenges, AI-driven security tools are costly, and the cybersecurity skills gap means that qualified professionals are in high demand, driving up salaries and making it difficult for many organizations to secure the expertise they need.

The involvement of nation-states in cyber operations adds another layer of complexity. State-sponsored attacks often target intellectual property, critical systems, and financial institutions, causing economic damage that can lead to significant economic losses for companies. These cyber campaigns are not only financially motivated but also serve geopolitical objectives, making them particularly difficult to deter or counter through conventional security measures.

In short, the cybersecurity landscape is evolving at an unprecedented pace. Threats are becoming more frequent, more sophisticated, and more strategic in nature. As attackers continue to innovate, defenders must do the same. Strengthening cybersecurity requires a combination of advanced technologies, skilled professionals, and robust international collaboration. The challenge ahead is significant, but failing to address it puts businesses, governments, and individuals at risk.

ENTERPRISE IT AND CYBERSECURITY STRATEGIES

IT and cybersecurity are critical for modern businesses and must be aligned with overall business strategies to operate effectively. Technology drives business growth, making it essential for IT investments to support organizational goals and protect against threats. Without proper coordination, security vulnerabilities and misaligned IT investments can leave a company exposed. A unified approach helps technology play a key role in achieving business objectives, ensuring that IT and cybersecurity efforts are integrated into the broader strategy. Cybersecurity alignment with business strategy extends beyond mere protection. It fosters continuity and resilience by addressing risks like cyberattacks and data breaches. A proactive approach integrates cybersecurity solutions into the business mission, such as embedding security into customer platforms to build trust. Without this alignment, even advanced security measures might not connect with the business goals, potentially leading to ineffective risk management.

IT must transition from being a cost center to a strategic asset, driving innovation and efficiency. Aligning IT initiatives with business goals ensures that projects like digital transformation and cloud migration support the company's objectives, such as market expansion or enhanced customer experience. By linking IT priorities with business strategy, organizations can ensure technology investments provide real value and contribute to achieving business outcomes. Adapting IT and cybersecurity strategies to fit the size and complexity of an organization includes understanding the strategy of the business, its inherent risk, the complexity of IT infrastructure, and selecting an appropriate alignment of frameworks and standards that reflect the specific needs of the organization.

Business Strategy Alignment

Due to the significance that IT and cybersecurity holds enterprises must ensure that their IT and cybersecurity initiatives align with their overall business strategy in order to operate effectively and safeguard the company. Technology is essential for business growth, making IT and cybersecurity more critical than ever. Without proper coordination, IT investments may not effectively support the organization's goals, and security vulnerabilities can leave the business exposed to potential threats. A unified approach helps bridge this divide, allowing technology to play a pivotal role in accomplishing business objectives.

Cybersecurity, when aligned with business strategy, goes beyond just protecting assets. It ensures continuity and resilience. Companies face constant risks from cyberattacks, data breaches, and regulatory challenges. A proactive cybersecurity strategy anticipates these risks and integrates solutions that support the overall business mission. For example, a business focused on customer trust and data protection must embed security in its customer-facing platforms to strengthen that trust. Without this alignment, even the most advanced security measures can seem disconnected from business outcomes.

IT, on the other hand, needs to evolve from being a cost center to a strategic asset. When IT initiatives are aligned with business goals, they drive innovation and efficiency. Digital transformation projects, cloud migration, and process automation should directly contribute to the company's objectives, whether expanding into new markets or enhancing customer experience. By connecting IT priorities with business strategy, organizations can ensure they are investing in technology that delivers tangible value.

Ultimately, aligning IT and cybersecurity with business strategy demands collaboration across the organization. Leaders from IT, security, and business functions must regularly communicate and assess how well their technology supports overall goals. This continuous dialogue helps ensure that as the business grows and changes, its technology and security capabilities keep pace, creating a secure and efficient foundation for long-term success.

Understanding Inherent Risk

Inherent risk is the natural or intrinsic risk that exists in any business activity or process before any controls or mitigations are put in place. According to the Sherwood Applied Business Security Architecture (SABSA)[1] framework, inherent risk represents the raw, unmanaged risk that is inherent to the nature of the business or operation. As an intrinsic part of doing business, inherent risk cannot be eliminated entirely, as it is fundamental to business activities and opportunities. Inherent risk exists at multiple levels within the business and for this reason, enterprise IT and cybersecurity teams need to consider both the potential negative impacts, as well as positive impacts of inherent risks and work together to deliver services that align with the business. By recognizing and analyzing inherent risks through this methodology, organizations can develop more effective, business-aligned security architectures and risk management strategies.

Managing Complexity

The complexity of IT environments and infrastructure in large enterprises significantly amplifies the challenges of cybersecurity. These environments typically encompass a vast array of hardware, software, networks, and data, often spread across multiple locations and integrated with numerous third-party services. Each of these components introduces potential vulnerabilities that can be exploited by cyber attackers. For instance, outdated software or unpatched systems can serve as entry points for malware, while misconfigured network devices can expose sensitive data. The sheer scale of large enterprise environments makes it difficult to maintain consistent security standards across all systems, leading to gaps that can be exploited.

Enterprises often have diverse IT infrastructures that include legacy systems alongside modern cloud-based solutions. Legacy systems, in particular, pose a significant risk because they are often no longer supported by the vendor, making it difficult to apply necessary systems patching and security updates. Additionally, the integration of these older systems with newer technologies can create complex dependencies and interoperability issues that further complicate security efforts. The transition to cloud services also introduces new security concerns, such as data breaches due to misconfigured cloud storage or vulnerabilities in third-party cloud applications. Managing these hybrid environments requires robust security strategies that account for the varying levels of risk associated with different components of the IT infrastructure.

Frameworks and Standards

Selecting the right IT framework for your organization is fundamental. There are many frameworks available, each designed to address different aspects of IT management, security, and governance. Choosing the one that aligns with your goals, industry requirements, and maturity level is key to maximizing value and ensuring long-term success. Among the most widely recognized frameworks are Center for Internet Security (CIS),[2] National Institute of Standards and Technology (NIST),[3] International Organization for Standardization (ISO), ITIL, Control Objectives for Information and Related Technologies (COBIT),[4] and Open Group Architecture Framework (TOGAF).[5] Each of these offers unique strengths depending on what you're looking to achieve and will be discussed in detail in further chapters.

CONCLUSION AND RECAP

In this chapter, we explored the various challenges and considerations that organizations face in managing IT and cybersecurity. The introduction provided a foundation by highlighting the complexities that arise when different business objectives and security goals come into conflict. As companies strive to protect their data and operations, they often encounter obstacles related to collaboration and communication between departments. These struggles are further amplified when different teams follow competing practices, which can hinder progress in achieving unified cybersecurity goals.

The issue of interconnected silos is another major theme. In large organizations, departments tend to operate in isolation, which can create barriers to effective communication and collaboration. This separation may seem like an efficient way to organize workflows, but it often leads to inefficiencies, especially when it comes to responding to security threats. While SMEs might experience fewer siloing issues, they face their own set of challenges, particularly due to limited resources and budget constraints.

We also examined the differences between large enterprises and smaller organizations. Large enterprises typically have more complex IT infrastructures and greater resources to manage cybersecurity, but they also face larger-scale challenges. SMEs, on the other hand, may have simpler setups but are often constrained by tighter budgets and fewer personnel, making it difficult to implement robust cybersecurity measures.

A key part of the discussion centered on common misconceptions about enterprise needs. Many assume that large organizations can easily handle cybersecurity because of their resources, but this overlooks the unique challenges they face, such as the complexity of their IT environments and the volume of data they must protect. Similarly, smaller organizations are often viewed as less vulnerable, but they are just as susceptible to cyber threats and may struggle even more due to their limited capabilities.

Regulatory compliance and legal considerations add another layer of complexity. Both large and small organizations must navigate a maze of regulations, which can vary across industries and regions. Failing to comply with these regulations can result in fines and other legal penalties, making it critical for organizations to stay up-to-date and ensure that their cybersecurity practices meet legal requirements.

IT operations also face numerous challenges. Managing the human element is often one of the most difficult tasks, as employees can unintentionally become the weakest link in an organization's cybersecurity chain. Ensuring that staff are properly trained and aware of potential risks is critical to maintaining security. Additionally, the sheer complexity of modern IT infrastructures, with outdated systems and a large volume of data, creates further hurdles for cybersecurity efforts.

Outdated systems, in particular, pose significant risks. Many organizations still rely on legacy technology that is difficult to secure and integrate with newer systems. The inability to scale or adapt to new cybersecurity threats adds to this problem, making flexibility an important consideration for organizations of all sizes.

For businesses operating internationally, the challenges multiply. Multinational operations introduce the need to comply with different regulations, manage diverse IT environments, and address varying cybersecurity risks across regions. Organizations must be agile enough to respond to threats that may arise in any part of their global operations.

Finally, we explored how organizations can align their cybersecurity strategies with their broader business objectives. Understanding inherent risks and managing the complexity of IT operations are central to this alignment. By adopting recognized frameworks and standards, organizations can create a structured approach to cybersecurity that is both scalable and adaptable to the changing threat landscape.

Managing enterprise IT and cybersecurity is a multifaceted challenge that requires careful planning, collaboration, and alignment with business goals. Organizations, whether large or small, must navigate competing practices, regulatory requirements, and operational complexities. By understanding these challenges and employing effective strategies, they can better protect their operations in an increasingly complex cybersecurity landscape.

NOTES

1 Sherwood, John, Andrew Clark, and David Lynas. *Enterprise Security Architecture: A Business-Driven Approach*. Boca Raton, FL: CRC Press, 2005.
2 Center for Internet Security (CIS). CIS Critical Security Controls v8. www.cisecurity.org/controls.
3 National Institute of Standards and Technology (NIST). *Framework for Improving Critical Infrastructure Cybersecurity*, Version 1.1. Gaithersburg, MD: NIST, 2018. www.nist.gov/cyberframework.
4 ISACA. *COBIT 2019 Framework: Introduction and Methodology*. Schaumburg, IL: ISACA, 2018. www.isaca.org/resources/cobit.
5 The Open Group. *The TOGAF® Standard, Version 9.2*. 2018. https://www.opengroup.org/togaf.

2 Enterprise IT Operations Management Essentials

LEARNING OBJECTIVES

- Understand the definition and key components of ITOM
- Comprehend infrastructure management and its importance
- Explore service management processes and their objectives
- Identify tools and technologies in ITOM

ENTERPRISE IT OPERATIONS MANAGEMENT (ITOM)

ITOM refers to a broad range of activities that ensure a company's technology functions properly. It covers all the systems, applications, and tools used by a business. ITOM teams focus on keeping these systems running efficiently, from maintaining data centers to overseeing the service desk. Their goal is to keep the technology infrastructure stable and reliable. This involves both reactive measures, like fixing problems when they occur, and proactive actions to prevent potential issues.

The people in ITOM play a key role in making sure everything runs as it should. They use their skills to manage a variety of physical and virtual systems, such as networks, storage, and endpoints. Security is another significant area they oversee, making sure that data remains safe. These responsibilities require a collaborative effort from multiple teams. Each team brings its expertise to support the organization's broader goals. Day-to-day tasks in ITOM include monitoring system performance, responding to IT incidents, and ensuring routine maintenance is completed. Enterprise systems are the backbone of many business processes, like payroll or production scheduling, and need to operate smoothly. To make sure these systems run effectively, companies integrate their core business functions into an enterprise platform. This integration makes it necessary for the systems to remain available with little downtime.

ITOM is responsible for ensuring that the business processes supported by IT systems perform well. When systems go offline, it can disrupt key operations. For example, if a payroll system crashes, employee payments might be delayed. To avoid this, IT operations teams monitor systems closely. They react quickly to alarms and work to resolve issues before they become bigger problems. This constant monitoring helps maintain business continuity. Reducing downtime is a major goal for ITOM teams because it can have a direct impact on business operations. By keeping systems running smoothly, ITOM helps ensure that the company can meet its operational goals. Many businesses rely heavily on their IT systems, making ITOM a critical part of day-to-day success. Quick responses to system issues keep things moving efficiently.

In addition to resolving problems, ITOM teams are constantly searching for ways to enhance performance and optimize operations. By placing great importance on monitoring system health and

DOI: 10.1201/9781003562153-3

executing efficient capacity planning strategies, these teams proactively aid the company in effectively preparing for future requirements. This rigorous approach not only significantly mitigates the risk of unexpected downtime but also ensures that the systems are fully equipped to seamlessly accommodate the ever-increasing demands as the business continues to expand and prosper.

Key Components of ITOM

ITOM covers many important tasks that help an organization's IT systems run smoothly. One key part of ITOM is monitoring and performance management. This involves constantly keeping an eye on things like servers, networks, and applications to make sure they're working as they should. By tracking performance in real time, issues can be spotted early, before they turn into bigger problems.

Incident management plays a vital role in how ITOM addresses and resolves unexpected disruptions. In situations where malfunctions occur, such as server failures, application crashes, or network outages, incident management swiftly intervenes to identify the problem, classify it appropriately, and promptly initiate corrective actions to minimize potential impact. Furthermore, it encompasses implementing well-structured strategies for effectively managing incidents and outlining the appropriate actions to undertake if the situation escalates. An essential component of this process is the incorporation of a comprehensive backup strategy. This ensures that, in the event of critical system failure or data loss, essential services can be quickly restored from secure backups, preserving business continuity and safeguarding against long-term damage. Regular testing and validation of backup systems also form a key part of this strategy, reinforcing preparedness and enabling IT teams to recover quickly and confidently. With a strong emphasis on efficiency, resilience, and minimizing downtime, incident management offers a reliable framework for maintaining seamless operations within the IT environment.

Change management is a huge factor when it comes to the successful management of updates to IT systems. Whether it entails the software upgrades, or the upgrading of hardware components, these transformations need to be meticulously executed without causing any form of disruption to ongoing business operations. ITOM plays a pivotal role in guaranteeing that these changes are flawlessly planned, diligently tested, and expertly implemented in a manner that impeccably avoids any and all disruptions to users or services. Its significance cannot be overstated as it ensures a smooth and uninterrupted transition during the entire change management process.

Capacity planning involves getting ready for the future. By analyzing historical data and grasping current IT usage trends, businesses can accurately predict the resources that will be required in the future. This prediction allows businesses to prevent the possibility of running out of capacity, ensuring smooth operations while avoiding unnecessary investments in superfluous resources, which can be a drain on funds. Effective capacity planning not only ensures that future IT needs are met but also aids in maintaining highly efficient and cost-effective IT operations. Proper foresight and analysis enable businesses to adapt and scale their resources appropriately.

Managing assets is another piece of the puzzle when it comes to effectively running an organization. It involves closely monitoring and overseeing all the hardware and software that the organization possesses, while actively ensuring their optimal utilization. By efficiently managing these assets, organizations can not only save money by preventing unnecessary overpurchasing or underutilization but also prolong the useful life of these valuable resources. This comprehensive asset management approach plays a vital role in maintaining a cost-effective and sustainable operational environment for an organization.

With network management ITOM is responsible for maintaining the reliability and performance of the organization's network. This pivotal role involves closely monitoring routers, switches, and firewalls to ensure stable connections and uninterrupted data flow throughout the network infrastructure. By meticulously overseeing these components, network managers guarantee uninterrupted network connectivity, enabling smooth communication and the efficient functioning of other

IT systems within the organization. Ultimately, a robust and effectively running network greatly enhances the overall productivity and performance of the entire organizational framework.

ITOM FRAMEWORKS

ITOM is more important now because IT teams face pressure to meet service expectations from business leaders. This has led to more use of best practice frameworks to manage IT services well. The Information Technology Infrastructure Library (ITIL) is a popular framework that helps companies match their IT services with business goals. It focuses on ways to improve service delivery while keeping costs down. Many big companies use ITIL to make their IT operations run smoother and work better.

Another useful framework is Control Objectives for Information and Related Technologies (COBIT), developed by ISACA. It helps make sure IT systems support business goals and follow rules. COBIT is good for managing risks and making sure IT systems work well. It's especially helpful in areas with strict rules, like banking and healthcare. International Organization for Standardization and International Electrotechnical Commission (ISO/IEC) standards like ISO 27001 work well for companies that operate in many countries or need to show they follow industry rules. Let's look at each of these frameworks to see how they're used and what benefits they offer.

ITIL

ITIL[1] helps organizations manage their IT services better. It gives advice on how to make IT services fit what businesses and customers need. By using these tips, organizations can set up standard ways to plan, deliver, and take care of their IT services. This leads to establishing a common well-defined vocabulary to ensure understandable communications between functions.

ITIL has five main parts, each dealing with a different stage of IT service: planning, design, transition, operation, and ongoing improvement. Each part helps businesses fit IT services into their overall goals. This approach also helps companies handle risks, work better, and spend less. ITIL includes key processes for managing different parts of IT services. These include making sure services meet agreed standards, planning for future needs, fixing problems, and making changes without causing trouble. Companies use ITIL to get better at managing IT services. It helps them understand IT costs better and use resources more wisely. ITIL also makes sure IT services support the company's bigger goals.

ITIL is good for managing change too. As companies grow and change, they need to adjust their IT services. ITIL gives a clear way to make these changes, lowering the risk of problems and keeping everyone on the same page.

COBIT

COBIT[2] helps organizations manage and control their IT systems. It shows how to make IT practices support business goals. Companies can use COBIT to make sure their IT plans help the business and follow rules. It's good for handling IT risks and meeting regulations. COBIT links technical issues, business risks, and control needs. COBIT has several key parts. It gives a structure for IT governance, showing what needs to be done. It breaks down IT activities into detailed steps. It sets goals for these processes and ways to check how well they're working. It also gives practical advice on how to reach these goals.

COBIT is based on five main ideas: meeting stakeholder needs, covering the whole business, using one framework across the organization, taking a complete approach, and keeping governance separate from management. COBIT helps organizations in several ways. It makes sure IT supports business goals. It helps manage IT risks better, reducing costly problems. It guides companies on following legal and industry rules. COBIT also helps companies get more value from their IT spending. It encourages ongoing improvement, pushing organizations to regularly check and make their IT processes better.

ISO/IEC

ISO/IEC[3] is a worldwide standard for managing IT services. It sets rules for delivering good IT services. It helps organizations create and maintain a good IT Service Management (ITSM) system. The aim is to make IT services fit business needs and keep getting better. ISO/IEC covers many important ITSM processes. These include managing service levels, capacity, and information security. It also deals with budgeting for IT services, handling problems, and making changes. Organizations can get certified to show they meet ISO/IEC standards. This can improve service quality and make customers happier. It can also boost a company's reputation, give it an edge over competitors, and make sure IT services support business goals. It can lead to better efficiency and cost savings too.

To get certified, organizations need to put the required processes in place. Then they go through a check by an official body. If any issues are found, they need to be fixed. The certification lasts for three years, with regular checks to make sure the standards are still being met.

ISO/IEC works well with other IT management frameworks. It fits nicely with ITIL practices, making ITSM smoother. It can also be used alongside other global standards, like ISO 9001 for quality management and ISO/IEC 27001 for information security. By using these frameworks together, organizations can make their IT operations excellent, ensuring good performance, security, and quality in their services.

Category	ITIL	COBIT	ISO/IEC
Purpose	Helps organizations manage IT services more efficiently.	Provides governance and management structure for IT.	Sets global standards for ITSM.
Key focus	Service management and alignment of IT with business needs.	IT governance, risk management, and regulatory compliance.	Standardization and certification of ITSM.
Core components	Five key stages: planning, design, transition, operation, and ongoing improvement.	Five key principles: stakeholder needs, enterprise-wide coverage, single framework, holistic approach, separation of governance and management.	Service level management, capacity planning, information security, budgeting, and change management.
Approach	Provides best practices for ITSM.	Focuses on governance and control of IT systems.	A structured and formalized approach to ITSM.
Business benefits	Improves efficiency, reduces costs, enhances communication.	Ensures IT supports business objectives, reduces operational risks.	Improves service quality, enhances reputation, ensures efficiency.
Risk management	Manages service risks through structured ITSM.	Comprehensive risk management framework for IT systems.	Focuses on continual service improvement and compliance.
Compliance and governance	Provides structured guidance but is not compliance focused.	Strong focus on regulatory compliance and industry best practices.	Strong compliance framework with certification requirements.
Certification	No official certification for organizations, but professionals can get ITIL certifications.	No formal certification for organizations, but professionals can obtain COBIT certifications.	Organizations can achieve ISO/IEC certification.

Category	ITIL	COBIT	ISO/IEC
Integration with other frameworks	Integrates well with ISO/IEC for ITSM.	Can be used alongside ITIL for governance and risk management.	Works well with ITIL and can be used alongside ISO 9001 and ISO/IEC 27001.

MULTIPLE ITOM FRAMEWORKS

Big companies often use more than one IT framework, especially if they've grown by joining with other companies. ITIL, COBIT, and ISO/IEC can be used together to manage IT services and governance well. Each one focuses on different things. ITIL is about best practices for ITSM, COBIT deals with IT governance and management, and ISO/IEC sets specific rules for ITSM systems. Together, they cover a lot of ground in managing IT processes.

Each framework does something different. ITIL gives detailed advice on handling various stages of service management. COBIT helps make sure IT operations support business goals and manage risks. ISO/IEC provides a standard way to check and certify ITSM systems. They work well for organizations that need to handle daily operations and long-term rule-following. Using these frameworks together gives thorough coverage. ITIL handles service management, COBIT takes care of governance, and ISO/IEC offers a way to get certified. This makes sure both day-to-day work and big-picture governance are taken care of. It helps IT support overall business goals better, leading to stronger performance.

For service quality, using ITIL's best practices with ISO/IEC's formal requirements can make service delivery better. ITIL focuses on working efficiently, while ISO/IEC emphasizes meeting standard requirements. This leads to happier customers. COBIT's focus on governance ensures risks are managed well and services follow necessary rules. To put this into practice, organizations might use COBIT for governance, ITIL for service management, and align those with ISO/IEC to get certified. This layered approach allows flexibility, as businesses can choose which parts of each framework to focus on. It also makes sure IT practices work well together across different areas.

Organizations don't have to use all three frameworks fully. They can pick the parts of ITIL, COBIT, or ISO/IEC that fit their needs best. This flexibility lets businesses create a custom approach that covers governance, service management, and standardization effectively, resulting in a well-rounded IT management strategy.

INFRASTRUCTURE MANAGEMENT

Infrastructure management is about taking care of all the technology a company uses every day. This includes physical things like servers and routers, as well as virtual systems, software applications, and cloud services. Good management makes sure everything works together to help the business run. As technology becomes more complex, it's typically harder to manage. Companies need to spend money on knowledge and tools to keep things running smoothly.

The main job of infrastructure management is to keep systems working well, safe, and able to grow with the business. This means fixing things that break and planning for the future. As technology gets better and there's more data, the infrastructure needs to be able to handle it. Companies need to check and upgrade components of their environment regularly to avoid slowdowns or breakdowns that could hurt work.

Network Infrastructure

Network infrastructure is all the equipment that helps a company share information. This includes routers, switches, firewalls, and other gear that connects devices inside the company and to the outside world. Routers send data where it needs to go. Switches connect different devices in a local network. Firewalls keep things safe by controlling what information can go in and out, protecting important stuff from people who shouldn't see it. Taking care of network infrastructure makes sure information flows smoothly between people, programs, and systems. Good management helps avoid delays, slowdowns, and security problems that can mess up work. This means watching how data moves, making things work better, and keeping security up to date. As businesses grow, their network needs to grow too, and managing this growth well is important for keeping communication fast and reliable.

Servers and Data Centers

Servers and data centers are places that hold all the computing power and storage a company needs. A data center can have hundreds or thousands of servers, all working together to store, process, and share information. Servers run important programs, handle data, and support systems that employees and customers use every day. These places need careful management to stay safe, use energy wisely, and handle more and more data.

Managing servers and data centers involves making sure there's enough power and cooling to keep everything running. When things break down, it can cost a lot of money, so backup systems are often used to prevent losing data or stopping services. As companies grow, they need more server space and processing power, which means they need to keep investing in data center management to make sure everything keeps working well for a long time.

Cloud Resources

Cloud resources let businesses use computing power, storage, and programs without owning the actual machines. Companies can use public clouds (shared with others), private clouds (just for them), or a mix of both, depending on what they need. Using cloud resources lets businesses grow quickly and easily. When they need more power or storage, they can just add it without buying new machines. This is really helpful for businesses that are growing fast or have busy seasons. Also, cloud services often come with built-in safety features, helping businesses protect their information and follow rules.

Storage Systems

Storage systems are really important for keeping all the information businesses create every day. These can be physical things like hard drives, or more complicated systems that connect to networks. Depending on what a company needs, they might use different types of storage. Each type has its own good points and is chosen based on things like how much it can hold, how fast it works, and how safe it is.

Good storage management makes sure information is easy to get to and is protected. As companies collect more and more information, they need to figure out how to handle it all. This includes making regular backups to avoid losing data and having extra copies in case something breaks. Many businesses also use cloud storage, which can grow as needed and means they don't have to take care of as much physical equipment.

Virtualization Platforms

Virtualization platforms let companies use their physical equipment more efficiently. Instead of using one server for one job, they can run several different programs or operating systems on the same machine. This means they need less space and use less energy and money on equipment, which is better for the environment.

Virtualization also makes it easier to manage IT resources. Virtual machines can be easily created, changed, or removed, letting companies adjust quickly when their needs change. This is really useful when a business's needs change a lot, as they can adjust without a lot of downtime or buying new equipment. Virtualization allows companies to spin up and down services that are dynamic and time-bound at little cost and effort. It also makes it easier to recover from disasters, as virtual machines can be backed up and restored more easily than physical servers.

IT SERVICE MANAGEMENT (ITSM)

ITSM forms the foundation of a well-orchestrated IT environment, encompassing the oversight of physical hardware and computing resources. This includes the provisioning, configuration, and lifecycle management of servers, storage, and endpoint devices, ensuring that every component is aligned with organizational needs and performance expectations. From capacity planning to asset optimization, effective management of these tangible resources enables scalability, cost-efficiency, and a predictable infrastructure baseline.

Beyond hardware, service management extends into the realm of network operations and security, foundational pillars in the delivery of seamless technical user experiences. Maintaining robust network connectivity, enforcing access controls, and implementing proactive security measures are essential to safeguarding data and maintaining business continuity. This domain not only addresses day-to-day operations but also supports compliance initiatives and risk mitigation strategies across the enterprise.

Another core aspect of service management lies in the continuous monitoring and maintenance of applications and systems. This involves leveraging observability tools, performance metrics, and alerting mechanisms to detect anomalies before they impact users. Routine updates, patch management, and performance tuning are carried out with precision to ensure optimal functionality across the application stack. These practices uphold system integrity while supporting agile change management and faster incident resolution.

Ultimately, the goal of service management is to ensure high availability, sustained performance, and operational efficiency throughout the entire infrastructure. Achieving this requires an integrated support framework that spans people, processes, and technology, enabling IT to meet service-level commitments and adapt to evolving business demands. Whether through automated workflows, cross-functional collaboration, or strategic governance, service management delivers the resilience and responsiveness essential for a modern digital enterprise.

Help Desk

Help desk operations represent a foundational component of ITSM, serving as the primary point of contact between end-users and IT services. As the frontline of support, the help desk is responsible for triaging a wide array of user-reported incidents ranging from application failures and connectivity disruptions to credential resets. Its role is not merely reactive; it is strategically positioned to maintain workforce productivity by ensuring swift resolution or escalation of issues that would otherwise impede business operations.

In enterprise environments, the help desk functions within a broader operational framework designed to ensure consistency, traceability, and accountability. Each service request or incident is logged and categorized within an ITSM platform, providing a structured approach to prioritization and resolution based on impact and urgency. This systematic documentation is not only essential for managing immediate workloads, but also for identifying recurring issues that may signal underlying systemic problems with insights that are critical for proactive problem management and continuous service improvement.

Beyond technical remediation, the help desk also plays a key role in service intelligence and operational visibility. The data collected from help desk interactions serves as a valuable input into performance metrics, service level objective adherence, and user experience trends. These insights inform decision-making at the architectural level, enabling alignment between IT support operations and enterprise-wide digital strategies. Furthermore, well-integrated help desk functions can contribute to knowledge management by capturing solutions and best practices for future reference.

An often-underemphasized aspect of help desk operations is its role in user engagement and education. Help desk personnel act as intermediaries between users and back-end IT teams, translating technical issues into understandable terms and guiding users toward more effective utilization of technology. This promotes digital literacy across the organization and fosters a culture of empowerment, where users feel more confident navigating IT systems and resolving minor issues independently.

Ultimately, the help desk is not just a support function, it is a strategic enabler of business continuity, user satisfaction, and operational resilience. When designed with scalability, integration, and knowledge sharing in mind, the help desk is a foundational component in the enterprise architecture. Its ability to adapt to evolving technologies, deliver consistent service, and feed intelligence back into ITOM and ITSM ecosystems ensures that the organization can respond effectively to change while maintaining a stable and efficient IT environment.

Incident Response

Incident response and management is another important process in service management. An incident is any unexpected event that disrupts normal IT operations, like a server crash or network failure. Incident management is about fixing service as quickly as possible to reduce problems for the business. The first step is finding the issue, which often happens through monitoring tools or when users report problems. Once found, the incident is given a priority based on how serious it is, and the right team is asked to fix it through an established escalation and prioritization process.

The next part of incident management involves finding and fixing the problem. Depending on how complex it is, the incident might be fixed quickly or need more investigation. For high-priority incidents, IT teams might work nonstop to restore service and limit any downtime. Good incident management needs clear communication between IT teams and others in the business to keep everyone informed about progress and when the issue might be fixed.

After the incident is resolved, the team usually looks back at what happened to understand what caused the problem and how to prevent it in the future. This review is a crucial part of always improving IT operations, helping organizations learn from incidents and make their processes better. Proper incident management ensures that IT disruptions are handled well, reducing the impact on business operations and worker productivity.

Problem Management

Problem management takes a different approach by trying to find and remove the root causes of recurring incidents. While incident management focuses on fixing services quickly, problem management tries to stop incidents from happening in the first place. This process involves a deeper look into underlying issues, often started when the same type of incident happens repeatedly. Problem management looks for trends and patterns in incidents to uncover deeper, system-wide issues within IT systems.

Once the root cause of a problem is found, the next step is to develop a permanent solution. This might involve fixing software, changing system settings, or upgrading hardware. The goal of problem management is to completely eliminate the issue, rather than just treating the symptoms. By addressing the root cause, problem management can greatly reduce the number of incidents over time, leading to more stable and reliable IT services.

Along with fixing the root cause, problem management also focuses on reducing the impact of known issues while a permanent solution is being developed. This could involve using temporary fixes that allow services to keep running while the underlying problem is being addressed. Through this proactive approach, problem management helps improve the overall quality of IT services and reduces how often incidents disrupt business operations.

Change Management

Change management is an important process in IT service management that focuses on controlling and managing changes to IT systems in an organized way. Changes to IT systems, whether it's upgrading software, replacing hardware, or adjusting settings, are unavoidable in any organization. However, unplanned or poorly executed changes can lead to serious disruptions, such as service outages or security vulnerabilities. Change management ensures that all changes are carefully planned, reviewed, and implemented with minimal disruption to ongoing operations.

A key part of change management is the change approval process. Before a change is made, it must be reviewed by a change advisory board (CAB), which is a group of people that assesses the potential risks and benefits of the change. The CAB ensures that the change aligns with the organization's goals, minimizes risks, and includes appropriate backup plans in case something goes wrong. This review process is critical for maintaining control over IT environments, especially in large organizations with complex systems.

Once a change is approved, it is implemented according to a predefined plan. The plan outlines who is responsible for the change, what steps will be taken, and how the change will be tested before being fully deployed. After the change is made, it is watched closely to ensure that it doesn't cause any unexpected problems. This organized approach to change management reduces the likelihood of disruptions and helps IT teams adapt to new technologies or business requirements without compromising service stability.

Service-Level Agreement (SLA) Monitoring

SLA monitoring and enforcement is another essential part of service management. SLAs are agreements between IT service providers and the business, outlining and measuring the expected level of service and performance. These agreements typically cover areas like uptime, response times, and issue resolution times. SLA monitoring involves tracking these measures to ensure that the IT services meet the agreed-upon standards. Regular monitoring helps identify potential areas where service may be falling short and allows teams to take corrective action before issues get worse.

In many cases, SLA enforcement requires clear communication and teamwork between IT teams and business stakeholders. If a service fails to meet the agreed performance levels, the IT team is responsible for investigating the root cause and addressing it quickly. Depending on the terms of the SLA, penalties or service credits may be applied if performance consistently falls below expectations. Effective SLA management ensures that IT services are reliable and meet the needs of the business, while also holding service providers accountable for their performance.

By consistently monitoring SLAs, organizations can gain valuable insights into how well their IT systems are performing and identify areas for improvement. SLA data can highlight trends, such as whether certain services are consistently underperforming or if specific teams need more resources. This ongoing feedback helps IT teams make data-driven decisions and continuously improve the quality of service they deliver to the business.

APPLICATION PERFORMANCE MANAGEMENT (APM)

APM is a way to watch, handle, and improve how software works. It uses tools and methods to keep applications running well. The main goal is to make sure applications work smoothly and are easy for people to use. This helps IT teams make sure their work matches what the business wants to achieve. APM lets IT teams watch applications as they're being used. If something goes wrong,

APM tools help find and fix the problem before it bothers users or messes up business work. This quick action is important for keeping users happy.

APM has several important parts. It can see how users are using the applications. It can figure out how applications are built and how they work. It can also look deeply at specific parts of applications to see how they're doing. APM can measure how well applications are working in real time. It can follow requests as they move through different parts of the system. It can look at the actual code to find slow spots. It also keeps an eye on the computers and databases that help run the application.

One big benefit of APM is that it makes applications more reliable. By fixing problems quickly, APM helps keep applications running more of the time. This makes users happier. APM also helps IT teams work in a way that helps the business reach its goals. This makes everything work better and helps stop problems before they get big. As technology changes, APM changes too. New APM tools can work with cloud systems and small, separate parts of applications, which are common now. They also use smart computer programs to predict problems before they happen. APM now looks at more things to understand application performance better.

Monitoring Application Performance in Real Time

Watching how applications perform in real time means keeping track of different measures all the time to see how well an application is working in real time. This uses special tools that collect information like how fast the application responds, how much work it's doing, how many errors it's making, and how much of the computer's power it's using. Real-time monitoring lets IT teams see how the application is working live, giving them a clear picture of how it's doing right now. By looking at this information, teams can quickly spot trends or unusual things that might mean there's a problem. This quick action helps keep the application healthy and makes sure any problems are dealt with fast.

Real-time monitoring also sets up alerts to tell IT staff about any problems as soon as they happen. These alerts are based on set levels or smart programs that notice when things aren't working normally. This quick feedback is important for fixing problems fast, which helps stop users from being affected. Basically, real-time monitoring acts like an early warning system, letting teams deal with problems before they get bigger and cause trouble for users or the business.

Detecting and Diagnosing Performance Problems

Finding and understanding complex performance problems needs a careful look at lots of different information. Big problems often involve many parts of the application, including the code, the computers it runs on, and other systems it works with. Advanced APM tools use methods like following requests through the system and looking closely at the code to find the root of performance problems. Following requests helps track them as they move through different parts of the system, showing where delays or failures happen. This lets IT teams see the path of a transaction across the whole system, finding slow spots and areas that aren't working well.

Understanding these problems means looking carefully at the collected information to see what's causing the application to perform poorly. This might mean reading logs, checking system settings, and seeing how well different parts are working. The goal is to find the specific things causing the problem, like slow code, overworked computers, or slow networks. By finding these issues accurately, IT teams can make targeted fixes to solve them, which makes the whole application work better and more reliably.

Availability and Optimal User Experience

Making sure applications are available and work well for users is a main goal of APM. Availability means the application stays working and users can access it without interruption. To keep applications highly available, IT teams must watch how well they're performing and how healthy they are, making sure they're always ready for users. This involves setting up backup systems, ways to keep working if something fails, and doing regular maintenance to prevent outages and minimize downtime. By actively managing these things, organizations can make sure their applications are always there for users.

Along with availability, making the user experience as good as possible is crucial for keeping users happy. This means making sure the application works well in different situations, like when lots of people are using it or when it's doing complicated tasks. Making things better includes speeding up how fast the application responds, reducing delays, and improving how well the application works overall. By focusing on these things, IT teams can give users a smooth and quick experience, which is important for keeping users and keeping them engaged. In the end, ensuring both availability and a good user experience helps achieve business goals and stay competitive.

Aligning IT Performance with Business Objectives

Making IT performance match business goals means making sure IT work and how well applications perform directly support what the organization wants to achieve overall. This matching needs an understanding of what the business is trying to do and turning those goals into specific measures and targets for IT. For example, if a business wants to make customers happier, IT teams might focus on making applications faster and more reliable. By connecting IT performance measures to business results, organizations can make sure their IT work helps achieve broader business goals.

This matching also means constantly checking and adjusting IT performance to meet changing business needs. As business priorities change or new goals are set, IT teams must change their performance measures and plans to match. This might mean using new technologies, making existing systems work better, or changing performance targets to better support what the organization wants to achieve. By keeping this match, IT departments can make sure their work not only helps day-to-day operations but also drives long-term success and growth for the business.

CAPACITY PLANNING AND RESOURCE OPTIMIZATION

Capacity Planning and Resource Optimization are important for companies to manage their resources well and meet changing demand. These processes work together to help operations run smoothly. Capacity Planning is about guessing future needs. Companies try to figure out how much capacity they'll need to meet customer demand. They look at what capacity they have now, spot any shortages, and make plans to fill these gaps. For example, a company might look at past sales to guess future needs. They also check if they have enough workers, equipment, and facilities.

Resource Optimization is about using available resources in the best way. This means doing the most important things first and cutting down on waste. For example, if a company finds some equipment isn't used much, they might use it for different projects or find new ways to use it. Making things work better is key. This could mean making processes simpler or helping employees learn new skills. Cutting costs while keeping quality good is another goal, done by using resources smartly and managing them well.

Capacity Planning and Resource Optimization work well together. Capacity Planning shows what resources will be needed in the future, while Resource Optimization makes sure those resources are used well. Together, these processes help companies use their resources to meet their goals. They help things work better and make customers happier by meeting demand more effectively.

Assessing Current Capacity

Checking current capacity means looking at a company's existing resources and setup to see if they can handle expected demand. This check usually includes looking at people, equipment, buildings, and technology. For example, a factory would look at its production lines, machines, and workers to see if they can make enough products. This check also means looking at how well these resources are working and being used to find any slow spots or unused things. This helps understand if the current setup can handle future growth or if changes are needed.

Companies might use different tools and methods to check their current capacity. They look at things like how much they can produce, how efficient they are, and how much of their resources they're using. They might also compare themselves to industry standards or similar companies to see if their capacity is good enough. The check should also think about possible limits, like when equipment needs fixing, how much space they have, or limits on workers. By looking carefully at these things, companies can see if they're ready to meet future demands and spot areas that might need to be improved or changed.

Forecasting Future Demand

Guessing future demand means trying to figure out how many products or services customers will want in the near and far future. This usually starts by looking at old information, like past sales, busy seasons, and how the market has acted before. Companies use different math methods and models to stretch this old information into future guesses. Getting these guesses right is really important because it affects all other planning decisions. For example, a store might look at sales from past years to guess how much they'll sell during busy times like holidays. They might also think about things like how the economy is doing, what's happening in their industry, and what their competitors are doing to make their guesses better.

Besides looking at old information, guessing future demand also means getting ideas from market research and what customers say. Surveys, group discussions, and looking at social media can give useful information about how customer likes are changing and new trends. Companies might also use sales and marketing guesses, as ads and new products can really change demand. By using both numbers and people's opinions, companies can make better guesses about demand. This helps them plan production, keep the right amount of stock, and use resources better, which helps them make better decisions and work more efficiently.

Improving Productivity and Performance

Making productivity and performance better means improving how efficiently resources are used to get better results. This can be done in various ways like using new technologies, making processes better, or improving employee skills. For example, using automation tools can speed up repeated tasks, letting employees focus on more complex, valuable work. Regular training programs can also help employees do their jobs better and contribute to overall productivity improvements.

Performance can be further improved by setting clear goals and ways to measure them. Regularly checking performance against these benchmarks allows companies to find areas to improve and make needed changes. Using performance management tools and techniques, like Key Performance Indicators (KPIs) and balanced scorecards, helps in tracking progress and staying focused on strategic goals. By always looking for ways to improve productivity and performance, companies can drive better results, achieve higher quality outcomes, and stay competitive in their industry.

TOOLS AND TECHNOLOGIES

Tools and technologies are very important for running IT operations smoothly. ITOM software suites help manage different parts of IT work from one place. These suites make it easier to watch different systems and keep everything running well. They work like control centers for IT departments. Network monitoring and management tools watch how the network is working. They help find and fix problems before they get big. These tools help keep the network stable and fast.

Configuration management databases keep track of all IT equipment and how it's set up. This makes it easier to manage and see changes. It's like a detailed list of everything in the IT system. Artificial Intelligence for IT Operations Platforms use smart computer programs to predict and fix issues by themselves. They can look at information quickly to see patterns and problems that people might miss. These platforms make IT management work better by using clever ways to solve problems.

Cloud management and orchestration tools help manage cloud services and resources. They make sure different cloud services work well together. Containerization and orchestration platforms let applications run smoothly in different places. Containers package applications with everything they need, making them easy to move and work the same everywhere. Orchestration tools help manage these containers, making sure they work well together. All these tools and technologies help keep IT systems running smoothly and efficiently.

Category	**Purpose**	**Key Capabilities**	**Benefits**
ITOM suites	Centralized management of IT infrastructure and operations	System monitoring, automation, dashboards, integration with business systems	Faster issue resolution, better visibility, improved efficiency
Network monitoring and management tools	Monitor and control network performance and stability	Traffic analysis, real-time alerts, automated tasks, network visualization	Improved uptime, quick issue identification, better network planning
Configuration management databases (CMDB)	Central repository for IT asset configuration and relationships	Asset tracking, dependency mapping, change impact analysis, audit support	Improved change management, faster root cause analysis, compliance readiness
AI for IT operations (AIOps)	Use AI to enhance IT operations with insights and automation	Anomaly detection, predictive analytics, automated remediation, system health correlation	Proactive issue resolution, reduced manual effort, enhanced operational visibility
Cloud management and orchestration tools	Manage cloud infrastructure and applications across environments	Resource scaling, cost tracking, automation, performance monitoring	Cost efficiency, easier cloud operations, better resource utilization
Containerization and orchestration platforms	Deploy and manage containerized applications	Container deployment, autoscaling, load balancing, microservices support	Consistent environments, scalable apps, fast updates and deployment
ITSM tools	Manage IT service delivery and support processes	Incident management, change management, service request handling, knowledge base	Streamlined service workflows, improved SLA compliance, enhanced user satisfaction
Backup and disaster recovery solutions	Protect and restore data in case of loss or disruption	Automated backups, snapshot management, failover systems, recovery testing	Minimized data loss, business continuity, rapid recovery from failures
Patch and vulnerability management tools	Identify and fix vulnerabilities in IT assets	Patch deployment, vulnerability scanning, remediation workflows	Reduced attack surface, improved system hygiene, proactive security management

Category	Purpose	Key Capabilities	Benefits
Remote monitoring and management (RMM) tools	Monitor and manage endpoints and IT systems remotely	Remote access, software deployment, performance monitoring, alerts	Scalable remote IT support, improved response time, reduced on-site interventions

IT SERVICE CONTINUITY AND DISASTER RECOVERY

IT Service Continuity makes sure technology systems and services keep working during and after problems. This means planning and getting ready for possible outages or failures. The main idea is to keep interruptions small and services running smoothly. Good continuity planning includes making detailed steps for different situations. These situations could be small glitches or big system failures. By writing down these steps, companies can recover quickly and keep services available.

Business Continuity Planning (BCP)

BCP is a way to make sure important business work keeps going during and after problems. This planning involves figuring out which business operations and resources are crucial for keeping the company running. To make a good BCP, companies start by doing a Business Impact Analysis (BIA). The BIA helps find out which processes are vital, how long they can be stopped before causing harm, and what resources they need. From this analysis, a continuity plan is made. This plan includes ways to keep operations going, other places to work, and plans to keep people informed.

After the plan is made, it's important to decide who does what. This means choosing a continuity team that will handle things during a problem. The team should have clear jobs, like working with outside vendors, managing resources, and talking to employees. The plan should also say how to protect and recover important things, like data and equipment. For example, it might include setting up ways to work from home or temporary offices so employees can keep working without big interruptions.

Testing and keeping the BCP up to date is ongoing work. Regular practice runs help make sure the plan works right and everyone knows what to do. It's important to look at and update the plan often, especially after big changes in how the business works or in technology. These updates make sure the BCP stays useful and can handle new risks or changes in business conditions. By keeping the plan current, companies can better deal with unexpected events and reduce how much they affect business operations.

Disaster Recovery (DR)

DR focuses on getting IT systems and data back after a big problem, like a natural disaster or cyberattack. The first step in making disaster recovery strategies is to do a risk assessment and impact analysis. This means finding possible threats, like hardware breaking down or data breaches, and seeing how they would affect business operations. This analysis helps decide which systems and data need to be recovered first. Based on this, companies can make a recovery plan that includes backing up data, having extra systems, and steps to restore systems.

One common way to do disaster recovery is to back up data. Regularly saving data, whether nearby or far away, makes sure recent information is available for recovery. Companies might use cloud storage or outside servers to store these backups, protecting against data loss. Besides backups, having extra systems, like spare servers or other network connections, can help quickly restore services if main systems fail. The recovery plan should also say how to set up systems and applications again to make sure they work right after recovery.

Testing and updating disaster recovery strategies is very important for them to work well. Regular testing, like practice runs, helps check that the recovery processes work as expected and finds any problems. This testing should be done in a controlled way to avoid messing up normal operations. After each test or real recovery event, the plan should be looked at and updated based on what was learned. By always improving disaster recovery strategies, companies can get better at handling problems and make sure they can respond faster and more efficiently to future disruptions.

CONCLUSION AND RECAP

In this chapter, we laid the groundwork for understanding Enterprise ITOM by introducing various frameworks and concepts. We began by exploring established frameworks such as the ITIL, COBIT, and ISO/IEC. ITIL provides a comprehensive set of practices for ITSM, emphasizing a structured approach to delivering high-quality IT services. COBIT focuses on governance and management of enterprise IT, helping organizations align IT goals with business objectives. ISO/IEC offers a global standard for ITSM, ensuring consistency and continuous improvement in service delivery. These frameworks form the backbone of ITOM by guiding organizations on best practices and procedures for managing their IT operations effectively.

We then examined infrastructure management, which is a cornerstone of ITOM. This includes various components such as network infrastructure, which encompasses routers, switches, and firewalls crucial for maintaining connectivity and security. Servers and data centers are pivotal for storing and processing data, and their management ensures that IT resources are available and functioning correctly. Cloud resources, including public, private, and hybrid clouds, offer scalable and flexible solutions for modern IT needs. Storage systems and virtualization platforms further enhance resource management by enabling efficient use of physical hardware and providing the ability to run multiple virtual instances on a single machine. Each of these components contributes to a robust IT infrastructure that supports the overall functionality of an organization's IT environment.

Service management was another significant topic in this chapter. We discussed how help desk operations serve as the frontline for user support, addressing issues and ensuring that users can effectively interact with IT services. Incident response and management involve detecting, analyzing, and resolving incidents that disrupt normal operations. Problem management focuses on identifying the root causes of recurring issues to prevent future occurrences. Change management ensures that modifications to the IT environment are implemented systematically, minimizing potential disruptions. Monitoring and enforcing SLAs help ensure that IT services meet predefined standards and expectations, contributing to overall service quality and user satisfaction.

APM was also highlighted, focusing on maintaining optimal performance for business-critical applications. Real-time monitoring tools are used to track the performance of applications, allowing for immediate response to any issues that arise. Detecting and diagnosing complex performance problems involves analyzing various metrics and logs to pinpoint the root cause of performance issues. Aligning IT performance with business objectives ensures that applications support organizational goals and deliver value. A well-managed APM strategy enhances the user experience and ensures that applications function efficiently and effectively.

Capacity planning and resource optimization were key areas of focus in this chapter. Forecasting future demand involves predicting the IT resource requirements based on current trends and anticipated growth. Assessing current capacity helps in understanding if existing resources are adequate to meet future needs. Identifying gaps between demand and capacity allows organizations to address potential shortages or overages. Developing strategies to address these gaps includes allocating resources to the most valuable activities and minimizing waste and idle time. By improving productivity and performance while reducing costs, organizations can achieve a balance that supports both operational efficiency and financial health.

We also explored a range of tools and technologies that support ITOM. ITOM software suites provide integrated solutions for managing various aspects of IT operations. Network monitoring and management tools help in tracking network performance and addressing issues. CMDB offers a centralized view of IT assets and their relationships. AIOps platforms use machine learning to automate and enhance IT operations, providing predictive analytics and intelligent insights. Cloud management and orchestration tools facilitate the efficient management of cloud resources, while containerization and orchestration platforms support the deployment and management of applications in containerized environments. These tools and technologies are instrumental in optimizing IT operations and maintaining a well-managed IT environment.

BCP and disaster recovery strategies are vital for ensuring that IT operations remain resilient in the face of disruptions. BCP focuses on maintaining essential functions during unexpected events, ensuring that critical operations continue without significant interruptions. Disaster recovery strategies, on the other hand, involve restoring IT services and data after a major incident, such as a natural disaster or cyberattack. Both approaches are important for minimizing the impact of disruptions and ensuring that the organization can recover and resume normal operations as quickly as possible.

This chapter provided an in-depth look at various aspects of ITOM, from frameworks and infrastructure management to service management and application performance. By understanding and integrating these elements, organizations can effectively manage their IT environments and align IT operations with business objectives. The chapter also emphasized the importance of modern tools and technologies, vendor management, and continuity planning in maintaining a well-functioning IT ecosystem.

Looking ahead, organizations must continue to evolve their ITOM practices to keep pace with technological advancements and changing business needs. Adopting new technologies and refining management practices will be key to achieving operational excellence and ensuring that IT supports organizational goals effectively. By staying informed and adaptable, organizations can navigate the complexities of IT operations and thrive in an ever-changing landscape.

NOTES

1 Axelos, *ITIL® Foundation: ITIL 4 Edition*, London: The Stationery Office (TSO), 2019. www.axelos.com.
2 ISACA, *COBIT 2019 Framework: Introduction and Methodology*, Schaumburg, IL: ISACA, 2018. www.isaca.org/resources/cobit.
3 International Organization for Standardization, *ISO/IEC 27001:2022: Information Security, Cybersecurity and Privacy Protection—Information Security Management Systems—Requirements*, Geneva: ISO, 2022.

3 Enterprise Risk Management and Cybersecurity Essentials

LEARNING OBJECTIVES

- Understand the distinctions between cybersecurity and risk management
- Analyze the impact of security incidents and breaches
- Apply cybersecurity frameworks and risk management strategies
- Navigate governance, compliance, and legal considerations

INTRODUCTION TO RISK MANAGEMENT AND CYBERSECURITY

Cybersecurity is about keeping computers, networks, and data safe from online attackers. Since the late 1990s the internet has become part of the essential foundation of all businesses, regardless of size or industry, by the ubiquity of email, word processors, spreadsheets, and presentation tools. The internet has changed how we talk to each other and do business, but it's also given criminals new ways to cause trouble. They find weak spots in software and hardware to steal personal info or spread computer viruses. Some of the activity is malicious vandalism, to stop organizations from conducting business. It is also used as political terrorism, exposing state or personnel information that is confidential. They may even use unauthorized access to damage critical infrastructure and endanger whole communities. People who work in cybersecurity try to stop these threats by finding weak spots, making better defenses, detecting when malicious activity occurs as soon as possible and fixing problems quickly. It's like a never-ending game of cat and mouse, with both sides always changing their plans.

A big idea in cybersecurity is the attack surface, which basically means all the ways a hacker might try to get into a system. The more ways a system connects to other things, the bigger its attack surface. Making this surface smaller and using strong defenses like encryption and firewalls are key to keeping important information safe. Cybersecurity experts need to know about different kinds of threats. Some tricks, like phishing, try to fool people into giving away personal information and stealing their credentials to allow access to bad actors. Others, like ransomware, lock people out of their computers until they pay money. There are also long-term attacks that try to steal secrets or damage important systems. Cybersecurity folks need to keep learning about these dangers as they change over time.

CYBERSECURITY VS. RISK MANAGEMENT: UNDERSTANDING THE DIFFERENCE

Cybersecurity focuses on protecting systems, networks, and data from cyber threats. It's about preventing unauthorized access, data breaches, and attacks that could compromise an organization's

DOI: 10.1201/9781003562153-4

digital infrastructure. Risk management, however, takes a broader approach. It looks at all potential threats a company might face—financial risks, legal liabilities, operational disruptions, and reputational damage. Cybersecurity is a key part of this, but risk management extends beyond IT security to ensure the business remains stable and resilient.

While cybersecurity teams work to defend against digital threats, risk management professionals consider the bigger picture. They assess how cyber risks connect to other vulnerabilities, such as supply chain disruptions, regulatory changes, or legal exposure. The goal is to anticipate problems, reduce their impact, and keep the organization running smoothly. Cybersecurity plays a critical role within the larger risk management framework, but they are not the same. Cybersecurity protects against digital threats, while risk management ensures the company is prepared for a wide range of challenges. Strong security requires both technical defenses to guard against cyber risks and a strategic approach to managing broader business threats.

Risk Management

Cybersecurity risk management is the process of identifying, analyzing, and mitigating risks to ensure the confidentiality, integrity, and availability of critical assets. It involves balancing security investments against potential threats while maintaining compliance with industry regulations, while ensuring users have the only right access to the right information and the right time. Cyber risks are not isolated to IT infrastructure, they stem from human behavior, operational processes, and supply chain dependencies. An effective risk management strategy assesses these interconnected factors to maximize the value of cybersecurity investments.

Risk management frameworks help organizations establish policies, define risk tolerance, and allocate resources efficiently. They provide a structured approach to identifying vulnerabilities, evaluating potential threats, and determining appropriate mitigation measures. By integrating risk management into business operations, organizations can minimize the impact of cyber threats while maintaining operational efficiency.

Identifying and Assessing Risk

A risk-based approach to cybersecurity empowers organizations to make informed decisions about where to apply security restrictions and implement controls. The foundation of any effective cybersecurity strategy begins with identifying and assessing risks. This process involves evaluating several key areas. First, understanding the threat landscape is essential, this includes both external and internal cyber threats that may target the organization. Next, assessing the potential business impact helps determine the financial, reputational, and operational consequences that could result from an attack. Compliance with regulatory requirements is also a critical factor, particularly when sensitive data is involved. Finally, organizations must analyze system vulnerabilities by identifying weaknesses across networks, applications, and existing security controls. This comprehensive risk assessment ensures that resources are allocated strategically, targeting the areas of greatest exposure and potential harm.

Risk assessment must be an ongoing process that integrates input from IT, compliance, legal, and business units. Cybersecurity teams must work alongside auditors and risk officers to ensure a holistic view of risk exposure. In many organizations, dedicated risk management professionals within IT security oversee the continuous evaluation of cyber risks.

Once risks are identified, organizations must determine risk tolerance—deciding which risks are acceptable and which require immediate mitigation. Risk assessments help organizations prioritize threats based on business needs, compliance obligations, and financial impact. Security policies should be tailored to the organization's unique risk profile, ensuring a balance between security and business efficiency.

ENTERPRISE RISK MANAGEMENT FRAMEWORKS

There are several risk management frameworks to guide organizations in structuring their security programs. These frameworks provide different methodologies for assessing and mitigating cyber risk. Highlighted below is a brief overview of two predominant frameworks, Enterprise Security Risk Management and Sherwood Applied Business Security Architecture, which is covered in greater completeness in Chapter 12.

ESRM

ESRM[1] aligns security efforts with business objectives by ensuring that cybersecurity enhances, rather than obstructs, operations. ESRM is a proactive approach that continuously monitors and reassesses risks, involves stakeholders from multiple business units, and prioritizes security controls based on business impact. ESRM follows a four-step process: Identify security risks across the organization, assess their severity and likelihood, prioritize mitigation measures based on risk exposure, and implement risk-based controls and monitoring. The key advantage is that ESRM ensures cybersecurity is business-driven, enabling security teams to work collaboratively with business units.

SABSA

SABSA[2] is a risk-driven security architecture framework that builds security strategies based on business requirements rather than technical specifications. It uses a layered security approach with six stages: Context, Concept, Logical, Physical, Component, and Operational. The key advantage is that SABSA integrates security into enterprise architecture, ensuring risk management is embedded into IT infrastructure.

CYBERSECURITY MANAGEMENT

The field of cybersecurity is continuously changing as threat actors become more sophisticated and their attacks gain more attention. This has led to an increase in the importance of cyber warfare on a global scale, with no one entity holding a dominant position. As a result, managing cybersecurity risk is a crucial aspect of decision-making and operational leadership for protecting enterprises, managing operations, and mitigating risk.

Key components of cybersecurity risk management include multilayered protection using various technologies and procedures to secure organizational IT systems and implementing security controls to enable business objectives while safeguarding against potential threats.

Frameworks can provide a centralized guide to implementing security controls; standards provide an implementation guide and key requirements to follow, and best practices provide proven mechanisms to achieve success. Many organizations use frameworks defined by their regulators or clients. However, other more complex regulated sectors, such as large banks or healthcare providers, are required to follow both a corporate governance standard and another sector-specific regulatory standard. This regulation presents a quandary: standards and best practices conflict, yet clearly the regulators desire that both be implemented.

IDENTIFYING THREATS AND VULNERABILITIES

There are different ways to categorize threats and vulnerabilities. In the cybersecurity realm, software developers and government agencies have traditionally used a basic model consisting of three elements to identify threat agents, including hackers, criminal hackers, and nation-states. This model helps to connect the threats and vulnerabilities in a cybersecurity risk model to at least one threat agent. However, as technology advances, it's important to consider whether this simple model covers all potential adversaries faced by an organization. Additionally, there is a concern that by focusing on more uncommon threats, it may overlook more common adversaries who could pose higher risks.

Looking beyond just the cybersecurity community could bring about a wider range of potential threat agents. Essentially, anyone with a vested interest in accessing vulnerable information could be considered a threat agent; typical examples include hackers, criminals, and even nation-state or corporate entities. While it may seem farfetched to view a corporation as a potential adversary, the accessibility of information within its data center is a significant concern for many enterprise risk managers.

CYBERSECURITY FRAMEWORKS

Cybersecurity frameworks provide structured methodologies for organizations to assess, manage, and mitigate security risks. These frameworks serve as blueprints for implementing security controls, ensuring regulatory compliance, and enhancing an organization's overall security posture. Understanding these frameworks is crucial for establishing a common security language and aligning cybersecurity efforts with business objectives. Below are three widely adopted cybersecurity frameworks that organizations rely on to strengthen defenses and build resilience against evolving threats.

Center for Internet Security (CIS)

The CIS[3] Controls framework is a practical, action-oriented security guide designed to improve cybersecurity for organizations of all sizes. It offers a prioritized set of security best practices, known as CIS Controls, which provide a structured, tiered approach to securing IT systems against prevalent cyber threats. These controls are divided into three implementation groups, tailored to the size, resources, and risk tolerance of an organization; Essential Cyber Hygiene, Intermediate Security Controls, and Advanced Security Practices.

The CIS framework's tiered model makes it highly scalable, enabling organizations with limited security resources to prioritize essential controls while allowing larger enterprises to implement advanced security measures such as continuous monitoring and incident response. One of the key advantages of the CIS framework is its alignment with other industry standards and compliance requirements, making it a cost-effective and adaptable solution for organizations seeking to enhance security posture without overcomplicating implementation.

NIST Cybersecurity Framework (CSF 2.0)

The NIST CSF 2.0,[4] released in 2024, builds upon the original NIST CSF, enhancing its adaptability to modern cybersecurity challenges. Originally designed for critical infrastructure, CSF 2.0 has evolved into a universal cybersecurity framework applicable across industries, regardless of size or maturity level. One of the key updates in CSF 2.0 is the expansion of its core functions. The framework now consists of six primary functions: Govern, Identify, Protect, Detect, Respond, and Recover.

The flexibility and scalability of CSF 2.0 make it a powerful tool for organizations across various industries, including finance, healthcare, defense, and technology. Whether an organization is just starting its cybersecurity journey or looking to refine an existing security program, CSF 2.0 provides a structured, risk-based approach to strengthening cybersecurity posture and resilience in an ever-evolving threat landscape.

ISO/IEC 27001

ISO/IEC 27001[5] is a globally recognized standard for establishing, implementing, maintaining, and continuously improving an Information Security Management System (ISMS). Unlike other frameworks that focus solely on technical controls, ISO/IEC 27001 integrates people, processes, and technology to provide a holistic approach to information security management. This standard follows a risk-based methodology, requiring organizations to identify security risks to sensitive data, implement controls to mitigate those risks, and continuously monitor and improve security processes to adapt to emerging threats.

ISO/IEC 27001 compliance demonstrates an organization's commitment to data security, enhancing trust with customers, business partners, and regulators. Achieving ISO certification involves a rigorous third-party audit, validating an organization's security maturity and resilience. This certification process is particularly valuable for companies handling sensitive data or operating in regulated industries, such as healthcare, finance, and technology.

ISO/IEC 27001's structured approach to risk management and compliance ensures that security measures are not just reactive but proactively embedded into business processes. Its emphasis on continuous improvement ensures organizations remain resilient against evolving cyber threats.

Category	CIS	NIST CSF 2.0	ISO/IEC 27001
Primary focus	Practical security controls and best practices for IT systems	Comprehensive, risk-based cybersecurity management	Holistic ISMS
Implementation approach	Three-tiered controls for different organizational sizes	Six core functions: Govern, Identify, Protect, Detect, Respond, Recover	Risk-based methodology covering people, processes, and technology
Best suited for	Organizations of all sizes, especially SMEs looking for structured controls	Organizations across industries, including SMEs and critical infrastructure	Enterprises handling sensitive data and requiring formal security governance
Certification requirement	No formal certification; organizations can self-implement	No formal certification; used as a framework for guidance	Requires third-party audit for certification
Scalability and flexibility	Highly scalable with implementation groups tailored to organization size	Flexible and adaptable across industries and business sizes	Structured and process-driven; requires ongoing compliance and auditing
Compliance and regulation alignment	Aligns with various standards (e.g., NIST, ISO, GDPR, HIPAA)	Widely recognized across industries and regulatory requirements	Designed to ensure compliance with global regulatory and legal requirements

There are also multiple specific cybersecurity frameworks which have been developed by the regulatory bodies that govern industries such as healthcare, credit card payments and government service providers. These can be referenced in the table below.

Category	HIPAA	PCI-DSS	CMMC 2.0
Purpose	Protect the privacy and security of health information	Protect cardholder data and secure payment card transactions	Safeguard Controlled Unclassified Information within the Defense Industrial Base

Category	HIPAA	PCI-DSS	CMMC 2.0
Applicability	Healthcare providers, health plans, clearinghouses, and business associates	Merchants, service providers, and organizations handling credit card transactions	Contractors and subcontractors doing business with the U.S. Department of Defense
Data protection scope	Protected Health Information (PHI), including electronic PHI	Cardholder Data, including PAN, CVV, etc.	Controlled Unclassified Information (CUI) and Federal Contract Information (FCI)
Core components	Privacy Rule, Security Rule, Breach Notification Rule	Twelve high-level requirements under six control objectives	Three maturity levels mapped to NIST 800-171 and NIST 800-172
Compliance requirements	Safeguards (admin, technical, physical); risk assessments; breach notification	Secure networks, access controls, system testing, monitoring, logging, policies	Varies by level: self-assessment (L1), third-party certification (L2), government-led (L3)
Enforcement authority	U.S. Department of Health and Human Services–Office for Civil Rights	Payment brands (e.g., Visa, MasterCard) via acquiring banks	U.S. Department of Defense, Office of the Under Secretary for Acquisition & Sustainment
Penalties for noncompliance	Civil and criminal penalties, up to $1.5 million per year per violation category	Fines, loss of processing privileges, reputational damage	Ineligibility to bid on DoD contracts requiring CMMC
Certification requirement	No formal certification, but audits may occur	No formal certification, validation required for some merchant levels	Formal certification required at Level 2 and above via accredited providers

Choosing the Right Cybersecurity Framework

Each of these frameworks serves distinct security needs:

- CIS—Best suited for organizations seeking a cost-effective, straightforward cybersecurity roadmap with tiered implementation guidance.
- NIST CSF 2.0—Ideal for businesses that require a flexible, risk-based approach to cybersecurity, especially those in regulated industries.
- ISO/IEC 27001—A comprehensive framework for organizations prioritizing formal security governance, risk management, and compliance.

Implementing a cybersecurity framework is not a one-size-fits-all approach. Organizations must evaluate their risk exposure, regulatory obligations, and security maturity to determine the best-fit framework, or integrate multiple frameworks to create a robust cybersecurity strategy. By leveraging these well-established standards, organizations can strengthen their defensive posture, ensure compliance, and build long-term resilience against cyber threats.

COMMON CYBERSECURITY PRACTICES AND TECHNOLOGIES

Cybersecurity is no longer a standalone function but an essential part of business operations, requiring a combination of technical controls, risk management strategies, and continuous monitoring. By integrating structured security practices enterprises can identify and mitigate risks before they escalate into full-scale breaches.

A strong security foundation begins with proactive risk assessments and secure application development. Vulnerability assessments and penetration testing help identify weaknesses in systems and applications, enabling organizations to remediate security gaps before attackers exploit them. Additionally, embedding security into the software development lifecycle through secure coding practices and DevSecOps ensures that applications remain resilient against emerging threats. These measures help minimize the attack surface and prevent exploitation at both the network and application layers.

Beyond technical defenses, human-centric security remains a crucial aspect of cybersecurity. According to prominent cybersecurity training and simulation technology firm KnowB4, 70–90%[6] of all attacks originate from social engineering and phishing attacks. These attacks continue to target employees as entry points into corporate networks. Security awareness training, phishing simulations, and ongoing education programs strengthen the human firewall by equipping employees with the knowledge to identify and respond to potential threats. By fostering a security-conscious culture, organizations can significantly reduce the risks associated with human error.

To further reinforce security, enterprises deploy a suite of cybersecurity technologies that provide continuous protection across network, endpoint, and data environments. Firewalls and intrusion detection systems serve as the first line of defense against external threats, while Virtual Private Networks (VPNs) secure remote communications. Endpoint security solutions, including antivirus, Endpoint Detection and Response, and device/data encryption, safeguard individual devices against malware and unauthorized access. Additionally, robust data protection mechanisms ensure that sensitive information remains secure.

Common Cybersecurity Practices

Cybersecurity should be an integral component of business operations, requiring a combination of technical controls, risk management frameworks, and continuous monitoring. Organizations implement structured security practices such as vulnerability assessments, penetration testing, secure software development, and incident response to mitigate cyber risks effectively. By integrating these measures, enterprises can enhance their security posture while maintaining operational resilience.

Vulnerability assessments and penetration testing play a crucial role in identifying and mitigating security gaps before attackers exploit them. Organizations conduct vulnerability assessments to systematically scan applications, networks, and infrastructure for weaknesses. Meanwhile, penetration testing simulates real-world cyberattacks, helping security teams evaluate existing defenses and uncover exploitable flaws. These proactive security assessments enable enterprises to prioritize remediation efforts and strengthen their overall security posture.

Application security is a fundamental component of modern cybersecurity frameworks, ensuring that software remains resilient against evolving threats. Secure coding practices, vulnerability assessments, and web application firewalls mitigate risks associated with common attack vectors such as injection flaws and cross-site scripting. By embedding security into the software development lifecycle, organizations can reduce their exposure to application-layer threats and enhance the integrity of digital assets. The adoption of DevSecOps further reinforces this approach by integrating security into agile development workflows. This methodology emphasizes shift-left security, automated security testing, and continuous integration and continuous delivery pipelines to enable rapid yet secure software releases.

Beyond technical controls, security awareness training empowers employees to recognize and defend against social engineering tactics. Phishing simulations, awareness campaigns, and ongoing education programs help mitigate human risk factors by fostering a security-conscious workforce. Attackers increasingly exploit human vulnerabilities rather than technical weaknesses, making employee awareness a critical defense layer. By equipping staff with the knowledge to identify phishing attempts and deceptive social engineering techniques, organizations can significantly reduce the likelihood of successful cyberattacks.

Robust incident response and recovery strategies ensure business continuity in the face of security breaches. Incident response planning establishes structured procedures for detecting, containing, and mitigating cyber threats, while disaster recovery strategies focus on restoring critical operations with minimal downtime. Effective response mechanisms, including defined escalation protocols and post-incident analysis, enable organizations to learn from security incidents and continuously improve their defenses. By integrating these cybersecurity best practices, enterprises can mitigate risks, maintain compliance, and build resilience against evolving cyber threats.

Cybersecurity Practice	Description
Network security	Network security is a critical component of an organization's cybersecurity strategy, designed to protect digital infrastructure from unauthorized access, data breaches, and cyber threats. Key components include firewalls, intrusion detection systems, VPNs, network segmentation, and endpoint protection.
Network segmentation	Network segmentation involves dividing an organization's network into smaller, isolated segments to limit lateral movement by attackers. Segmentation strategies include VLANs, microsegmentation, and zero-trust network architecture. By enforcing access controls and restricting intersegment communication, organizations can contain breaches and prevent unauthorized access to critical systems.
Vulnerability assessments and penetration testing	Organizations conduct vulnerability assessments to identify weaknesses in their applications and infrastructure. Penetration testing simulates real-world attack scenarios to evaluate security defenses and uncover exploitable flaws.
Application security	Application security encompasses measures to identify and remediate vulnerabilities in software applications. Secure coding practices, vulnerability assessments, and web application firewalls help mitigate risks associated with application-layer attacks.
DevSecOps	DevSecOps promotes security integration throughout the software development lifecycle. It incorporates security automation, continuous testing, and compliance monitoring to enhance software security. By aligning security with development and operations, DevSecOps accelerates secure software delivery and reduces vulnerabilities.
Secure coding practices	Developers follow secure coding guidelines (e.g., OWASP Top 10) to mitigate common vulnerabilities such as SQL injection and cross-site scripting (XSS). Regular code reviews and automated security testing enhance software integrity.
Security awareness training	Cybersecurity training programs educate employees on recognizing threats such as phishing and social engineering attacks.
Incident response and recovery	Incident response planning and disaster recovery strategies ensure organizations can quickly recover from security incidents.

Common Cybersecurity Technologies

Cyber adversaries continuously develop new attack vectors, making it imperative to implement robust defense mechanisms across networks, endpoints, applications, and data. To address these challenges, cybersecurity professionals leverage a suite of technologies designed to detect, prevent, and mitigate cyber threats. These solutions work in tandem to enforce security policies, minimize attack surfaces, and enhance overall resilience. Understanding the role of core security technologies is essential for building a comprehensive cybersecurity strategy that aligns with business objectives and regulatory requirements.

Network security remains the first line of defense against external threats. Firewalls serve as a gatekeeper, filtering traffic based on predefined rules to prevent unauthorized access. Traditional firewalls operate at the packet level, while next-generation firewalls incorporate advanced capabilities such as deep packet inspection and intrusion prevention. Complementing firewalls, intrusion detection systems monitor network activity, identifying malicious patterns through signature-based and anomaly-based detection methods. Together, these technologies enhance an organization's ability to detect and respond to cyber threats in real time. Additionally, VPNs provide encrypted communication channels, ensuring data confidentiality for remote users and internetwork connectivity.

Endpoint security plays a critical role in safeguarding individual devices against malware, unauthorized access, and data breaches. Antivirus and antimalware solutions form the foundation of endpoint protection, while Endpoint Detection and Response (EDR) solutions provide real-time monitoring and advanced threat-hunting capabilities. Device encryption mitigates risks associated with data loss by rendering stolen data unreadable, and access controls enforce authentication policies to prevent unauthorized use. By integrating endpoint security with network defenses, organizations establish a cohesive security posture that extends across all access points.

Beyond network and endpoint security, data protection is a cornerstone of any cybersecurity strategy. Organizations must implement encryption, data loss prevention, and access controls to prevent unauthorized data access, leakage, and tampering. Encryption ensures that sensitive information remains secure, whether in transit or at rest. Data loss prevention solutions monitor data movement and enforce compliance policies, reducing the risk of accidental or intentional leaks. Access control frameworks, including Role-Based Access Control and Attribute-Based Access Control, ensure that users only have access to the data necessary for their role. These measures collectively reduce the risk of data breaches and regulatory noncompliance.

Identity and access management solutions provide centralized control over user authentication and authorization, mitigating the risks associated with credential compromise. Multifactor Authentication strengthens authentication by requiring multiple forms of identity verification, while Single Sign-On streamlines access management without sacrificing security. Privileged access management enforces strict controls over high-risk accounts, preventing attackers from escalating privileges within an environment. Combined with web application firewalls, which defend against application-layer threats, identity and access management (IAM) solutions enhance an organization's ability to protect both internal and external resources. By deploying these cybersecurity technologies strategically, enterprises can build a resilient security framework that adapts to emerging threats while maintaining operational efficiency.

Cybersecurity Technology	Description
Firewalls	Firewalls act as a barrier between trusted internal networks and untrusted external environments, such as the internet. They analyze network traffic based on predefined security rules, blocking or allowing packets accordingly. Traditional firewalls filter traffic at the packet level, while next-generation firewalls incorporate deep packet inspection, application-layer filtering, and intrusion prevention capabilities.
Intrusion detection systems	Intrusion Detection Systems solutions continuously monitor network activity to detect and respond to suspicious behavior. They operate in two primary forms: network-based (monitors traffic across entire network segments) and host-based (focuses on activities within specific devices).
VPNs	VPNs encrypt network traffic, ensuring secure communication over public or untrusted networks. They provide confidentiality, integrity, and authentication, preventing eavesdropping and man-in-the-middle attacks.

Cybersecurity Technology	Description
Endpoint protection	Endpoint security encompasses various defense mechanisms to safeguard individual devices from cyber threats. End point protection includes Antivirus and Antimalware (solutions that detect and remove malicious software), EDR (real-time monitoring), Device Encryption (protect sensitive data in case of device theft or loss), and Access Controls (enforce authentication and authorization policies).
Data security	Data security focuses on protecting information from unauthorized access, tampering, and loss. Organizations implement encryption, data loss prevention, access controls, and classification frameworks to mitigate risks associated with data exposure.
Data encryption	Encryption transforms plaintext into ciphertext, ensuring that only authorized users can decrypt and access sensitive data. Common encryption standards include Advanced Encryption Standard for data storage and Transport Layer Security for secure network communication.
Data loss prevention	Data Loss Prevention solutions monitor and control data movement to prevent accidental or malicious leaks. They enforce policies to restrict data transfers via email, cloud services, and removable media.
Access controls and data classification	Access control mechanisms, including role-based access control and attribute-based access control, limit data exposure to authorized users.
Web application firewalls	Web Application Firewalls solutions filter and monitor HTTP traffic to protect web applications from threats such as SQL injection and cross-site request forgery.
Identity and access management	IAM solutions manage user identities, authentication, and authorization processes to enforce security policies.
Multifactor authentication	Multifactor Authentication strengthens authentication by requiring users to verify their identity through multiple factors (e.g., passwords, biometrics, security tokens).
Single sign-on	Single Sign-On enables users to access multiple applications with a single authentication session, improving security and user experience

Emerging Technologies in Cybersecurity

Innovative technologies are reshaping cybersecurity, providing advanced threat detection and mitigation capabilities.

- User and Entity Behavior Analytics (UEBA) is a cybersecurity solution designed to detect anomalous and potentially malicious behavior within an organization's network. It leverages machine learning, statistical analysis, and automation to establish baseline behavior patterns for both users and nonuser entities, such as servers, routers, Internet of Things (IoT) devices, and endpoints. By continuously monitoring activity and comparing it to these baselines, UEBA identifies deviations that may signal insider threats, compromised accounts, or cyberattacks.
- Artificial Intelligence and Machine Learning enhance threat intelligence, automate anomaly detection, and predict cyber threats. These technologies improve security efficiency by analyzing vast datasets and identifying suspicious patterns.
- Blockchain Technology enhances data integrity and transparency, reducing risks associated with centralized databases. It offers applications in identity management, secure transactions, and decentralized security solutions.

CYBERSECURITY AND RISK MITIGATION STRATEGIES

A robust risk mitigation plan is essential for organizations to effectively manage cyber threats while maintaining operational stability. Risk mitigation should be integrated throughout every stage of an IT system's lifecycle, ensuring that security measures are preventive, detective, and corrective. Preventive controls, such as firewalls, encryption, and multifactor authentication (MFA), serve as the first line of defense, reducing the likelihood of unauthorized access. Detective controls, including intrusion detection systems (IDS) and continuous monitoring, help identify potential threats before they cause significant damage. In cases where a breach occurs, corrective controls—such as incident response plans and disaster recovery strategies—ensure rapid containment and recovery, minimizing the impact on business operations.

Proactive Risk Planning

Cybersecurity risks must be addressed proactively rather than reactively. Regular security assessments help organizations identify vulnerabilities before they can be exploited. Implementing a zero-trust security model further strengthens defenses by ensuring that access is granted only after thorough verification, reducing the risk of unauthorized access. In addition, employee security training is critical for mitigating threats like phishing and social engineering, which often exploit human error as an entry point for attackers. Another key component of proactive risk management is third-party risk assessment, which ensures that external vendors and partners adhere to stringent security standards, protecting the organization's supply chain from potential cyber threats.

Continuous Risk Monitoring

With cyber threats evolving at an unprecedented pace, organizations must adopt real-time threat intelligence and continuous monitoring to stay ahead of emerging risks. Security Information and Event Management (SIEM) tools help detect anomalies by aggregating and analyzing security logs, providing early indicators of suspicious activity. Artificial Intelligence for IT Operations (AIOps) further enhances monitoring by automating threat analysis, allowing security teams to respond faster to potential incidents. Collaboration with industry partners and regulatory bodies through cyber threat intelligence sharing and integration into the systems, such as IDS/IPS and SIEM, improves situational awareness and enhances collective defense, strengthening the organization's ability to anticipate and counter threats.

Incident Response and Business Continuity

Despite best efforts to prevent attacks, organizations must be prepared to respond swiftly and effectively when incidents occur. A structured Incident Response Plan (IRP) provides a clear roadmap for handling cyber incidents, ensuring a coordinated and efficient response. To validate the effectiveness of response procedures, tabletop exercises should be conducted regularly, simulating real-world attack scenarios to assess readiness and identify gaps. Automated threat containment mechanisms can further limit the spread of malware or unauthorized access, reducing the impact of an attack. Additionally, redundant backup solutions play a crucial role in business continuity, ensuring that critical data can be quickly restored following a security breach or system failure. By implementing these measures, organizations can strengthen their resilience against cyber threats while minimizing disruption to operations.

Cybersecurity Threat Landscape

The cybersecurity threat landscape is constantly evolving, with adversaries refining their tactics and developing new attack vectors. As digital dependency grows across industries and everyday life, cybercriminals exploit expanding attack surfaces, targeting individuals, businesses, and even governments. The sophistication and frequency of attacks continue to escalate, creating a high-stakes environment where security professionals must remain proactive to mitigate risks.

Ransomware: A Persistent and Escalating Threat

Ransomware remains one of the most disruptive cyber threats today. Attackers use malicious software to encrypt critical data, demanding payment, typically in cryptocurrencies like Bitcoin, to restore access. The stakes are even higher with double extortion tactics, where attackers not only encrypt files but also exfiltrate sensitive data, threatening to leak it unless their demands are met. Ransomware operators increasingly target high-value entities, including hospitals, government agencies, and infrastructure providers, knowing that these organizations cannot afford prolonged downtime.

Nation-State Cyber Operations

State-sponsored cyber threats have become a central concern for national security and economic stability. Adversaries such as Russia, China, North Korea, Iran and some eastern European countries engage in cyber espionage, intellectual property theft, and disruptive cyberattacks to further strategic objectives. These operations can destabilize industries, compromise critical infrastructure, and escalate geopolitical tensions. Unlike financially motivated cybercriminals, nation-state actors have access to vast resources, including advanced malware and zero-day exploits, making their campaigns highly effective and difficult to attribute.

Phishing Attacks

Despite increased awareness, phishing remains one of the most successful attack methods. Cybercriminals continuously refine their social engineering tactics, crafting highly convincing emails and messages that deceive users into revealing credentials or executing malware. Business email compromise scams have also surged, where attackers impersonate executives or vendors to trick employees into authorizing fraudulent wire transfers. AI-driven phishing attacks further complicate detection, enabling attackers to personalize and automate large-scale campaigns.

Spear-phishing is a sophisticated form of phishing that targets specific individuals or organizations using tailored, personal information to increase the likelihood of success. Unlike generic phishing attempts, spear-phishing leverages publicly available data such as job titles, social connections, or corporate affiliations, often gathered from social media or company websites. The attacker then crafts a convincing email, usually appearing to originate from a trusted contact like a colleague or business partner. These messages often contain malicious links or attachments designed to harvest login credentials, exfiltrate sensitive data, or deliver malware. The ultimate goal may be to compromise systems, commit financial fraud, or gain persistent access to protected environments.

Smishing is another variant of phishing that uses SMS text messages as the attack vector. These messages are crafted to look like legitimate communications from trusted institutions such as banks, delivery companies, or government agencies. They often rely on urgency or fear tactics such as warnings about compromised accounts, to prompt recipients to click on malicious links or download harmful applications. Once engaged, victims may inadvertently disclose personal information like passwords or credit card numbers, or expose their devices to malware. The intent behind smishing is typically financial theft, identity fraud, or the establishment of a foothold for broader attacks.

The Security Risks of IoT Devices

The proliferation of IoT devices, ranging from smart home systems to industrial sensors, introduces significant security risks. IoT devices are often based on open source code, like Linux-based distributions, that have less detailed software development lifecycle (SDLC) approaches and lack robust security controls, making them easy targets for attackers seeking entry points into corporate networks. Compromised IoT devices are frequently harnessed for Distributed Denial-of-Service (DDoS) attacks, overwhelming online services with traffic from vast botnets. As IoT adoption grows, so does the urgency for enforcing stronger authentication, regular patching, and network segmentation.

Zero-Day Vulnerabilities

Zero-day vulnerabilities, previously unknown software flaws that hackers exploit before patches are available, pose severe risks to organizations. These vulnerabilities are prized assets for cybercriminals, nation-state actors, and even intelligence agencies. Threat actors exploit zero-days to infiltrate networks undetected, often leveraging them in targeted attacks against high-value entities. Security teams must rely on proactive threat intelligence, continuous monitoring, behavior-based analysis, and rapid patch management to minimize exposure.

Supply Chain Attacks

Cybercriminals increasingly focus on supply chain attacks, infiltrating organizations by compromising third-party vendors, software providers, or managed service providers. Instead of attacking enterprises directly, adversaries inject malware or backdoors into trusted software updates, affecting thousands of downstream users. The SolarWinds breach exemplifies the scale of these attacks, highlighting the need for stringent vetting of third-party partners, software integrity checks, and Zero Trust security frameworks.

Cloud Security Challenges

As businesses migrate workloads and sensitive data to cloud environments, cloud security misconfigurations remain a leading cause of breaches. While cloud service providers implement robust security measures, customers are responsible for securing their own cloud assets. Inadequate access controls, overly permissive storage settings, and poor identity management frequently lead to data leaks and unauthorized access. Organizations must enforce strong cloud security policies, including MFA, encryption, and continuous compliance monitoring.

Artificial Intelligence in Cyber Warfare

AI and machine learning are dual-use technologies in cybersecurity, while they enhance threat detection and response, adversaries weaponize them for more sophisticated attacks. AI-powered malware can autonomously evade detection, adapt to security defenses, and launch automated phishing campaigns. Cybercriminals can also manipulate AI-driven decision-making systems, potentially disrupting financial markets, misinformation campaigns, and even autonomous infrastructure.

Defenders must leverage AI responsibly, ensuring it is used for proactive security rather than falling into adversaries' hands.

Human Factor

Despite technological advancements, human error remains the most significant cybersecurity vulnerability. Poor password hygiene, falling for phishing scams, misconfigurations, and accidental data exposure contribute to a large percentage of breaches. While security awareness training is essential, it must be supplemented with strong IAM, behavioral analytics, and automated security enforcement to minimize human risk.

The Wide-Ranging Impact of Security Incidents and Breaches

Security breaches and cyber incidents don't just disrupt individual organizations, they can ripple across industries, economies, and even national security landscapes. When unauthorized actors infiltrate networks, steal data, or manipulate systems, the consequences extend far beyond a single compromised database. While the initial impact might seem limited to data loss or corruption, the broader implications are often severe and long-lasting.

Financial Fallout

The most immediate and measurable consequence of a security breach is financial loss. Organizations must deal with forensic investigations, legal fees, regulatory fines, and remediation costs. Beyond direct financial penalties, businesses face lost revenue from disrupted operations, decreased consumer confidence, and reputational damage that can drive customers to competitors. Publicly traded companies may see stock prices plummet, while smaller businesses often struggle to recover, with some never reopening after a significant breach.

Erosion of Trust

Customer and stakeholder confidence is difficult to build but easy to lose. A single security breach can permanently alter the way consumers view an organization, especially when sensitive personal data is exposed. Industries handling highly confidential information, such as healthcare, finance, and e-commerce, are particularly vulnerable to this trust erosion. A hospital that suffers a breach compromising patient records, for example, may not only lose patients to competitors but also face increased scrutiny from regulators and insurers.

Regulatory and Legal Consequences

Cybersecurity is now a legal and regulatory issue as much as it is a technical one. Organizations failing to protect sensitive data can be held liable under laws like GDPR, CCPA, and various sector-specific regulations such as HIPAA for healthcare and PCI-DSS for payment security. Noncompliance can result in severe fines, mandatory security reforms, and increased oversight, adding to the long-term financial strain on the affected business.

Operational Disruptions

A well-coordinated cyberattack can cripple an organization's ability to function. Ransomware attacks, for example, have the potential to paralyze operations for days or even weeks, as seen in high-profile incidents targeting hospitals, financial institutions, and supply chain networks. When critical systems go offline, productivity grinds to a halt, and the cost of downtime escalates rapidly. In sectors like banking or emergency services, even a short-term disruption can have life-threatening consequences.

Reputational Damage and Market Positioning

Brand perception is an invaluable asset that can take years to cultivate but seconds to destroy. Once a security incident becomes public, the narrative often revolves around an organization's failure to safeguard its customers' information. Even after the issue is resolved, long-term damage can persist, affecting customer retention, partnerships, and future revenue opportunities. Companies that fail to respond transparently or mitigate the impact quickly may suffer an even greater reputational hit.

Intellectual Property Theft and Competitive Disadvantage

For businesses in technology, pharmaceuticals, defense, and manufacturing, cybersecurity breaches can expose intellectual property, proprietary research, and trade secrets to adversaries. Cyber espionage campaigns targeting high-value data can erase years of investment in innovation, allowing competitors, both domestic and foreign, to gain an unfair advantage. The theft of strategic plans, patents, and proprietary software can have long-term ramifications, weakening an organization's market position and profitability.

CASE STUDY: CYBERSECURITY INTELLECTUAL PROPERTY THEFT AT AMERICAN SUPERCONDUCTOR

Background

American Superconductor (AMSC), a Massachusetts-based infrastructure provider specializing in wind turbine technology, suffered a major cybersecurity breach that had long-term financial and operational consequences. The company's largest customer, Sinovel Wind Group (SWG), a Chinese wind turbine manufacturer, illicitly acquired AMSC's proprietary source code and software, allowing them to bypass licensing agreements and install pirated versions of the software into their turbines.

The Incident

The intellectual property theft was orchestrated through an insider attack. A former AMSC employee, recruited by SWG, illicitly transferred critical source code and control software that powered AMSC's wind turbine systems. This unauthorized access enabled Sinovel to implement AMSC's technology without paying for licenses, effectively cutting the company out of its own market. The impact was immediate and severe. Sinovel, once AMSC's biggest client, canceled outstanding contracts and stopped purchasing software and components from the company. This led to an estimated revenue loss of approximately $100 million annually, a significant blow to AMSC's financial stability.

Consequences

The theft of proprietary software caused several major setbacks for AMSC:

- Financial loss: The abrupt loss of SWG as a customer caused a dramatic revenue decline. AMSC had to lay off employees and restructure its business operations to survive.
- Competitive disadvantage: By leveraging stolen technology, SWG gained an unfair market advantage. They were able to produce wind turbines using AMSC's software

without investing in its research and development. This allowed them to reduce costs and undercut AMSC in the global wind energy market.

- Operational disruption: AMSC had to shift its business strategy, refocus on new product offerings, and pursue costly legal action to mitigate the damage. The breach also undermined investor confidence, further impacting the company's stock and valuation.

Legal and Regulatory Fallout

Following the incident, AMSC pursued legal action against SWG in both U.S. and Chinese courts. In 2018, a U.S. court found Sinovel guilty of trade secret theft and ordered the company to pay over $59 million in restitution and fines. However, the financial damage to AMSC far exceeded this amount, and the company continued to struggle with its market position in the years that followed.

Lessons Learned

This case underscores the high stakes of intellectual property protection in the cybersecurity landscape:

- The need for strong insider threat management: The breach was enabled by an insider with privileged access. Implementing stricter access controls, employee monitoring, and data loss prevention strategies could have mitigated the risk.
- The impact of IP theft on market position: When a competitor illicitly acquires proprietary technology, the victimized company loses not only revenue but also its ability to compete fairly in the industry.
- Legal remedies are not always sufficient: Even with successful litigation, the financial and reputational damage caused by IP theft can far exceed the restitution received. Proactive cybersecurity defenses are essential to prevent such incidents from occurring.

Conclusion

American Superconductor's experience highlights how cybersecurity failures, particularly those involving intellectual property, can lead to devastating financial and strategic consequences. For companies operating in technology-driven industries, protecting proprietary software and trade secrets must be a top priority to avoid losing market share, revenue, and competitive edge.

Source: www.justice.gov/archives/opa/pr/chinese-company-sinovel-wind-group-convicted-theft-trade-secrets.

Employee Morale and Productivity Decline

Beyond external impacts, cyber incidents affect an organization internally. Employees often find themselves dealing with system outages, increased security protocols, and fears of personal data exposure. Strict post-breach security policies, such as MFA requirements, restricted access, additional monitoring, and phishing simulations may create friction in workflows, slowing down business processes. This heightened scrutiny can lead to frustration, disengagement, and even higher turnover among employees, further compounding business challenges.

National Security and Geopolitical Risks

Cybersecurity incidents aren't just a corporate or financial issue; they can escalate into matters of national security. Attacks on critical infrastructure, including power grids, transportation systems, healthcare facilities, and military networks, have the potential to cause widespread disruption, economic instability, and even loss of life. Nation-state cyber operations are increasingly sophisticated, blurring the lines between cybercrime, espionage, and acts of war. Governments worldwide are investing heavily in cyber defense strategies to counter these growing threats, reinforcing the notion that cybersecurity is now a fundamental aspect of national security policy.

Evolving Industry Regulations and Security Standards

High-profile security breaches often serve as catalysts for stricter industry regulations and enhanced security measures. Companies may be required to adopt more robust encryption standards, implement stricter access controls, and enhance their security monitoring and auditing capabilities. While these regulations aim to strengthen overall cybersecurity postures, they also introduce additional compliance costs. Businesses must weigh these expenses against the potential risks of noncompliance, ensuring they strike the right balance between security and operational efficiency.

CONCLUSION AND RECAP

In this chapter, we explored the fundamental aspects of enterprise cybersecurity risk management, laying the groundwork for understanding the critical role cybersecurity plays in modern organizations. Cybersecurity, at its core, is the practice of protecting systems, networks, and data from digital attacks, theft, or damage. It is an essential component of any enterprise, as the digital threat landscape continues to evolve with increasing complexity. Understanding what cybersecurity entails and how it functions is vital for organizations seeking to protect their assets in a constantly changing environment.

We examined the major components of cybersecurity, such as network security, endpoint protection, data security, application security, and IAM. Each of these components plays a unique role in defending an organization against potential threats. The broader threat landscape is vast, with attacks ranging from data breaches to ransomware, and phishing to insider threats. This landscape emphasizes the importance of robust cybersecurity measures and the potential impact that security incidents can have on business operations, finances, and reputation.

One of the key areas of focus was cybersecurity frameworks, which provide structured approaches for identifying, assessing, and managing threats. These frameworks, such as the NIST CSF, offer best practices for preventing and mitigating cybersecurity incidents. By identifying vulnerabilities and implementing appropriate safeguards, organizations can reduce their risk exposure. The role of risk management frameworks was also highlighted, with an emphasis on how enterprises can identify, assess, and prioritize risks in alignment with their overall business objectives.

Risk planning and mitigation strategies are critical components of enterprise cybersecurity. Organizations must develop a proactive approach, integrating both preventive measures and incident response plans to address potential threats. Whether securing networks or safeguarding endpoints, businesses must assess the risk factors and put mitigation strategies in place. Having a structured risk management framework ensures that an enterprise is better equipped to handle cybersecurity threats before they escalate into full-blown crises.

In addition to technical solutions, the importance of cybersecurity management and training was emphasized. Employees play a crucial role in maintaining a secure environment, making security awareness training an indispensable part of any cybersecurity strategy. Effective incident response and recovery plans are also vital, as they enable organizations to quickly address and minimize the damage from breaches or attacks. Legal and compliance considerations add another layer of complexity to cybersecurity, ensuring that organizations adhere to regulations and maintain good governance practices.

Finally, we looked toward the future of cybersecurity, exploring emerging technologies that may shape how we defend against new threats. As technologies evolve, so do the strategies that enterprises must adopt to stay ahead of cybercriminals. From artificial intelligence to blockchain, these innovations hold the potential to further enhance cybersecurity measures in the years to come. As we move forward, it is clear that a comprehensive approach to cybersecurity risk management is essential for ensuring that enterprises remain resilient and secure in the face of ever-growing challenges.

NOTES

1 ASIS International, *Enterprise Security Risk Management (ESRM): Concepts and Strategies*, Alexandria, VA: ASIS International, 2020.

2 John Sherwood, Andrew Clark, and David Lynas, *Enterprise Security Architecture: A Business-Driven Approach*, Boca Raton, FL: CRC Press, 2005.

3 Center for Internet Security, *CIS Critical Security Controls v8*. www.cisecurity.org/controls.

4 National Institute of Standards and Technology (NIST), *Framework for Improving Critical Infrastructure Cybersecurity, Version 1.1*, Gaithersburg, MD: NIST, 2018. www.nist.gov/cyberframework.

5 International Organization for Standardization, *ISO/IEC 27001:2022—Information Security, Cybersecurity and Privacy Protection—Information Security Management Systems—Requirements*, Geneva: ISO, 2022.

6 Grimes, Roger. 2025. "If Social Engineering Accounts for Up to 90% of Attacks, Why Is It Ignored?" March 15, 2025. KnowBe4 Security Awareness Training Blog. https://blog.knowbe4.com/social-engineering-accounts-for-90-of-attacks-why-is-it-ignored.

4 Exploring the Evolving Landscape of Technology in Large Enterprises

LEARNING OBJECTIVES

- Understand how modern enterprise infrastructure and applications are being rearchitected to support agility, resilience, and digital transformation
- Explore key architectural trends that are shaping the future of enterprise IT
- Gain insight into the strategic role of application modernization, cloud computing, and low-code/no-code platforms in enabling business innovation and operational efficiency
- Recognize the importance of aligning IT strategy with business objectives and how emerging technologies contribute to long-term enterprise value

The enterprise technology landscape is rapidly transforming as organizations accelerate digital initiatives to drive efficiency, innovation, and competitive advantage. Technology is no longer just a support function confined to IT departments, it now permeates every facet of business, from operations and finance to customer engagement and supply chain management. However, despite this evolution, enterprises still grapple with legacy challenges, such as manual processes, complex architectures, and siloed systems that hinder agility and scalability.

IT leaders must align technology investments with business objectives, ensuring that enterprise systems not only support operations but actively contribute to strategic growth. The proliferation of cloud computing, big data analytics, artificial intelligence, and the Internet of Things has ushered in a new era of digital transformation, making it imperative for enterprises to rethink their IT strategies and embrace a more integrated and forward-thinking approach.

MODERN ENTERPRISE INFRASTRUCTURE

The legacy enterprise IT paradigm, characterized by monolithic applications, proprietary hardware, and centralized on-premises data centers, is no longer sufficient to meet the demands of a digital-first business landscape. In its place, we are witnessing the emergence of composable, cloud-native architectures that enable agility, scalability, and operational efficiency.

This evolution is not simply a matter of adopting new technologies, it reflects a fundamental rearchitecture of enterprise infrastructure to align more tightly with business outcomes. Leading organizations are embracing hybrid cloud models, containerized workloads, microservices, and software-defined networking to create environments that are adaptive by design and resilient under pressure.

The modern enterprise infrastructure is shaped by a cohesive integration of several core components: hybrid IT environments, edge computing, AI-driven automation, and Zero Trust

DOI: 10.1201/9781003562153-5

security. These pillars provide the foundation for infrastructure strategies that are inherently more scalable, secure, and aligned with the demands of continuous innovation.

Hybrid IT Environments

Hybrid IT has become the architectural standard for enterprises requiring both control and flexibility. By bridging on-premises systems with public and private cloud services, hybrid models enable organizations to optimize workload placement based on latency, regulatory, performance, and cost considerations. A well-architected hybrid environment supports workload portability, dynamic resource allocation, and business continuity. However, complexity increases as IT must manage a distributed estate. Success depends on robust orchestration layers, API-driven automation, policy-based governance, and end-to-end visibility across the infrastructure.

Edge Computing

As data volumes grow and latency requirements tighten, edge computing is reshaping how enterprises process information. By bringing compute and storage closer to data generation points, whether factory floors, retail locations, or IoT ecosystems, organizations can unlock real-time decision-making and localized intelligence. From a design perspective, edge architectures require a decentralized model with strong interoperability, local processing capabilities, and hardened security. Architects must address challenges such as device authentication, secure data transmission, and lifecycle management of distributed nodes—all while integrating edge seamlessly with core and cloud infrastructure.

AI-Driven Automation (AIOps)

Current infrastructure landscapes are too complex for manual intervention alone. AIOps introduces machine learning into operations, enabling proactive detection of anomalies, intelligent root-cause analysis, and autonomous remediation. The result is a shift from reactive maintenance to predictive, data-driven operations. To operationalize AIOps, organizations must ensure high-quality telemetry, integrate with ITSM platforms, and establish feedback loops for continuous learning. Enterprise architects play a critical role in defining the data architecture and control plane that supports automation across compute, storage, and network layers.

Zero Trust Security Models

Traditional perimeter-based security models are obsolete in a world of remote users, SaaS applications, and interconnected systems. Zero Trust offers a new architectural paradigm, built on the principle of never trust, always verify. Implementing Zero Trust requires a holistic security architecture that integrates identity and access management (IAM), continuous authentication, microsegmentation, and real-time policy enforcement. Rather than treating security as an overlay, enterprise architects must embed Zero Trust principles into the fabric of infrastructure design, ensuring that access is contextual, least-privileged, and dynamically enforced.

Key Component	Description	Purpose	Benefits
Multifactor Authentication (MFA)	Requires users to provide two or more verification factors (e.g., password + OTP or biometrics) before accessing systems.	Ensures that only authorized users gain access to resources, even if credentials are compromised.	Strengthens identity verification, reduces risk of unauthorized access, and credential abuse.

Key Component	Description	Purpose	Benefits
Microsegmentation	Divides the network into small, isolated zones or segments, each with its own access controls.	Limits an attacker's ability to move laterally within the network after initial compromise.	Contains breaches, improves visibility, and enhances granular access control.
Continuous monitoring and behavior analytics	Continuously observes user, device, and system behavior to detect anomalies or threats in real time.	Quickly identifies abnormal activity that could indicate malicious intent or compromised assets.	Enables rapid response, supports threat hunting, and improves situational awareness.
Least-privilege access	Grants users and systems only the access necessary to perform their specific functions or roles.	Reduces the attack surface by minimizing unnecessary permissions and access.	Prevents privilege abuse, limits potential damage from compromised accounts or insider threats.

From System Maintenance to Strategic Enablement

The role of IT is shifting from operational upkeep to strategic enablement. Infrastructure teams must evolve from system custodians to business enablers, delivering platforms that are not only reliable and secure but also capable of supporting continuous innovation. Modernizing infrastructure requires more than capital investment, it calls for an architectural mindset. This includes reskilling teams, adopting automation-first practices, and designing systems for adaptability and business alignment from the outset.

ENTERPRISE APPLICATIONS

Enterprise applications are no longer confined to monolithic, rules-driven systems supporting routine back-office functions. Today, they are rapidly evolving into intelligent, adaptive platforms that serve as strategic enablers of business transformation. This shift reflects a broader architectural movement, one that integrates AI, automation, and cloud-native principles into the digital fabric of the enterprise.

As technology ecosystems become more distributed, data-driven, and experience-centric, enterprise applications must be designed to support not only operational excellence but also innovation, scale, and continuous change. This evolution is marked by the rise of intelligent enterprise resource planning and customer relationship management platforms, democratized development via low-code/no-code tools, and a focused investment in modernization as a prerequisite for digital transformation.

Enterprise Resource Planning (ERP)

ERP systems have long formed the transactional backbone of the enterprise, managing finance, procurement, supply chain, and workforce operations. However, traditional ERP implementations have historically been plagued by rigid schemas, complex customizations, and poor data interoperability. ERP 2.0 represents a fundamental rearchitecture of enterprise planning systems. Cloud-native,

API-first, and augmented with AI and real-time analytics, modern ERP platforms are no longer passive systems of record. Instead, they serve as dynamic systems of intelligence, designed to sense, respond, and adapt to real-time business conditions.

Key architectural advancements include:

- Embedded AI/ML for predictive analytics (e.g., demand forecasting, cash flow optimization)
- Event-driven architectures to support responsive workflows and real-time decisioning
- Composable modules that allow for agile deployment and integration of capabilities
- Cloud-native design for scalability, elasticity, and faster upgrade cycles

Organizations must ensure that ERP modernization initiatives align with broader digital transformation objectives, particularly around data integration, business agility, and cost optimization. The focus should be on minimizing legacy technical debt while maximizing platform extensibility and user-centric design.

Customer Relationship Management (CRM)

CRM platforms have evolved into strategic intelligence engines that go far beyond contact management. Current CRM architectures incorporate customer data platforms, AI-driven analytics, behavioral modeling, and automated engagement workflows to deliver deeply personalized, omnichannel experiences.

CRM systems are architected to:

- Ingest and unify multisource customer data in real time
- Apply machine learning for lead scoring, churn prediction, and next best action
- Automate engagement through AI-powered chatbots, virtual agents, and email orchestration
- Integrate seamlessly with sales, service, and marketing platforms for a 360-degree customer view

This shift requires enterprise architects to rethink CRM not as a single system, but as an ecosystem of composable, intelligent services, each playing a role in delivering frictionless, high-value customer experiences. Data governance, API management, and identity integration are foundational concerns in designing secure, scalable CRM environments that span both internal and third-party platforms.

Low-Code/No-Code Platforms

The rise of low-code and no-code platforms signals a profound shift in how enterprise software is conceived, built, and maintained. These platforms enable citizen developers, nontechnical business users, to create and iterate on applications rapidly, reducing pressure on central IT and accelerating time to value. While low-code development improves agility, it introduces new architectural considerations:

- Platform governance: Ensuring role-based access, audit trails, and change control
- Integration architecture: Enabling low-code apps to interface securely with core systems
- Lifecycle management: Establishing patterns for DevOps, CI/CD, and automated testing
- Security and compliance controls: Preventing shadow IT and enforcing policy adherence

Organizations must define a governed innovation framework, balancing autonomy with oversight, to ensure that low-code initiatives contribute to enterprise-scale agility without compromising architectural integrity or compliance posture.

The Role of Application Modernization in Digital Transformation

Modernizing legacy applications is not simply a technical upgrade, it is a business imperative. Legacy systems often represent the single largest source of friction in digital initiatives due to their inflexibility, performance constraints, and security vulnerabilities. Modernization should be approached as a portfolio-driven transformation, targeting high-value, high-risk systems with strategies such as:

- Refactoring monoliths into modular services
- Rehosting workloads onto cloud platforms
- Replatforming applications for containerized orchestration
- Rewriting where necessary to enable innovation and extensibility

This transformation is intrinsically linked to a set of strategic enterprise objectives. It drives the acceleration of cloud adoption and the advancement of hybrid deployment strategies, enabling organizations to scale more efficiently and respond to changing demands. At the same time, it enhances cybersecurity by standardizing IAM practices across increasingly distributed environments. Modernization also plays a critical role in reducing technical debt, which in turn improves cost transparency and predictability. Furthermore, by streamlining data flow and orchestration across applications, it empowers real-time business intelligence and more informed decision-making at every level of the enterprise.

CLOUD COMPUTING

Cloud computing has evolved from a disruptive innovation into a foundational pillar of enterprise architecture. It represents a paradigm shift in how organizations provision, consume, and manage technology resources, transforming IT from a capital-intensive function into a strategic enabler of agility, scale, and innovation. At its core, cloud computing enables organizations to access shared pools of configurable resources, including compute, storage, and applications, via the internet, on demand, and with minimal management overhead. But beyond this technical definition lies a broader architectural opportunity: the ability to architect for change.

Enterprises are no longer adopting cloud solely to reduce infrastructure costs; they are leveraging it as a platform for continuous transformation. Cloud computing allows organizations to modernize legacy environments, accelerate digital product delivery, harness advanced analytics and artificial intelligence, and support distributed global operations without having to purchase, implement, and maintain physical hardware.

Cloud as an Operational Model, Not Just a Location

When we architect for the cloud, we're not merely relocating workloads to a hyperscaler's data center, we are embracing a new operational paradigm. Cloud introduces a dynamic, service-oriented approach where infrastructure becomes programmable, environments are ephemeral, and innovation is constrained only by architectural foresight. In this model, IT moves from being a gatekeeper to becoming an orchestrator of services. The cloud enables real-time provisioning, rapid experimentation, and self-service access to development platforms. For enterprise architects, this demands a rethink of traditional governance, integration, and security models. It requires an architecture that is modular, automated, and capable of evolving alongside business priorities.

On-Demand Responsiveness and Real-Time Scalability

A defining characteristic of cloud computing is its ability to deliver IT services in real time. Traditional infrastructure models are burdened by procurement cycles, static capacity planning, and manual provisioning processes. In contrast, cloud platforms empower enterprises to deploy compute, storage, and network resources precisely when and where they are needed. This just-in-time responsiveness transforms business agility. Whether entering new markets, scaling digital services, or responding to unforeseen spikes in demand, enterprises can leverage cloud elasticity to remain responsive and cost-effective. Applications can be deployed in minutes, not weeks; environments can scale automatically in response to real-time telemetry. This fluidity is essential in the current business environment, where speed to market and operational resilience are nonnegotiable.

Efficiency and Optimization through Intelligent Resource Management

Cloud-native infrastructure is designed for efficiency at scale. It eliminates the waste associated with underutilized hardware, shifting the enterprise from fixed-cost provisioning to consumption-based pricing models. By dynamically allocating resources based on workload demands, cloud platforms drive optimal utilization and energy efficiency. Moreover, cloud providers continually invest in infrastructure modernization, offering enterprises access to state-of-the-art computer architectures, high-speed storage, and global content delivery networks without recovering some of the sunk costs of physical hardware through depreciation. These capabilities would be prohibitively expensive to replicate in-house but are made available through cloud as part of the service.

Interoperability and the Rise of Composable Architectures

Modern cloud environments support a high degree of interoperability, allowing organizations to integrate services and platforms across diverse providers. This flexibility is vital in a multicloud or hybrid-cloud strategy, where different workloads may be best suited to different environments based on compliance, latency, or functional requirements.

Through the use of Application Programming Interfaces (APIs), container orchestration, and event-driven architectures, enterprises can build composable systems that span clouds, data centers, and edge locations. This level of interoperability reduces the risk of vendor lock-in and supports innovation by enabling best-of-breed service integration. It also calls for a unified control plane, architected for visibility, policy enforcement, and identity federation across a heterogeneous ecosystem.

Scalability and Elasticity as Design Principles

Perhaps the most transformative attribute of cloud computing is its inherent scalability. Enterprises can architect systems to scale horizontally across multiple instances or regions, ensuring high availability and fault tolerance. Elasticity ensures that resources are automatically adjusted in real time, scaling out to absorb peak demand or scaling in to control cost. This is particularly impactful in industries with dynamic workloads, such as e-commerce, media, financial services, and digital health. Elasticity reduces the need to overprovision resources for the worst-case scenario and instead enables capacity to follow demand curves.

Cloud as a Strategic Asset in Economic Uncertainty

In times of economic volatility, the cloud becomes more than a cost-saving mechanism, it becomes a strategic buffer. Its pay-as-you-go model allows enterprises to scale down nonessential workloads, defer capital expenditures, and rapidly reallocate resources to areas of growth. Built-in capabilities such as automated failover, backup, and disaster recovery further enhance business continuity. As economic conditions fluctuate, organizations that are cloud-native are better equipped to weather disruption. They can pivot faster, experiment more freely, and derisk innovation. This resilience is not incidental, it is architectural.

A Rapidly Evolving Competitive Landscape

The cloud provider ecosystem continues to mature, offering a spectrum of services from global hyperscalers like AWS, Azure, and Google Cloud to specialized providers targeting vertical industries or sovereign data requirements. These platforms now offer capabilities far beyond basic infrastructure, encompassing advanced analytics, artificial intelligence and machine learning services, IoT frameworks, and industry-specific compliance solutions. Enterprises must evaluate cloud vendors not just on technical merit but on strategic alignment, considering data residency, ecosystem integration, regulatory alignment, and long-term roadmap compatibility. As cloud strategies become more complex, architecture must guide the selection and orchestration of these services to ensure coherence and value realization.

The Cloud-Centric Future

The trajectory of cloud computing is toward greater intelligence, decentralization, and autonomy. The integration of artificial intelligence and machine learning into cloud operations, often referred to as Artificial Intelligence for IT Operations, enables predictive scaling, intelligent anomaly detection, and automated remediation. Meanwhile, edge computing pushes data processing closer to where it is generated, enabling real-time analytics and autonomous decision-making in manufacturing, logistics, healthcare, and beyond. Emerging technologies such as 5G, serverless computing, and quantum-as-a-service will further redefine what's possible. For the enterprise architect, the challenge and opportunity lie in designing cloud-native systems that are not only scalable and efficient but also capable of evolving in response to new technology paradigms.

DIGITAL TRANSFORMATION

Digital transformation has moved from a conceptual aspiration to a strategic imperative. Enterprises across industries are embracing digital capabilities to fundamentally reshape how they deliver value, manage operations, and engage with customers. This evolution involves more than adopting emerging technologies; it requires a reimagining of core business models, organizational processes, and the role of enterprise IT itself. The convergence of cloud computing, advanced analytics, and digital engagement platforms is driving a systemic shift in how enterprises operate in the digital economy.

At the center of this shift is the CIO, whose role has expanded from overseeing infrastructure and cost control to orchestrating enterprise-wide transformation initiatives. The modern CIO is far more engaged and relevant to the business as both a technology strategist and a business leader, guiding organizations through complex change journeys while ensuring that technology investments directly support growth, innovation, and resilience. This elevated role requires close collaboration with executive leadership, a deep understanding of evolving business dynamics, and the ability to translate enterprise goals into scalable digital architectures.

A decade ago, cloud computing was viewed as a tactical convenience, useful for noncritical workloads and pilot programs, but not ready to support the core operational needs of large enterprises. Today, that view has been fundamentally overturned. The cloud is now recognized as the foundation of digital transformation. It enables elastic scalability, supports continuous delivery, and offers access to a rapidly expanding suite of services that power automation, AI, and data intelligence. What was once met with caution is now embraced as a strategic necessity.

The early skepticism around cloud adoption, particularly for mission-critical applications, was rooted in concerns over security, control, and performance. Those concerns have been addressed through the maturity of cloud platforms, regulatory clarity, and the adoption of governance frameworks tailored for distributed environments. As a result, CIOs who once resisted cloud migration are now leading the charge, pushing forward enterprise-wide cloud strategies that enhance agility, lower operational overhead, and enable faster innovation cycles. Cloud adoption has become an inflection point for rethinking legacy architectures.

This transformation has fundamentally altered the operating model of enterprise IT. Once characterized by centralized control, ticket-driven workflows, and lengthy procurement cycles, IT is now evolving into a service-oriented, product-centric organization. DevOps practices, agile methodologies, and automation pipelines are replacing rigid, siloed approaches to system delivery. The role of IT is no longer limited to keeping systems running, it is about building the digital capabilities and developing business solutions that allow the enterprise to compete, adapt, and scale in real time.

Enterprises are now focused not simply on migrating to the cloud but on maturing their cloud ecosystems. This involves moving beyond infrastructure lift-and-shift to embrace cloud-native architectures, designing applications with containerization, microservices, serverless computing, and platform automation in mind. Mature organizations are investing in cloud governance, observability, and cost optimization practices that allow them to scale usage without losing visibility or control. In this context, cloud becomes more than a deployment model, it becomes a continuously evolving platform for innovation.

As enterprises move deeper into digital transformation, hybrid and multicloud strategies are emerging as dominant architectural patterns. Organizations are choosing to run certain workloads in public cloud environments for scalability and reach, while retaining others in private or on-premises environments for latency, control, or compliance. Multicloud strategies further enable flexibility by avoiding vendor lock-in and allowing organizations to match workloads to the strengths of each platform. This distributed landscape introduces new architectural complexities, requiring a unified management approach to ensure interoperability, performance, and security across all environments.

Alongside these changes, the strategic value of data has never been greater. Enterprises are building integrated data pipelines and leveraging real-time analytics to inform every aspect of business decision-making, from customer engagement to supply chain optimization. The shift toward AI-driven enterprises demands cloud platforms that can process large volumes of structured and unstructured data at scale, support model training and inference, and integrate seamlessly into operational workflows. Data architecture, once treated as a back-end concern, is now a central pillar of digital competitiveness.

Security and compliance considerations have also evolved. The perimeter-based models of the past are insufficient in a cloud-centric world where users, devices, and applications operate far beyond the boundaries of traditional networks. Enterprises must now adopt Zero Trust security models, enforce strong identity and access controls, and embed security into the fabric of cloud architectures. Proactive threat detection, policy-based enforcement, and continuous monitoring have become essential components of a resilient security posture. The architecture must account not only for technological complexity but also for evolving regulatory requirements and cyber threats.

The purpose of digital transformation is not technology for its own sake, but the creation of a more intelligent, adaptive, and customer-centric business environment. IT is no longer a back-office function, it is the core enabler for the success of the enterprise. For CIOs the path forward involves aligning infrastructure with business priorities, building composable platforms, and fostering a culture of innovation and agility. Those who treat enterprise IT as a lever for business acceleration, not just operations, will be best positioned to lead their organizations into a future defined by constant change and exponential opportunity.

THE CONVERGENCE OF IT AND OPERATIONAL TECHNOLOGY (OT)

The convergence of IT and OT is fundamentally reshaping how industrial enterprises and critical infrastructure operators design, manage, and secure their environments. Once distinct in purpose and architecture, these domains are now merging into unified ecosystems that support intelligent automation, continuous monitoring, and real-time, data-driven decision-making.

Historically, IT systems have served the enterprise layer, governing business applications, data management, and user services, while OT systems have focused on the physical domain, controlling industrial processes through SCADA, DCS, and MES platforms. IT has prioritized cybersecurity, uptime, and data integrity; OT has focused on deterministic performance, safety, and system availability. Their separation was intentional, born from differing operational priorities and risk models. Today, however, the rapid infusion of Internet of Things devices, cloud platforms, AI analytics, and edge computing into industrial environments is erasing these boundaries.

This convergence is not merely a technical shift, it is an architectural transformation that demands a holistic rethinking of how cyber-physical systems are designed, secured, and governed. The benefits are compelling: improved visibility, predictive maintenance, autonomous operations, and enhanced situational awareness. But these gains also bring complexity and risk, especially in terms of security, interoperability, and operational continuity.

Industrial IoT (IIoT)

The proliferation of Industrial IoT is a primary catalyst for IT–OT convergence. IIoT extends traditional OT by embedding intelligence at the edge, enabling machines, sensors, and devices to collect, process, and transmit real-time operational data. This data, when integrated with enterprise IT systems, enables deep insight into asset performance, environmental conditions, and system behaviors. In manufacturing, IIoT-enabled sensors can monitor vibration, temperature, and energy consumption to detect early signs of equipment fatigue, enabling predictive maintenance and minimizing unplanned downtime. In the energy sector, smart grid systems ingest telemetry from distributed energy resources to optimize load balancing and prevent outages.

These use cases illustrate the architectural value of IIoT, providing a digital bridge between operational assets and enterprise decision-making systems. However, this expansion of connected devices significantly enlarges the attack surface. Architecturally, enterprises must adopt zero-trust models, secure device onboarding, and encrypted communication channels, alongside continuous monitoring and threat detection, to mitigate risk while preserving operational gains.

Cyber-Physical Systems (CPS)

The maturation of CPS marks a critical inflection point in the evolution of industrial architecture. CPS tightly integrates computational algorithms with physical processes, enabling systems to sense, compute, and actuate in coordinated, autonomous ways. These systems form the foundation of next-generation capabilities such as smart manufacturing, autonomous vehicles, and intelligent utility grids.

In an industrial context, CPS powers production environments where robots dynamically collaborate with humans, adjusting workflows based on real-time feedback and demand shifts. In utilities, CPS enables self-healing grids that can isolate faults and reroute power autonomously. These systems are highly adaptive, combining edge intelligence, centralized orchestration, and real-time responsiveness.

From an architectural standpoint, CPS introduces a complex interdependence between software logic, hardware behavior, and environmental inputs. This requires a systems engineering mindset, ensuring that control loops, communication protocols, safety mechanisms, and machine learning models are cohesively designed and governed. Furthermore, as these systems become more autonomous, the implications for safety, reliability, and cybersecurity intensify, necessitating robust validation, simulation, and failure recovery frameworks.

AI-Driven Analytics

AI and advanced analytics are foundational to unlocking the full potential of IT–OT convergence. These technologies enable real-time correlation of data from across operational and enterprise systems, driving smarter decisions and proactive interventions. In manufacturing, AI models analyze production metrics to dynamically optimize resource utilization, detect bottlenecks, and adjust schedules. In the energy sector, machine learning algorithms forecast demand with high accuracy, allowing providers to calibrate generation in real time and reduce operational waste. Across industries, AI-enabled anomaly detection systems flag deviations in physical processes, enabling preemptive response before faults escalate.

From an enterprise architecture perspective, these capabilities hinge on the seamless flow of data across disparate systems. Achieving this requires architectural investment in data integration platforms, common semantic models, and scalable analytics infrastructure. Governance becomes critical: data lineage, model transparency, and access control must be embedded at every layer. Furthermore, edge-to-core data orchestration must balance latency, bandwidth, and compute availability to ensure real-time insights without overburdening networks or systems.

Balancing Innovation and Risk in IT–OT Convergence

While the promise of IT–OT convergence is compelling, it introduces a multidimensional risk landscape that cannot be ignored. Historically isolated OT systems, once protected by air gaps, are now interconnected with IT networks, creating pathways for lateral movement and exposing critical infrastructure to cyber threats that were never part of the OT threat model. This new exposure demands a rethinking of risk frameworks. Traditional perimeter security must give way to microsegmentation, continuous authentication, and behavior-based anomaly detection. Legacy OT devices, which often lack built-in security controls, must be protected through compensating controls such as protocol isolation, secure gateways, and passive monitoring.

Organizations must guide this transition by defining security blueprints that span both cyber and physical domains. This includes unified identity management, secure configuration baselines, and convergence-aware incident response playbooks. Just as importantly, organizational alignment is essential: IT and OT teams must break down silos, establish shared operational objectives, and codevelop governance models that reflect the hybrid nature of modern industrial environments.

AI AND ML ARE TRANSFORMING ENTERPRISE

AI and ML are no longer experimental technologies confined to isolated innovation labs, they are foundational elements of the modern enterprise IT architecture. These capabilities are now deeply embedded across enterprise systems, introducing predictive analytics, intelligent automation, and adaptive security into the core of digital operations. As organizations move toward becoming data-native, AI and ML serve as key enablers, transforming how data is interpreted, how services are delivered, and how decisions are made at scale.

At the architectural level, AI and ML are redefining IT as not just a provider of infrastructure and applications, but as a proactive intelligence layer that senses, learns, and evolves alongside the business. These technologies are enabling real-time insight generation, self-healing systems, and experience-centric service delivery. From AI-driven service management to dynamic data analytics and automated business processes, enterprises are shifting from static systems of record to intelligent systems of action.

Rearchitecting IT Service Management with AI: From Reactive to Predictive

Traditional IT service management has long depended on manual triage, static workflows, and human-led escalation paths. In contrast, AI is enabling a shift to proactive, context-aware, and self-optimizing service management. AI-powered virtual agents now perform first-line support, handling a wide range of user queries using natural language processing and contextual awareness.

Intelligent ticketing platforms leverage machine learning models to autoclassify incidents, assign appropriate priority levels, and route tickets to the right support tiers, drastically reducing mean time to resolution. More advanced use cases include anomaly detection systems that analyze infrastructure telemetry in real time to flag early warning signals, enabling IT teams to remediate issues before they disrupt business services.

This transformation requires architects to design for data flow across systems, establish AI model training pipelines, and implement feedback loops to improve performance over time. ITSM platforms must become interoperable with AI/ML engines and integrated with observability and Artificial Intelligence for IT Operations tools to create a cohesive, adaptive support environment.

AI-Driven Analytics: Architecting for Real-Time Business Intelligence

The traditional enterprise analytics stack, anchored by data warehouses and scheduled reporting, struggles to meet the demands of real-time decision-making. AI and ML are transforming data analytics by enabling continuous, automated insight generation from both structured and unstructured data sources. AI-powered analytics engines ingest massive data volumes across disparate systems and apply statistical models and deep learning techniques to uncover patterns, correlations, and actionable insights. Predictive analytics allows enterprises to forecast future outcomes with confidence, whether optimizing supply chains, anticipating customer churn, or mitigating financial risk. These insights are not static; they adapt as new data is ingested, creating a feedback loop of continuous learning and decision refinement.

Organizations must design data architectures that support real-time ingestion, model deployment, and explainable AI. This includes scalable data pipelines, metadata management, and secure access controls. The goal is to architect an analytics ecosystem that is not only performant but also trustworthy and aligned with governance requirements.

AI-Augmented Automation

Robotic Process Automation (RPA) has long been a cornerstone of digital operations, but when combined with AI, it evolves into intelligent automation. While traditional RPA executes rule-based tasks, AI-augmented automation extends this capability to more dynamic and cognitive functions, understanding intent, interpreting unstructured inputs, and adapting to exceptions.

In the enterprise IT context, AI-enabled automation can manage software patching, system health monitoring, log analysis, and compliance checks without human intervention. Business teams leverage these capabilities to automate complex workflows such as contract analysis, claims processing, or customer onboarding, improving speed, accuracy, and compliance. Organizations must think beyond tactical automation and instead design scalable automation frameworks. This includes establishing a unified orchestration layer, ensuring integration with business applications, and embedding control mechanisms that govern automation logic, auditability, and exception handling.

Challenges and Strategic Considerations: Navigating the AI Adoption Curve

Despite its transformative potential, AI adoption introduces significant architectural and organizational complexity. Data privacy remains a critical concern, especially as AI systems consume sensitive or regulated information. Algorithmic bias and explainability are also key issues, enterprises must be able to validate the fairness, accuracy, and accountability of automated decisions. Furthermore, the AI talent gap presents a structural challenge. Building and maintaining AI capabilities requires not only data scientists but also engineers, architects, and domain experts who can align models with real-world operational contexts.

To navigate these challenges, organizations must advocate for an ethical AI governance framework, one that incorporates model lifecycle management, bias monitoring, transparency, and compliance. Equally important is the development of training and enablement programs to upskill the existing workforce and embed AI literacy across the organization.

Challenge Area	Description	Enterprise Considerations	Recommended Actions
Data privacy and security risks	AI systems require access to large volumes of data, often including sensitive or personal information.	Risk of data breaches, noncompliance with regulations (e.g., GDPR, CCPA), and reputational harm.	– Implement robust data governance – Encrypt data in transit and at rest – Conduct regular compliance audits
Algorithmic bias and ethics	Biases in training data can lead to unfair or discriminatory AI outcomes.	May result in regulatory scrutiny, legal liability, and loss of customer trust.	– Conduct bias assessments – Incorporate fairness metrics – Ensure diverse training data – Establish ethical AI review boards
Skills gap and workforce readiness	AI initiatives require skilled professionals, which are often in short supply.	Delayed deployment, misalignment of AI strategy, and underutilization of AI tools.	– Invest in training and certifications – Promote cross-functional AI literacy – Partner with academic institutions
Integration with legacy systems	Existing legacy IT infrastructure may not support AI workloads or real-time data integration.	Increased complexity, reduced performance, and higher costs for modernization.	– Assess system compatibility – Use APIs and microservices – Leverage cloud-native AI platforms
Explainability and trust in AI	AI models often operate as "black boxes," making decisions that are difficult to interpret or justify.	Limits user adoption, raises governance concerns, and hinders regulatory compliance.	– Apply Explainable AI (XAI) techniques – Document model decisions – Maintain audit trails and governance logs

AI and ML are not peripheral technologies; they are becoming embedded as strategic layers across enterprise IT architectures. They serve as the connective tissue that links data to insight, infrastructure to intent, and user experience to business outcomes. Organizations that can seamlessly integrate AI into their IT fabric will unlock new levels of agility, innovation, and operational intelligence. However, realizing this vision requires deliberate architectural planning. AI capabilities must be designed for scalability, trustworthiness, and adaptability. When embedded within service management, analytics, automation, and cybersecurity, AI becomes not just a tool, but a strategic asset driving digital transformation.

BLOCKCHAIN IN THE ENTERPRISE

Blockchain technology has evolved well beyond its initial role as the foundation for cryptocurrencies. It is now emerging as a foundational element in the enterprise technology stack, offering a decentralized, tamper-resistant architecture capable of solving persistent challenges related to trust, transparency, and data integrity. At its core, blockchain is a ledger system for immutable and verifiable records across distributed systems, making it particularly valuable in environments where data assurance, transactional accountability, and auditability are nonnegotiable.

Although enterprise adoption remains in the exploratory or early deployment stages across many sectors, the strategic interest in blockchain is accelerating. Organizations are beginning to view distributed ledger technologies not just as experimental tools but as integral components of next-generation digital infrastructure, enabling secure data exchange, streamlining cross-organizational workflows, and mitigating systemic risks. However, the path to adoption is not without complexity. Scalability, regulatory ambiguity, interoperability with existing enterprise systems, and governance considerations must all be addressed through a pragmatic architectural lens.

Supply Chain Visibility and Trust

Global supply chains are inherently complex, multiparty ecosystems that depend on accurate, timely, and trustworthy information exchange. Traditional supply chain architectures, often built on siloed systems and manual processes, are susceptible to fraud, data inconsistencies, and lack of real-time traceability. These limitations hinder operational efficiency and introduce risk, particularly in high-stakes sectors such as pharmaceuticals, food production, and aerospace.

Blockchain provides a single source of truth across distributed participants. Each transaction, whether it's a shipment confirmation, quality inspection, or customs clearance, is cryptographically recorded in an immutable ledger that is visible to all authorized parties. This shared visibility enhances accountability, ensures the authenticity of goods, and prevents tampering or counterfeiting. Smart contracts embedded within the blockchain can automatically enforce compliance with contractual terms, regulatory thresholds, or logistical milestones. For instance, a smart contract might release payment only upon verified delivery, or trigger alerts when temperature-sensitive goods fall outside acceptable parameters.

Decentralized Identity

As enterprises confront an increasingly complex threat landscape, IAM has become a linchpin of both security and user experience. Traditional IAM approaches, rooted in centralized repositories and federated trust models, create high-value targets for attackers. A single compromise can expose millions of user identities, leading to cascading impacts across systems and services. Blockchain introduces a decentralized identity model, referred to as Self-Sovereign Identity, where individuals or entities retain control over their identity attributes. Rather than storing personally identifiable information in a centralized database, identity credentials are stored in users' digital wallets and verified cryptographically on-chain. Trust is established not through a central authority, but via consensus and cryptographic proofs.

For enterprises, blockchain-based identity frameworks offer a transformative alternative to legacy authentication systems. They can be applied across a range of scenarios, including employee onboarding, contractor verification, multifactor authentication, and other business processes. Moreover, decentralized identity aligns with emerging privacy regulations by minimizing data collection and enhancing consent management. From an architectural perspective, integrating decentralized identity requires a shift in IAM strategy, adopting verifiable credentials, integrating with blockchain registries, and ensuring compatibility with existing directory services and identity providers.

USE CASE: SELF-SOVEREIGN IDENTITY (SSI) REAL-WORLD APPLICATIONS

SSI has several real-world applications in the finance sector, addressing challenges such as regulatory compliance, fraud prevention, and customer experience. Below are some key use cases:

Know Your Customer (KYC) and Anti-Money Laundering (AML)

- SSI enables a reusable KYC process, allowing customers to verify their identity once and reuse it across multiple financial institutions. This reduces onboarding friction while maintaining compliance with regulatory requirements.
- With SSI, personally identifiable information (PII) is securely stored and shared only with user consent, enhancing privacy and reducing the risk of data breaches.

Mortgage Applications

- SSI can streamline mortgage processes by providing verifiable digital credentials. This eliminates the risk of fraudulent applications using fake identities and reduces paperwork and processing time.

Decentralized Finance (DeFi) and Crypto

- SSI bridges centralized finance and decentralized finance by providing a secure identity layer. It enables identity verification for peer-to-peer transactions, KYC-compliant loan pools, and wallet authentication without compromising user privacy.
- It also facilitates secure transactions in crypto ecosystems by allowing users to share minimal identity data, such as a verified handle, to prove authenticity.

Mobile Banking

- SSI simplifies the onboarding process for mobile banking users by verifying identities digitally without extensive paperwork. This enhances customer experience while ensuring security through blockchain-based authentication.

Fraud Prevention

- By leveraging blockchain technology, SSI ensures that credentials are immutable and verifiable, significantly reducing identity fraud risks in financial transactions.

Regulatory Compliance

- Financial institutions can use SSI to comply with complex regulatory requirements such as GDPR or PSD2 by enabling selective disclosure of data. This ensures that only necessary information is shared while maintaining user privacy.

Securing Transactions and Combating Financial Fraud

The traditional financial transaction ecosystem is heavily reliant on intermediaries, banks, payment processors, clearinghouses, that introduce latency, operational cost, and potential failure points. Additionally, fraud, money laundering, and transactional manipulation remain persistent risks, exacerbated by fragmented systems and inconsistent oversight.

Blockchain offers a fundamentally different model: peer-to-peer transactions secured by cryptographic validation, consensus algorithms, and immutable audit trails. Every transaction recorded on the ledger is time-stamped, tamper-resistant, and independently verifiable, reducing opportunities for fraud and enabling real-time reconciliation. Smart contracts extend this model by automating the enforcement of business logic within transactions. For example, escrow conditions can be encoded directly into the blockchain, releasing funds automatically upon verified delivery or compliance with regulatory criteria. This reduces reliance on third-party arbiters and enhances trust between counterparties.

Financial institutions, insurers, and fintech organizations are actively piloting blockchain to enhance the transparency and resilience of payment processing, digital asset management, trade finance, and antifraud measures. However, enterprise adoption must be approached with architectural rigor, balancing performance, throughput, compliance, and integration with existing financial systems and regulatory reporting frameworks.

Architectural Considerations for Blockchain

Blockchain's introduction into the enterprise environment demands a multidimensional architectural approach. It is not simply another database or transactional layer, it redefines data ownership, distribution, and validation across ecosystem boundaries. As such, successful adoption requires addressing several foundational questions:

- Governance: Who operates and maintains the blockchain network? What permissions are granted to each participant?
- Integration: How will blockchain systems interoperate with ERP, CRM, IAM, and analytics platforms?
- Data strategy: What data is stored on-chain versus off-chain? How is privacy maintained while ensuring auditability?
- Security: How are cryptographic keys managed? What protections are in place against consensus attacks?
- Regulatory compliance: How are blockchain transactions aligned with data protection laws, financial regulations, and industry-specific mandates?

Organizations must learn to better collaborate across IT, legal, security, and business domains to develop reference architectures, pilot use cases, and maturity models that guide blockchain implementation from concept to production.

THE STRATEGIC HORIZON OF ENTERPRISE IT

Enterprise IT stands at an inflection point. As technological disruption accelerates and the complexity of digital ecosystems deepens, the enterprise IT function is evolving from a traditional service provider to a strategic orchestrator of innovation, resilience, and business value. The convergence of hyperautomation, quantum computing, decentralized architectures, cyber resilience, and sustainable IT is redefining what it means to architect systems for competitive advantage in the decade ahead.

In this future state, IT leaders must embrace a mindset shift, from managing infrastructure to designing ecosystems, from reacting to disruptions to anticipating change, and from supporting operations to shaping the business itself. The IT function must become inherently agile, intelligent, and environmentally responsible, capable of evolving in lockstep with both market dynamics and stakeholder expectations. Those organizations that can integrate these emerging technologies into a unified, scalable IT strategy will position themselves not just to survive in a complex digital economy, but to lead it.

Hyperautomation

Hyperautomation is not merely the next step in automation, it represents a transformational leap. It is the strategic integration of AI, machine learning, RPA, and low-code technologies to automate complex, end-to-end business and IT workflows. Unlike traditional automation, which is confined to deterministic rule execution, hyperautomation enables systems to learn, adapt, and optimize in real time. For enterprise IT, the implications are profound. IT service management is moving from reactive incident handling to predictive and preventive models. Through AI-driven observability and root cause analysis, infrastructure teams can detect anomalies and remediate issues autonomously, minimizing downtime and improving service quality. RPA bots can provision resources, manage user access, and resolve Level 1 helpdesk tickets at scale and with precision.

Beyond IT operations, hyperautomation empowers business functions across finance, HR, and customer service to improve decision velocity, reduce errors, and respond faster to changing demands. As enterprises move toward AI-first operating models, hyperautomation becomes an architectural foundation, blending people, processes, and platforms into adaptive digital workflows. To succeed, organizations must ensure the integration of hyperautomation into the broader enterprise architecture landscape, governing automation pipelines, securing data flows, and enabling seamless interoperability across business domains.

Quantum Computing

Quantum computing represents a paradigm shift in computational capability. By leveraging quantum bits and the principles of superposition and entanglement, quantum systems are poised to perform calculations that are infeasible for even the most powerful classical supercomputers. For enterprise IT, quantum computing is no longer a theoretical curiosity, it is a strategic frontier. The potential impact spans cybersecurity, optimization, AI, and simulation. Quantum algorithms could decrypt conventional encryption in seconds, necessitating a transition to quantum-safe cryptography and zero-trust models resilient to quantum threats. In finance, logistics, and life sciences, quantum models could transform portfolio optimization, supply chain logistics, and drug discovery through unprecedented processing speed and complexity handling.

Although enterprise-grade quantum systems are still in very early stages, the window for preparation is now. IT leaders must begin evaluating quantum-readiness, engaging in research partnerships, assessing encryption dependencies, and exploring hybrid quantum-classical workloads. Integration with existing enterprise platforms will require new protocols, middleware, and governance mechanisms. Organizations should lead the development of quantum adoption frameworks that align with long-term digital strategy, balancing innovation opportunity with the practical realities of infrastructure, security, and skill development.

Decentralized Architectures

The traditional model of centralized IT infrastructure is increasingly incompatible with the demands of modern, distributed business operations. To support latency-sensitive applications, data sovereignty requirements, and operational resilience, enterprises are moving toward decentralized architecture models. Edge computing exemplifies this shift, enabling data processing and analytics to occur at or near the data source. In industries such as manufacturing, healthcare, and transportation, edge deployments reduce latency, enhance responsiveness, and offload bandwidth-intensive tasks from centralized data centers. From predictive maintenance in industrial equipment to real-time telemetry in autonomous vehicles, edge computing is unlocking new frontiers of operational intelligence.

Simultaneously, blockchain and distributed ledger technologies are enabling new models of decentralized trust. These platforms support secure, tamper-evident recordkeeping across untrusted parties, driving innovation in digital identity, cross-border transactions, and decentralized finance. Decentralized architectures also strengthen business continuity by eliminating single points of failure and supporting geographic diversity in compute and storage. For architects, the design of such systems must consider not only performance and scalability, but also orchestration complexity, data consistency models, and the edge-to-core security continuum.

Sustainable IT

Sustainability is no longer a peripheral concern, due to the heightened global awareness around climate change, it is a growing enterprise consideration. As environmental, social, and governance (ESG) frameworks have become part of some investor and consumer expectations, the IT function must lead in reducing digital carbon footprints while maintaining service excellence. Enterprise IT consumes a significant portion of global energy, particularly through data center operations. To address this, organizations are investing in energy-efficient infrastructure, migrating workloads to renewable-powered cloud environments, and leveraging AI to optimize resource consumption and thermal management.

At the architectural level, sustainability must be engineered into the software lifecycle. This includes designing applications for computational efficiency, adopting serverless and event-driven models to minimize idle resource usage, and leveraging containerization to reduce deployment overhead. Sustainable IT also requires carbon accounting tools, green service level agreements, and reporting dashboards that provide transparency across the technology stack. Moreover, regulatory pressures around emissions disclosure and e-waste management are intensifying. IT architects must work in tandem with sustainability officers and procurement teams to ensure that technology decisions align with broader climate commitments and corporate responsibility goals.

CONCLUSION AND RECAP

The transformation of enterprise IT is not simply a matter of adopting new tools or modernizing legacy systems, it is a comprehensive, architectural reinvention. We are witnessing the evolution of IT from a tactical function into a strategic capability that underpins business agility, resilience, and innovation. This shift has been catalyzed by advancements in cloud computing, intelligent infrastructure, application modernization, AI integration, and emerging technologies such as blockchain and quantum computing. For enterprise architects, the challenge is no longer how to build for today, but how to architect for continuous reinvention.

The modernization of enterprise infrastructure marks a critical first step in this evolution. Legacy, monolithic systems have given way to modular, scalable, cloud-native architectures that support real-time responsiveness and platform extensibility. Hybrid IT, edge computing, and Zero Trust security have emerged as foundational design pillars, enabling infrastructure that is not only operationally efficient but also aligned with modern digital demands. These components are no longer optional, they are baseline requirements for organizations seeking to remain competitive in an always-on, data-intensive economy.

This infrastructural shift is matched by a parallel transformation in enterprise applications. ERP and CRM platforms have evolved from passive systems of record into intelligent systems of action, capable of real-time analytics, decision automation, and personalized engagement. The rise of low-code/no-code platforms has further democratized development, enabling rapid innovation while introducing new governance and integration challenges. Application modernization is now a continuous architectural practice, one that unlocks agility and ensures that digital capabilities scale in tandem with business ambition.

Cloud computing, once viewed as a cost optimization tool, has become the backbone of enterprise transformation. It delivers on-demand scalability, global reach, and access to cutting-edge services, from AI to IoT to advanced analytics. As enterprises mature their cloud strategies, architectural patterns are shifting from lift-and-shift to fully cloud-native. Composability, observability, elasticity, and multicloud interoperability are emerging as core design principles. The cloud is no longer a destination; it is an operating model and a strategic platform for innovation.

The convergence of IT and OT further amplifies the role of architecture in enabling enterprise-wide intelligence. Industrial IoT, CPS, and edge analytics are unifying physical and digital domains, creating real-time feedback loops between operations and strategy. Yet with this convergence comes increased complexity and risk. Architects must design systems that balance determinism and agility, enforce cybersecurity across domains, and ensure resilience in mission-critical environments. The IT–OT boundary is dissolving, and with it, traditional architectural silos must disappear as well.

Artificial intelligence and machine learning are emerging not as isolated innovations but as systemic enablers embedded across the enterprise stack. From predictive service management to real-time business intelligence and intelligent automation, AI is shaping a new generation of self-optimizing systems. Enterprise architects must ensure that AI is governed responsibly, integrated seamlessly, and scaled sustainably. AI is not simply a technical capability, it is an architectural force that reshapes how value is delivered, how operations are executed, and how organizations learn and evolve.

Hyperautomation extends this intelligence by orchestrating AI, RPA, and analytics into cohesive digital workflows. It is redefining the scope of what can be automated, shifting IT operations from reactive firefighting to proactive innovation. For architects, this demands new patterns of orchestration, observability, and policy enforcement. Hyperautomation is not about replacing people; it is about augmenting human decision-making and liberating teams to focus on higher-value strategic initiatives.

Meanwhile, quantum computing and blockchain technologies are expanding the strategic horizon of enterprise IT. Quantum computing offers unprecedented potential in optimization, simulation, and cryptography, requiring organizations to begin preparing today for its eventual integration into enterprise workflows. Blockchain introduces a decentralized model of trust and transparency, transforming data assurance, identity, and transaction integrity across value chains. Enterprise architects must guide their organizations through pragmatic experimentation, developing the frameworks and interoperability needed to bring these technologies from concept to production.

Across all of these domains, a recurring theme is clear: the architecture must evolve. Static frameworks, siloed systems, and reactive governance models are no longer viable. The future demands dynamic, composable, intelligence-driven architectures that can scale, adapt, and learn. Enterprise architects are uniquely positioned to orchestrate this transformation, translating business vision into technology reality and ensuring that every investment in IT drives measurable, strategic value.

As we look forward, the organizations that succeed will be those that view IT not as a cost center, but as a strategic enabler of growth, differentiation, and resilience. These enterprises will build platforms that are modular, secure, intelligent, and sustainable. They will embed agility not only in their development practices but in their operating models and governance frameworks. And they will place architecture at the center of transformation and ensure that change is not just embraced but architected by design.

Part II

Enterprise IT and Cybersecurity Complexity

5 The Role of IT and Cybersecurity Process, Policies, and Controls

LEARNING OBJECTIVES

- Understand the foundational role of policies, processes, and controls in managing enterprise IT operations and cybersecurity, and how they interconnect to support governance, risk management, and compliance
- Differentiate between processes, policies, and controls, including the types of controls and explain how each contributes to the security and efficiency of IT operations
- Recognize the importance of aligning IT practices with business goals through frameworks like Information Technology Infrastructure Library (ITIL), Control Objectives for Information and Related Technologies (COBIT), ISO 27001, and NIST CSF, and understand how these frameworks help drive continuous improvement and regulatory compliance
- Apply knowledge of how policies influence control objectives, implementation, and enforcement, ensuring traceability, standardization, and adaptability in a rapidly evolving threat and business landscape

The management of enterprise IT operations and cybersecurity relies heavily on processes, policies, and controls. These elements form the backbone of strong governance, effective risk management, and regulatory compliance. To fully grasp their importance, we need to delve into each component and examine how they work together to create a well-functioning IT environment.

Processes are step-by-step procedures that define how tasks should be completed. In IT and cybersecurity, they ensure consistency and efficiency by standardizing workflows. Documented processes also facilitate knowledge sharing and continuous improvement, allowing teams to learn from past actions and optimize their responses. For example, incident response processes help guide swift and coordinated reactions to security breaches.

Policies, on the other hand, provide the overarching guidelines that steer an organization's approach to IT operations and security. They communicate expectations to employees; help meet regulatory requirements and serve as the foundation for risk management. A data security policy, for example, outlines how data should be handled, classified, and protected, ensuring that everyone follows best practices.

Controls are the specific tools and measures used to enforce policies and manage risks. These are often divided into administrative, technical, and physical controls. Whether through security training, encryption systems, or surveillance cameras, controls provide concrete ways to safeguard

DOI: 10.1201/9781003562153-7

systems and data. They also allow organizations to measure their security effectiveness and adjust where needed.

These three elements are interconnected, with policies setting direction, processes defining how to implement controls, and controls enforcing policies. This relationship ensures a comprehensive and structured approach to IT operations and security, making it easier to manage risks and maintain compliance. By aligning processes, policies, and controls, organizations benefit from improved security, operational efficiency, compliance, and reduced risk. This framework not only strengthens the organization's security posture but also fosters accountability and clarity in roles and responsibilities, which are crucial for long-term success.

UNDERSTANDING IT OPERATIONS MANAGEMENT POLICIES, PROCESSES, AND CONTROLS

Enterprise IT operations and cybersecurity rely on three key pillars: processes, policies, and controls. These elements work together to create strong governance, manage risks, and ensure compliance with regulations. Let's explore each component and see how they interconnect to build a robust IT environment.

IT Processes

Processes form the core of any well-run IT operation. They provide structured steps that guide employees through various tasks and procedures. In IT and cybersecurity, processes ensure everyone follows a standard approach, regardless of their team or location.

One major advantage of established processes is the uniformity they bring to an organization. When all staff members follow the same steps to complete a task, it reduces variation and boosts consistency. This is especially important in large companies where teams may be spread across different locations or time zones. By adhering to standardized processes, a technician in New York will handle a security incident the same way as their colleague in London, ensuring a unified approach to problem-solving.

Well-crafted processes can significantly improve efficiency and cut down on errors. When employees have a clear, step-by-step guide to follow, they're less likely to skip important steps or make mistakes. This is particularly valuable in high-stress situations, such as responding to a data breach or managing a system outage, where clear thinking and methodical approaches are critical.

Picture a scenario where a company detects a potential security breach. A well-defined incident response process would guide the team through each critical step: from initial detection and assessment, through containment and elimination, to recovery and post-incident review. This structured approach ensures that no vital steps are overlooked in the heat of the moment.

Processes play a key role in preserving and transferring organizational knowledge. They serve as a repository of best practices, capturing the collective wisdom and experience of the organization. This makes processes invaluable tools for training new employees and bringing them up to speed quickly. For example, a detailed process for setting up new user accounts ensures that even a newly hired IT support technician can correctly set up access rights, create email accounts, and install necessary software, all while following the organization's security standards.

It's worth noting that processes aren't set in stone. They should evolve over time, reflecting new insights, technologies, and best practices. Regular review and refinement of processes allow organizations to learn from their experiences and adapt to new challenges. For instance, a software development team might regularly review and update their coding and testing processes based on lessons learned from previous projects. This cycle of continuous improvement helps the team become more efficient and produce higher-quality code over time.

IT Policies

While processes dictate how things should be done, policies provide the overarching framework for why things are done a certain way. Policies are high-level guidelines that set the tone for an organization's approach to IT operations and security. Policies play an essential role in setting clear expectations for everyone in the organization, from entry-level employees to top executives. They define the "what" and "why" of organizational practices, providing a foundation for decision-making and aligning actions with the company's broader objectives. For example, a data classification policy might outline different levels of data sensitivity (e.g., public, internal, confidential, highly confidential) and provide guidelines on how each category should be handled. This policy would then inform more specific processes and controls for data handling across the organization.

One of the primary functions of policies is to ensure compliance with laws, regulations, and industry standards. In today's complex regulatory environment, having clear policies in place is essential for avoiding legal pitfalls and potential fines. Consider a healthcare organization subject to Health Insurance Portability and Accountability Act (HIPAA) regulations. Their information security policy would need to address specific requirements for protecting patient data, including guidelines on data access, storage, and transmission. This policy would then drive the implementation of specific controls and processes to ensure HIPAA compliance.

Policies provide a framework for identifying potential vulnerabilities and implementing measures to mitigate them. A comprehensive set of IT and security policies helps organizations take a proactive approach to risk management, addressing potential threats before they materialize. For instance, a Bring Your Own Device (BYOD) policy might outline the security measures required for personal devices used for work purposes. This policy would help mitigate the risks associated with employees accessing sensitive company data on potentially unsecured personal devices.

While policies need to be thorough, they also need to be practical and enforceable. Overly restrictive or complex policies can lead to employee frustration and noncompliance, while policies that are too vague may not provide enough guidance. Finding this balance often requires input from various stakeholders across the organization. For example, when developing a remote work policy, IT and security teams might need to collaborate with HR and legal departments to ensure the policy addresses security concerns while also considering employee rights and productivity needs.

IT Controls

Controls are the practical implementation of policies and the enforcers of processes. They are the tangible actions, tools, and measures that organizations use to manage risk and ensure compliance with their established guidelines. Let's review the three common control categories:

1. *Administrative controls:* Administrative controls focus on management-driven initiatives and procedures. These are often the "soft" controls that shape organizational behavior and culture. Security awareness training is a prime example of administrative control. Regular training sessions can educate employees about common cyber threats, such as phishing attacks, and teach them best practices for maintaining a secure environment. This kind of control helps create a security-conscious culture throughout the organization. Another important administrative control is the principle of least privilege. This ensures that users only have access to the resources they absolutely need to perform their job functions. Implementing this principle requires careful consideration of job roles and responsibilities, and regular review of access rights.
2. *Technical controls:* Technical controls are the technological safeguards that protect an organization's assets and data. As cyber threats become increasingly sophisticated, organizations must continually evaluate and update their technical controls. Firewalls and

intrusion detection systems form the first line of defense against external threats. These tools monitor network traffic, identifying and blocking potential attacks before they can cause damage. Encryption is another crucial technical control, protecting sensitive data both in transit and at rest. Whether it's encrypting emails containing sensitive information or securing data stored in the cloud, encryption plays a vital role in maintaining data confidentiality. Multifactor authentication (MFA) has become an increasingly important technical control in recent years. By requiring multiple forms of verification before granting access, MFA significantly reduces the risk of unauthorized access, even if passwords are compromised.

3. *Physical controls:* While it's easy to overlook the importance of physical security. However, physical controls remain a critical component of overall security strategy. Access control systems, such as key cards or biometric scanners, ensure that only authorized personnel can enter sensitive areas. This is particularly crucial for data centers or areas where critical infrastructure is housed. Surveillance cameras serve both as a deterrent to potential intruders and as a tool for investigating security incidents. Proper placement and monitoring of these cameras can significantly enhance an organization's physical security posture. Even seemingly simple measures, like proper disposal of physical documents through shredding, play an important role in maintaining overall security. In an era of increasing environmental awareness, many organizations are also implementing controls around the secure disposal of electronic devices to prevent data leaks and reduce e-waste.

The Interplay of Processes, Policies, and Controls

While we've discussed processes, policies, and controls separately, in practice, they form an interconnected system that drives effective IT operations and cybersecurity management.

Policies set the overall direction, defining what needs to be done to ensure security and operational effectiveness. From these high-level guidelines, more specific standards and procedures are developed, providing detailed instructions on how to meet policy requirements.

Controls are then implemented to enforce these standards and ensure compliance with the policies. For example, a policy might state that all sensitive data must be encrypted. The corresponding control would be the actual encryption software and protocols put in place to protect the data.

Processes tie everything together by providing the step-by-step framework for how these controls are used and how policies are carried out in daily operations. They ensure that everyone in the organization knows exactly what to do to maintain security and efficiency, from how to handle a customer data request to the proper steps for reporting a suspected security breach.

The effectiveness of this triad depends on its ability to adapt to changing circumstances. As technology evolves and new threats emerge, organizations must be ready to update their approach accordingly. Regular audits and assessments play a crucial role in this adaptive process. By regularly evaluating the effectiveness of their processes, policies, and controls, organizations can identify areas for improvement and stay ahead of potential threats. For instance, the rise of cloud computing has required many organizations to rethink their data storage and access policies. This, in turn, has led to the implementation of new controls (like cloud access security brokers) and the development of new processes for managing cloud resources securely.

While robust processes, clear policies, and strong controls are essential, their effectiveness ultimately depends on the people implementing them. The best-designed system can be undermined by human error or intentional misuse. This is why ongoing training and communication are vital components of any IT and security strategy. Regular security awareness training helps employees understand the importance of following established processes and adhering to security policies.

By understanding and implementing enterprise IT operations and cybersecurity, processes, policies and controls effectively, organizations can better protect their assets, comply with regulations, and position themselves for long-term success in an increasingly digital world. As the technological landscape continues to evolve, the importance of these fundamental components will only grow, making it essential for organizations to invest time and resources in developing and maintaining robust processes, clear policies, and effective controls.

IMPORTANCE OF ITOM PROCESSES, POLICIES AND CONTROLS

Managing IT systems and services is essential to keeping a company's technology running smoothly and aligned with its goals. Here's a straightforward look at the key IT processes and why they matter.

First, companies need a solid service strategy. This is where decisions are made about which IT services to offer and how those services fit the company's overall goals. For instance, a retail company might decide to develop a mobile app if they see more customers shopping on their phones. Aligning IT services with business needs ensures that resources are used wisely. A key part of this strategy is the service catalog. Think of it as a menu that lists all the available IT services for different departments, from basic things like email to more advanced tools like data analysis. This helps IT teams manage resources and set clear expectations.

Next is service design, where ideas start to become real plans. The goal here is to make sure services are reliable, secure, and easy to use. Designers plan for backup systems to handle high demand, put security measures in place, and make sure the services can scale as the business grows. Once the design phase is complete, service transition begins. This is where new systems are rolled out or existing ones are updated. Change management plays a big role in ensuring a smooth transition—communicating with everyone involved and having backup plans ready if things don't go as expected. Testing is vital to make sure the new systems work well and securely before they go live. After a new system is launched, it's important to train staff and provide support. This could involve user guides or training sessions to help people adapt to the changes.

Then comes service operation, which is the day-to-day management of IT services. The service desk is the first point of contact for any IT issues. It's about more than just fixing problems quickly; it's about maintaining trust and providing a good experience for users. When problems arise, incident management steps in to resolve them fast. The aim isn't just to fix the problem but also to understand why it happened, so it doesn't happen again. Problem management goes a step further by looking for underlying issues and fixing them before they become bigger problems.

Managing who has access to what is another key responsibility. It's important to make sure the right people have the right access while keeping everything secure.

Lastly, continual service improvement focuses on constantly reviewing and improving IT services to make them more efficient. This could be small updates or bigger changes like implementing new technology, but the aim is always to keep improving and adapt to the company's needs.

IT processes work together to support the business from planning through daily operations, always with an eye on improving. Fine-tuning these processes helps companies get the most out of their technology, move forward with innovation, and stay competitive in a digital world.

THE IMPORTANCE OF ITOM PROCESS

Efficient ITOM processes are essential for supporting organizations in various advantageous ways. They improve overall operations, resulting in a marked increase in efficiency, which can lead to considerable savings in time and financial costs. When services are provided consistently and reliably, user satisfaction and contentment with the service tend to increase. Furthermore, having clear and effective processes established is critical for managing risks and proactively preventing potential issues that could occur in the future.

- By effectively streamlining various operations, IT teams can devote their attention and resources to more crucial and rewarding work instead of getting bogged down in repetitive, time-consuming tasks that consume their energy and focus. This strategic approach leads to enhanced productivity levels across the entire company, fostering a more efficient working environment and ultimately driving better outcomes for the organization as a whole. When IT services are reliable, consistently efficient, and meet or even exceed expectations, everyone involved benefits greatly. Users can count on receiving exactly what they need right when they need it most. This reliability fosters trust and enhances productivity across the board.

- Effective and intelligent utilization of resources presents yet another significant advantage of implementing good IT processes within organizations. By strategically eliminating waste and streamlining inefficiencies, companies can manage to keep their overall costs down while still ensuring the delivery of top-notch, high-quality services to their customers and clients.
- Proactive monitoring and effective risk management significantly contribute to preventing small issues from evolving into larger, more complex problems. This proactive approach leads to reduced downtime and minimizes the occurrence of security headaches, resulting in a much smoother operational experience.
- Aligning IT efforts with company goals is absolutely crucial for overall success. Well-designed processes ensure that technology effectively supports the business objectives instead of merely running in the background without purpose. This alignment can lead to greater efficiency and improved outcomes.
- Standardization is absolutely key to significantly reducing errors and enhancing overall efficiency in any system. When everyone consistently follows the same playbook, processes and operations run much more smoothly, leading to better outcomes and increased productivity across the board.

Ultimately, effective IT processes are crucial in assisting companies to adapt and flourish in an ever-evolving landscape. As business requirements continually shift and expand, IT can seamlessly scale up operations to effectively meet these new demands without missing a beat or causing disruptions.

THE ROLE OF IT FRAMEWORKS

In Chapter 2 we had a high-level look at IT frameworks and how these provide structured approaches to managing operations and integrating security measures. They help organizations align their IT strategy with business goals while keeping everything secure. In this chapter we are going to do a deeper dive on the two most commonly used frameworks are ITIL and COBIT. ITIL focuses on managing IT services and keeping customers happy. COBIT takes a broader view, helping align IT processes with business objectives and manage risks. Understanding the differences between these frameworks helps companies choose the right one for their needs. While both offer valuable tools, they serve different purposes and can be used in different ways to improve IT management.

Let's break down the key distinctions between them in a way that highlights their unique focuses and applications.

ITIL

ITIL is a comprehensive framework that helps organizations manage their IT services more effectively.[1] It aims to ensure IT services are chosen, planned, delivered, and maintained in a way that meets specific business needs. By standardizing processes, ITIL helps companies achieve more consistent and predictable outcomes in their IT operations.

Aspect	Details
Purpose	Standardize IT processes to achieve consistent, predictable outcomes and support business objectives.
Origins	Developed by the UK's Central Computer and Telecommunications Agency to standardize ITSM.
Core components	1. Service Strategy 2. Service Design 3. Service Transition 4. Service Operation 5. Continual Service Improvement
Approach	Bottom-up—focuses on the IT department's perspective to ground practices in daily operational realities.
Flexibility	Adaptable framework—organizations can choose relevant elements to suit their needs.
Key benefits	– Improved service quality – Higher customer satisfaction – Cost reduction – Better alignment with business goals
Continuous improvement	Regular evaluation and updates through the Continual Service Improvement phase.

COBIT

COBIT[2] is a framework designed to help organizations manage and govern their enterprise IT systems. COBIT provides tools to enhance the value of IT investments while balancing benefits, risks, and resources. The framework aligns IT goals with broader business objectives, positioning technology as a strategic enabler rather than just a support function.

Aspect	Description
Purpose	Framework for IT governance and management to maximize value and minimize risk in IT investments.
Origins	ISACA
Core components	– Governance & management objectives – Process reference model – Control objectives – Maturity models
Approach	Align IT goals with business objectives, treating IT as a strategic enabler.
Flexibility	Adaptable to organizations of any size or industry
Key benefits	– Aligns IT initiatives with business strategy – Enhances decision-making – Optimizes IT resources and investments
Continuous improvement	Encourages regular reviews and enhancements of IT services

Comparison of ITIL and COBIT

ITIL is designed with a strong focus on IT Service Management (ITSM). It offers detailed guidance on how to manage the full lifecycle of IT services, from planning and delivery to ongoing support and improvement. A major part of the ITIL philosophy is ensuring that services evolve and improve over time, always aiming for high levels of customer satisfaction. On the other hand, COBIT casts a wider net. Its primary concern is with IT governance, focusing on making sure that IT processes not only run smoothly but also align closely with a company's broader business objectives. COBIT also takes into account regulatory requirements, ensuring that organizations remain compliant with external rules and standards.

Aspect	ITIL	COBIT
Primary focus	ITSM	IT Governance and Business Alignment
Scope	Narrower focus on optimizing IT service lifecycle	Broader scope covering IT governance, risk management, and compliance
Approach	Bottom-up approach, improving IT processes from within	Top-down approach, aligning IT with overall business strategy
Implementation	Implemented mainly by ITSM teams	Involves a wide range of stakeholders, including executives
Structure	Structured around five stages of IT service lifecycle	Organized around governance and management objectives in five domains
Regulatory compliance	Less emphasis on regulatory compliance	Strong emphasis on meeting regulatory requirements
Orientation	Service-oriented, focused on improving IT service delivery	Business-oriented, ensuring IT aligns with broader business goals
Best For	Organizations aiming to improve IT service quality and customer satisfaction	Organizations needing to align IT governance with business strategies and compliance needs

Can ITIL and COBIT Be Implemented Simultaneously?

ITIL and COBIT can indeed be implemented together within an organization. These two frameworks often complement each other well, each bringing its own strengths to create a more comprehensive approach to managing and governing IT. When used in tandem, these frameworks offer a range of benefits. ITIL drives operational excellence by improving IT service processes, while COBIT ensures these processes align with business strategy and governance. COBIT provides a framework for managing risks, compliance, and regulatory requirements, while ITIL offers detailed process guidance for effective ITSM and high-quality outcomes.

Organizations can approach the implementation of both frameworks in a way that leverages their respective strengths. For instance, ITIL might be used to streamline IT service delivery, enhance customer satisfaction, and improve incident management processes. Meanwhile, COBIT can ensure these IT efforts align with broader business goals like risk management, compliance, and strategic objectives. This dual focus bridges the gap between tactical and strategic perspectives. ITIL provides practical, detailed guidelines for daily ITSM, while COBIT ensures these services deliver value and contribute to broader organizational goals. Together, they help IT teams manage operations effectively while supporting long-term business success.

Both frameworks are flexible and adaptable, allowing organizations to tailor their use based on specific needs. This customization is crucial, as no two organizations are identical, and IT needs vary depending on factors like size, industry, and business goals. By selecting relevant elements from both frameworks, organizations can create a comprehensive and effective governance and service management strategy. For example, a company might use ITIL to manage incident and problem resolution processes, ensuring efficient handling of IT issues with minimal customer impact. Simultaneously, COBIT could be used to ensure these processes comply with risk management and regulatory requirements, protecting the organization from potential risks.

Integrating ITIL and COBIT offers a more comprehensive IT management approach. ITIL handles the operational side, focusing on delivering high-quality services, while COBIT ensures these services align with business goals and governance requirements. This combination can lead to continuous improvement, operational excellence, and a more strategic, well-rounded approach to IT management.

IMPORTANCE OF CYBERSECURITY PROCESSES, POLICIES, AND CONTROLS

Cybersecurity processes, policies, and controls are the core of any organization's defense against digital threats. These elements work together to protect systems, networks, and sensitive information from cyberattacks. Each plays a distinct role, and understanding their functions is essential for building a solid security foundation.

Cybersecurity Processes

Processes are the detailed steps that guide how security-related tasks are carried out within an organization. Having well-defined processes ensures that everyone follows the same procedures, which leads to more consistent and efficient results. For example, a company might have a process for regularly updating its software to protect against vulnerabilities, making sure the entire organization is on the same page. In the case of a security breach, these processes become even more critical. They provide clear instructions on how to respond, who needs to be contacted, and what actions must be taken to contain and resolve the issue. By following these established steps, the organization can reduce the impact of an incident and recover more quickly.

Cybersecurity Policies

Policies are high-level statements that outline how an organization approaches security. They offer direction and set expectations for how information should be protected. For instance, a policy might state that all customer data must be encrypted to ensure privacy. These policies also play a vital role in identifying and managing risks. They guide the organization in assessing where vulnerabilities may exist and what measures should be taken to address them. Policies also ensure compliance with industry standards and legal requirements, helping avoid fines and protecting the company's reputation. Additionally, they set clear expectations for employees, making it easier for everyone to understand their responsibilities when it comes to security.

Cybersecurity Controls

Controls are the specific actions and tools put in place to enforce policies and reduce risks. They include both technical measures, like firewalls and antivirus software, and administrative actions, such as employee training. Controls ensure that the organization's security policies are not just words on paper but are actively implemented to protect against threats. As mentioned earlier in this chapter there are three main types of ITOM and cybersecurity controls: Administrative Controls, Technical Controls, and Physical Controls.

Why Cybersecurity Processes, Policies, and Controls Matter

When combined, these elements form a robust defense strategy. Together, they help organizations identify and manage risks, ensuring potential threats are handled promptly and effectively. By following these structured approaches, companies stay compliant with legal and industry regulations, which helps avoid penalties and preserve their reputations. In the event of a security incident, well-established processes and policies enable a rapid, coordinated response. This minimizes damage and reduces downtime, helping the organization get back to normal operations as quickly as possible. Controls, in turn, provide the practical tools needed to limit the impact of any breach.

Another key benefit is consistency and awareness. By standardizing security practices across the organization, risks stemming from inconsistent procedures are greatly reduced. Everyone in the company knows what to do, how to do it, and why it matters, which strengthens the overall security posture. Employees understand their roles in protecting the organization, and regular updates to these elements ensure that the company stays ahead of emerging threats. This creates a continuous improvement cycle, allowing the organization to evolve its security measures as needed to keep pace with changing technology and risks.

THE ROLE OF CYBERSECURITY FRAMEWORKS

In Chapter 2 we introduced cybersecurity frameworks from a very high-level perspective. In this chapter we will take a much deeper look at the two of the most commonly used cybersecurity frameworks today are the NIST Cybersecurity Framework (NIST CSF) and ISO 27001. Both are widely respected and have been adopted by organizations across industries for their comprehensive approach to managing cyber threats. Let's take a closer look at each of these frameworks.

NIST Cybersecurity Framework (NIST CSF)

The NIST CSF is an important set of guidelines and best practices. Developed by the U.S. National Institute of Standards and Technology, it helps organizations improve how they manage cybersecurity risks. The framework serves as a roadmap for businesses looking to strengthen their defenses against cyber threats. The primary purpose of the NIST CSF is to assist organizations in assessing their current cybersecurity measures. It also helps them enhance their ability to prevent, detect, and respond to potential risks. This structured approach is especially valuable in today's digital landscape, where threats are constantly evolving.

Aspect	Description
Purpose	Helps organizations manage and reduce cybersecurity risk. Provides a structured, voluntary framework for assessing and improving cybersecurity posture.
Core elements	– Framework Core: Key cybersecurity activities organized into Functions, Categories, and Subcategories. – Implementation Tiers: Measures maturity (Tiers 1–4). – Framework Profiles: Aligns current vs. target cybersecurity states.
Implementation	– Tier 1: Partial – Tier 2: Risk Informed – Tier 3: Repeatable – Tier 4: Adaptive
Framework profiles	Aligns business goals with cybersecurity outcomes. Used to compare "Current" vs. "Target" states and identify improvement opportunities.
Approach	Prioritizes resources and efforts based on specific risks and business needs.
Flexibility	Can be adapted to any size organization or industry. Not mandated by law.

The NIST CSF 2.0 is organized around six essential functions including Govern, Identify, Protect, Detect, Respond and Recover. These functions work together in a continuous cycle to help organizations establish, implement, and improve their cybersecurity posture. The Govern function provides the overarching strategy and direction, while the other five functions focus on the operational aspects of cybersecurity risk management. Let's explore these in more detail:

Function	Purpose
Govern	Sets strategic direction, policy, roles/responsibilities, and integrates cybersecurity into enterprise risk management. Includes third-party risk.
Identify	Understands assets, risks, and vulnerabilities. Focuses on knowing what to protect and the context of threats.
Protect	Implements safeguards to ensure service delivery. Prevents or limits cybersecurity events through controls and defense mechanisms.
Detect	Monitors and identifies anomalies or cybersecurity events in real time. Ensures timely discovery of threats.
Respond	Takes immediate actions once a threat is detected. Coordinates incident response to contain and mitigate damage.
Recover	Restores capabilities or services after an incident. Focuses on resilience, learning, and continuous improvement.

International Organization for Standardization (ISO) 27001

ISO 27001 is the international standard that provides requirements for an information security management system (ISMS), which was jointly published by ISO and IEC. The standard outlines a framework for organizations to manage and protect their information assets. At its core, ISO 27001 helps organizations identify and protect valuable information. It encourages a thoughtful approach to managing security risks, emphasizing that each organization should assess its specific vulnerabilities.

ISO 27001 is founded on three essential principles known collectively as the CIA triad: confidentiality, integrity, and availability. These principles form the backbone of the standard's approach to securing information and are central to building an effective ISMS. Each element addresses a distinct aspect of information protection, ensuring that data remains secure, reliable, and accessible within an organization.

Confidentiality focuses on preventing unauthorized access to sensitive information. This means ensuring that only those with proper authorization can view or handle specific data, such as personal information or proprietary business assets. Implementing access controls is one foundational method, defining which users or roles are permitted to access which data and under what circumstances. Encryption also plays a critical role, transforming readable information into a secure format that requires a decryption key to interpret. Authentication mechanisms, such as strong passwords or biometric verification, further strengthen confidentiality by confirming that users are who they claim to be. Together, these measures reduce the risk of data breaches and unauthorized disclosure.

Integrity is about maintaining the accuracy and trustworthiness of information over its entire lifecycle. Data must remain unchanged unless alterations are authorized and traceable. Integrity is protected through mechanisms like input validation, dual authorization processes, and cryptographic checksums, codes that detect even minor alterations to data. Digital signatures are also used to confirm that data originates from a verified source and has not been tampered with. Without integrity controls, organizations risk basing decisions on corrupted or manipulated information, which can lead to financial loss, reputational damage, and operational disruption.

Availability ensures that authorized users can access the data and systems they need, when they need them. Business continuity depends on the reliability of IT infrastructure, and any interruption, from hardware failure to cyberattacks, can impact productivity. To uphold availability, organizations must perform regular maintenance, implement system redundancy, and maintain up-to-date backups. Disaster recovery planning is also crucial, detailing how to restore critical operations quickly after an incident. By proactively safeguarding availability, organizations can avoid downtime, ensure operational efficiency, and maintain trust with stakeholders.

Aspect	Description
Purpose	To establish, implement, maintain, and continually improve an ISMS to protect the confidentiality, integrity, and availability of information.
Core elements	CIA Triad (Confidentiality, Integrity, Availability), Risk Assessment, Annex A Controls (114 controls in ISO/IEC 27001:2013; revised in 2022 to 93 controls), Management Commitment, Continual Improvement
Implementation	Based on the PDCA (Plan-Do-Check-Act) cycle; requires risk assessment, setting objectives, implementing controls, internal audits, and management reviews.
Framework profiles	No predefined profiles like NIST CSF; instead, organizations tailor their ISMS scope and controls based on specific risks, regulatory requirements, and business context.
Approach	Risk-based and process-driven; focuses on aligning security controls with organizational risks and integrating security into business processes.
Flexibility	Highly adaptable across industries and organization sizes; scalable from small businesses to multinational enterprises; compatible with other frameworks like NIST, COBIT, and GDPR.

Beyond the CIA triad, ISO 27001 provides a structured framework for implementing an ISMS. The standard consists of 11 main clauses that outline requirements for establishing, operating, monitoring, and continually improving information security processes. In addition, Annex A of the standard offers a catalog of security controls that organizations can select and apply based on their specific risk landscape. Together, these components guide organizations in building a resilient and adaptive security program aligned with international best practices. The latest version of ISO 27001 published in 2022 contains 93 controls grouped into four main themes.

One of the significant advantages of ISO 27001 is that organizations can achieve certification from accredited bodies. This certification signifies compliance with the standard and demonstrates a commitment to information security. Achieving this status can enhance an organization's reputation, showing clients and stakeholders that they take data protection seriously. Implementing ISO 27001 not only strengthens information security but also boosts resilience against cyberattacks.

Globally, ISO 27001 is recognized as the leading standard for information security management. Its wide acceptance underscores its importance and reliability in promoting best practices in information security. ISO 27001 is designed to work alongside other management system standards, making it easier for organizations to integrate their various management practices.

Comparison of NIST CSF and ISO 27001

Both NIST CSF and ISO 27001 serve to enhance cybersecurity but adopt distinct methodologies. NIST CSF offers a flexible framework, ideal for organizations beginning to shape their cybersecurity strategies. In contrast, ISO 27001 provides a structured approach that is certifiable and acknowledged worldwide. Many organizations find that utilizing both frameworks together can create a robust cybersecurity strategy tailored to their unique requirements.

Aspect	NIST CSF	ISO 27001
Primary focus	Flexible cybersecurity framework for risk management	Structured ISMS
Scope	Initially for U.S. critical infrastructure, now widely adopted	International standard applicable to all industries
Framework structure	Five core functions: Identify, Protect, Detect, Respond, Recover	Specific clauses with Annex A containing 93 security controls

Aspect	NIST CSF	ISO 27001
Certification	No official certification; self-implemented	Formal certification available via third-party audits
Cost	Freely accessible with no certification costs	Involves documentation and audit costs
Maturity level suitability	Best suited for organizations beginning cybersecurity programs	Ideal for organizations with established security practices
Technical depth	More technical, providing detailed implementation guidance	Broader approach, focusing on risk-based security management
Global recognition	Primarily recognized in the United States	Globally recognized, often required for international business
Customization and flexibility	Highly flexible and adaptable across industries	Provides structured compliance but allows some flexibility
Risk management approach	Risk-based approach with focus on threat identification and response	Comprehensive risk assessment and management process

Can NIST CSF and ISO 27001 Be Implemented Simultaneously?

Implementing the NIST Cybersecurity Framework (CSF) and ISO 27001 together is not only possible, but it also offers several advantages. First, these two frameworks complement each other very well. Both focus on similar processes for managing risks related to information security. They share common goals: identifying potential risks, implementing suitable controls to mitigate those risks, and continuously monitoring the performance of these controls.

Another important point to note is the significant overlap between the two frameworks. For organizations that are already certified under ISO 27001, they find that they have met around 83% of the requirements set forth by the NIST CSF. On the flip side, organizations that comply with the NIST CSF have completed about 61% of what is necessary for ISO 27001 compliance. This overlap means that working on one framework can substantially ease the burden of fulfilling the requirements of the other.

Taking on both frameworks at the same time allows organizations to adopt a more comprehensive approach to managing information security risks. It helps in building a stronger overall cybersecurity posture and enhancing resilience against potential threats. The NIST CSF offers flexibility by serving as a baseline for creating a cybersecurity program. In contrast, ISO 27001 provides a more structured path that culminates in certification.

Each framework has its own strengths. The NIST CSF is more technical and is particularly beneficial during the initial phases of a cybersecurity risk management program. Meanwhile, ISO 27001 is less technical and focuses more on risk-based management, making it ideal for organizations that have already matured in their operational capabilities.

Organizations can also find integration possibilities between the two frameworks. Many of the requirements from both standards can be woven into the same set of policies and procedures. This integration minimizes duplicated efforts and improves overall efficiency. Additionally, although not flawless, there are crosswalks and mapping tools available that can assist organizations in aligning the NIST CSF with ISO 27001.

To successfully implement both frameworks at the same time, organizations should first ensure they have a solid understanding of each framework. Next, they should conduct a gap analysis to identify any areas where they fall short. After that, developing a clear integration plan is crucial. This plan should outline the necessary controls and policies that need to be put in place. Continuous monitoring and improvement are essential to ensure ongoing compliance and effectiveness.

Finally, organizations should leverage the benefits of being compliant with both standards when communicating with stakeholders. Although the journey to implement both frameworks can be challenging, the rewards can be significant. In the long run, it can lead to a stronger security posture and save both time and resources.

NOTABLE MENTION: CLOUD SECURITY ALLIANCE CLOUD CONTROLS MATRIX (CSA CCM)

The CSA CCM[3] is an important framework focused on cybersecurity in cloud computing. Its main aim is to establish fundamental security principles that help both cloud vendors and potential customers. For businesses exploring cloud technology, grasping these principles is important for evaluating the overall security risks linked to different cloud providers. By providing clear guidance, the CSA CCM supports organizations in making educated choices about which vendors they can trust to handle their sensitive data.

A key aspect of the CSA CCM is its clarity regarding responsibilities between cloud service providers and customers. This shared responsibility model is essential for ensuring both parties know their roles in maintaining security. By defining who is responsible for what, the framework reduces confusion and helps ensure effective implementation of security measures across the cloud environment.

The latest version, CCM v4, is quite detailed, comprising 197 control objectives organized into 17 distinct domains. Each domain tackles critical aspects of cloud technology. This organized structure allows organizations to pinpoint specific concerns and address them effectively.

Control #	Domain	Description
1	Application & Interface Security	Secures cloud applications and APIs by embedding security throughout development—coding, testing, deployment.
2	Audit and Assurance	Ensures cloud services meet standards and regulations, identifying any security gaps.
3	Business Continuity Management and Operational Resilience	Prepares for disruptions with disaster recovery plans to maintain critical operations.
4	Change Control and Configuration Management	Manages infrastructure/app changes with documentation, approvals, and testing.
5	Data Security and Privacy Lifecycle Management	Secures data through classification, encryption, and privacy compliance across its lifecycle.
6	Datacenter Security	Protects physical cloud data centers using access controls and surveillance.
7	Cryptography, Encryption, and Key Management	Applies encryption and secure key management to safeguard sensitive data.
8	Governance, Risk Management, and Compliance	Sets up governance for cloud use, risk assessment, and regulatory compliance.
9	Human Resources Security	Mitigates insider threats through background checks, training, and access controls.
10	Identity and Access Management	Controls access to cloud resources using strong identity verification and authorization.
11	Security Infrastructure and Virtualization	Secures virtual/cloud infrastructure through segmentation and secure configurations.
12	Interoperability and Portability	Facilitates data portability and multicloud compatibility to prevent vendor lock-in.
13	Universal Endpoint Management	Secures user devices (e.g., mobile, laptops) with endpoint protection and MDM.

Control #	Domain	Description
14	Security Incident Management, E-Discovery, and Cloud Forensics	Enables incident response, investigation, and legal discovery during breaches.
15	Supply Chain Management, Transparency, and Accountability	Manages third-party risk, ensures transparency, and strengthens supply chain security.
16	Threat and Vulnerability Management	Continuously scans and patches vulnerabilities to reduce exposure.
17	Logging and Monitoring	Collects logs and enables real-time monitoring to detect/respond to threats quickly.

Organizations can utilize the CCM as a valuable resource for assessing their cloud implementations. This framework offers practical guidance on the necessary security controls, depending on the roles of different participants in the cloud supply chain. Whether a business is a cloud service provider or a customer using cloud services, the CCM provides insights into best practices and recommended measures to bolster security.

COMMON ELEMENTS OF IT AND CYBERSECURITY PROCESS, POLICIES, AND CONTROLS

Across most established IT and cybersecurity frameworks, such as NIST CSF, ISO/IEC 27001, COBIT, and ITIL, there are consistent foundational elements that form the backbone of effective security and operational governance. These frameworks aim to address the full lifecycle of risk, operations, and assurance, enabling enterprises to manage digital threats while aligning technology with business goals. Leveraging the strengths of multiple frameworks often allows organizations to tailor their controls to meet their unique risk profile and compliance requirements.

Risk management is a recurring pillar in every framework. Effective programs depend on continuous assessment and mitigation of threats to infrastructure, data, and operations. These frameworks promote proactive identification of vulnerabilities and the application of controls before exploitation occurs. Alongside risk, strong governance is emphasized, where executive leadership plays an integral role in setting security priorities, funding initiatives, and establishing organizational accountability for cybersecurity.

Operational elements such as asset management, access control, and incident response are universally present. Enterprises must maintain an accurate inventory of their IT assets, including data, software, and hardware, to effectively protect and govern them. Access to these assets must be tightly controlled through identity and access management practices. When incidents occur, organizations are expected to have mature detection and response capabilities, enabling them to recover quickly and limit damage.

Another shared focus is continuous improvement. Frameworks like ITIL and ISO 27001 stress the need for iterative process refinement and regular evaluations. This philosophy ensures that controls evolve alongside the threat landscape and that lessons learned from audits or incidents are incorporated into future operations. Equally important is the formalization of policy and procedure. Documented, enforceable guidance provides structure to operations and ensures consistency across teams and functions.

Human factors are also a critical theme. Training and awareness programs are essential to foster a security-conscious culture. These frameworks recognize that even the most advanced technical controls can be undermined without informed and vigilant personnel. Compliance with laws and regulations is another shared expectation, requiring organizations to demonstrate due diligence in meeting industry standards, protecting data, and reporting as needed to regulators and stakeholders.

Finally, robust data protection, vendor management, and business continuity capabilities are fundamental. Organizations must protect data confidentiality, integrity, and availability at all stages. They must also manage third-party risk by vetting vendors and enforcing contractual security standards. Additionally, a mature disaster recovery and business continuity strategy ensures operational resilience in the face of disruptions, whether technical, environmental, or malicious. Together, these principles support a secure and adaptable enterprise environment.

HOW POLICIES SHAPE CONTROL OBJECTIVES, CONTROLS, AND CONTROL ENFORCEMENT

Policies play a crucial role in guiding how organizations manage their security and risk strategies. They serve as a foundation, influencing every layer of an organization's security framework, from setting objectives to ensuring enforcement. Let's take a closer look at how policies shape these critical elements:

How Policies Shape Control Objectives

Policies are the starting point for defining what an organization needs to protect and how far that protection must go. They set the direction and establish priorities, ensuring everyone knows the expectations for security and risk management. For example, a policy might state that sensitive customer information should be encrypted. From that broad directive, specific control objectives are created, such as classifying data based on its sensitivity, ensuring encryption is in place, and managing the keys used for that encryption. The objectives are, in essence, the steps needed to meet the policy's requirements. These objectives guide the practical work, ensuring that the organization's policies are followed in everyday operations.

How Policies Shape Controls

Once the control objectives are in place, policies further guide the selection and implementation of the specific mechanisms, or controls, needed to meet those objectives. These controls are the tangible actions or systems that enforce the organization's security measures. For instance, if a policy requires strong password protection, the controls might include setting rules for password complexity, establishing account lockout procedures after failed login attempts, and defining how often passwords should expire and be updated. The policy doesn't just say "secure the system"; it provides the framework that influences every technical and procedural step needed to make that happen. It sets the boundaries and requirements, ensuring controls are not only implemented but aligned with the broader goals.

How Policies Shape Control Enforcement

Policies also establish who is responsible for ensuring that controls are followed and what happens if they aren't. They create the structure for enforcing compliance, outlining the roles of individuals or teams responsible for monitoring and taking action when necessary. A well-written policy will also detail the consequences of failing to meet control requirements and provide a system for managing exceptions when compliance isn't possible. For example, if a user violates an acceptable use policy, the enforcement mechanism might include monitoring user activities, issuing warnings, or revoking access. This enforcement ensures that the organization not only sets rules but has the means to ensure they are followed in practice.

Alignment and Traceability

One of the key strengths of well-defined policies is that they ensure a direct link between the high-level organizational goals and the day-to-day technical operations. This alignment means that the control objectives, the controls themselves, and their enforcement all trace back to the core values and risk tolerance of the organization. Every technical safeguard or rule can be linked to a broader business requirement, ensuring that nothing is implemented in isolation. Policies provide this structure, helping organizations maintain focus and ensuring that security efforts are consistent with their overall mission.

Continuous Improvement

Policies are not static. Organizations grow, change, and face new risks, and policies must evolve with them. Many policies include guidelines for regular review and updates, which ensures that control objectives and controls stay relevant and effective. As new threats emerge or regulations change, policies drive the necessary adjustments, making sure that the security framework is always improving. This built-in process of regular assessment means that the organization is constantly refining its approach to risk and security.

Compliance and Standardization

In addition to shaping internal practices, policies help ensure that the organization adheres to external standards and regulations. Many industries have specific legal or regulatory requirements that must be met, and policies are the mechanism for embedding those requirements into the organization's everyday operations. By shaping control objectives and guiding control implementation, policies make sure that these standards are consistently applied across the organization, creating a unified approach to security that can withstand external scrutiny.

Policies are the backbone of an organization's security strategy. They don't just set the rules; they influence every part of the security process, from defining what needs to be protected, to guiding the implementation of controls, to ensuring those controls are properly enforced. This holistic approach ensures that the organization's security efforts are cohesive, effective, and aligned with its overall goals and risk appetite.

CONCLUSION AND RECAP

The successful management of enterprise IT operations and cybersecurity hinges on the integration and alignment of three foundational components: processes, policies, and controls. These elements are not stand-alone constructs but operate in concert to build resilient, secure, and compliant environments that support both day-to-day operations and long-term strategic objectives. Their effective implementation underpins every aspect of IT governance and risk management, enabling organizations to operate with confidence in a rapidly evolving threat landscape.

Processes form the operational backbone, providing structure and repeatability to critical IT and security tasks. From incident response to change management and access provisioning, well-documented processes create consistency, reduce errors, and drive efficiency. They also institutionalize knowledge, ensuring that expertise is not lost when personnel transitions occur. Critically, mature process frameworks allow organizations to respond swiftly to disruptions, enabling business continuity even under pressure.

Policies, meanwhile, define the organization's intent, risk tolerance, and expectations. They articulate the "why" behind the "how," translating executive directives into actionable guidance for technology teams. Well-crafted policies reflect legal, regulatory, and business requirements and serve as the foundational drivers for both process design and control implementation. They align business objectives with operational execution and act as the connective tissue between governance and operations.

Controls are the practical enablers that enforce policy and operationalize processes. These can be administrative (e.g., training, role-based access), technical (e.g., firewalls, encryption), or physical (e.g., facility access systems), each playing a vital role in managing enterprise risk. The most effective control environments are layered, aligned to risk priorities, and continuously tested for effectiveness. Without these tangible safeguards, even the most comprehensive policies and processes remain theoretical.

As organizations adopt frameworks like ITIL, COBIT, NIST CSF, ISO 27001, and CSA CCM, they encounter consistent themes: the importance of governance, risk management, continuous improvement, and compliance. These frameworks reinforce the same message, security and operational excellence must be embedded into the fabric of organizational culture. When implemented thoughtfully, they offer a structured path for aligning IT functions with business needs while keeping risk exposure in check.

It's also critical to recognize the human element. No matter how advanced the tools or mature the processes, security is only as strong as the people operating within it. Regular training, clear communication, and a culture of accountability must reinforce the policies and controls in place. Frameworks across the board emphasize security awareness, insider threat mitigation, and the role of leadership in modeling and enforcing best practices.

Another core takeaway is the importance of agility and continuous improvement. Enterprise environments, regulatory landscapes, and threat vectors are constantly shifting. Static policies and rigid processes quickly become liabilities. Leading organizations bake review cycles into their governance models, using audits, metrics, and lessons learned to iterate and evolve. This is particularly important in dynamic domains like cloud security, where the shared responsibility model and technology velocity demand rapid adaptation.

The value of aligning multiple frameworks cannot be overstated. ITIL and COBIT together create a synergy between service management and governance. NIST CSF and ISO 27001 complement each other by blending flexibility with certification-ready structure. CSA CCM adds precision in cloud-specific risk controls. When organizations integrate the strengths of these frameworks into a unified model, they gain better visibility, scalability, and assurance.

Moreover, the chapter has shown that policies are not just static documents, they're the blueprint from which control objectives are defined, controls are enforced, and compliance is assured. They provide the traceability required for internal audits, regulatory inspections, and board-level reporting. Without clearly defined policies, control selection becomes reactive and fragmented, weakening the organization's security posture.

The strategic interplay between processes, policies, and controls is the cornerstone of secure and efficient IT operations. They provide structure in complexity, clarity in ambiguity, and resilience in disruption. As organizations continue to digitize, adopt cloud services, and face escalating cyber threats, the foundational knowledge covered in this chapter will remain essential. Leaders who understand how to operationalize these elements holistically will be best positioned to guide their organizations toward secure, scalable, and compliant growth.

NOTES

1 TechTarget. "ITIL (Information Technology Infrastructure Library)." SearchDataCenter. Accessed June 16, 2025. www.techtarget.com/searchdatacenter/definition/ITIL.

2 ISACA. n.d. *COBIT Framework*. Accessed June 16, 2025. www.isaca.org/resources/cobit.

3 Cloud Security Alliance. *Cloud Controls Matrix (CCM)*. Accessed June 16, 2025. https://cloudsecurityalliance.org/research/cloud-controls-matrix.

6 The Use of Compensating Controls in Enterprise IT

LEARNING OBJECTIVES

- Understand that compensating controls are carefully designed alternatives used only when primary security controls can't be implemented
- Learn that effective compensating controls require validation, governance, and lifecycle management
- Identify that overuse or poor implementation leads to risk accumulation
- Understand that security, risk, compliance, and business units must work together to ensure compensating controls align with business objectives, and regulatory expectations

A fundamental aspect of security management involves recognizing and addressing the risk of doing business. Every organization must make informed decisions regarding risk acceptance and mitigation, particularly when compensating controls come into play. This discussion delves into the core philosophy behind compensating controls, which is an approach that mirrors the concept of insurance, where businesses take proactive measures to mitigate potential losses even when complete security cannot be achieved. By exploring the relationship between risk, security, and operational efficiency, organizations can develop a more nuanced understanding of how compensating controls fit within their broader security strategy.

Compensating controls form a foundational component of an enterprise's overall security and compliance strategy, serving as alternative measures when primary security controls are not feasible or fully effective. These controls provide organizations with a means to mitigate security risks while maintaining compliance with industry standards and regulatory frameworks. However, their implementation requires careful consideration to ensure they offer an equivalent level of security and do not introduce additional risks.

This document provides comprehensive guidance on the design, implementation, and documentation of compensating controls within an enterprise environment. It aims to clarify misconceptions surrounding these controls by illustrating the limitations of built-in security mechanisms and emphasizing the importance of collaboration with information security teams. Understanding the organizational structure of a typical security program is essential in ensuring compensating controls are appropriately integrated and effectively managed.

The characteristics of compensating controls must be clearly defined to ensure they function as intended. A well-structured framework for their application ensures that organizations can implement these measures without undermining the integrity of their security posture. This document outlines the essential considerations necessary for identifying and applying compensating controls that align with an enterprise's business objectives, operational needs, and critical infrastructure

DOI: 10.1201/9781003562153-8

requirements. By doing so, organizations can ensure that these controls support broader security initiatives while maintaining business continuity and regulatory compliance.

DEFINITION AND PURPOSE OF COMPENSATING CONTROLS

In cybersecurity and compliance, a compensating control is an alternative security measure used in place of a primary control that cannot be fully implemented. These controls are designed to provide equivalent or comparable protection against threats, ensuring that security objectives are met even when primary controls are unavailable. The application of compensating controls is especially relevant in industries that operate under stringent security requirements, such as finance, healthcare, and government. These industries require continuous risk management, monitoring, and adherence to standardized frameworks to safeguard sensitive data and critical infrastructure.

Although compensating controls can serve as valuable security measures, relying on them excessively is considered a poor security practice. Their overuse may indicate systemic security weaknesses, as they often act as workarounds rather than comprehensive solutions. Unlike primary controls, which are typically proactive and preventive, compensating controls may function as reactive risk mitigations, addressing security gaps but not necessarily eliminating the underlying vulnerabilities. If not carefully designed, documented, and continuously monitored, compensating controls can lead to security blind spots, compliance violations, and increased exposure to cyber threats.

A key concern in the implementation of compensating controls is auditability. If these controls are not well documented or fail to demonstrate effectiveness during an audit, they may be classified as false positives, leading to regulatory noncompliance or security deficiencies. Auditors assess whether compensating controls provide a level of protection equivalent to the original security requirements. If a compensating control does not adequately address the intended risk, organizations may face penalties, security breaches, or operational disruptions.

CASE STUDY: MAJOR RETAILER USES COMPENSATING CONTROLS FOR PCI DSS

Background

RetailCo, a mid-sized e-commerce retailer, processes 50,000+ credit card transactions monthly. During a PCI DSS audit, they identified a critical gap with their legacy inventory management system that couldn't support encryption for stored cardholder data (PCI DSS Requirement 3.4). A full system overhaul would take 18 months due to budget and technical constraints.

Problem

Without encryption, RetailCo risked noncompliance, fines, and data breaches. They needed an interim solution to mitigate risks while planning the system upgrade.

Compensating Controls Implemented

To address the gap, RetailCo deployed the following compensating controls, aligned with PCI DSS criteria:

1. Network segmentation
   - Isolated the legacy system from other networks to limit exposure.
   - Implemented strict firewall rules to block unauthorized access.
2. Enhanced access controls
   - Enforced MFA for all administrative access to the legacy system.
   - Restricted access via MAC address filtering and IP whitelisting.
3. Continuous monitoring
   - Deployed intrusion detection systems (IDS) with real-time alerts for suspicious activity.
   - Conducted daily log reviews and quarterly penetration testing.
4. Data minimization
   - Reduced stored cardholder data retention from 12 months to 48 hours.
   - Masked PANs (Primary Account Numbers) in all internal logs.

Validation and Documentation

RetailCo followed PCI DSS guidelines for validating compensating controls:

- Risk assessment: Quantified residual risk (low) after controls, validated by a third-party QSA.
- Documentation: Created a Compensating Control Worksheet (CCW) detailing:
  - o Rationale for controls.
  - o Evidence of implementation (e.g., firewall logs, MFA activation records).
- Testing: Simulated attack vectors (e.g., SQL injection, unauthorized access) to verify control effectiveness.

Outcome

- Compliance achieved: The QSA approved the controls as meeting PCI DSS intent, rigor, and defense levels.
- Cost savings: Delayed the $500K system overhaul by 12 months.
- Risk reduction: No breaches occurred during the interim period.

Key Lessons

- Alignment with intent: Controls must directly address the original requirement's purpose (e.g., MFA reduced unauthorized access risk as encryption would have).
- Temporary ≠ Permanent: RetailCo maintained a transition plan to implement encryption within 18 months.
- Holistic approach: Combining segmentation, monitoring, and access controls provided layered security

THE ROLE OF COMPENSATING CONTROLS IN CYBERSECURITY AND RISK MANAGEMENT

In the context of enterprise cybersecurity and risk management, compensating controls represent deliberate, risk-informed security measures implemented when standard or prescribed security controls cannot be applied due to legitimate business, operational, financial, or technological constraints. Far from being ad hoc workarounds, compensating controls must be strategically designed to deliver a level of protection that is equivalent, if not functionally superior, to the primary controls they replace or supplement.

These alternative safeguards are often necessary in complex enterprise environments where prescriptive control implementations are impeded by legacy technologies, third-party constraints, technical debt, or regulatory ambiguity. The role of compensating controls becomes particularly critical in highly regulated industries, such as finance, healthcare, and critical infrastructure, where adherence to frameworks like NIST 800-53, ISO/IEC 27001, PCI DSS, HIPAA, and SOX is not optional, but mandated by law or industry standard. Despite their utility, compensating controls must be deployed with precision and strategic oversight. They are not long-term substitutes for mature security architectures, but rather temporary, risk-aware control implementations that buy time while permanent solutions are developed or while systemic constraints are resolved.

Designing Effective Compensating Controls

To be effective, a compensating control must meet three critical enterprise criteria:

- Comparable risk reduction: It must demonstrably address the same threat vectors or risk scenarios as the control it replaces.
- Operational feasibility: It must function within the current business and IT operating model without creating friction or new vulnerabilities.
- Strategic alignment: It must align with the organization's overarching security architecture, risk appetite, and compliance objectives.

Enterprise security architects must ensure these controls are intelligently scoped, technically sound, and sustainably maintainable. Poorly implemented compensating controls often result in "control illusions," where perceived protection is not matched by actual efficacy, leaving organizations exposed to cascading risks. Moreover, compensating controls should avoid introducing undue operational complexity. If the control requires excessive manual intervention, extensive user training, or customized integrations, it may present more risk than reward. Automation, scalability, and integration into existing Security Orchestration, Automation, and Response (SOAR) and Security Information and Event Management (SIEM) platforms should be considered baseline requirements.

Governance, Monitoring, and Lifecycle Management

The strategic value of compensating controls is realized only through continuous validation and lifecycle governance. These controls must be treated as living components within the security architecture, which is subject to change, deprecation, or replacement as the threat landscape evolves or as enabling technologies are introduced. Key activities that ensure governance maturity include:

- Formal risk assessments to validate that the control continues to mitigate identified risks adequately.
- Periodic control testing, including automated validation routines and red/blue team exercises.
- Continuous monitoring of effectiveness, often integrated with telemetry and behavioral analytics.
- Documented exception handling processes that formally approve the use of compensating controls under defined conditions.

Enterprise risk and compliance teams must ensure all compensating controls are fully documented within governance repositories such as the GRC platform or control register, including their justification, control owner, dependencies, and expiration/review date. This documentation ensures transparency for internal stakeholders and external auditors alike.

Defining Boundaries and Preventing Overuse

A recurring risk in enterprise environments is the overextension of compensating controls beyond their intended scope. This usually stems from expediency, organizations applying a temporary fix to multiple systems or use cases rather than addressing root architectural or process-level deficiencies. This phenomenon results in risk diffusion, where latent vulnerabilities shift across the enterprise and become increasingly difficult to detect or remediate. To avoid such outcomes, organizations should define strict criteria and governance gates for the deployment of compensating controls, including:

- Trigger conditions: When is a compensating control permissible?
- Control duration: What is the maximum lifecycle before reassessment or replacement?
- Scope limitation: What systems, data classes, or business functions are covered?
- Exit strategy: What conditions must be met to retire the compensating control?

These parameters must be enforced through policy-level control frameworks and embedded within the organization's enterprise security architecture (ESA) and risk management processes.

Managing the Residual Risk of Control Substitution

Every compensating control inherently represents a deviation from standard best practices or regulatory expectations. As such, there is always residual risk, and in some cases, risk transfer, associated with their use. Security leaders must therefore assess the cumulative impact of compensating controls across the environment, particularly in scenarios involving:

- Legacy systems with unpatched vulnerabilities
- Cloud services with provider-imposed limitations
- OT environments where downtime is unacceptable
- Third-party integrations lacking security transparency

For example, replacing an MFA requirement with enhanced logging and anomaly detection introduces a time lag between breach and detection, a gap that must be acknowledged and mitigated through accelerated response capabilities. Thus, compensating controls should never be viewed in isolation but instead as part of a broader, interconnected control ecosystem, where control dependencies, failure modes, and escalation paths are well understood.

Compensating Controls as Strategic Risk Instruments

In mature cybersecurity programs, compensating controls are not shortcuts or exemptions, they are strategically governed instruments of risk management that enable business continuity, innovation, and regulatory alignment amid real-world constraints. When designed and managed effectively, they allow enterprises to maintain defensible security postures even in the presence of legacy debt, shifting compliance requirements, and complex operating environments. Organizations should ensure that compensating controls are not only technically effective but also strategically integrated, risk-informed, and architecturally aligned. Their role is to balance agility with control, enabling the organization to adapt without compromising its resilience.

TYPES OF COMPENSATING CONTROLS IN IT SECURITY AND COMPLIANCE

In the realm of enterprise cybersecurity and regulatory compliance, compensating controls serve as strategic stopgap measures that enable organizations to maintain an acceptable security posture when a required primary control is either infeasible, delayed, or temporarily ineffective. Unlike baseline controls that are often prescriptive and broadly applied, compensating controls are context-specific, designed to address precise security deficiencies driven by operational constraints, legacy system limitations, budgetary restrictions, or transitional states in an evolving architecture.

These controls are not intended to be permanent replacements for foundational security mechanisms; rather, they are risk-based adaptations that ensure business continuity and compliance alignment while primary controls are under development, in migration, or awaiting integration. They must provide a security level that is equivalent to or greater than the control they substitute and must be thoroughly documented, rigorously tested, and continuously monitored to validate their effectiveness. Understanding the strategic implementation of compensating controls is critical for enterprise security architects, particularly within risk management frameworks, where control adequacy is continuously measured against defined risk appetites and tolerance thresholds.

Types of Compensating Controls

Compensating controls generally fall into three primary categories, technical, administrative, and physical, each with distinct roles in safeguarding enterprise assets. Their implementation should always reflect a layered defense approach, reinforcing the principle of defense-in-depth.

Technical Compensating Controls

Technical compensating controls are system-enforced security mechanisms implemented through software, hardware, or automation frameworks. These controls are preferred for their precision, consistency, and scalability in high-velocity enterprise environments. For instance, when full deployment of Multifactor Authentication (MFA) for remote access cannot be immediately realized, perhaps due to incompatibility with legacy VPN clients, a compensating control may involve real-time anomaly detection, centralized login monitoring, and automated alerting. These measures enable rapid identification of suspicious login patterns or geolocation anomalies, allowing incident responders to act swiftly and prevent credential misuse.

Another scenario involves systems lacking full-disk encryption due to technical debt. In such cases, a layered compensating strategy may include:

- File integrity monitoring
- Endpoint detection and response solutions
- Privileged access workstations
- Immutable logging mechanisms

These controls, when orchestrated effectively, provide visibility, traceability, and mitigation in lieu of native encryption, though they must be accompanied by strict access governance and auditability. The enterprise value of technical compensating controls lies in their ability to automate detection, reduce human error, and provide measurable outputs for audit and compliance reporting. However, architects must ensure that these controls are not only well integrated but also periodically validated against evolving threat landscapes and business requirements. Misconfigured or noisy controls can lead to alert fatigue, false positives, and ultimately a diluted security posture.

Administrative Compensating Controls

Administrative compensating controls are policy-driven, human-centric security practices that guide behavior, enforce accountability, and create procedural safeguards. While lacking direct technical enforcement, these controls play a pivotal role in shaping a culture of security within the organization. For example, when software limitations prevent the use of automatic session timeouts, the organization may enforce a written policy mandating users to manually log off after a specific duration of inactivity. This is reinforced by mandatory security awareness training, periodic reminders, and disciplinary procedures for noncompliance.

In another scenario, consider a legacy system that lacks role-based access control capabilities. A compensating administrative control could involve:

- Manual access reviews on a biweekly basis
- A structured access request and approval workflow
- Periodic audits performed by the internal GRC or IT compliance team
- Segregation of duties policies

These controls introduce governance mechanisms that ensure accountability, even in the absence of robust automation. While administrative controls are often more cost-effective and faster to deploy, their effectiveness hinges on organizational discipline, continuous user engagement, and managerial oversight. They are inherently more susceptible to circumvention and inconsistencies, especially in decentralized or fast-paced operational environments. Thus, administrative controls should ideally complement technical safeguards, not replace them entirely.

Physical Compensating Controls

Physical compensating controls are measures designed to prevent unauthorized physical access to critical infrastructure, systems, and data-bearing assets. In an enterprise context, particularly within data centers, network closets, or hybrid work environments, these controls serve as the first line of defense against tampering, theft, or sabotage. If the organization lacks electronic access control systems or biometric authentication due to cost or infrastructure limitations, compensating measures might include:

- Manual entry logs
- 24/7 on-site security personnel
- Visitor escort policies
- Periodic physical audits of server rooms and critical infrastructure

Similarly, if encryption cannot be implemented due to hardware compatibility issues, the compensating strategy may enforce:

- Locked and monitored server enclosures
- Offline storage of cryptographic keys in secured safes
- Restricted physical access via badge authorization or keycard rotation schedules

In environments where data sovereignty or regulatory frameworks like HIPAA or CJIS apply, physical controls may also involve tamper-evident seals, surveillance systems, environmental controls (e.g., fire suppression), and geofencing. Although physical controls are highly effective at deterring or delaying attacks, they are best utilized in conjunction with administrative and technical layers. A physical security breach, if unmonitored or poorly logged, can bypass multiple digital defenses, making integrated monitoring and response mechanisms critical.

HOW COMPENSATING CONTROLS WORK TOGETHER

Compensating controls work by providing alternative security measures across technical, administrative, and physical domains to address gaps when primary controls cannot meet requirements. These controls maintain risk mitigation equivalence through coordinated implementation across security layers. Here's how they integrate:

Technical Compensating Controls

Purpose	Examples
Address vulnerabilities in systems/software when primary technical safeguards are impractical.	• Deploying MFA when network segmentation isn't feasible. • Implementing enhanced logging and monitoring to detect anomalies if intrusion prevention systems (IPS) are outdated. • Using data encryption to compensate for weak physical security in data storage.

Administrative Compensating Controls

Purpose	Examples
Mitigate risks through policy adjustments or procedural changes when standard governance measures fall short.	• Manual audit reviews replacing automated compliance checks in legacy systems. • Security awareness training to offset gaps in technical access controls. • Revised incident response plans during system upgrades to maintain operational continuity.

Physical Compensating Controls

Purpose	Examples
Strengthen physical security when primary safeguards (e.g., biometric access) are unavailable.	• Adding security guards or surveillance cameras to compensate for inadequate door-locking mechanisms. • Implementing environmental controls (e.g., fire suppression) where structural upgrades are delayed.

Integration across Control Types

Scenario	Primary Control Gap	Compensating Controls
Legacy system unable to support MFA	Technical	Administrative (stricter password policies) + Technical (login monitoring).
Budget constraints prevent facility upgrades	Physical	Technical (encryption) + Administrative (access log reviews).
Incompatible automated patch management	Technical	Administrative (manual patch validation) + Physical (restricted server room access).

Key principles for effective integration include:

1. Equivalence: Compensating controls must match or exceed the risk reduction of the original requirement.
2. Documentation: Justify why primary controls aren't feasible and validate compensatory measures.
3. Cross-domain synergy: Combine technical monitoring, administrative policies, and physical restrictions to create layered defenses.

Strategic Application and Lifecycle of Compensating Controls

For security architects, the implementation of compensating controls should be guided by a formalized risk assessment and gap analysis. These controls must be:

- Documented in policy and control libraries
- Mapped to applicable compliance frameworks
- Monitored through metrics or KPIs
- Periodically reevaluated for necessity and effectiveness

It is essential to communicate clearly to stakeholders, including auditors, that compensating controls are transitional and not indicative of design flaws, but rather deliberate, risk-informed decisions made to balance business agility with security assurance. Wherever feasible, architects should develop sunset timelines or transition plans that define when and how the primary control will be implemented or restored. This ensures that compensating controls do not become permanent crutches that erode long-term security maturity.

IMPLEMENTATION OF COMPENSATING CONTROLS

In complex enterprise environments, there are instances where certain baseline security controls, whether mandated by policy, standards, or regulation, cannot be implemented due to technological constraints, legacy system dependencies, operational requirements, or budgetary limitations. In such scenarios, compensating controls serve as alternative safeguards. However, their implementation must be strategic, risk-informed, and compliant with applicable regulatory frameworks. As a matter of enterprise security governance, every compensating control, whether technical, administrative, or physical, must satisfy the following critical principles:

1. *Risk equivalence to the original control:* Compensating controls must demonstrably mitigate risk to a level equivalent to that provided by the original control they replace or supplement. This is not a matter of convenience or subjective judgment; it requires a formalized risk assessment and quantitative or qualitative analysis to validate equivalency. Where equivalence cannot be fully achieved through a single measure, a layered approach involving multiple compensating controls may be necessary to reach acceptable residual risk levels.
2. *Clear justification and comprehensive documentation:* Organizations must maintain thorough documentation that explicitly outlines:
   - The rationale for not implementing the original control.
   - The nature, scope, and function of the compensating control.
   - How the compensating control addresses the underlying risk.
   - The timeline and roadmap for transitioning to the originally required control, where applicable.

This documentation should be maintained within the enterprise's Governance, Risk, and Compliance program and be readily available for internal review and external audit.

3. *Verifiability through testing and auditing:* A compensating control that cannot be empirically tested or independently audited cannot be trusted to perform its intended function under real-world conditions. Controls must be subjected to routine validation, including:
   - Functional testing to verify operational effectiveness.
   - Control assessments as part of internal risk reviews.
   - Formal audits aligned with the organization's audit cadence and compliance obligations. Controls failing to meet these criteria may be deemed noncompliant and invalidate audit assertions.
4. *Regulatory alignment and auditor acceptance:* Compensating controls must map directly to the intent and risk mitigation goals of the original regulatory requirements. For example:
   - In PCI DSS, compensating controls must meet the criteria.
   - In frameworks like NIST SP 800-53, ISO/IEC 27001, or HIPAA Security Rule, compensating controls must align with the control objectives and demonstrate similar assurance levels.

     Enterprises must proactively engage with internal compliance teams and external auditors to confirm that any compensating control is acceptable within the specific regulatory context. Failure to secure agreement in advance can result in audit exceptions, fines, or increased residual risk exposure.

Temporary by Design, Not by Default

While compensating controls are a valid and often necessary component of enterprise cybersecurity strategy, they must never become institutionalized as long-term replacements for core security controls. Their role is to act as transitional safeguards, providing temporary risk mitigation while the enterprise works toward implementing fully compliant, standardized, and ideally automated security mechanisms.

Organizations should continuously reassess all compensating controls as part of their control lifecycle management and prioritize their retirement as capabilities mature and constraints are resolved. The long-term objective should always be to converge on a resilient, standards-based security architecture that minimizes exceptions and maximizes alignment with security best practices.

By rigorously selecting, implementing, and governing compensating controls within a well-defined enterprise risk management framework, security leaders can uphold the integrity of the organization's security posture, maintain audit readiness, and ensure adaptability in the face of evolving technological and regulatory landscapes.

STRATEGIC EVALUATION OF COMPENSATING CONTROLS IN THE ESA

In the context of a mature enterprise security program, the evaluation of compensating controls is not simply a technical exercise, it is a strategic decision point within the broader risk governance process. Compensating controls, when applied correctly, can provide effective risk mitigation in scenarios where standard security controls are infeasible due to operational, technical, or financial constraints. However, their effectiveness must be rigorously validated to ensure they do not degrade the organization's security posture or introduce unmanaged residual risk.

While industry frameworks allow for the use of compensating controls, none prescribes a one-size-fits-all method for evaluating their adequacy. Therefore, it falls upon security architects and risk management leaders to establish consistent, defensible evaluation criteria that ensure compensating controls meet or exceed the intent of the original control. This requires a holistic understanding of the threat landscape, business context, and the interdependencies across the organization's control environment.

Principles for Evaluating Compensating Controls

At the foundation of any evaluation is the principle of control equivalence: a compensating control must deliver comparable risk mitigation to the prescribed baseline control. This means the alternative control must address the same threat vectors, operate with similar or greater reliability, and integrate seamlessly with the organization's broader security architecture. Key evaluation criteria include:

- Risk equivalence: Does the compensating control neutralize the same threat vectors as the original control with similar effectiveness?
- Security impact: Does the control introduce new vulnerabilities, reduce the layered defense posture, or create interdependencies that weaken resilience?
- Business alignment: Is the control aligned with enterprise risk tolerance, compliance mandates, and operational priorities?
- Feasibility justification: Has the organization documented a defensible rationale for why the primary control is impractical, and why the alternative is the best viable solution?

Critically, compensating controls must not be used as tactical workarounds to bypass compliance mandates. Instead, they should be implemented as part of a well-documented, risk-based exception process that is subject to governance oversight and continuous reassessment.

Architectural Considerations and Interdependencies

Enterprise security architectures are inherently interlinked. Introducing a compensating control in one domain can have cascading effects across others, especially when controls intersect with identity management, data protection, and incident response workflows. Organizations must analyze:

- Control interaction: How does the compensating control affect adjacent systems and controls? Could it inadvertently create control gaps or dependencies?
- Cumulative risk: If multiple compensating controls are deployed across the organization, do they collectively elevate systemic risk or reduce defense-in-depth?
- Resilience and recovery: Does the compensating control support failover, redundancy, and post-incident forensics in the same manner as the original control?

An example of this might involve replacing host-based EDR with network-based anomaly detection due to limitations in legacy systems. While network visibility may offer compensating insights, it may lack the forensic fidelity and real-time containment capabilities of endpoint-based tools, demanding additional layers of control and compensatory response mechanisms.

Challenges in Measuring Compensating Control Effectiveness

One of the most persistent challenges in evaluating compensating controls lies in quantifying their efficacy. Unlike primary controls, which often have deterministic outcomes, compensating controls frequently rely on probabilistic or behavioral indicators, human intervention, or contextual risk analysis. This inherently introduces variability, subjectivity, and potential for latent failure. Organizational control owners must assess:

- Detection fidelity: Does the control exhibit high false positive/false negative rates? Is it prone to evasion techniques?
- Human reliance: How dependent is the control on manual processes or analyst judgment? What are the risks of fatigue or inconsistency?
- Bypass risk: Can threat actors easily identify and circumvent the control? Is it resilient against insider threat vectors?
- Operational burden: Does the control introduce inefficiencies, degrade user experience, or obstruct core business functions?

For instance, a compensating control replacing automated data loss prevention enforcement with manual data review may meet compliance in theory, but in practice, it introduces significant delays, inconsistency, and fatigue, ultimately reducing control reliability.

Establishing Key Performance Indicators (KPIs) to Quantify Effectiveness

To maintain accountability and ensure continuous improvement, compensating controls must be supported by clearly defined KPIs. These metrics enable security leadership to evaluate the ongoing relevance, performance, and business impact of the controls, informing both operational tuning and strategic control lifecycle decisions. Recommended KPIs include:

- Threat detection time: Time-to-detect compared to baseline controls. Are threats identified within acceptable response windows?
- Incident containment rate: Success rate of the control in preventing or limiting real-world attacks.
- Audit conformance: Frequency and severity of audit findings tied to the compensating control.
- User compliance trends: Rates of adherence, exception requests, and policy violations related to the control.
- Cost efficiency: Comparative analysis of resource consumption (human, technological, and financial) relative to the original control.

These metrics must be reviewed within the context of the organization's risk appetite and recalibrated as new threats emerge or business conditions evolve.

Monitoring, Incident Response, and Adaptive Validation

A control that is not continuously monitored is a control that cannot be trusted. Compensating controls, particularly those adopted under duress or constraint, must be subjected to aggressive real-time validation. This requires robust telemetry, behavioral analytics, and integration with incident response workflows. Examples of compensating control validation mechanisms include:

- Log correlation and behavioral analysis: Leveraging SIEM and SOAR platforms to detect anomalies that suggest control evasion or failure.
- Red team testing and threat emulation: Periodically testing compensating controls against simulated adversarial techniques to validate their effectiveness.
- Secure enclave monitoring: Using tamper-resistant enclaves to ensure integrity and nonrepudiation of control-related telemetry and logs.

- Resilience engineering: Stress-testing compensating controls under failure conditions to understand their behavior during outages or attacks.

These mechanisms help security teams detect control drift, identify systemic weaknesses, and iteratively improve compensating strategies.

Lifecycle Management and Strategic Integration

Compensating controls are, by design, transitional, not permanent solutions. Their use should be governed by a structured lifecycle framework that aligns with enterprise architecture methodologies and control governance models. The lifecycle should include:

- Risk-based justification: Document why the control is needed, what risk it addresses, and how it aligns with enterprise risk tolerance.
- Design and deployment: Architect the control for integration into existing workflows, with minimal disruption and clear boundaries of responsibility.
- Monitoring and assurance: Implement continuous monitoring, testing, and reporting mechanisms to verify control efficacy over time.
- Sunset and transition planning: Develop a roadmap for replacing the compensating control with the prescribed standard control when constraints are resolved.

Organizations should incorporate these controls into enterprise governance tooling, GRC platforms, and audit workflows to ensure transparency, repeatability, and accountability.

Stewardship of Compensating Controls

Compensating controls, when strategically designed and rigorously validated, serve as essential tools in maintaining security and compliance amidst evolving constraints. However, their use must be deliberate, temporary, and anchored in enterprise risk strategy. As stewards of the security architecture, it is our responsibility to ensure that these controls do not become institutionalized band-aids, but rather carefully managed instruments of risk mitigation, constantly monitored, continuously evaluated, and ultimately replaced with more robust and permanent safeguards. By embedding compensating controls within a broader architectural and governance context, organizations can sustain both operational agility and security integrity, even in the face of constraint and complexity.

CHALLENGES AND BEST PRACTICES IN USING COMPENSATING CONTROLS

In today's rapidly evolving regulatory landscape and complex IT environments, the strategic use of compensating controls has become a necessary component of mature enterprise security and compliance programs. While the implementation of prescribed, baseline controls remains the gold standard, real-world constraints often hinder an organization's ability to fully comply with mandated security requirements. In such scenarios, compensating controls serve as alternative safeguards designed to meet the intent and objectives of the original control, enabling risk mitigation while maintaining compliance posture. However, deploying compensating controls is not a simple matter of substitution. It requires a deliberate, risk-informed approach that considers the broader impact on the organization's security architecture, compliance obligations, and operational continuity. Often, enterprises are prompted to evaluate compensating measures following audit findings, deficiency notices, or formal management letters from external assessors. These moments present both a challenge and an opportunity: a challenge in terms of addressing control gaps under duress, and an opportunity to strengthen the control environment through thoughtful design and stakeholder engagement.

One of the primary complexities in adopting compensating controls lies in reconciling compliance imperatives with business priorities. Enterprise leadership may be reluctant to disrupt existing processes, especially when those workflows are tightly coupled with revenue generation, customer experience, or operational efficiency. As such, compensating controls are frequently proposed as a means to satisfy regulatory requirements without imposing undue friction on business operations. Yet this approach must be treated with caution. Overreliance on compensating measures can lead to a fragmented or brittle control environment if not anchored in a coherent security strategy.

To ensure compensating controls are both effective and sustainable, organizations must apply the same rigor to their evaluation and implementation as they would for primary controls. This includes:

- Objective alignment: Validating that the compensating control satisfies the intent and security objectives of the control it replaces. This is a nonnegotiable starting point.
- Risk assessment: Conducting a comprehensive risk analysis to determine residual risk exposure, potential attack vectors introduced by the compensating measure, and its overall impact on the threat landscape.
- Operational feasibility: Ensuring the control can be consistently applied and monitored within existing processes and technology stacks without introducing operational bottlenecks.
- Documentation and justification: Maintaining clear, auditable documentation that articulates the rationale, design, and effectiveness of the compensating control. This is critical for both internal assurance and external audit readiness.
- Periodic review and testing: Establishing a cadence for reassessment to validate ongoing relevance and effectiveness, particularly as the organization's environment or threat model evolves.

A mature implementation also necessitates cross-functional collaboration. Effective compensating control strategies are the product of joint efforts between business process owners, IT operations, cybersecurity architects, risk management professionals, and compliance leads. Only through such interdisciplinary coordination can organizations ensure that these controls do not serve as superficial workarounds, but as risk-aligned, strategically integrated components of the broader security program.

Compensating controls should not be viewed as shortcuts or temporary patches, but as intentional, thoughtfully crafted mechanisms to uphold security and compliance when traditional controls are not feasible. Their successful adoption hinges on architectural discipline, risk-centric thinking, and continuous stakeholder engagement. By approaching compensating controls with the same strategic intent as any core security investment, enterprises can turn constraint into resilience and compliance into a catalyst for operational excellence.

STRATEGIC AND OPERATIONAL CHALLENGES IN IMPLEMENTING COMPENSATING CONTROLS

In complex enterprise IT environments, compensating controls serve as critical risk mitigation mechanisms when primary security controls are infeasible due to technical debt, budget constraints, or operational realities. While compensating controls enable organizations to maintain security assurance and regulatory compliance, their implementation is fraught with strategic and tactical challenges that, if unaddressed, can erode their effectiveness and create long-term security liabilities.

Misalignment between Risk Objectives and Control Intent

A foundational challenge is the misalignment between the intended security outcomes of compensating controls and their actual risk mitigation value. Too often, organizations adopt compensating controls with a narrow focus on audit compliance, neglecting to assess whether those controls truly neutralize the original risk vectors. This checkbox mentality leads to an illusion of security, compliance is achieved, but critical exposures remain unaddressed. Organizations should develop a risk-first mindset. Every compensating control should be explicitly mapped to the threat vector it aims to mitigate, with demonstrable equivalency to the intended primary control. Control decisions must be guided by threat modeling, attack surface analysis, and risk quantification, not just auditor expectations.

Static Controls in a Dynamic Threat Environment

Another prevalent issue is the static nature of many compensating controls. Once implemented, these controls are often treated as permanent solutions, with little consideration for the evolving threat landscape. Given the velocity of threat evolution, ransomware-as-a-service, AI-assisted phishing, supply chain compromises, controls that were sufficient at implementation may rapidly become obsolete. Enterprise programs must embed compensating controls within a broader continuous control validation strategy. This requires integration with threat intelligence, security testing, and continuous monitoring frameworks to assess ongoing control efficacy. Compensating controls should be subject to the same cadence of reassessment and validation as primary controls.

Documentation Deficiency and Audit Risk

Poorly documented compensating controls introduce audit friction and undermine accountability. In many cases, control design rationales, implementation records, effectiveness metrics, and risk acceptance decisions are scattered, or worse, undocumented. From a compliance standpoint, this not only weakens the organization's audit defensibility but also makes it difficult to determine if the control is still justified or effective. Organizations must ensure that compensating controls are incorporated into their security governance framework. This includes maintaining robust control documentation repositories that capture the risk context, justification, control objectives, technical configurations, and validation evidence. Automated governance, risk, and compliance platforms should be leveraged to centralize and streamline this process.

Resource Burden and Operational Complexity

Compensating controls often impose unintended operational burdens. Unlike preventive controls that are typically embedded into system design, compensating controls are frequently implemented as external mechanisms or manual procedures. These can introduce process complexity, increase alert fatigue, and strain limited cybersecurity resources. To address this, organizations should prioritize the automation of compensating controls wherever feasible. SOAR, policy-as-code, and machine-readable compliance controls enable scalable enforcement with reduced manual overhead. Architectural alignment with zero trust principles and secure-by-design methodologies further reduces the need for compensating workarounds in the first place.

Overuse and Compensating Control Creep

Compensating controls are meant to be exceptions, not foundational elements of a security architecture. However, in many environments, what begins as a stopgap becomes institutionalized. Over time, these controls accumulate, creating a brittle architecture of band-aids and bypasses rather than a cohesive, risk-aligned security model. Cybersecurity teams must enforce lifecycle governance for compensating controls. Every compensating control should have a sunset plan linked to the remediation of the root issue. This requires strong coordination between security, IT operations, architecture, and finance to ensure technical debt is reduced over time and compensating controls are decommissioned when primary controls become feasible.

Architectural Best Practices for Effective Compensating Controls

To operationalize compensating controls as a strategic risk management mechanism, organizations should adopt a principled, architecture-driven approach rooted in defense-in-depth and zero trust philosophies.

- *Risk-driven control design:* Compensating controls must be grounded in risk analytics. Security architects should define a structured process for evaluating residual risk and determining whether the proposed control achieves control equivalency. Leveraging threat modeling, kill chain analysis, and quantitative risk assessment, organizations can rationalize the control's effectiveness relative to the threat it is mitigating.
- *Engineering for control validation:* Control efficacy should be measurable and testable. Integrating compensating controls into a security testing program, including adversarial emulation, behavioral analytics, and automated regression testing, enables organizations to validate that the control performs under realistic threat scenarios. Wherever possible, compensating controls should include embedded telemetry to facilitate real-time monitoring, anomaly detection, and policy enforcement.
- *Regulatory alignment and auditor engagement:* Regulatory compliance should be a design consideration, not an afterthought. Each compensating control should be explicitly mapped to relevant control frameworks with alignment validated through collaboration with compliance and legal stakeholders. Engaging third-party auditors during the design phase reduces audit friction and builds consensus on control sufficiency.
- *Scope control and context-aware enforcement:* Enterprise security architects must ensure that compensating controls are scoped precisely to the systems, applications, and risk scenarios for which they are intended. Overly broad application can create blind spots, propagate technical debt, and introduce new vulnerabilities. Control enforcement should be adaptive, leveraging contextual signals to dynamically adjust policies and permissions.

COMPENSATING CONTROLS IN CLOUD ENVIRONMENTS

The shift to hybrid cloud, mobile-first, and decentralized architectures introduces new complexities for compensating control design. Cloud platforms introduce shared responsibility models that redefine how controls are implemented. Cybersecurity teams should map compensating controls across IaaS, PaaS, and SaaS layers, leveraging cloud services provider native services such as IAM, encryption-at-rest, key management, and workload isolation to achieve equivalent security outcomes. Examples include using cloud-native encryption services when endpoint full-disk encryption is not feasible and leveraging SIEM integrations with cloud services provider telemetry to create compensating visibility in ephemeral environments.

CASE STUDY: HEALTHCARE PROVIDER ENHANCES HIPAA COMPLIANCE USING AWS COMPENSATING CONTROLS

Background

A U.S.-based healthcare technology company managing sensitive patient data faced challenges implementing traditional IDS across its AWS infrastructure. Regulatory obligations under HIPAA and HITRUST required continuous monitoring of protected health information, but technical constraints in AWS EC2 limited network-level visibility.

Challenge

The organization needed to:

- Meet HIPAA's requirement for monitoring malicious activity.
- Address AWS EC2's inability to provide full network traffic access without operational disruption.
- Maintain compliance during rapid cloud migration of critical applications like EHR systems.

Compensating Control Implementation

- Constraints:
  - Native AWS tools couldn't capture all network traffic without performance impacts.
  - Legacy systems required gradual migration, creating temporary security gaps.
- Solution design:
  - The company implemented layered compensating controls:

Control objective	Compensating measure	AWS services used
Network monitoring	OS-level log analysis + management plane auditing	Amazon CloudWatch, AWS Config
Access control	Enhanced IAM policies with session logging	AWS IAM, CloudTrail
Data protection	Automated encryption validation	AWS KMS, Lambda
System integrity	Immutable backup/recovery system	AWS Backup, Elastic Disaster Recovery

Key Implementation Steps

1. Deployed centralized log collection for all EC2 instances using AWS Systems Manager.
2. Implemented real-time analysis of OS security logs for attack patterns using Amazon Detective.
3. Established automated validation of encryption states through AWS Config rules.
4. Created immutable backups with two-hour RTO using AWS Elastic Disaster Recovery.

Validation and Maintenance

- Conducted weekly automated compliance checks using AWS Audit Manager.
- Implemented CI/CD pipeline with Terraform to enforce control consistency.
- Integrated with AWS Security Hub for unified monitoring.

Outcomes

- Achieved HITRUST certification while migrating servers to AWS.
- Reduced incident response time through enhanced logging.
- Maintained uptime with zero PHI breaches post-migration.
- Cut disaster recovery costs compared to on-prem solutions.

THE FUTURE OF COMPENSATING CONTROLS

Looking ahead, compensating controls will be increasingly shaped by intelligent automation and adaptive security paradigms. AI/ML models enable compensating controls that dynamically adapt to risk conditions. Behavioral analytics, continuous authentication, and anomaly-based intrusion detection provide context-aware security that compensates for missing preventive controls. These models reduce false positives, improve detection speed, and support just-in-time enforcement.

Confidential computing is redefining compensating controls for data-in-use. By isolating workloads in hardware-based trusted execution environments, organizations can mitigate risks of memory scraping, insider threats, and OS-level compromise, particularly useful in untrusted or multitenant cloud environments. As regulatory expectations grow more stringent and real-time, organizations must shift from periodic audits to continuous compliance validation. Regulatory technology platforms offer solutions to automate, perform data analysis, and other tools designed to simplify and automate the process of meeting regulatory requirements that integrate with continuous integration and continuous delivery pipelines, policy engines, and cloud security posture management tools enable compensating controls to be monitored and enforced continuously.

CONCLUSION AND RECAP

Compensating controls, when properly understood and strategically implemented, are far more than temporary fixes or compliance shortcuts. They represent deliberate, risk-informed design decisions that allow organizations to uphold their security and compliance posture in the face of practical limitations. From legacy system dependencies to evolving regulatory obligations, compensating controls provide the flexibility to bridge gaps without compromising on protection. This chapter has outlined not only the mechanics of these controls, but also the architectural discipline required to ensure they fulfill their intended purpose.

Central to their effectiveness is a thorough understanding of the risk context in which they operate. A compensating control must do more than appear functional—it must mitigate risk to a degree that is equivalent to, or greater than, the original control it supplements or replaces. Achieving this requires rigorous assessment, evidence-based justification, and a strategic alignment with both the enterprise's threat model and its risk tolerance. Controls implemented without this depth of evaluation tend to introduce risk rather than reduce it, often lulling organizations into a false sense of security.

One of the key themes emphasized throughout this work is the importance of architectural integration. Compensating controls cannot be implemented in isolation; they must be woven into the broader security fabric of the organization. Whether the control interacts with identity systems, data protection workflows, or incident response mechanisms, its impact must be fully understood and accounted for. Security architects must analyze not only the control's immediate effect, but also its cascading influence across adjacent systems and business processes.

Governance and lifecycle management are equally critical. Compensating controls should be treated as dynamic elements within the ESA, subject to continuous reassessment and refinement. They are, by design, temporary responses to current constraints, not long-term substitutes for well-architected solutions. Without defined ownership, expiration timelines, or review mechanisms, these controls often persist beyond their period of relevance, slowly degrading the integrity of the security program and contributing to technical debt.

As discussed, compensating controls can take many forms, technical, administrative, or physical. Each serves a distinct purpose, and each presents unique strengths and limitations. Technical controls provide automation and consistency, administrative controls govern user behavior and procedural compliance, and physical controls secure tangible access points. No single category is universally superior; rather, their effectiveness is maximized when deployed as part of a layered defense strategy, tailored to the enterprise's specific operational environment.

The evolving nature of enterprise IT, particularly the shift to hybrid cloud, distributed workforces, and ephemeral computing, demands a new level of agility in control design. In these contexts, compensating controls must be elastic, portable, and context aware. Cloud-native services, real-time policy enforcement, and telemetry-driven decision-making have become core to modern security architectures. The enterprise must ensure that its compensating strategies are adaptable to these shifts, or risk obsolescence in the face of architectural transformation.

Compensating controls must also be measurable. A control that cannot be tested, validated, or monitored provides little assurance to either security teams or auditors. Metrics such as detection time, audit readiness, and user compliance trends must be used to continuously evaluate the relevance and performance of each control. These metrics not only demonstrate effectiveness but also help inform strategic decisions about whether a control should be retained, enhanced, or phased out.

At the human level, administrative compensating controls demand cultural reinforcement. These controls are inherently vulnerable to inconsistency, circumvention, and human error. While they can be rapidly deployed and are often cost-effective, they rely on the discipline and awareness of the people who operate within their scope. Therefore, education, training, and executive sponsorship are essential to reinforce their importance. However, whenever possible, manual procedures should be supplemented or replaced with technical controls to reduce the potential for deviation.

A persistent tension in the field is the balancing act between security integrity and compliance requirements. There is often pressure to implement compensating controls purely to satisfy audit checklists or avoid regulatory penalties. This compliance-first mindset can result in controls that meet formal criteria without delivering real security value. Security architects must resist this tendency by ensuring that every compensating control deployed is rooted in risk reduction, not just documentation or optics.

An equally dangerous pitfall is the normalization of compensating controls. When exceptions become the rule, the control environment becomes brittle and incoherent. This chapter has emphasized the importance of avoiding compensating control creep, where temporary controls are never revisited or replaced. Strong governance, stakeholder engagement, and technical roadmaps must converge to ensure that these controls remain transitional and do not become institutionalized weaknesses.

Looking forward, the future of compensating controls will be shaped by intelligent automation, behavioral analytics, and AI-enhanced detection and response. Adaptive controls that respond dynamically to changes in user behavior, threat intelligence, and risk conditions are rapidly becoming viable replacements for static compensating mechanisms. These technologies hold the potential to reduce false positives, accelerate containment, and offer a higher degree of risk equivalency than ever before.

Ultimately, compensating controls are only as effective as the intent and discipline behind their implementation. When governed with foresight, integrated with architectural rigor, and validated with metrics, these controls serve as essential enablers of security resilience in constrained environments. However, their long-term value depends on their temporary nature and the enterprise's commitment to maturing past the limitations that made them necessary in the first place. As security architects, our mandate is clear: to use compensating controls judiciously, manage them strategically, and retire them decisively, ensuring they serve as bridges to better security, not barriers to it.

7 Cybersecurity Resourcing Strategies for Enterprise Organizations

LEARNING OBJECTIVES

- Learn that cybersecurity must be treated as a core business priority, not just an IT issue
- Understand that organizations must invest in resourcing based on risk to get the most security value from your budget
- Explore how to build and maintain a skilled, well-supported cybersecurity workforce
- Gain an appreciation for how organizations can stay flexible and continuously adapt to new threats and technologies

Enterprise organizations face persistent and evolving challenges in resourcing, developing, and sustaining robust cybersecurity programs. To mitigate these challenges, organizations must adopt best practices and establish mature methodologies that ensure the resilience of their IT infrastructure. Effective cybersecurity resourcing is a multifaceted issue, requiring answers to two fundamental questions:

1. What level of resourcing is sufficient to stay ahead of adversaries and adapt to rapidly changing technologies?
2. How can organizations deploy these resources most effectively?

A strategic and integrated approach to cybersecurity resourcing aligns business risk management, technology investments, and workforce development. This alignment maximizes security effectiveness while optimizing resource utilization. A Cybersecurity Governance Framework serves as a foundational structure for managing enterprise cybersecurity risk, focusing on operational resourcing, business alignment, executive support, and performance monitoring.

This chapter outlines key considerations for organizations seeking to enhance the security of their networked systems and data assets. However, cybersecurity is a dynamic field with no one-size-fits-all solutions. Threat actors continuously evolve their tactics, techniques, and procedures, while organizations introduce new technologies that expand both capability and risk exposure. To maintain an effective security posture, cybersecurity programs must proactively adapt and evolve beyond static best practices.

THE RESOURCING IMPERATIVE

Ensuring that cybersecurity programs are properly staffed, well trained, and strategically organized is not just a best practice, it is an essential operational necessity. Despite this widely acknowledged

DOI: 10.1201/9781003562153-9

principle, many organizations underinvest in cybersecurity, treating it as a discretionary cost rather than a fundamental business enabler. This shortfall frequently becomes a root cause of security program failures. When cybersecurity is inadequately resourced or misaligned with organizational needs, the ability to manage cyber risk is compromised. This misalignment often leads to material financial losses, operational disruptions, and reputational damage, consequences that extend far beyond IT and into the core of business operations.

Cybersecurity resilience requires more than reactive defense; it demands strategic investment in people, processes, and technology. Boards and executive leadership must recognize that cybersecurity is not simply an IT issue, it is a business risk issue. As digital transformation accelerates, reliance on digital assets, e-commerce, and interconnected supply chains exposes organizations to new vulnerabilities. Meanwhile, legacy systems and outdated skill sets further impede efforts to assess and strengthen security capabilities.

STRATEGIC CYBERSECURITY RESOURCING

To address modern cybersecurity challenges, organizations must move beyond reactive security measures and adopt a proactive cybersecurity resourcing strategy. This strategy must be comprehensive, aligning business objectives with risk management, workforce development, and technological investment. The key to effective cybersecurity resourcing is not just about spending more but ensuring that resources are deployed efficiently and effectively to maximize security impact. Given the growing complexity of cyber threats, enterprises must integrate cybersecurity into their core business functions, ensuring it is treated as a critical business enabler rather than a secondary IT concern.

An effective cybersecurity resourcing strategy should be risk-driven, prioritizing investments in areas that provide the highest security return. Organizations must also focus on workforce development, ensuring that security teams are adequately trained and equipped to counter evolving threats. Additionally, technology optimization is essential, as many enterprises suffer from tool sprawl, leading to inefficiencies and security gaps. Executive and board engagement is another key factor, as strong leadership support is essential for aligning cybersecurity initiatives with business priorities. Finally, continuous assessment and adaptation ensure that cybersecurity programs remain resilient and agile in response to emerging threats.

By strategically aligning cybersecurity resourcing with these key areas, enterprises can strengthen their security posture while maintaining operational efficiency. This approach not only mitigates financial and reputational risks but also ensures compliance with industry regulations and best practices. Organizations that fail to adopt a structured cybersecurity resourcing strategy risk falling behind, leaving critical assets exposed to cyberattacks. As cyber threats become more sophisticated, the ability to adapt and optimize security resources will define the success or failure of an enterprise's cybersecurity program.

RISK-BASED INVESTMENT

Cybersecurity investment should be guided by a risk-based approach, ensuring that financial and technical resources are allocated to areas that offer the highest security impact. Instead of arbitrarily increasing budgets or spreading resources thinly across multiple initiatives, organizations must conduct thorough risk assessments to identify their most critical vulnerabilities. These assessments should consider external factors such as industry-specific threats, regulatory requirements, and geopolitical risks, as well as internal factors like existing security controls and incident response capabilities.

A well-defined risk management framework helps organizations prioritize investments in high-value areas such as critical infrastructure protection, threat intelligence, and incident response capabilities. By focusing on these key areas, enterprises can proactively mitigate threats before they escalate into major security incidents. Additionally, risk-based budgeting ensures that cybersecurity investments are aligned with overall business objectives, reducing the likelihood of unnecessary expenditures on low-impact security measures.

To implement an effective risk-based investment strategy, organizations must leverage real-time threat intelligence and analytics. By continuously monitoring the threat landscape, enterprises can dynamically adjust their security investments based on emerging risks. This adaptive approach ensures that cybersecurity spending remains relevant and responsive to the constantly evolving threat environment. Furthermore, organizations should adopt cyber risk quantification models to measure the potential financial impact of cyber threats, helping executives make informed decisions about cybersecurity funding.

Regulatory compliance is another critical factor in cybersecurity investment. Organizations operating in highly regulated industries, such as finance, healthcare, and critical infrastructure, must ensure that their security programs meet stringent regulatory requirements. Noncompliance not only increases security risks but also exposes enterprises to legal penalties and reputational damage. Investing in compliance-driven security measures, such as data protection, encryption, and audit readiness, is essential for maintaining regulatory adherence.

Ultimately, a risk-based investment approach enables organizations to optimize their security budgets while maximizing protection against cyber threats. By focusing on the areas that matter most, enterprises can enhance their cybersecurity resilience without overspending or misallocating resources. This strategic approach transforms cybersecurity from a reactive cost center into a proactive business enabler that supports long-term enterprise growth and stability.

WORKFORCE DEVELOPMENT

A skilled and well-trained cybersecurity workforce is the foundation of a successful security program. As cyber threats become more advanced, organizations must invest in their employees' skills and knowledge to ensure they can effectively detect, prevent, and respond to attacks. Workforce development should not be viewed as a one-time initiative but as an ongoing process that evolves alongside the cyber threat landscape.

Organizations should implement continuous education and training programs to keep security professionals up to date with the latest attack techniques, defense strategies, and regulatory changes. This includes offering cybersecurity certifications, hands-on training exercises, and simulated attack scenarios to improve technical proficiency. Additionally, participation in industry conferences and knowledge-sharing initiatives can help security teams stay informed about emerging threats and best practices.

Beyond technical training, cybersecurity teams must also develop cross-functional collaboration skills. Cybersecurity cannot operate in isolation, rather it must be integrated with IT, compliance, and business units to ensure a holistic security strategy. Encouraging interdepartmental cooperation helps security teams better understand business priorities, improving their ability to align security initiatives with enterprise goals.

The ongoing cybersecurity skills shortage presents a major challenge for enterprises. To address this issue, organizations must focus on both talent retention and recruitment. Competitive salaries, career development opportunities, and a positive work environment are essential for attracting and retaining top cybersecurity talent. Additionally, investing in internal upskilling programs allows organizations to develop talent from within, reducing dependency on external hiring.

A robust workforce development strategy also includes cybersecurity awareness training for nonsecurity employees. Human error remains one of the leading causes of security breaches, making it essential for all employees to understand fundamental security practices such as phishing prevention, password hygiene, and data protection. By fostering a culture of cybersecurity awareness across the organization, enterprises can significantly reduce their overall risk exposure.

TECHNOLOGY OPTIMIZATION

Many enterprises struggle with technology sprawl, accumulating security tools without a cohesive strategy. This results in operational inefficiencies, redundant systems, misaligned staffing, and visibility gaps that adversaries can exploit. Instead of continuously adding new security products, organizations should focus on optimizing and integrating their existing technology stack.

A streamlined security architecture enhances visibility and coordination across the security operations center, allowing teams to detect and respond to threats more effectively. Security teams must regularly assess their tools' effectiveness, ensuring that each solution contributes to a comprehensive defense strategy rather than operating in isolation. Organizations should also consolidate overlapping functionalities to reduce complexity and cost.

Automation and AI-driven analytics play an essential role in modern cybersecurity operations resourcing. By leveraging machine learning and behavioral analytics, enterprises can improve threat detection, accelerate incident response, and reduce analyst workload. Automated security orchestration streamlines repetitive tasks such as log analysis, patch management, and access control enforcement, freeing up human resources for more complex security challenges.

Technology optimization is not just about selecting the right tools but ensuring they are effectively deployed and maintained. Organizations must establish a security governance framework to evaluate technology performance, enforce policies, and ensure alignment with business objectives. By continuously refining their technology stack, enterprises can enhance security efficiency while reducing operational overhead.

EXECUTIVE AND BOARD ENGAGEMENT

For cybersecurity to be effective, it must have strong executive and board-level sponsorship. Cybersecurity is no longer a purely technical concern, it is a critical business risk that impacts an organization's financial stability, regulatory compliance, and reputation. Executive leaders must recognize that cyber threats pose significant risks to business continuity and must allocate the necessary resources to mitigate these threats. Without senior leadership buy-in, security initiatives often lack direction, funding, and long-term viability.

One of the key challenges in executive engagement is bridging the communication gap between security professionals and business leaders. Technical teams often focus on security metrics, while executives prioritize financial and operational outcomes. Security leaders must learn to translate cybersecurity risks into business language, demonstrating how specific threats could lead to financial loss, regulatory fines, or reputational damage. Using real-world case studies and industry benchmarks can help executives understand the tangible impact of cybersecurity investments.

To ensure sustained board-level attention, cybersecurity should be a standing agenda item in executive meetings. Boards should receive regular reports on the organization's security posture, incident response capabilities, and emerging threats. These reports should include key performance indicators such as mean time to detect, mean time to respond, security control effectiveness, and compliance status. By tracking these metrics over time, executives can make informed decisions about cybersecurity funding and strategic direction.

Accountability is another essential aspect of executive engagement. Organizations should establish a clear governance model that defines roles and responsibilities for cybersecurity at all levels of leadership. A dedicated Chief Information Security Officer should have direct reporting lines to executive leadership and the board, ensuring that cybersecurity concerns receive the attention they deserve. Additionally, assigning risk ownership to business units encourages a security-first mindset across the organization, rather than leaving cybersecurity solely in the hands of IT teams.

Beyond internal governance, executives must also stay informed about regulatory requirements and industry best practices. Many industries are subject to stringent cybersecurity regulations and failure to comply can lead to substantial legal penalties and loss of customer trust. By proactively integrating compliance into cybersecurity strategy, organizations can reduce regulatory risks while strengthening their overall security posture. Board members should undergo periodic cybersecurity awareness training to ensure they understand their role in overseeing cyber risk management.

Optimizing the Chief Information Security Officer (CISO) Reporting Structure for Effective Risk Management

The role of the CISO has expanded beyond technical security oversight to encompass enterprise risk management, regulatory compliance, and business continuity. The effectiveness of a CISO is significantly influenced by their reporting structure, which dictates their ability to secure resources, align cybersecurity with business objectives, and influence decision-making at the executive level. This case study examines different CISO reporting models, evaluating their advantages, drawbacks, and the current industry trends that shape how organizations position their cybersecurity leadership.

The placement of the CISO within an organization's hierarchy can define how cybersecurity is perceived whether as a business risk function or merely a subset of IT operations. The following models highlight the most common reporting structures and their implications.

CISO Reports to:	Benefits	Challenges
Chief Executive Officer (CEO)	– Strategic influence at the executive level – Direct visibility to top leadership – Stronger resource allocation – Peer status among C-suite executives – Better advocacy for security investment	– Potential conflict with Chief Information Officer (CIO) – Budget and authority disputes – CEO may lack time/depth in cybersecurity operations
CIO	– Clear IT chain of command – Leverages CIO's tech expertise – Integrated approach to IT and security	– Cybersecurity seen as subset of IT – Limited cross-functional visibility – Potential conflict of interest (security vs. performance) – Security priorities may be overridden by IT goals
Chief Risk Officer (CRO)	– Cybersecurity treated as business risk – Aligns with enterprise risk management – Enhances risk communication to executives – Focused, risk-based investments	– Not all organizations have a CRO – Risk of viewing cybersecurity only as compliance – May lose influence in strategic business innovation
Chief Financial Officer (CFO)	– Aligns cybersecurity with financial risk – Encourages cost-efficiency in security – Focus on ROI for security investments	– Risk of underfunding security – Focus on short-term ROI over long-term resilience – Security viewed as a cost center

Current Industry Trends in CISO Reporting Structures

As the regulatory landscape evolves and cybersecurity threats become more complex, organizations are reassessing where the CISO should sit within the executive hierarchy. The role of the CISO has shifted from compliance-focused security oversight to strategic business leadership. Increasingly, organizations are adopting a risk-centric approach to cybersecurity, requiring CISOs to engage directly with executive leadership and boards of directors. This shift is reflected in a trend toward CISOs reporting directly to CEOs, CROs, or other C-suite executives rather than being embedded within IT structures. Additionally, regulatory pressures are driving changes in reporting structures. Regulations such as the SEC's cybersecurity disclosure rules, GDPR, and industry-specific mandates emphasize board-level accountability for cybersecurity risks. This has increased the demand for greater CISO visibility at the highest levels of corporate governance, ensuring that security strategies align with legal and compliance requirements.

Selecting the Optimal Reporting Structure

The ideal CISO reporting structure varies by organization, depending on business size, industry, regulatory requirements, and risk profile. Reporting directly to the CEO provides the greatest strategic influence and visibility, ensuring that cybersecurity is embedded in executive decision-making. However, for organizations with strong risk management frameworks, a reporting line to the CRO can enhance alignment with enterprise risk strategies. Conversely, keeping the CISO under the CIO is increasingly seen as an outdated model, as it often limits cybersecurity's independence and effectiveness. The CIO–CISO relationship is still critical, but reporting structures must ensure that security is not subordinated to IT operational goals. Meanwhile, reporting to the CFO may work in finance-driven industries, but it requires careful balancing of security priorities against financial constraints. Ultimately, the most effective CISO reporting structure is one that preserves the independence of cybersecurity decision-making, ensures access to executive leadership, and aligns cybersecurity investments with overall business risk. Organizations must continuously evaluate and refine their reporting structures to ensure they support a proactive, business-driven approach to cybersecurity.

CONTINUOUS ASSESSMENT AND ADAPTATION

The cybersecurity landscape is in a constant state of evolution, with new attack vectors, vulnerabilities, and adversarial tactics emerging daily. A static security program that relies on outdated controls and periodic audits is insufficient to combat modern threats. Organizations must adopt a continuous assessment and adaptation approach, ensuring that security measures are regularly tested, refined, and updated to address emerging risks.

One of the most effective ways to continuously assess cybersecurity posture is through penetration testing and red teaming. Penetration tests simulate real-world cyberattacks to identify weaknesses in an organization's defenses, while red team exercises go a step further by emulating advanced persistent threats to test an organization's detection and response capabilities. Conducting these exercises on a regular basis allows enterprises to identify vulnerabilities before malicious actors exploit them and refine their incident response plans accordingly.

In addition to offensive security testing, organizations should leverage cyber threat intelligence to stay ahead of adversaries. Threat intelligence platforms aggregate real-time data on new attack trends, malware strains, and threat actor tactics, enabling security teams to proactively adjust their defenses. Integrating threat intelligence into Security Information and Event Management (SIEM) systems enhances detection capabilities and ensures that Security Operations Centers (SOCs) remain informed about relevant threats.

Regulatory compliance audits and risk assessments should be conducted on an ongoing basis, rather than as one-time events. Compliance frameworks provide structured methodologies for assessing and improving cybersecurity posture. However, compliance alone does not equate to security, organizations must go beyond minimum regulatory requirements and adopt a risk-based approach to continuously strengthen their defenses.

Lastly, organizations must foster a culture of continuous improvement within their cybersecurity teams. Cyber resilience exercises, tabletop simulations, and post-incident reviews provide valuable insights that can be used to refine policies and procedures. Cybersecurity is not a static discipline; it requires constant learning, adaptation, and evolution. By embedding continuous assessment and adaptation into their security strategy, enterprises can stay ahead of emerging threats and maintain long-term resilience in an increasingly hostile cyber landscape.

CHALLENGES IN CYBERSECURITY RESOURCING

Developing a comprehensive cybersecurity resource preparedness strategy requires a deep understanding of the current resourcing challenges within the industry. The cybersecurity profession is facing significant workforce shortages, with millions of unfilled positions worldwide. This talent gap directly affects an organization's ability to secure critical systems, respond to threats, and maintain resilience. Without a sufficient number of cybersecurity professionals, enterprises are left vulnerable to increasing attack volumes and evolving adversarial tactics. Addressing this gap necessitates strategic workforce planning, recruitment, and skills development.

Beyond sheer numbers, the cybersecurity workforce lacks readiness in many cases. Many professionals entering the field do not have the necessary technical proficiency, hands-on experience, or cross-disciplinary knowledge to effectively counter modern cyber threats. Organizations must recognize that hiring alone is not a solution; they must invest in continuous learning, mentorship, and competency-based training programs. Cybersecurity roles require a mix of technical expertise, strategic risk management, and incident response capabilities, yet current educational pipelines do not fully prepare professionals to meet these demands.

Furthermore, the skills shortage extends beyond traditional information security disciplines. Cybersecurity today intersects with cloud computing, DevSecOps, AI-driven threat detection, and regulatory compliance. A multifaceted skill set is essential, and enterprises must adopt role-based training models to build specialized talent pools within their security teams. Additionally, enterprises must establish cross-functional partnerships between IT, security, legal, and business units to ensure security is not an isolated function but an integrated part of the organization's digital strategy.

One of the major obstacles for cybersecurity professionals is the difficulty in career advancement and retention. The field is notorious for burnout due to high-stress environments, long hours, and overwhelming workloads. Organizations must address this by implementing well-structured career paths, mentorship programs, and work–life balance initiatives. A lack of professional growth opportunities leads to attrition, skill drain, and loss of institutional security knowledge, which exacerbates resourcing issues.

Securing the right cybersecurity resources at the right time is becoming increasingly difficult due to budget constraints and competing organizational priorities. Decision-makers must recognize that cybersecurity investment is not a cost center but a business enabler. Enterprises need to move beyond reactive security spending and adopt a proactive, risk-based funding model that aligns cybersecurity investments with business goals and threat intelligence insights.

IDENTIFICATION OF RESOURCE CONSTRAINTS IN CYBERSECURITY

Enterprises must continuously evaluate their cybersecurity posture to determine whether current resources, people, processes, and technology, are sufficient to counter evolving threats. This assessment involves measuring operational effectiveness, incident response readiness, and risk exposure. However, identifying security gaps is only the first step, securing the necessary resources to address them is an ongoing challenge.

A major constraint is funding allocation, as cybersecurity budgets often compete with other business priorities. Security leaders must effectively communicate the return on investment of cybersecurity spending, linking them to business risk reduction and regulatory compliance. Organizations that underfund cybersecurity risk higher incident costs, legal repercussions, and reputational damage. A structured budget planning process should prioritize high-impact security initiatives, such as threat intelligence integration, workforce development, and security automation.

Another resource constraint is scalability. As enterprises expand, security teams struggle to keep pace with the growing attack surface. New digital transformation initiatives introduce additional security risks, requiring adaptive security models that scale with business operations. Cloud adoption, IoT integration, and remote work policies further complicate security resourcing, requiring dynamic security frameworks that evolve alongside enterprise architecture.

Legacy security structures also pose constraints. Many organizations operate with fragmented security tools, siloed teams, and outdated technologies that limit their ability to respond effectively to cyber threats. A lack of interoperability between security systems can slow down threat detection and response, leading to prolonged dwell times for attackers within enterprise networks. A modernized, integrated security approach is necessary to break down these barriers and improve overall efficiency.

Lastly, constraints are not just internal but also external. The global cybersecurity workforce shortage means that even organizations with the budget and strategic alignment to expand their teams struggle to find and retain qualified professionals. This reality underscores the importance of automation, artificial intelligence, and managed security services to supplement in-house capabilities. Cybersecurity leaders must explore alternative sourcing models, including public–private partnerships, security-as-a-service solutions, and industry-wide intelligence sharing, to address these limitations.

ADDRESSING THE SKILLS SHORTAGE IN CYBERSECURITY

The demand for cybersecurity professionals continues to outpace supply. According to an article published in *Cybercrimes Magazine*,[1] as of 2025, there are over 457,000 unfilled cybersecurity positions in the U.S., with a global shortage estimated at around 3.5 million. This gap is exacerbated by rapid technological advancements and evolving cyber threats, which require a diverse set of skills that traditional education systems struggle to keep up with.

Larger companies, such as those in the Fortune 500, often attract and retain top talent, leaving smaller businesses with limited access to skilled cybersecurity professionals. According to an article published by Industrial Cyber[2] critical sectors like banking, public, energy, and insurance report low confidence in having the necessary cybersecurity talent. The article goes on to explain that the shortage leads to increased workload and burnout among existing cybersecurity professionals, affecting productivity and effectiveness. It also hinders innovation and progress within and outside the cybersecurity industry.

To close the cybersecurity skills gap, enterprises must redesign their workforce development strategies to build the right mix of technical, strategic, and operational expertise. Traditional hiring models are insufficient; instead, organizations should embrace a hybrid approach that includes internal training, mentorship, and cross-disciplinary knowledge sharing.

Building cybersecurity skills must begin with structured training programs that align with enterprise security needs. Organizations should develop role-based learning tracks covering areas such as cloud security, threat intelligence, digital forensics, and incident response. Offering practical, hands-on training, such as capture-the-flag competitions, simulated attack scenarios, and red teaming exercises, helps professionals develop real-world competencies.

Collaboration with academic institutions, cybersecurity boot camps, and certification programs is critical to creating a pipeline of qualified professionals. Organizations can sponsor cybersecurity education programs, provide internships, and develop apprenticeship models to equip new talent with the necessary skills. Additionally, enterprises should offer tuition reimbursement and skill development incentives to retain existing employees and encourage continuous learning.

Cybersecurity workforce planning must also include diversity initiatives. The field has historically lacked diversity, which limits the range of perspectives and problem-solving approaches. By actively recruiting from underrepresented demographics and nontraditional career backgrounds, organizations can broaden the cybersecurity talent pool and introduce new thinking into security problem-solving.

Enterprises should adopt automated security solutions to compensate for workforce shortages. By leveraging AI-driven threat detection, security orchestration, and automated incident response, organizations can reduce the dependency on human intervention for routine security operations, allowing security teams to focus on higher-value tasks.

Cyber PIVOTT Act Reintroduced to Address Critical Cybersecurity Workforce Gaps

The Cyber PIVOTT Act of 2025[3] (Providing Individuals Various Opportunities for Technical Training to Build a Skills-Based Cyber Workforce) is a legislative proposal aimed at expanding cybersecurity education and workforce development. To amend the Homeland Security Act of 2002 and create the PIVOTT Program, a skills-based cybersecurity workforce development initiative administered by the Cybersecurity and Infrastructure Security Agency (CISA).

Category	Details
Program name	PIVOTT (Providing Individuals Various Opportunities for Technical Training to Build a Skills-Based Cyber Workforce)
Administered by	CISA
Target institutions	Community colleges, technical schools, and other two-year institutions
Student eligibility	– New or first-semester students in cyber/cyber-relevant two-year programs – Career changers with a high school diploma – Technical cert programs (<2 years)
Scholarship coverage	Full tuition, academic/lab fees, travel, lodging, stipends, per diem, certification fees, internship costs
Service obligation	Two years in a cyber or cyber-relevant government role (Federal, State, Tribal, Local, Territorial); exceptions for military service or further education
Skills-based exercises	At least four required (e.g., labs, hackathons, tabletop exercises, virtual programming); at least one must be in-person
Internship requirements	Internships in government, critical infrastructure (rural/high risk), or federal agencies; support for clearances and prioritization for federal roles
Outreach activities	– Regional outreach and industry engagement – Annual skills report – Federal recruitment fair at 5+ campuses
Post-completion benefits	– Access to cyber job/training database – Up to three cyber certification vouchers – Scholarships for federal employees with 7+ years of service
Compliance monitoring	Participating institutions must monitor scholarship recipients for service and academic requirements
Repayment terms	Treated as Federal Stafford Loans if obligations aren't met; potential waivers for hardship or unavailability of government jobs

Category	Details
Program growth targets	– Year 1: 250 students – Year 2+: double each year until 1,000/year – Goal: 10,000 students/year within ten years
Reports required	– CISA program review within 90 days of enactment – Annual reporting if enrollment quotas aren't met
Additional promotion	Support for CyberCorps® Scholarship for Service as a national benchmark

ADAPTABILITY AND FLEXIBILITY IN RESOURCE ALLOCATION

Cybersecurity resource allocation must be dynamic, risk-based, and scalable to support evolving business and threat landscapes. Static security budgets and rigid resourcing models fail to address emerging vulnerabilities and attack trends. Organizations must implement adaptive security investment frameworks that align with real-time threat intelligence and business priorities.

A risk-driven resource allocation strategy requires continuous evaluation of security effectiveness. Enterprises should leverage risk assessments, security audits, and incident trend analysis to adjust resource distribution as needed. Scenario-based modeling can help organizations anticipate security gaps and proactively allocate resources before incidents occur.

Security budgets must also be flexible enough to support emerging technology adoption. As organizations transition to cloud-based architectures, AI-driven security models, and zero-trust frameworks, cybersecurity funding should be adjusted accordingly. Legacy security models must evolve to keep pace with digital transformation.

By fostering a culture of adaptability and proactive risk management, organizations can ensure that cybersecurity resource preparedness remains aligned with business growth, evolving threats, and regulatory requirements.

CONCLUSION AND RECAP

Cybersecurity resourcing is one of the most pressing and persistent challenges facing modern enterprises. As threats grow more sophisticated and technology environments become increasingly complex, the question is no longer whether to invest in cybersecurity, but how to invest wisely. This chapter dissects the intricacies of cybersecurity resourcing, urging organizations to move from reactive spending to proactive, risk-aligned strategies. It underscores the need to view cybersecurity not as an IT issue but as an essential component of enterprise risk management, one that underpins business continuity, brand trust, and long-term strategic viability.

A central theme is the imperative to elevate cybersecurity resourcing beyond tactical staffing to strategic capability building. Too often, organizations underresource security programs or misallocate funds, leading to gaps that adversaries are quick to exploit. Boards and executives must recognize that inadequate cybersecurity investment directly translates to operational risk. Resilient programs are those that not only secure current operations but anticipate future threats through forward-looking resource planning.

Risk-based investment emerges as the keystone of effective cybersecurity spending. Rather than distribute funds evenly or haphazardly, enterprises must identify their most critical risks and invest in controls that offer the greatest risk reduction. This targeted approach helps avoid waste and aligns security priorities with business outcomes. Real-time threat intelligence, risk quantification, and regulatory awareness are indispensable tools in this prioritization process. Without them, even generous budgets can be misdirected.

Another focal point is workforce development. The shortage of cybersecurity professionals is both a capacity issue and a capability issue. Organizations must cultivate a pipeline of skilled talent through structured training, internal upskilling, and collaboration with academic institutions. But talent alone isn't enough. Continuous professional development, career pathing, and burnout mitigation are essential to sustain a high-performing security workforce. This applies to both technical practitioners and business stakeholders who play roles in governance and compliance.

Technology optimization, not expansion, is advocated as a best practice. Enterprises often suffer from tool sprawl, where overlapping technologies drain budgets and increase complexity. A more mature approach focuses on integration, automation, and governance. Security tools should communicate effectively, align with workflows, and be measured for efficacy. AI and automation can offset workforce shortages and accelerate response times, but they must be thoughtfully implemented and continuously tuned.

Executive engagement is nonnegotiable. Cybersecurity leadership must have visibility and influence at the highest levels of the organization. The chapter explores reporting structures for the CISO, emphasizing that alignment with the CEO or CRO enhances strategic decision-making and risk visibility. Boards must not only be informed of cyber risks but actively participate in governance. This shift requires CISOs to communicate in the language of risk, compliance, and business impact rather than technical minutiae.

Continuous assessment and adaptation are necessary to keep pace with evolving threats. Static controls and infrequent audits are no longer sufficient. Red teaming, threat hunting, and real-time intelligence integration ensure that security programs remain agile. Post-incident reviews, tabletop exercises, and adversarial simulations foster a culture of learning and resilience. Security teams must adopt a mindset of continuous improvement, using insights from real-world threats to refine controls and strategies.

The chapter also examines structural resource constraints, such as budget limitations, scalability issues, and legacy system dependencies. These barriers are often compounded by external challenges, including the global cybersecurity talent shortage. To overcome them, enterprises must embrace flexible sourcing models, such as managed services and public–private partnerships. Strategic investment in automation and orchestration can help bridge capability gaps, ensuring coverage even when human capital is limited.

A significant portion of the chapter is dedicated to addressing the cybersecurity skills gap, which is both a strategic threat and a growth inhibitor. Organizations must move beyond reactive hiring and develop comprehensive workforce development plans. These include role-based training, diverse hiring practices, and collaborative initiatives with universities and training bootcamps. The shortage of qualified professionals cannot be addressed by salary alone; it requires investment in the long-term growth and well-being of the workforce.

Finally, the chapter concludes by highlighting adaptability and flexibility in resource allocation as the cornerstone of modern cybersecurity strategy. Rigid budgets and inflexible planning cycles leave enterprises exposed in a fast-moving threat environment. By embedding cybersecurity into business planning, enabling dynamic reallocation of resources, and staying ahead of adversaries through continuous monitoring and refinement, organizations can build cybersecurity programs that are not only resilient but also scalable, responsive, and future-ready.

NOTES

1 Morgan, Steve. 2021. "Cybersecurity Jobs Report: 3.5 Million Unfilled Positions in 2021." *Cybersecurity Ventures*, November 9, 2021. https://cybersecurityventures.com/jobs-report-2021.

2 Industrial Cyber. "Cyber PIVOT Act Reintroduced to Address Critical Cybersecurity Workforce Gaps." *Industrial Cyber*, June 13, 2024. https://industrialcyber.co/regulation-standards-and-compliance/cyber-pivott-act-reintroduced-to-address-critical-cybersecurity-workforce-gaps.

3 U.S. House of Representatives, Committee on Homeland Security. *Report on Cyber PIVOTT: A Strategy for Strengthening America's Cybersecurity Workforce*. February 3, 2025. https://homeland.house.gov/wp-content/uploads/2025/02/Cyber-PIVOTT-2.3.25.pdf.

8 Outsourcing and Third-Party Risk Management

LEARNING OBJECTIVES

- Learn how to align cybersecurity outsourcing with business strategy to enhance resilience, rather than treating it as a cost-cutting measure
- Understand how to evaluate third-party providers using five critical dimensions: trust, responsiveness, integration, transparency, and capability maturity
- Gain insight into building proactive third-party governance, including continuous oversight, contractual enforcement, and operational integration
- Discover how to sustain long-term cyber resilience through shared responsibility, internal leadership, and adaptive vendor partnerships

CONSIDERATIONS IN CYBERSECURITY OUTSOURCING

Cybersecurity today is no longer a self-contained function. It has evolved into a multifaceted operational discipline that intersects with compliance, business continuity, digital transformation, and enterprise risk management. Despite this growing complexity, most organizations still lack the internal depth, both in expertise and resources, to manage all aspects of security effectively. As cyber threats become more sophisticated and regulatory expectations increase, outsourcing has become a pragmatic strategy to augment internal capabilities. Yet, outsourcing security is not a silver bullet. It must be grounded in a deliberate strategy that aligns with business objectives, preserves operational resilience, and minimizes third-party dependencies that may introduce systemic risk.

Effective cybersecurity operations require more than just tools, they demand situational awareness, threat intelligence integration, and rapid response. These capabilities rely on niche skill sets that are increasingly difficult to source and retain in-house. As such, organizations are faced with a critical decision: which security functions should remain internal, and which can be entrusted to external partners? Cybersecurity outsourcing is often pursued out of necessity, but the decision to delegate key security functions to an external party must be governed by more than just operational need or cost-effectiveness. Enterprises must evaluate potential outsourcing arrangements through a set of core constraints that ultimately determine whether the relationship strengthens the security posture or introduces latent vulnerabilities. These constraints including trust, responsiveness, integration, transparency, and capability maturity, form the foundation for evaluating and managing third-party security engagements.

DOI: 10.1201/9781003562153-10

Trust

Trust is the bedrock of any third-party relationship, particularly in cybersecurity, where external providers may gain access to sensitive systems, confidential data, and critical infrastructure. This trust must be earned, not assumed. It begins with a thorough vetting process that examines a provider's security posture, reputation, regulatory standing, and historical performance. However, initial due diligence is not sufficient on its own. Trust must be continuously reinforced through contractual obligations, technical controls, and regular validation of the provider's operational behaviors.

Trust is also contextual as it varies depending on the nature of the services being outsourced and the level of access granted. For example, a vendor providing patch management support may require a different level of assurance compared to one managing privileged access or incident response. Zero trust principles should be applied, even within trusted third-party relationships, to minimize the blast radius in the event of a breach.

Responsiveness

In cybersecurity, speed is often the difference between containment and escalation. The responsiveness of a third-party provider is essential to effective risk mitigation. A well-defined incident response protocol must be built into the outsourcing arrangement, including predefined escalation paths, communication procedures, and response time thresholds.

Responsiveness must also account for time zone alignment, staffing coverage, and the provider's ability to handle simultaneous or multitenant incidents without degradation in service quality. Organizations should conduct real-world incident response simulations involving the provider to validate responsiveness under pressure. If the service provider is unable to act quickly and decisively in the early stages of an incident, the consequences may be irreversible.

Integration

A service provider's value is significantly diminished if its operations cannot be seamlessly integrated into the enterprise's existing security architecture, IT infrastructure, and business workflows. Effective integration includes data sharing, alert correlation, workflow alignment, and unified reporting. A disjointed or siloed security service often creates operational friction, duplicated efforts, and security blind spots.

Organizations must assess a provider's ability to work within existing systems such as SIEMs, ITSM platforms, endpoint detection tools, and compliance management solutions. Integration should also extend to governance structures, enabling security teams to maintain unified oversight across both internal and external operations. A lack of integration can be inefficient and downright dangerous, as it obscures visibility and weakens coordinated responses.

Transparency

Transparency governs how much insight the enterprise has into the provider's operations, security practices, and incident handling. A lack of transparency undermines situational awareness and can obscure early warning signs of compromise or service degradation. Providers must be willing to share telemetry, control plane logs, audit findings, security metrics, and performance reports in a timely and accessible manner.

Transparency also includes candid communication around limitations, failures, or emerging risks. Service providers that obscure or downplay issues introduce unnecessary risk and delay remediation. Enterprises must embed transparency requirements into contracts and service-level agreements (SLAs), with provisions for routine security briefings, audit rights, and post-incident reviews. Without transparency, even a technically capable provider may become a liability.

Capability Maturity

Not all providers possess the same level of operational maturity. Some may offer baseline services with little depth, while others bring extensive threat intelligence, automation capabilities, and mature governance models. Capability maturity reflects the provider's ability to scale, adapt, and proactively manage evolving threats. This includes their internal controls, staffing qualifications, technology stack, and ability to align with the organization's risk management strategy.

Organizations must evaluate providers using established maturity models, such as the Capability Maturity Model Integration (CMMI)[1] or NIST Tiers.[2] Providers should demonstrate continuous improvement, internal compliance mechanisms, and investment in innovation. A provider that lacks maturity may struggle to keep pace with complex enterprise needs, particularly as threats become more advanced and persistent.

Together, these five constraints form the strategic lens through which outsourcing decisions must be evaluated. An outsourcing engagement that scores high across all five dimensions is more likely to deliver long-term security value. Conversely, gaps in any one area can amplify risk and reduce the effectiveness of the broader cybersecurity program. As such, security leaders must institutionalize these criteria within their third-party risk management (TPRM) framework, ensuring that outsourcing decisions support the integrity of the enterprise security architecture.

THE OUTSOURCING SPECTRUM AND VENDOR REALITIES

The cybersecurity services landscape spans a wide spectrum, from ad hoc consulting engagements to comprehensive MDR solutions. While short-term engagements may offer strategic value or compliance readiness, longer-term managed services provide consistent monitoring, incident handling, and data correlation. Security Operations Center-as-a-Service (SOCaaS) providers are especially attractive for enterprises that need 24/7 oversight without building it internally. However, not all service providers are created equal. Many are optimized for sales rather than sustained operational performance. Glossy marketing brochures and impressive dashboards often mask immature service delivery models. To cut through the noise, organizations must prioritize technical depth, reliability, and the provider's ability to integrate with the existing ecosystem over superficial market positioning.

Cost also plays a determinative role. Cybersecurity is typically classified as a protective, rather than revenue-generating, function, which means that many organizations operate under tight budgets. Full-spectrum in-house security programs, complete with round-the-clock monitoring and threat hunting, are simply out of reach for most enterprises. Outsourcing provides a path to resilience without disproportionately straining financial resources. Yet it must be preceded by a rigorous risk assessment process.

This assessment should identify which functions are suitable for externalization, which must remain under direct control, and what security obligations must be codified. It must also account for regulatory exposure, breach impact, incident response readiness, and vendor oversight structures. Without this clarity, outsourcing can become a source of fragmentation and blind spots.

ESTABLISHING EFFECTIVE THIRD-PARTY RISK GOVERNANCE

Third-party relationships are often deeply embedded within the fabric of business operations. From cloud service providers and identity platforms to MDR partners, external entities now play an active role in maintaining the confidentiality, integrity, and availability of critical systems and data. As this reliance grows, so does the exposure to third-party risk. The complexity of these relationships demands a structured and disciplined approach to governance, one that is integrated into the organization's broader security and risk management framework.

Establishing effective governance begins with visibility. Organizations must maintain a current and comprehensive inventory of all third-party engagements, including direct vendors, subcontractors, and any service providers with access to sensitive data or network infrastructure. This inventory should include information on what data is shared, what systems are accessible, and the extent of service integration. Without this foundational awareness, organizations are unable to assess their actual exposure or apply appropriate controls.

Once visibility is established, the next step is classification. Not all third parties represent the same level of risk. A security camera vendor, a payroll processor, and a cloud infrastructure provider all carry vastly different implications for operational security. Risk classification frameworks should consider factors such as data sensitivity, access privileges, business criticality, and geographic regulatory exposure. These criteria allow enterprises to segment vendors into appropriate risk tiers and allocate governance resources accordingly.

Governance must be a continuous process, not a one-time assessment conducted during vendor onboarding. Threat actors evolve their tactics, vendors modify their service delivery models, and regulatory requirements shift frequently. As a result, third-party relationships must be monitored and reassessed on an ongoing basis. This includes conducting regular security reviews, requiring periodic attestations of compliance, scheduling independent audits, and performing technical assessments such as penetration tests or code reviews when warranted.

Integration with internal security operations is another essential requirement. A third party that is not aligned with the organization's incident response process or fails to communicate during a cyber event introduces operational fragility. Governance must ensure that vendors are integrated into incident response playbooks, threat intelligence sharing mechanisms, and change management processes. Response readiness cannot be assumed; it must be validated through joint exercises, coordinated simulations, and formal testing.

Clear ownership is necessary to maintain accountability. Every third-party relationship should have a designated internal sponsor who is responsible for overseeing risk posture, service quality, and contractual compliance. This responsibility includes reviewing performance metrics, coordinating assessments, escalating risks to governance committees, and maintaining open communication with both internal stakeholders and the vendor. Governance is most effective when it is anchored in clearly defined roles and supported by strong cross-functional collaboration among security, procurement, legal, and operational teams.

The contractual foundation of third-party governance must be solid and enforceable. Contracts should go beyond generic clauses and include specific provisions related to security controls, breach notification timelines, audit rights, data handling procedures, and legal compliance requirements. These agreements must reflect the organization's risk appetite and regulatory obligations. However, contracts alone are not sufficient. Organizations must have the operational capability to monitor compliance, enforce terms, and respond to nonconformance when it occurs.

Metrics provide the basis for informed oversight. Governance frameworks should include clearly defined performance indicators such as incident response times, the number of unresolved security findings, audit outcomes, and adherence to SLAs. Dashboards and vendor scorecards can support executive decision-making by providing real-time insight into third-party performance and emerging risks. Metrics should be actionable and aligned with enterprise risk priorities.

Cultural alignment enhances governance maturity. Organizations that treat vendors as strategic partners rather than transactional suppliers often realize better long-term security outcomes. Collaboration, transparency, and mutual commitment to improvement create an environment where security objectives are met more consistently. Vendors should be engaged in joint planning, security exercises, and continuous feedback cycles. Security is not only a technical function; it is also a shared responsibility built on trust and alignment.

As enterprises grow more dependent on digital ecosystems, third-party governance must evolve into a proactive and predictive function. Static checklists and outdated assessment models cannot keep pace with the velocity and complexity of external relationships. The future of third-party risk governance lies in real-time monitoring, automated risk intelligence, and integrated platforms that connect vendor oversight with enterprise security operations.

Ultimately, third-party governance is not just about reducing exposure. It is about enabling the organization to grow securely, engage with external innovators, and scale operations without compromising trust. When designed and executed effectively, third-party risk governance becomes a core capability of the security architecture, reinforcing resilience across every layer of the business.

STRUCTURING THIRD-PARTY RELATIONSHIPS THROUGH SLAS

The cornerstone of any successful outsourcing arrangement is the SLA. This is not merely a contractual formality, it is the operational expression of expectations, obligations, and measurable outcomes. A well-structured SLA defines the scope of services, delineates roles and responsibilities, and establishes performance thresholds that reflect business priorities and risk tolerances.

SLAs must clearly outline the services being provided, from incident response timelines and log retention to system uptime and threat intelligence updates. They should include quantifiable metrics, such as mean time to detect (MTTD), mean time to respond (MTTR), and false positive ratios, to ensure that performance can be measured and continuously improved.

Security-specific provisions are also necessary. These may include requirements for breach notification, data sovereignty, encryption standards, and compliance reporting. In addition, organizations must reserve audit rights to independently verify that service providers are adhering to the agreed-upon standards. Because the threat landscape is fluid, SLAs must be living documents. They should be reviewed regularly to reflect changes in the regulatory environment, threat intelligence insights, and shifts in business strategy. Without this ongoing recalibration, SLAs lose their effectiveness and expose the organization to unforeseen risks.

Domain	Key Elements	Purpose
Scope of services	– Defined services and boundaries – In-scope systems, functions, and data	Clarifies what the provider is responsible for; prevents assumption gaps
Performance metrics	– MTTD – MTTR – Uptime SLAs	Enables measurable accountability and comparison across providers
Incident response	– Notification timelines – Escalation paths – Roles and responsibilities	Ensures alignment during security events and accelerates coordinated response
Threat intelligence and detection	– Frequency of signature updates – Intelligence source integration	Keeps security measures up to date with evolving threats
Compliance and regulatory alignment	– Data protection requirements – Logging and audit controls – Breach notification	Ensures the provider supports compliance with laws like GDPR, HIPAA, PCI-DSS
Reporting and transparency	– Monthly/quarterly reporting – KPI dashboards – SLA compliance reporting	Facilitates transparency and ongoing governance
Data handling and privacy	– Data residency – Encryption standards – Access control policies	Addresses confidentiality, integrity, and compliance risks associated with sensitive data

Domain	Key Elements	Purpose
Audit and assessment rights	– Third-party audits – On-site inspections – Vulnerability disclosures	Allows enterprises to verify provider compliance and security posture
Change management	– Notification of changes – Impact assessment – Approval workflows	Reduces operational risks from uncontrolled changes in tools, configurations, or infrastructure
Termination and exit strategy	– Data handover procedures – Retention and deletion policies – Transition support	Ensures continuity and protection during disengagement or provider transitions
Continuous improvement	– SLA review frequency – Update mechanisms – Security roadmap integration	Keeps the agreement aligned with evolving risks and business objectives

DEFINING SHARED RESPONSIBILITY AND OPERATIONAL CLARITY WITH SHARED RESPONSIBILITY MODELS

Outsourcing cybersecurity functions introduces operational complexity, especially around ownership, accountability, and response coordination. One of the most common failure points in third-party security relationships is the assumption that responsibility transfers entirely to the provider. This misconception often leads to gaps in coverage, mismanaged incidents, and audit failures. To address this, organizations must adopt a clear and enforceable Shared Responsibility Model tailored to each provider relationship.

In a shared responsibility construct, both the enterprise and the service provider are accountable for different layers of the security stack. While the provider may manage infrastructure, tools, or specific workflows, such as threat monitoring or log correlation, the enterprise retains responsibility for governance, strategic decision-making, and regulatory compliance. Understanding where the provider's responsibilities end and where the organization's responsibilities begin is critical to preventing overlap or, worse, blind spots.

For example, a Managed Detection and Response (MDR) services provider may monitor endpoints and generate alerts, but if incident containment, legal notification, or cross-departmental communication plans are not the enterprise's responsibility by design, the response effort will stall. Similarly, a cloud service provider may secure the underlying platform, but customer-specific configurations, identity management, and data classification remain squarely within the enterprise domain.

To operationalize shared responsibility, organizations should develop and maintain matrix for each major outsourced security function following RACI, which stands for Responsible, Accountable, Consulted, and Informed. This matrix defines who is:

- Responsible: The party executing the task or process.
- Accountable: The entity ultimately answerable for its outcome.
- Consulted: Stakeholders who provide input or guidance.
- Informed: Parties that must be kept apprised of progress or incidents.

By applying RACI to third-party engagements, enterprises gain visibility into decision rights, communication workflows, and performance obligations.

Activity	Responsible	Accountable	Consulted	Informed
Initial alert triage	MDR Provider	MDR Provider	Enterprise SOC	CISO, Legal
Incident containment	Enterprise SOC	Enterprise CISO	MDR Provider, Legal	IT Ops, Executive Team

Activity	Responsible	Accountable	Consulted	Informed
Regulatory notification	Enterprise Legal	General Counsel	CISO, Compliance	Board, Communications
Root cause analysis	MDR Provider	MDR Provider	Enterprise SOC	Internal Audit
Remediation and hardening	IT Operations	CIO	Security Architecture	Risk Committee

This structure removes ambiguity and streamlines collaboration between internal teams and external providers. It also ensures the organization maintains control over risk decisions while leveraging third-party expertise for execution. Moreover, RACI matrices should not be static documents. As vendor roles evolve, threat environments shift, and internal capabilities mature, these models must be reviewed and updated regularly to reflect current realities. Enterprises should incorporate RACI validation into their vendor governance routines and test role clarity during tabletop exercises or red team simulations.

Ultimately, defining and enforcing shared responsibility through structured RACI models strengthens operational resilience. It ensures that all parties understand their roles during both routine operations and high-stakes incidents. More importantly, it reinforces the enterprise's leadership position in security governance, regardless of how many operational tasks are externalized.

SUSTAINING LONG-TERM CYBER RESILIENCE THROUGH OUTSOURCING

Building long-term cyber resilience through outsourcing requires more than transactional vendor agreements or cost-based decisions. It calls for a strategic posture that integrates outsourced security services into the broader enterprise risk management framework. Cyber threats continue to evolve in complexity and frequency, and regulatory expectations are becoming increasingly demanding. In this context, outsourcing must be approached not as a temporary fix, but as a sustainable component of the organization's cybersecurity operating model.

Successful long-term outsourcing relationships are anchored in continuous alignment between the enterprise and its service providers. This alignment must be maintained not only at the onset of the relationship but throughout its lifecycle. Security leaders must regularly assess the effectiveness of outsourced functions, reevaluate the risk landscape, and recalibrate expectations as business priorities shift. Static contracts and outdated service definitions are no longer sufficient in a threat environment that is constantly in motion.

Enterprises must establish governance mechanisms that provide visibility into the performance of third-party security providers. These mechanisms should include structured performance reviews, periodic audits, and collaborative planning sessions to address emerging risks and identify areas for improvement. Metrics such as detection and response times, false positive rates, threat intelligence value, and incident resolution effectiveness must be tracked and analyzed as part of a continuous feedback loop. The goal is to foster an adaptive relationship where both parties contribute to the evolution of security capabilities.

Long-term resilience also depends on the organization's ability to retain strategic control. While outsourcing enables access to specialized tools and expertise, the enterprise must maintain oversight of critical decision-making processes. This includes defining acceptable risk thresholds, approving incident response protocols, and retaining control over identity and access management policies. Security governance must remain in-house, ensuring that the organization can act decisively in the event of a breach, regulatory inquiry, or contractual dispute.

Another dimension of resilience lies in talent development. Although outsourcing addresses immediate staffing shortages, it should not lead to the erosion of internal cybersecurity expertise.

Organizations must invest in training and upskilling their internal teams, particularly in areas such as threat modeling, risk assessment, incident coordination, and compliance oversight. A knowledgeable in-house team serves as both a strategic interface with vendors and a safeguard against overdependence on external providers.

Technology interoperability is also essential. Outsourced services must be integrated with the enterprise's existing security infrastructure. This includes compatibility with logging platforms, identity services, ticketing systems, and orchestration tools. Fragmented systems create blind spots and slow down response times. A cohesive, interoperable architecture ensures that outsourced services function as extensions of the enterprise's security operations rather than isolated silos.

Additionally, the organization must maintain resilience by ensuring contractual agility. This means that outsourcing agreements must be designed with flexibility to accommodate changing business needs, emerging threats, and shifts in regulatory requirements. Contractual clauses should include provisions for scope expansion, service evolution, termination rights, and financial accountability in case of service failures or noncompliance. The ability to pivot or renegotiate agreements quickly can be critical in a volatile risk environment.

Lastly, long-term cyber resilience depends on establishing a culture of shared accountability. Both the enterprise and its service providers must view security as a joint responsibility. Trust must be earned through transparency, responsiveness, and a demonstrated commitment to continuous improvement. Vendors should be evaluated not just on cost and service levels, but also on their ability to adapt, innovate, and contribute to the enterprise's long-term security objectives.

When outsourcing is managed strategically, it enhances the organization's ability to detect, respond to, and recover from cyber threats. It provides scalability and operational depth that internal teams may struggle to achieve alone. However, this value is only realized through deliberate governance, continuous oversight, and a focus on long-term outcomes. Cyber resilience is not the product of a single decision but the result of sustained collaboration between internal and external security stakeholders, working in concert to protect the enterprise's digital ecosystem. This is where an alignment checklist is valuable.

Domain	Checklist Item	Y/N
Strategic alignment	Confirm that outsourced services align with enterprise risk management and security objectives	
	Validate that security requirements are integrated into business and digital transformation roadmaps	
	Ensure outsourced functions support long-term resilience, not just short-term capacity gaps	
Governance and oversight	Establish clear governance frameworks for outsourced security services	
	Define internal roles for vendor oversight and accountability	
	Schedule quarterly performance reviews and annual strategic planning sessions with providers	
	Implement executive-level reporting on third-party security performance	
Performance and metrics	Define and monitor key performance indicators (MTTD, MTTR, detection accuracy, etc.)	
	Ensure metrics are tied to business impact and risk tolerance levels	
	Continuously review service level performance against agreed benchmarks	
	Include breach simulations or tabletop exercises as part of vendor performance evaluation	

Domain	Checklist Item	Y/N
Security integration	Verify technical integration with internal SIEM, SOAR, IAM, and ticketing systems	
	Ensure bidirectional data sharing between internal and external security teams	
	Validate secure API use, data flow restrictions, and log ingestion consistency	
	Map outsourced functions to internal incident response plans and escalation paths	
Regulatory and contractual controls	Ensure contracts include data residency, breach notification, and compliance clauses	
	Include rights for independent audits and security assessments	
	Define clear exit strategies and data return or destruction procedures	
	Update contracts periodically to reflect new regulatory requirements and threat scenarios	
Risk management and adaptability	Conduct regular risk assessments of outsourced functions	
	Classify vendors by criticality and apply tiered risk management controls	
	Ensure flexibility in contracts to adjust scope, terminate services, or add capabilities	
	Establish procedures to onboard or replace vendors with minimal disruption	
Talent and internal capability	Invest in internal security talent to interface with and govern third-party providers	
	Maintain in-house expertise in risk assessment, threat intelligence, and incident coordination	
	Provide cross-training for internal teams to reduce dependency on specific providers	
	Develop career pathways and succession plans for key security governance roles	
Shared accountability and trust	Establish transparent communication channels and escalation procedures	
	Align vendors on shared security goals, ethics, and continuous improvement mindset	
	Include third-party roles in enterprise-wide security drills and incident simulations	
	Promote cultural alignment and responsiveness through joint planning and retrospectives	

CONCLUSION AND RECAP

Cybersecurity outsourcing, when approached with strategic intent, becomes far more than a cost-saving maneuver. It transforms into a deliberate extension of enterprise security architecture, enabling organizations to augment capability, expand operational reach, and address the scarcity of specialized talent. But this transformation hinges on rigorous planning, execution discipline, and a clear understanding of shared responsibilities.

Throughout this chapter, we've examined the foundational considerations that must inform any outsourcing initiative. Decisions around delegation of security functions are not just technical, they are governance-driven, risk-aligned, and rooted in a deep understanding of organizational priorities. Outsourcing, in this light, is not merely about service delivery. It is about reinforcing resilience and expanding the security perimeter without diluting accountability.

The five evaluation constraints including trust, responsiveness, integration, transparency, and capability maturity, form the strategic lens through which outsourcing partnerships must be assessed. These are not soft attributes. Each one directly influences how effectively the provider can protect enterprise assets under real-world pressure. Weakness in any dimension can compromise the integrity of the entire security ecosystem.

Trust, in particular, cannot be overstated. It underpins every aspect of a third-party relationship. Without continuous validation and earned assurance, even the most technically competent vendor becomes a risk. Trust must be operationalized through rigorous due diligence, persistent monitoring, and the enforcement of zero trust principles, even with trusted partners.

Responsiveness defines the tempo of defense. In cyber operations, delays translate directly into exposure. Providers that cannot act with speed and precision during a live incident introduce more than friction, they introduce systemic risk. Validation of responsiveness, through simulation and regular drills, is a nonnegotiable component of any outsourcing engagement.

Integration ensures that third-party services do not function as isolated nodes. A provider must plug into the enterprise's infrastructure, processes, and communication channels. Without this connective tissue, alerts go unactioned, context is lost, and coordination fails. Integration is both a technical and operational imperative.

Transparency provides the visibility needed to govern outsourced services effectively. Vendors must be willing to expose the inner workings of their operations, not just provide SLA dashboards. Opacity, in this context, can be inconvenient and very dangerous. Security cannot be maintained in the dark.

Capability maturity is the differentiator between providers that merely respond and those that anticipate. Mature vendors align with the organization's strategic direction, demonstrate operational excellence, and evolve in step with the threat landscape. Immature providers often become liabilities masked behind automation scripts and marketing collateral.

The outsourcing spectrum itself is broad, and vendor performance varies widely. The most successful organizations resist the allure of polished sales pitches and instead prioritize technical competence, service alignment, and the provider's ability to support long-term resilience. The decision to outsource must follow a structured assessment of internal gaps, external dependencies, and business continuity risks.

Third-party risk governance is the mechanism that binds these efforts together. Inventory, classification, continuous monitoring, and integration with internal operations create the scaffolding necessary for responsible outsourcing. Governance is not a checkpoint; it is an operating model, which should be adaptive, data-driven, and infused into the enterprise security fabric.

Service Level Agreements provide the contractual articulation of these expectations. But an SLA is only as effective as its specificity and enforceability. It must be dynamic, quantitative, and aligned with security priorities. The inclusion of meaningful metrics, breach protocols, and audit rights elevates SLAs from legal formalities to instruments of operational accountability.

Responsibility models such as RACI clarify where decision rights lie. They eliminate the dangerous ambiguity that often plagues third-party engagements. Outsourcing does not absolve the enterprise of responsibility, it redistributes it. Without clear delineation, risk falls through the cracks, often surfacing only during moments of crisis.

Sustained cyber resilience is the endgame. Outsourcing contributes to this goal only when it is embedded into the broader strategy. Static contracts and isolated services cannot keep pace with dynamic threats. Organizations must build living partnerships, driven by metrics, shared insights, and mutual adaptability.

Internal capability development remains essential. Outsourcing should never replace institutional knowledge, as it should complement it. A competent in-house team serves as the anchor, the translator, and the enforcer of the enterprise's risk posture. No provider can substitute for strategic ownership.

Technological interoperability closes the loop. The ability to exchange data, automate workflows, and correlate signals across internal and external systems defines whether outsourced services become true extensions of enterprise operations or disconnected add-ons. Architecture must be intentionally designed with this in mind.

Ultimately, cybersecurity outsourcing is not a shortcut. It is a discipline. One that, when executed with rigor and foresight, enhances agility, strengthens defenses, and provides scale in a resource-constrained world. But it is also unforgiving. Missteps in selection, oversight, or alignment can have far-reaching consequences.

NOTES

1 CMMI Institute, *CMMI Models and Services*, accessed June 16, 2025. https://cmmiinstitute.com.
2 National Institute of Standards and Technology, *Cybersecurity Framework Components*, accessed June 16, 2025. www.nist.gov/cyberframework/cybersecurity-framework-components.

Part III

The Case for Cybersecurity and Operational Alignment

9 Cybersecurity and IT Operations Alignment

LEARNING OBJECTIVES

- Understand how the lack of coordination between security and IT teams leads to delayed incident response, compliance gaps, and operational disruptions
- Learn how integrating cybersecurity into IT operations improves threat detection, response times, and overall system stability
- Learn that unifying monitoring tools, automating security enforcement, and establishing cross-team workflows are essential strategies for bridging the operational–security gap
- Gain an understanding of how aligning cybersecurity with IT operations helps organizations stay compliant, eliminate redundancies, and accelerate innovation without compromising security

Organizations rely on both cybersecurity and IT operations to keep systems secure and running smoothly. However, these two critical functions often operate in silos, leading to inefficiencies and vulnerabilities. As cyber threats grow more sophisticated, aligning cybersecurity with IT operations is no longer just an option, it's a necessity for maintaining security, compliance, and business continuity.

When cybersecurity and IT operations are misaligned, organizations face significant risks. Security teams may detect threats, but without close collaboration, IT operations may struggle to implement fixes quickly, increasing the risk of breaches. Likewise, IT teams might roll out system updates or performance optimizations that inadvertently weaken security controls. These disconnects lead to delayed incident response, operational disruptions, and potential compliance violations.

A unified approach to cybersecurity and IT operations offers numerous advantages. Proactively integrating security within IT workflows reduces system vulnerabilities while ensuring performance remains stable. This alignment enables faster detection and remediation of threats, enhances system reliability, and ensures compliance with industry regulations. When both teams work together, organizations can shift from reactive security measures to a proactive, risk-based strategy.

To achieve this integration, organizations must adopt key strategies that promote collaboration and automation. Shared visibility through unified monitoring tools helps both teams identify and address risks in real time. Automated security controls ensure consistent enforcement of policies without burdening IT teams with manual tasks. Cross-team communication, joint incident response exercises, and embedding security within IT processes through Infrastructure as Code and DevSecOps further strengthen alignment.

By breaking down barriers between cybersecurity and IT operations, organizations create a more resilient and efficient security posture. Security no longer becomes a last-minute add-on but a core

DOI: 10.1201/9781003562153-12

component of IT decision-making. This shift enables businesses to reduce risks while maintaining operational agility, ensuring that security and performance go hand in hand. It also provides cross-training between the organizations and creates alternative career paths by exposing both teams to the different specialties and allowing them some level of understanding and proficiency (or at minimum, exposure) that they would otherwise not have.

As cyber threats continue to evolve, the need for cybersecurity and IT operations alignment will only grow. Organizations that successfully integrate these functions will not only enhance their security defenses but also improve system efficiency, compliance, and overall business resilience. The future of cybersecurity depends on a collaborative approach, one where security and IT operations work as partners, not as separate entities.

MISALIGNMENT BETWEEN CYBERSECURITY AND ITOM

The disconnect between cybersecurity and IT operations creates a range of challenges that can weaken an organization's security posture and operational efficiency. While both teams play critical roles in maintaining secure and reliable systems, their conflicting priorities and lack of collaboration often lead to vulnerabilities, delays, and inefficiencies. Without a well-coordinated approach, organizations struggle to defend against modern cyber threats while ensuring seamless IT performance.

One of the most significant challenges of misalignment is delayed incident response. Security teams may detect threats in real time, but without direct coordination with IT operations, remediation efforts can be slow. IT teams, focused on system performance and availability, might not have the necessary context to prioritize security threats appropriately. As a result, critical vulnerabilities may remain unpatched, giving attackers more time to exploit weaknesses.

Another issue is operational disruptions caused by security measures. Cybersecurity teams often implement policies and controls designed to protect systems, but these measures can sometimes conflict with IT operations' need for speed and efficiency. For example, security updates, patches, or access restrictions might be deployed without considering their impact on system performance, leading to unintended downtime or degraded user experience.

A lack of collaboration also increases the risk of compliance failures. Many industries require organizations to meet strict regulatory standards for data protection and security. However, if IT operations teams are unaware of these compliance requirements, they may inadvertently implement changes that put the organization at risk of noncompliance. Similarly, security teams might enforce policies without consulting IT, leading to inefficiencies or unnecessary restrictions that slow down business processes.

Visibility gaps between cybersecurity and IT operations further complicate security efforts. Without shared access to monitoring tools and logs, security teams may struggle to detect threats hidden within IT infrastructure, while IT teams might overlook security concerns in their daily operations. This lack of visibility makes it difficult to maintain a unified response to threats and weakens the organization's ability to identify potential security incidents early.

Additionally, inconsistent security enforcement across IT systems creates vulnerabilities. If IT teams implement changes without aligning with security policies, security controls may be inconsistently applied across different environments. This fragmented approach leaves gaps that attackers can exploit, especially in hybrid or multicloud environments where security configurations may vary between platforms.

The absence of a unified strategy can also lead to inefficiencies in resource allocation. Security teams and IT operations may duplicate efforts or work at cross-purposes, leading to wasted time and resources. For example, IT teams might deploy security patches without fully understanding the risks, while security teams may conduct independent vulnerability scans that do not align with

IT workflows. These inefficiencies not only increase operational costs but also slow down overall security improvements.

Another challenge is poor communication between teams, which leads to misunderstandings and conflicting priorities. Security teams often focus on risk reduction, while IT operations prioritize system uptime and performance. Without clear communication channels, each team may view the other as an obstacle rather than a partner, making it difficult to develop a cohesive security strategy. This misalignment fosters a reactive rather than proactive security culture.

Resistance to change is another major hurdle. IT operations teams may be hesitant to adopt new security measures that they perceive as burdensome or disruptive to existing workflows. Likewise, security teams may resist modifying their policies to accommodate IT operations' needs. Overcoming this resistance requires a cultural shift, where both teams recognize the value of working together toward shared goals.

Finally, the growing complexity of IT environments exacerbates the misalignment problem. Organizations increasingly rely on cloud services, remote workforces, and third-party vendors, expanding the attack surface and making security management more challenging. If cybersecurity and IT operations teams do not work together to secure these dynamic environments, vulnerabilities can go unnoticed, leading to greater exposure to cyber threats. Addressing these challenges requires more than just technical solutions, it demands a shift in mindset and organizational culture. By fostering collaboration, implementing shared security tools, and aligning their goals, cybersecurity and IT operations teams can overcome these barriers and create a stronger, more resilient security posture.

CASE STUDY: CROSS-SECTOR MISALIGNMENT BETWEEN CYBERSECURITY AND IT OPERATIONS

Organizations that fail to align IT and cybersecurity face heightened risks of breaches, financial penalties, and operational paralysis. Successful alignment requires cultural shifts, shared accountability, and technology that bridges gaps between teams.

Key challenges	Impact
Conflicting priorities	– IT Operations often prioritize system availability and user productivity, while Cybersecurity focuses on risk mitigation and compliance. This disconnect can lead to delayed security updates or overridden access controls to maintain uptime. – Example: In an intelligence agency, an engineer retained access to sensitive systems despite being moved to another team, leading to a major data leak.
Tool and process incompatibility	– IT teams may deploy tools without considering cybersecurity requirements, resulting in fragmented visibility and unmanaged risks. For instance, 75% of organizations report integration challenges between security tools and existing IT infrastructure. – A retail company's advanced security tools failed to align with business processes, contributing to a massive data breach.
Access management failures	– Inconsistent privilege revocation and poor monitoring enable insider threats. A misaligned saboteur exploited dormant accounts and audit log deletions to leak classified data.
Delayed incident response	– Siloed teams struggle with coordinated responses. A healthcare provider's ransomware recovery was hampered because cybersecurity tools weren't integrated with disaster recovery plans.

Key challenges	Impact
Resource misallocation	– Without aligned goals, organizations overspend on redundant tools or neglect critical vulnerabilities. Surveys reveal that 42% of UAE/KSA companies faced delayed investments due to misalignment.

Intelligence Agency Insider Threat

Scenario	Root cause	Impact
An engineer with a history of policy violations retained system access after being reassigned, leading to data theft and leaks.	Incomplete access revocation and lack of cross-departmental communication between IT and security teams.	Leaked intelligence endangered personnel and damaged national security missions.

Retail Data Breach

Scenario	Root cause	Impact
A major retailer's cybersecurity tools were not integrated with IT operations, resulting in undetected vulnerabilities.	Security strategies were siloed from business processes, delaying threat detection.	$1+ billion in recovery costs, lawsuits, and reputational damage.

Healthcare Ransomware Attack

Scenario	Root cause	Impact
A hospital's disaster recovery plan lacked alignment with cybersecurity protocols, prolonging downtime.	IT and cybersecurity teams operated independently, with no joint risk assessments.	Operational shutdowns and regulatory fines.

POTENTIAL OF ALIGNING ITOM AND CYBERSECURITY

Bridging the gap between cybersecurity and IT operations delivers numerous benefits, transforming security from a reactive burden into a proactive and integrated part of business operations. When these teams work together effectively, organizations experience stronger security, improved efficiency, and reduced operational risks. Instead of treating security as an afterthought, a unified approach embeds it within IT workflows, ensuring that systems remain both secure and high performing.

One of the most immediate advantages of aligning cybersecurity with IT operations is proactive threat management. Instead of reacting to security incidents after they occur, organizations can identify and mitigate risks before they lead to breaches. With both teams sharing data, insights, and tools, security vulnerabilities can be detected and addressed early in the development or deployment process, significantly reducing exposure to cyber threats.

Faster incident response is another key benefit. When security and IT operations teams operate in silos, responding to incidents often involves delays due to miscommunication, lack of visibility, or conflicting priorities. A unified approach ensures that both teams have access to real-time threat intelligence and can coordinate responses immediately. This reduces downtime, minimizes damage, and prevents minor security issues from escalating into major breaches. By embedding security into IT workflows, organizations also achieve improved system reliability. Many security incidents result from misconfigurations, unpatched vulnerabilities, or poorly managed access controls. When IT operations and security teams collaborate, they can proactively implement security best practices within IT processes, reducing the likelihood of system failures caused by security oversights.

A strong cybersecurity and IT operations alignment also helps organizations maintain compliance with regulatory requirements. Many industries, such as finance and healthcare, are subject to strict data protection laws that require continuous monitoring and reporting. A coordinated approach ensures that security controls are properly implemented and that IT operations maintain necessary documentation, reducing the risk of compliance violations and associated penalties.

Beyond regulatory compliance, a unified approach also enhances audit readiness. Security teams often struggle to gather the necessary logs, reports, and configurations needed for audits, while IT operations may not always prioritize compliance-related tasks. By working together, both teams can streamline audit preparation, ensuring that organizations can quickly provide evidence of their security controls and risk management strategies by leveraging (or coordinating) the strengths of both teams.

Cost efficiency is another major advantage. When security and IT operations work in isolation, organizations often spend money on redundant tools, overlapping processes, or inefficient security measures that disrupt business operations. By aligning efforts, businesses can reduce waste, optimize resources, and make smarter investments in security technologies that enhance IT operations.

In addition to cost savings, organizations benefit from greater operational agility. Traditional security models often slow down IT deployments due to lengthy security reviews, unscheduled vulnerability fixes, or conflicts between security policies and IT processes. By integrating security into IT workflows from the start, organizations can accelerate software development, cloud adoption, and infrastructure changes without introducing unnecessary risks.

A unified cybersecurity and IT operations approach also fosters better risk management. Instead of treating security as an isolated function, organizations can adopt a risk-based approach where security decisions align with business objectives. IT operations teams gain a better understanding of security risks, while security teams become more aware of operational constraints, leading to balanced decisions that prioritize both security and efficiency.

Enhanced visibility into security and IT environments is another fundamental benefit. Security teams rely on monitoring tools, logs, and analytics to detect threats, while IT operations use performance monitoring to maintain system uptime often using some of the same data, making these systems redundant. By integrating these monitoring solutions, both teams gain a comprehensive view of potential threats, performance issues, and vulnerabilities, leading to more effective security strategies.

Reduced downtime and disruption is another significant advantage. Security incidents, such as ransomware attacks or misconfigured firewalls, can lead to extended outages that impact business continuity. When cybersecurity and IT operations teams work together, they can quickly contain threats, restore systems, and implement preventive measures to minimize future disruptions.

A unified approach also improves third-party and supply chain security. Many organizations rely on external vendors, cloud providers, and third-party services, which introduce additional security risks. By ensuring that security and IT operations teams collaborate on vendor risk assessments, compliance checks, and secure integration processes, organizations can better protect their supply chains from cyber threats.

Another key benefit is stronger endpoint security and device management. With the rise of remote work and bring-your-own-device policies, IT operations must manage an increasing number of devices, while security teams must ensure these devices are properly secured. A unified strategy ensures that endpoint security measures, such as patching, access controls, and threat detection, are consistently enforced across all devices.

A well-integrated cybersecurity and IT operations strategy also builds greater trust among employees and stakeholders. When security policies are seen as obstacles, employees may try to bypass them, leading to risky behaviors. However, when security is seamlessly integrated into IT processes, employees experience fewer disruptions, making them more likely to follow security best practices. This trust extends to stakeholders, including customers, investors, and regulators, who see the organization as more secure and reliable.

Lastly, cybersecurity and IT operations alignment supports long-term digital transformation initiatives. As organizations adopt emerging technologies such as artificial intelligence, cloud computing, and automation, security must be embedded into these advancements from the start. A unified approach ensures that security and IT teams collaborate on new technology rollouts, reducing risks while enabling innovation and growth. By addressing these benefits, organizations can create a security-first culture where cybersecurity is not a bottleneck but a strategic enabler of business success. A unified cybersecurity and IT operations approach not only strengthens security but also enhances efficiency, compliance, and overall business resilience, preparing organizations for the challenges of an evolving threat landscape.

USE CASE: ALIGNING CYBERSECURITY AND IT OPERATIONS IN FINANCIAL SERVICES

Overview

Financial services companies face unique challenges due to their vulnerability to cyberattacks and stringent regulatory requirements. Aligning cybersecurity and IT operations can deliver significant benefits, including enhanced risk management, operational efficiency, compliance adherence, and improved customer trust. This case study explores how financial institutions can achieve these benefits through strategic alignment.

Challenges Faced by Financial Institutions

1. Sophisticated cyber threats: Financial institutions are prime targets for cybercriminals employing tactics such as ransomware, credential stuffing, and phishing attacks.
2. Regulatory compliance: Adhering to standards like PCI DSS and GDPR is critical but resource intensive.
3. Operational silos: Disjointed IT and cybersecurity functions can lead to inefficiencies and gaps in protection.
4. Resource constraints: Smaller IT teams often struggle to manage complex security environments effectively.

Strategic Alignment of Cybersecurity and IT Operations

Aligning cybersecurity with IT operations involves integrating processes, technologies, and teams to create a unified approach to risk management.

Key Strategy	Benefits
Unified risk management	– Consolidating first party and third-party cyber risk management on a single platform enhances visibility across internal and external threats. – Standardized metrics streamline risk assessments, enabling consistent evaluations across the organization.
Proactive threat detection	– Implementing AI-driven security platforms for real-time anomaly detection ensures rapid identification of threats. – Managed Security Operations Centers (SOCs) provide 24/7 monitoring, logging, and threat hunting capabilities.
Enhanced collaboration	– Bridging communication gaps between technical teams and business leaders improves decision-making by presenting risks in financial terms that resonate with stakeholders. – Integrated dashboards enable IT teams to provide auditors with comprehensive cybersecurity reporting.
Operational efficiency	– Automating processes such as log analysis reduces manual workload for security analysts, allowing them to focus on high-priority tasks. – Streamlined incident response protocols minimize downtime during security breaches.
Compliance optimization	– Tailored solutions simplify audits by generating detailed reports aligned with regulatory standards like PCI DSS within a short timeframe. – Continuous monitoring ensures adherence to evolving compliance requirements

CONSIDERATIONS FOR CYBERSECURITY AND ITOM ALIGNMENT

Aligning cybersecurity with IT operations is becoming more and more a strategic imperative. The proliferation of hybrid infrastructures, the sophistication of threat actors, and the increasing weight of regulatory scrutiny have rendered siloed security and IT functions obsolete. A modern enterprise must adopt an integrated approach where cybersecurity objectives are tightly interwoven into IT operational processes, ensuring that resilience, compliance, and performance are achieved without compromise.

Establishing Unified Visibility across Security and IT Domains

The foundation of operational synergy lies in converged visibility. Traditionally, security teams focus on threat intelligence and incident detection, while IT operations prioritize performance and availability. These distinct vantage points often lead to fragmented responses. To overcome this, enterprises must deploy a unified observability layer that fuses security telemetry with infrastructure and application monitoring. Implementing platforms such as Security Information and Event Management (SIEM) or Extended Detection and Response (XDR) integrated with AI Operations (AIOps) tools provides real-time correlation across security incidents and system health metrics. This convergence allows IT teams to understand the impact of cyber events on system performance, while security teams gain deeper context into vulnerabilities rooted in infrastructure misconfigurations or degradation.

Automating Security Controls to Enhance Operational Agility

Manual security enforcement mechanisms, such as ad hoc patching, periodic compliance audits, or legacy vulnerability management processes, are no longer sustainable in an environment demanding real-time responsiveness. Automation must be embedded at the core of operational workflows to ensure continuous compliance, rapid threat mitigation, and consistent control enforcement across distributed environments. By leveraging automated patch orchestration, vulnerability remediation, and configuration compliance tools, enterprises can maintain security hygiene without incurring operational bottlenecks or introducing human error.

Driving Cross-Functional Collaboration through Shared Workflows

Security and IT operations must operate under a shared mission: ensuring business outcomes. Yet, organizational silos often impede this goal, creating disconnects during incident response and delaying risk mitigation efforts. A mature security architecture mandates the institutionalization of cross-functional collaboration through integrated workflows, shared tooling, and routine joint exercises. Collaboration should extend beyond communication platforms. It requires the development of unified runbooks, which are step-by-step instructions for executing procedures, integrated ticketing systems, and cross-functional accountability during incident investigations and change management cycles.

Embedding Security into DevOps through DevSecOps Methodologies

Security must be embedded throughout the software development lifecycle. DevSecOps enforces this principle by integrating security validations into every phase of the Continuous Integration/Continuous Delivery (CI/CD) pipeline, from code commit to infrastructure provisioning. This approach ensures that applications are designed and deployed with inherent security, reducing the attack surface introduced by late-stage patches or configuration drift. By leveraging tools such as Static Application Security Testing (SAST), Dynamic Application Security Testing (DAST), and Infrastructure as Code (IaC) scanning solutions, security becomes a continuous, automated quality gate rather than a reactive afterthought.

Security as Code (SaC)

SaC formalizes the definition and enforcement of security policies using version-controlled, declarative templates. This approach allows enterprises to standardize access controls, firewall rules, encryption policies, and logging configurations across all environments with minimal manual intervention. By coupling SaC with IaC frameworks, such as Terraform or AWS CloudFormation, organizations can ensure consistent security posture, simplify audits, and detect drift in real time.

Institutionalizing Joint Incident Response Exercises

Integrated incident response capabilities are critical to minimizing dwell time and business disruption during cyber events. Enterprises should operationalize tabletop exercises and live-fire simulations that involve both security and IT operations teams, ensuring clear communication, rapid containment, and effective recovery. Drills should simulate a variety of threat scenarios, from data exfiltration and ransomware to insider threats and supply chain compromise, tailored to the organization's threat landscape and business priorities.

Harmonizing Cybersecurity and IT Risk Management Frameworks

To effectively manage enterprise risk, cybersecurity and IT operational risks must be evaluated through a single lens. Integrated risk management frameworks ensure that decision-makers can assess the cumulative impact of both security threats and IT performance issues on business objectives. By aligning cybersecurity risk assessments with IT governance frameworks, organizations gain a unified understanding of operational resilience, regulatory exposure, and business continuity.

Operationalizing Compliance within IT Workflows

Compliance can no longer be treated as a periodic checkbox exercise because the risk to the business has accelerated significantly. Instead, it must be continuously embedded into IT workflows using automated policy enforcement and continuous compliance monitoring. Tools that assess configurations against regulatory baselines in real-time reduce audit fatigue and improve response times to policy violations.

Leveraging AI for Proactive Security and Operational Intelligence

Artificial Intelligence and Machine Learning introduce new capabilities in both cybersecurity and IT operations. From anomaly detection to predictive maintenance, AI-driven platforms can augment human decision-making and reduce response times. Security analytics platforms leveraging ML can correlate vast amounts of telemetry data, identifying potential insider threats or compromised accounts long before they trigger conventional alerts.

Embedding Security KPIs into IT Operational Metrics

Security must be measured and managed with the same rigor as performance and availability. Embedding cybersecurity KPIs into IT scorecards reinforces shared accountability and ensures that risk reduction is a measurable objective. Metrics such as mean time to detect/respond, patching cadence, phishing susceptibility rates, and audit readiness should be evaluated alongside uptime, latency, and incident closure rates.

Enforcing Policy Uniformity across Hybrid and Multicloud Environments

Disparate security policies across cloud and on-premises environments create blind spots and introduce unnecessary complexity. Centralized policy enforcement ensures consistency in access controls, encryption, logging, and threat detection, regardless of where workloads reside. Unified policy orchestration through tools such as cloud security posture management, policy-as-code, and API-based configuration managers enables enterprises to maintain a hardened posture across their digital estate.

Strategy	Use Case
Establishing unified visibility across security and IT domains	A global financial services firm integrates authentication logs, endpoint telemetry, and behavioral analytics into its SIEM platform. This enables early detection of lateral movement associated with credential abuse, while simultaneously alerting IT of potential service degradation tied to the affected systems.
Automating security controls to enhance operational agility	A retail enterprise operating in multicloud environments deploys policy-as-code frameworks and automated remediation playbooks that continuously enforce security baselines. This ensures that workloads are hardened and compliant at all times, even as infrastructure scales dynamically during peak business periods.
Driving cross-functional collaboration through shared workflows	A healthcare provider establishes a Security–Operations Coordination Board that conducts monthly risk review sessions. During these sessions, teams jointly assess patching cadences, upcoming infrastructure changes, and emerging threats to ensure cohesive and timely mitigation strategies.

Strategy	Use Case
Embedding security into DevOps through DevSecOps methodologies	A SaaS startup implements security gates within its GitLab CI/CD pipeline, automating code scans, dependency checks, and infrastructure policy validations. Any deviation from secure coding or deployment standards results in pipeline failures, preventing vulnerable assets from reaching production.
Implementing SaC for standardization and auditability	A multinational cloud service provider embeds security modules into its Terraform blueprints, enforcing uniform encryption standards and access control lists across thousands of virtual machines. Any policy drift is automatically flagged and remediated via CI/CD-integrated enforcement mechanisms.
Institutionalizing joint incident response exercises	A manufacturing conglomerate conducts quarterly ransomware simulations in its OT and IT environments. These exercises evaluate detection speed, escalation paths, containment procedures, and restoration capabilities, refining its cyber resilience strategy over time.
Harmonizing cybersecurity and IT risk management frameworks	A banking institution embeds NIST CSF controls within its IT service management platform. This allows it to evaluate infrastructure changes not only for technical impact, but also for their implications on regulatory compliance and data protection.
Operationalizing compliance within IT workflows	An e-commerce enterprise managing PCI-DSS scope integrates Cloud Security Posture Management (CSPM) tools with its cloud deployment pipeline. Every infrastructure change is evaluated against PCI benchmarks before deployment, and deviations are remediated automatically or flagged for review.
Leveraging AI for proactive security and operational intelligence	A telecom provider deploys an AI-driven behavioral analytics platform that monitors user and entity behavior. The system autonomously identifies anomalous access patterns indicative of credential theft and triggers step-up authentication measures, neutralizing the threat before data exfiltration occurs.
Embedding security KPIs into IT operational metrics	A global logistics firm incorporates security SLAs into its IT operations dashboard. Performance bonuses and team evaluations are tied not only to system uptime, but also to vulnerability remediation cycles and incident containment effectiveness.
Enforcing policy uniformity across hybrid and multicloud environments	A global SaaS provider standardizes firewall configurations, IAM policies, and logging rules across AWS, Azure, and Google Cloud using a centralized control plane. This uniformity reduces attack surfaces and streamlines compliance with international regulations.

CHALLENGES IN ALIGNING ITOM AND CYBERSECURITY

Achieving cohesive alignment between ITOM and cybersecurity remains one of the most persistent and complex challenges facing modern enterprise architecture. At the core of this misalignment lies a divergence in mission objectives: ITOM is driven by the imperative to maintain availability, performance, and operational efficiency, whereas cybersecurity is fundamentally tasked with protecting confidentiality, integrity, and availability through risk mitigation, regulatory compliance, and threat defense.

Aligning IT operations and cybersecurity is not a matter of compromise; it is a matter of architectural convergence. This requires an intentional strategy that fuses visibility, automation, governance, and risk management into a cohesive operational fabric. Enterprise security architects must lead this transformation by designing frameworks that align people, process, and technology toward a unified goal: securing the enterprise without sacrificing agility, availability, or performance. By embedding security into the fabric of operations, organizations can shift from reactive silos to proactive resilience, where ITOM and cybersecurity function not as adversaries, but as strategic partners in enabling business outcomes.

Conflicting Objectives and Priority Misalignment

Operational teams often emphasize velocity, rapid deployments, minimal downtime, and streamlined service delivery. In contrast, security teams emphasize due diligence, control validation, and measured change implementation. This natural tension creates friction, especially during change management cycles. For example, ITOM may push for aggressive system rollouts, while cybersecurity imposes security gating functions such as risk assessments and control verification, which may introduce delays. Aligning these priorities requires a risk-informed operational model where business impact, risk tolerance, and mission criticality guide decision-making, rather than siloed KPIs.

Fragmented Visibility across Toolsets

Visibility is the cornerstone of effective management, yet ITOM and cybersecurity often operate with distinct tooling ecosystems. ITOM relies on telemetry and performance monitoring solutions, while cybersecurity depends on SIEM, XDR, and threat intelligence platforms. The lack of integration between these toolsets creates operational blind spots, where infrastructure changes or performance degradations occur without security context, or security alerts are generated in isolation from the operational state. Bridging this divide demands converged observability platforms that provide correlated insights across operational and security domains.

Organizational Silos and Inefficient Collaboration Models

Traditional organizational structures often isolate ITOM and cybersecurity under separate reporting lines, fostering communication breakdowns and fragmented incident response. Without a shared operating model or governance structure, policies may be enforced unilaterally by security teams, while ITOM may implement changes without security validation undermining resilience. The adoption of integrated frameworks such as DevSecOps, Site Reliability Engineering with embedded security roles, and centralized governance models are essential to break down these silos and drive cohesive execution.

Patch Management and Change Control Conflicts

Vulnerability remediation and patch management are operationally complex and politically sensitive. Security teams often issue remediation mandates based on severity and exploitability, while ITOM assesses patches through the lens of stability, dependencies, and change risk. This disconnect results in frequent bottlenecks, delays in patch application, bypassed updates, or emergency deployments that disrupt services. A mature, risk-based patch management strategy that jointly evaluates business impact, threat landscape, and service dependencies is vital to reconcile these competing pressures.

Inconsistent Asset Inventory and Configuration Management

Accurate and real-time asset inventory is foundational to both operational and security domains. Yet, discrepancies in asset discovery, configuration management database (CMBD) updates, and lifecycle tracking introduce risks ranging from unpatched systems to unmanaged endpoints. These inconsistencies not only create security exposure but also undermine ITOM's ability to perform effective capacity planning, root cause analysis, and lifecycle management. Organizations must invest in continuous asset discovery, unified CMDB strategies, and integrated configuration baselines to maintain operational and security fidelity.

Misaligned Incident Response and Root Cause Analysis

Incidents are often diagnosed through different lenses, ITOM investigates performance degradation, while security teams analyze potential compromises. Without a unified incident response framework, the two functions may respond in parallel but disconnected workflows, leading to prolonged recovery times and incomplete root cause analysis. Establishing a joint incident lifecycle model, supported by integrated playbooks, which document how to handle incidents, and shared forensics capabilities, enables comprehensive resolution and prevents recurrence.

Security–Performance Tradeoffs and Operational Resistance

Security controls often introduce system overhead, whether through deep packet inspection, endpoint detection and response, encrypted traffic analysis, or data encryption. ITOM may view these controls as impediments to performance service level agreements and user experience, prompting attempts to disable or circumvent them. This tension underscores the need for collaborative control design that accounts for performance baselines, as well as architectural solutions that balance protection with performance.

Regulatory Compliance Friction

Regulatory mandates require stringent access controls, audit logging, data retention, and segmentation. These requirements can significantly impact operational workflows, storage overhead, and system complexity. ITOM teams may resist these changes, viewing them as nonfunctional burdens. Security architects must translate regulatory requirements into operationally feasible designs and embed compliance controls into ITOM workflows to minimize friction and ensure audit readiness.

Cloud and Hybrid Environment Complexity

As enterprises migrate toward hybrid and multicloud architectures, the heterogeneity of infrastructure increases dramatically. Cloud-native security tools may not align with traditional ITOM platforms, creating disjointed monitoring, misaligned policies, and inconsistent configuration baselines. Enterprise security architecture must define cloud governance frameworks that include integrated monitoring, consistent control objectives, and automation pipelines that span both legacy and cloud-native environments.

Siloed Automation and Orchestration

Automation is a force multiplier, but only when orchestrated across domains. Many organizations deploy automation in isolation: ITOM automates ticketing and provisioning, while cybersecurity automates alert triage and threat response. Without orchestration, automation becomes fragmented, and handoffs between teams remain manual. Implementing unified orchestration frameworks, such as Security Orchestration, Automation, and Response (SOAR) integrated with ITSM and event-driven infrastructure, enables coordinated response, closed-loop remediation, and improved operational tempo.

Shadow IT and Unmanaged Technology Risk

The proliferation of shadow IT, driven by business units adopting SaaS, cloud, or unmanaged hardware without IT or security oversight, introduces systemic risk. ITOM may struggle to support or manage these assets, while cybersecurity teams remain blind to their existence. Continuous asset discovery, policy enforcement via cloud access security brokers, and governance frameworks are essential to reclaim visibility and control over shadow assets.

Vendor and Supply Chain Risk Divergence

Third-party risk management is a joint concern but often approached differently. ITOM evaluates vendors for Service Level Agreement (SLA) performance and supportability, while cybersecurity assesses them for software assurance, breach history, and security posture. Misalignment during procurement or onboarding phases can lead to systemic exposure. Integrated vendor risk frameworks, backed by shared due diligence processes and third-party risk scoring, ensure both performance and security are accounted for in sourcing decisions.

Disparate Risk Models

Perhaps most fundamentally, ITOM and cybersecurity often operate under different risk models. ITOM evaluates risk through the lens of service disruption, capacity, and user impact. Cybersecurity evaluates risk through threat vectors, exploitability, and impact severity. Without a harmonized enterprise risk framework, prioritization becomes misaligned. By adopting a unified risk management framework organizations can ensure that both functions evaluate risk with a shared taxonomy and business context.

Delayed Detection Due to Misaligned Monitoring

A spike in CPU or network utilization may be dismissed as a benign performance anomaly by ITOM, while cybersecurity might interpret it as lateral movement or data exfiltration. Without a shared monitoring strategy and contextual correlation, early indicators of compromise are easily missed. Integrated security and operational analytics platforms, backed by shared playbooks and contextual alerting, enable faster detection and response.

Cultural Divide and Resistance to Integration

Finally, cultural inertia remains one of the most difficult challenges to overcome. ITOM teams may view security as an impediment to innovation, while security teams may impose controls without understanding operational constraints. Overcoming this requires a top-down cultural shift, one that embraces a security-by-design philosophy while empowering operations teams to contribute to security outcomes. Leadership must drive alignment through shared objectives, incentives, and performance metrics that reward collaboration, not silos.

CONCLUSION AND RECAP

As the digital enterprise evolves, the once-parallel tracks of IT operations and cybersecurity must now converge into a single, integrated discipline. Gone are the days when uptime and security could be treated as separate success metrics. Today, system performance without security is fragile; security without operational alignment is ineffective. This chapter has explored not only the necessity but the strategic value of unifying these critical functions across the modern enterprise.

The root of the misalignment lies in conflicting operational mandates. IT operations traditionally prioritize availability, speed, and service quality, while cybersecurity focuses on protecting assets, data, and users from evolving threats. These diverging mandates frequently lead to tactical clashes, patches delayed due to uptime concerns, security tools deactivated to preserve performance, and compliance mandates overlooked in the name of agility. The result is a fragmented security posture and a brittle IT ecosystem.

These tensions are exacerbated by a fragmented visibility landscape. ITOM relies on performance telemetry and health dashboards, while cybersecurity consumes threat intelligence and anomaly detection feeds. Without unified observability, teams are navigating the same enterprise terrain with different maps. This disconnect leads to slower incident detection, misaligned response strategies, and a reactive security culture. Integrated monitoring, built atop converged data pipelines, must be a foundational architectural goal.

Collaboration breakdowns are not merely process issues; they are architectural liabilities. Siloed ticketing systems, disconnected runbooks, and uncoordinated change approvals contribute to delayed remediation, policy drift, and audit gaps. Cross-functional coordination must be institutionalized through shared workflows, integrated toolchains, and governance structures that treat cybersecurity and ITOM as equal stakeholders in service delivery and risk mitigation.

Automation holds promise, but not in isolation. ITOM has matured its automation runbooks for provisioning and scaling; cybersecurity has done the same for alert triage and threat containment. Yet without orchestration across domains, automation remains fragmented. A truly resilient architecture demands unified workflows where SOAR platforms integrate with ITSM systems, enabling real-time remediation that spans detection to resolution with minimal human intervention.

Asset inventory and configuration management are the linchpins of both operational integrity and security hygiene. Inconsistent inventories, unmanaged devices, and configuration drift expose gaps attackers can exploit and operations teams cannot troubleshoot. Continuous discovery, automated configuration enforcement, and unified CMDBs must become nonnegotiable for enterprises seeking full-spectrum visibility and control.

Incidents offer a sobering lens into organizational readiness and misalignment. Security and operations teams often respond to the same incident from different perspectives, leading to fragmented diagnostics, prolonged recovery, and root cause uncertainty. A joint incident lifecycle supported by shared tooling, playbooks, and war rooms, is essential for true operational resilience and breach containment.

Cultural resistance remains one of the most enduring obstacles. IT operations may see security as a constraint; cybersecurity may treat ITOM as a source of risk. This adversarial mindset must be replaced with a shared mission model, where every change, deployment, or response is evaluated for both its business value and its risk implications. Executive leadership must champion this cultural transformation through incentives, joint KPIs, and consistent messaging.

Cloud and hybrid architectures magnify the cost of misalignment. With decentralized infrastructure, ephemeral workloads, and divergent control models, inconsistencies across environments are inevitable without a unified security–operations fabric. Centralized policy orchestration, consistent enforcement mechanisms, and cloud-native visibility tools must be architected into the operating model from the ground up.

Risk must be the shared language between teams. While cybersecurity evaluates threats and vulnerabilities, ITOM assesses service disruption and operational loss. A unified risk management framework ensures that all functions operate from a common understanding of risk exposure, enabling prioritization based on business impact rather than isolated technical metrics.

The benefits of alignment are profound. Organizations that embed security into IT operations experience faster threat detection, streamlined compliance, lower operational costs, and improved business agility. Security becomes an enabler, not an obstacle, to innovation, cloud adoption, and digital transformation. Employees face fewer disruptions, stakeholders gain confidence, and the enterprise moves forward with both speed and assurance.

Aligning cybersecurity with IT operations is not a project, it is an enterprise transformation. It requires architectural convergence, operational discipline, cultural realignment, and executive sponsorship. Enterprises must lead this shift, designing systems and processes where security is not bolted on, but built in. Only then can organizations achieve the resilience, agility, and trustworthiness demanded by the modern digital landscape.

10 Alignment of DevOps and DevSecOps for Greater Assurance

LEARNING OBJECTIVES

- Understand the shift from DevOps to DevSecOps and its role in addressing modern security challenges
- Learn how collaboration between development, operations, and security teams strengthens the development pipeline
- Discover how automation in DevSecOps integrates security testing into continuous integration and continuous delivery/deployment (CI/CD) pipelines without slowing development
- Explore how DevSecOps improves incident response, compliance, and alignment between security and business goals

IT capabilities underpin the core value delivery mechanisms of modern enterprises, government institutions, and every industry. Whether enabling citizen services, facilitating business operations, or supporting internal workforce productivity, technology serves as a foundational enabler. However, as the reliance on software systems continues to grow, so too does the attack surface. Software is no longer just a tool; it is the operational backbone of digital strategy. As such, the security of software systems is not a peripheral concern, but a fundamental business and mission-critical requirement.

The accelerating frequency and sophistication of cyber threats, ranging from nation-state actors to financially motivated cybercriminals, demands a paradigm shift in how organizations approach software development and security. Traditional models that treat security as a final step or an external overlay are no longer sufficient. Security must be intrinsic, continuous, and automated. This is where DevSecOps emerges as not just a methodology, but a cultural and architectural transformation.

DevSecOps integrates security practices directly into the Development and Operations (DevOps) pipeline, enabling organizations to detect, remediate, and prevent vulnerabilities early in the software development lifecycle (SDLC). This proactive approach enhances system resilience and enables the secure delivery of capabilities at speed and scale. When implemented properly, DevSecOps ensures that security is not a bottleneck, but a shared responsibility woven into every phase, from planning and design, through development, testing, deployment, and continuous operations.

One of the most pressing challenges organizations face is the adversarial nature of modern threat environments. Weaponized malware, AI-driven attack automation, and supply chain compromises transform software security into a persistent battleground. Defensive strategies must evolve to meet this reality. Unfortunately, many organizations still over-index on post-development security assessments, leaving exploitable design and implementation flaws unaddressed until it is too late. Evidence shows that a significant portion of vulnerabilities are introduced during the design and coding phases, not through user error or operational misconfiguration, but through systemic weaknesses embedded in the application architecture itself.

DOI: 10.1201/9781003562153-13

This is a call to evolve from reactive security models to proactive, integrated security engineering. DevSecOps when aligned with architectural governance, threat modeling, secure coding practices, and continuous monitoring can bridge the gap between development agility and enterprise security. By doing so, we not only reduce risk but enable the rapid and secure delivery of digital services that our stakeholders increasingly demand.

DEFINING DEVOPS AND DEVSECOPS

In order to keep up with the demands of the business, organizations require rapid software delivery without compromising security. DevOps emerged as a collaborative, agile approach that unifies development, operations, and quality assurance to enable continuous, high-velocity deployment. DevSecOps extends this model by embedding security as a core component throughout the development lifecycle, shifting security left to detect and mitigate risks earlier, reduce costs, and improve system resilience. By integrating security into DevOps practices, organizations can align faster delivery with effective risk management, ensuring scalable, secure, and compliant software systems.

What Is DevOps?

DevOps represents a transformative paradigm shift in how enterprises approach the delivery and operation of software systems. It is not merely a set of tools or practices—it is an organizational philosophy that breaks down traditional silos between development, IT operations, and quality assurance. By fostering cross-functional collaboration, automation, shared accountability, and continuous feedback loops, DevOps enables organizations to deliver business value at speed, while maintaining system reliability and scalability.

At its core, DevOps is designed to support agile, iterative development lifecycles with a strong emphasis on CI and CD. This integrated approach empowers teams to rapidly deploy changes into production environments with minimal manual intervention. The result is a software development capability characterized by high velocity, low risk, and increased system resilience. DevOps does not eliminate the need for control, it redefines how control is implemented by embedding it into automated, version-controlled, and testable pipelines.

DevOps involves several important practices.[1] Continuous integration ensures that each new piece of code is automatically tested and combined with the existing system. Continuous delivery makes it possible to roll out updates quickly and consistently. Infrastructure as Code (IaC) automates how systems are set up, while microservices break larger applications into smaller parts that can be managed independently. Monitoring and logging are also essential, providing insights into how software is performing.

From an enterprise architecture perspective, DevOps aligns with business goals by accelerating time-to-market, reducing mean time to recovery, and enabling faster adaptation to changing market or regulatory requirements. However, without security embedded into this cycle, the pace of change can become a vector for risk.

History of DevOps

The origins of DevOps can be traced back to the early 2000s, during which the Agile Software Development movement emerged. Agile methodologies emphasized iterative development and collaboration, which highlighted the need for a more integrated approach between DevOps teams.

- Key Milestones
  - Agile Movement (2001): The publication of the Agile Manifesto[2] marked a shift toward iterative development, encouraging collaboration and customer feedback. However, this approach did not fully address operational challenges in deploying software.

  - o Emergence of DevOps (2009): The term "DevOps" was coined during the first DevOpsDays[3] conference in Ghent, Belgium. This event brought together developers and operations professionals to discuss bridging gaps between their roles.
  - o Rise of Continuous Integration/Continuous Delivery (CI/CD): The adoption of CI/CD practices in the early 2010s allowed for automated testing and deployment, significantly improving the speed and reliability of software releases.
  - o Mainstream Adoption: By 2014, major organizations like Amazon and Netflix were implementing DevOps practices to enhance their software delivery processes. This period also saw the integration of security practices into DevOps, leading to the concept of DevSecOps.
- Evolution
  - o Over time, DevOps has evolved with technological advancements such as cloud computing and automation tools, which have further streamlined development processes. Today, it encompasses a variety of practices that promote continuous improvement and collaboration across teams.

What Is DevSecOps?

DevSecOps is the logical and necessary evolution of the DevOps model, introducing security as a core, continuous, and collaborative discipline throughout the software delivery lifecycle. Rather than treating security as a gating function at the end of development, DevSecOps advocates for embedding security controls, testing, and assurance mechanisms from the earliest stages of planning through to deployment and operations.

In practice, DevSecOps integrates security capabilities, including static and dynamic analysis, threat modeling, compliance scanning, container security, and IaC validation, into the automated toolchains that power modern CI/CD pipelines. This enables teams to identify and remediate vulnerabilities as early as possible, dramatically reducing both the cost and complexity of fixing security defects post-deployment.

From an architectural standpoint, DevSecOps is not just about tooling, it represents a cultural realignment. Security becomes a shared responsibility, not an external function. This shift requires educating developers, empowering operations with security visibility, and integrating risk management practices into agile workflows. DevSecOps also supports the proactive identification of misconfigurations, insecure code patterns, and third-party risks before they escalate into enterprise-level threats.

History of DevSecOps

The evolution of DevSecOps is rooted in the transformation of software development practices over the decades:

- Waterfall Era (1990s–2000s): Software development followed a linear, sequential model where security was addressed only at the end of the development process. This approach often led to costly and time-consuming fixes for vulnerabilities discovered late in the cycle.
- Agile and DevOps (2010s): The Agile methodology introduced iterative development, emphasizing collaboration and speed. DevOps further bridged the gap between DevOps teams, enabling faster delivery cycles. However, security remained siloed, often treated as a separate phase.
- Shift-Left Movement (2012): The Shift-Left paradigm encouraged integrating security earlier in the SDLC, making it a proactive rather than reactive process.

- Emergence of DevSecOps (2014–present): DevSecOps was born out of the need to embed security into every phase of SDLC, combining DevOps principles with continuous security practices. It emphasizes a collaborative culture where developers, operations, and security teams share responsibility for secure software delivery

DevSecOps represents a significant evolution in software development by integrating security into every phase of the SDLC. Its history reflects a shift from reactive to proactive security measures, driven by the need for faster yet safer software delivery. The benefits, ranging from early vulnerability detection to enhanced collaboration, make it an essential practice for modern organizations aiming to balance agility with robust cybersecurity.

Strategic Importance of Security Integration in the SDLC

In today's hypercompetitive digital landscape, the pressure to deliver features and systems to market rapidly can inadvertently deprioritize robust security controls. This creates a dangerous dichotomy between velocity and assurance. However, security need not be a bottleneck; rather, it can be a force multiplier when integrated seamlessly into DevOps processes.

Delaying security validations until the final stages of development, or worse, after deployment, introduces significant architectural and financial risk. Studies consistently show that the cost to remediate a vulnerability increases exponentially the later it is discovered in the lifecycle. Furthermore, reputational damage resulting from a breach or compliance failure can have far-reaching impacts on customer trust, investor confidence, and regulatory standing.

The adoption of DevSecOps enables risk-aware software delivery, where security is treated as a design requirement, not a compliance afterthought. It introduces threat-informed decision-making early in development and enables organizations to build resilient architectures that can withstand evolving threat landscapes. By shifting security left, organizations are able to:

- Reduce Mean Time to Detect (MTTD) and Mean Time to Respond (MTTR) for security issues.
- Leverage automated security testing as part of every code commit or infrastructure change.
- Ensure compliance is continuous, auditable, and aligned with cybersecurity and regulatory frameworks.

Make informed risk tradeoffs based on both the likelihood of a threat and the impact severity, recognizing that even small improvements in either dimension can dramatically reduce enterprise risk exposure.

Security by Design in the DevOps Era

The integration of DevSecOps is a business enabler and not merely an operational enhancement. Organizations that successfully adopt DevSecOps are better positioned to respond to change, scale securely, and innovate without sacrificing governance. This requires not only the adoption of security tooling, but a holistic rethinking of enterprise security architecture. Security architects must define guardrails that are enforceable through policy-as-code, align security requirements with business goals, and ensure architectural consistency across hybrid or multicloud environments. In short, DevSecOps empowers enterprises to build secure, reliable, and compliant systems at the speed of business, reinforcing the strategic role of security as both a protector of value and an enabler of innovation.

SECURITY CHALLENGES IN THE SDLC

As the enterprise software landscape continues to evolve, attackers have significantly shifted left, targeting the development process itself as a primary avenue for compromise. Vulnerabilities embedded within the SDLC, whether through flawed code, misconfigured environments, exposed secrets, or third-party dependencies, present an expanding attack surface that traditional security controls cannot effectively mitigate alone.

Security engineering, once a downstream discipline in the release process, has evolved into a critical enabler of agile and resilient digital transformation. Yet, despite years of advancement, secure coding principles and design patterns are often subordinated to the urgency of rapid software delivery. The convergence of DevOps introduced tremendous gains in agility and velocity, but frequently at the expense of architectural rigor and embedded security assurance.

As DevSecOps gains traction, enterprise architects must guide its integration, not as a bolt-on solution, but as a strategic alignment of security architecture with CI/CD pipelines, development practices, and runtime environments. This paper explores the current landscape of DevOps and DevSecOps, assessing their maturity, architectural gaps, and the path toward embedding security as a continuous and automated function. We will outline actionable guidance to operationalize security across the software supply chain while maintaining development velocity and business agility.

CI/CD Pipeline Vulnerabilities

CI/CD pipelines have become strategic assets—and attractive targets—for threat actors. These automation frameworks often operate with elevated privileges and access to sensitive systems, secrets, and artifacts. A successful compromise of a CI/CD toolchain can result in the distribution of malicious payloads across production environments, effectively weaponizing the software delivery process itself. The CI/CD threat model must account for:

- Toolchain Compromise: Attackers targeting tools used for automating the software development process with the aim of injecting malicious jobs or exfiltrating secrets.
- Credential Leakage: Secrets stored insecurely in pipeline configs or environment variables.
- Supply Chain Attacks: Compromised third-party dependencies entering the pipeline via package managers or registries.
- Privilege Escalation: Over-permissioned service accounts used by pipeline runners.

A secure CI/CD architecture should include isolated build environments, policy-as-code enforcement, immutable artifacts, and signed provenance metadata. Moreover, containerization and sandboxing of build jobs reduce lateral movement opportunities. Adoption of zero trust principles within the DevOps toolchain, such as identity-based access, just-in-time privilege elevation, and continuous authentication, provides foundational resilience against compromise.

Advanced strategies such as push–resistance indices and image hardening ensure that container images are verifiably built from trusted sources, layered securely, and scanned for vulnerabilities pre-deployment. When automated threat modeling and vulnerability prioritization are integrated, organizations can reduce remediation costs and accelerate secure delivery compared to manual processes.

Code Repositories and Version Control

Source code repositories and version control systems are the custodians of an enterprise's intellectual property and a critical component of its digital supply chain. Compromising a repository can grant adversaries persistent access to sensitive business logic, cryptographic secrets, and embedded credentials. Security architecture for version control systems must enforce:

- Granular Access Control: Role-Based Access Control (RBAC) with principle of least privilege, enforced down to the repository or even branch level.
- Strong Authentication: Single Sign-On (SSO) integrated with identity governance platforms, coupled with mandatory Multifactor Authentication (MFA).
- Audit Logging and Anomaly Detection: Continuous monitoring for anomalous check-ins, privilege escalations, and bypassed reviews.

Beyond access management, data governance plays a foundational role. Source code should never contain personally identifiable information or regulated data. Developers must be trained and tooling must be in place to detect and prevent the inadvertent check-in of sensitive data. In regulated environments, this also includes the enforceable deletion of any compliance-relevant data mistakenly added to the codebase, unless retention policies legally justify preservation.

Code must be treated as an immutable artifact. Once committed and peer-reviewed via pull request workflows, the approved source should be cryptographically signed, scanned for vulnerabilities, and stored with version history intact for audit and rollback purposes. Integration with artifact repositories further enforces integrity and consistency across build pipelines.

BEST PRACTICES FOR IMPLEMENTING DEVSECOPS

As enterprises increasingly integrate security into the SDLC, the DevSecOps model has emerged as a critical framework for balancing speed, agility, and security. Unlike traditional security approaches that introduce security controls late in the development cycle, DevSecOps mandates a shift-left approach, embedding security from the initial stages of software development. Additionally, effective DevSecOps implementation relies on cross-functional collaboration between development, operations, and security teams to ensure a unified security posture.

Aligning DevSecOps with DevOps

DevSecOps is not merely a security overlay on DevOps, it is a transformative approach that requires cultural, technical, and architectural alignment. For enterprise adoption to succeed, security leaders must collaborate with DevOps teams to embed security objectives into key performance indicators, developer tooling, and platform architecture. Key architectural enablers include:

- Security as Code (SaC): Declarative security policies versioned and enforced alongside application code.
- Policy-Driven Controls: Policy engines applied at deployment gates.
- Security Telemetry: Centralized observability into build integrity, dependency health, and attack surface metrics.
- Shift-Left Automation: Integration of Static Application Security Testing (SAST), Dynamic Application Security Testing (DAST), and Software Composition Analysis (SCA) tools into Integrated Development Environment (IDE) and pre-commit stages.

Enterprise architects must also define governance models for DevSecOps maturity, establishing secure development baselines, pipeline reference architectures, and automated controls that enable compliance-by-design. This ensures security does not slow delivery, but rather, enhances reliability and trust.

Looking ahead, the convergence of AI/ML and platform engineering will introduce new complexities and opportunities for DevSecOps. Enterprise security architects must stay ahead of this curve by designing resilient, composable, and self-defending DevOps ecosystems. Emphasis should be placed on software bill of materials visibility, dependency provenance, and runtime behavioral baselining. DevSecOps must evolve from tactical tool integration to strategic capability development. This requires enterprise-wide alignment, executive sponsorship, and a risk-informed approach to software innovation. Only then can organizations deliver software at speed, without compromising the trust that underpins their digital future.

Shift-Left Security

The shift-left principle lies at the core of DevSecOps, advocating for the integration of security early and continuously throughout the development lifecycle. By embedding threat detection, static analysis, and policy enforcement in the initial phases of design, coding, and integration, enterprises can drastically reduce the cost, complexity, and risk of post-deployment vulnerabilities. Here are some key actions to follow:

- Embed security gates in every CI/CD stage.
- Automate early feedback loops to accelerate remediation.
- Integrate policy-as-code frameworks to enforce governance from the start.

This paradigm shift not only aligns with agile and continuous delivery models but also enhances organizational resilience against the growing velocity and sophistication of cyber threats.

Automated Security Testing & Code Analysis

Scalability and consistency in modern software delivery require automation. SAST, SCA, DAST, and container scanning must be fully integrated into CI/CD pipelines. Here are some recommended practices:

- Automate scans at every code commit using tools like GitHub Advanced Security.
- Leverage SCA tools to assess third-party libraries and dependencies for Common Vulnerabilities and Exposures (CVE) and licensing risks.
- Ensure security testing is nonblocking yet informative, failing fast only when critical risks are identified.

The goal is not just early detection, but contextual remediation. Developers must receive actionable, just-in-time security feedback without friction to their workflows.

Developer Enablement and Secure Coding Practices

Security must be developer centric. A secure SDLC is only sustainable when developers are empowered with knowledge, tools, and contextual support to write secure code. The following are some strategic initiatives for DevOps teams:

- Implement secure coding guidelines and conduct regular threat-awareness training.
- Integrate security plugins into integrated development environments to offer inline guidance.

- Establish security champions programs within development tribes to create distributed accountability.

By building a culture of shared responsibility and providing developers with the resources they need, enterprises can significantly reduce the prevalence of common vulnerabilities like cross site scripting, injection, or insecure deserialization.

IaC and Policy Enforcement

As cloud-native architectures mature, IaC has become a double-edged sword; it enables rapid provisioning but introduces potential risks if misconfigured. DevSecOps requires rigorous governance over IaC templates, Kubernetes manifests, and Terraform modules. The following are architectural controls as guidance:

- Enforce pre-deployment scanning using tools.
- Integrate policy engines to enforce organizational policies declaratively.
- Apply drift detection tools to ensure runtime environments match intended configurations.

Treating infrastructure as immutable code brings consistency but must be paired with automated guardrails to prevent configuration drift and compliance violations.

Unified DevSecOps Toolchain Integration

Security tools must not exist in silos. Enterprises should aim for a fully integrated DevSecOps ecosystem where visibility, automation, and orchestration span the entire SDLC. Following these best practices is a good start:

- Consolidate tooling into cohesive platforms that integrate with GitOps workflows, CI/CD orchestrators, and container orchestration platforms like Kubernetes.
- Integrate findings into centralized dashboards and SIEM platforms to unify visibility.
- Use correlation and deduplication logic to reduce alert fatigue and prioritize critical findings.

Tool rationalization and orchestration are essential to avoid the chaos of fragmented visibility and inconsistent enforcement.

Threat Modeling and Risk-Based Prioritization

Security must align with business risk and formal threat modeling methodologies enable teams to identify attack vectors early and assess risks based on impact and exploitability. Threat modeling execution strategies such as these are key to reducing development risk:

- Embed threat modeling sessions into agile planning cycles.
- Leverage architectural risk assessments to inform sprint backlogs.
- Adopt risk-scoring frameworks to prioritize remediation, focusing efforts where they yield the most risk reduction.

This ensures that security is not only early and automated, but also intelligent and prioritized.

USE CASE: THREAT MODELING FRAMEWORK IN DEVSECOPS

STRIDE[a]**:** Developed by Microsoft is a widely adopted threat modeling framework that categorizes threats into six types: Spoofing, Tampering, Repudiation, Information Disclosure, Denial of Service, and Elevation of Privilege. It is especially effective during the design phase of development, enabling teams to systematically identify and classify potential threats based on their impact on core security principles such as authentication, integrity, and confidentiality.

Role in DevSecOps	Key Contributions
Proactive threat identification	Categorizes threats into six types: Spoofing, Tampering, Repudiation, Information Disclosure, Denial of Service, Elevation of Privilege. Supports early-stage threat modeling aligned with "Shift Left" principles.
Structured security integration	Uses data flow diagrams to map threats to system components, enabling systematic vulnerability analysis and targeted mitigation.
Team collaboration	Encourages joint threat modeling sessions, enhancing communication between development, operations, and security teams.
Continuous security	Can be embedded into sprints and iterative DevOps cycles for ongoing threat modeling and mitigation.

PASTA[b]**:** Process for Attack Simulation and Threat Analysis (PASTA) is a risk-centric threat modeling framework that aligns technical security measures with business objectives through a comprehensive seven-step process. This includes defining objectives, profiling applications, analyzing threats and vulnerabilities, modeling attacks, and conducting risk analysis. Its strategic and in-depth approach makes it especially well-suited for large organizations that need detailed, lifecycle-integrated threat modeling to support secure software development.

Role in DevSecOps	Key Contributions
Risk-Centric Approach	Focuses on simulating attack scenarios based on business context and aligning security priorities with organizational risk tolerance.
Comprehensive Threat Analysis	Uses a seven-step methodology to deeply analyze threats, attack paths, and impacts, ideal for complex and high-risk systems.
Early Detection and Mitigation	Identifies vulnerabilities and defines security requirements early in the design phase, supporting proactive defense strategies.
Collaboration Across Teams	Promotes engagement between developers, security professionals, architects, and operations to ensure robust and accurate threat modeling.
Integration into CI/CD Pipelines	Enables continuous threat assessment and risk analysis within automated development workflows.

[a] Adam Shostack, *Threat Modeling: Designing for Security*, Wiley, 2014.[b] Tony UcedaVélez and Marco M. Morana, *Risk Centric Threat Modeling: Process for Attack Simulation and Threat Analysis*, Wiley, 2015.Secrets Management and Identity Governance

Hardcoded secrets, Application Programming Interface (API) keys, and ungoverned credentials remain one of the most common causes of breaches. A mature DevSecOps practice mandates robust secrets management so it's important to:

- Use centralized vault solutions to manage and rotate secrets.
- Apply fine-grained access controls using RBAC and ABAC models.
- Enforce MFA and use identity federation to control access across services.

Authentication and authorization should be foundational, not an afterthought, ensuring secure-by-design access control across environments.

Container and Kubernetes Security

Containerized microservices are a cornerstone of modern software delivery, but they also introduce a new attack surface. DevSecOps must extend to container security and Kubernetes runtime protection such as:

- Scan images during build and deploy stages.
- Sign images to enforce integrity.
- Apply Kubernetes security policies and monitor runtime activity.

Secure containerization requires a layered defense approach, from image provenance to runtime anomaly detection.

Observability, Monitoring, and Incident Response

Continuous security requires real-time observability and actionable intelligence. DevSecOps practices must include advanced telemetry and automated response capabilities with a focused implementation on:

- Instrument applications and infrastructure with tools like OpenTelemetry for telemetry.
- Use extended Berkeley Packet Filter (eBPF) based runtime security tools in Linux for low-level behavioral monitoring.
- Build automated incident response playbooks within SOAR platforms to reduce MTTD and MTTR.

Security operations must evolve from reactive to anticipatory, rooted in real-time data and automated workflows.

Compliance Automation and Auditability

Regulatory compliance mandates impose nonnegotiable requirements on enterprise software delivery. DevSecOps must enable and support automated, continuous compliance such as:

- Codify policies and controls using frameworks like Policy as Code (PaC), which is an approach that defines and enforces policies using code.
- Automate evidence collection and audit trail generation.
- Integrate compliance dashboards with Governance, Risk, and Compliance (GRC) platforms to provide real-time assurance to auditors and executives.

Audit readiness should be a natural output of the DevSecOps pipeline, not a retrospective burden.

Security Culture and Executive Alignment

No toolchain or policy can compensate for a poor security culture. Enterprise leadership must lead the support for embedding security into the organization's core culture, positioning it as a strategic enabler, not a barrier through things like:

- Promoting blameless postmortems to encourage transparency and learning.
- Celebrating security wins and gamifying secure coding challenges.
- Include security Key Performance Indicators (KPI) in executive dashboards and team objectives.

A DevSecOps initiative will only succeed when it's championed by executives, understood by developers, and embedded in daily operations.

EMERGING TRENDS IN DEVSECOPS

As organizations accelerate their adoption of DevSecOps, the landscape is undergoing a profound transformation fueled by advances in artificial intelligence, virtualization technologies, and predictive analytics. These emerging capabilities are reshaping how security is embedded into the SDLC, moving from reactive controls to proactive, intelligence-driven safeguards. Enterprise security architects must keep pace with this evolution by evaluating which innovations can be operationalized effectively within their environments without sacrificing trust, control, or compliance.

One notable advancement is fuzz testing at scale, now enhanced through the integration of machine learning algorithms. Traditional fuzzing often relies on brute-force input generation and lacks contextual awareness. Modern intelligent fuzzers, however, can prioritize inputs based on probabilistic models, code coverage metrics, and behavioral learning, allowing security teams to uncover deep logic flaws and edge-case vulnerabilities more efficiently. This capability is particularly useful in validating APIs, parsers, and microservices where traditional static testing methods may fall short.

Another trend gaining momentum is the use of AI-assisted code reviews. Large language models trained on secure coding patterns and historical vulnerability data are now being deployed to augment security analysts and developers alike. These tools can detect semantic issues, risky design decisions, and logic bugs that are often missed by conventional scanners. By integrating AI into code review pipelines, enterprises can significantly enhance their ability to identify vulnerabilities earlier and at a lower cost without overburdening developers or slowing release cycles.

Further strengthening this proactive testing posture is the emergence of stateful testing and replay systems, powered by advanced kernel instrumentation and system call tracing. These technologies allow teams to capture runtime behavior, rewind execution, and analyze interactions between applications and operating systems with precision. Such capabilities are essential for root-cause analysis in complex, distributed systems where transient failures or race conditions may otherwise be untraceable. They also offer new opportunities for security researchers to simulate exploit scenarios and test resiliency against sophisticated threat models.

Finally, predictive vulnerability detection is ushering in a new era of anticipatory security. By training machine learning models on vast repositories of source code and vulnerability databases, these tools can forecast potential weak points in new code, even before formal testing begins. This predictive insight enables teams to make design adjustments early in development, reducing downstream rework and improving overall security posture. However, while these innovations offer significant efficiency gains, they are not a silver bullet. Automation and AI must be treated as force multipliers, not replacements for human expertise. The strategic oversight of experienced security professionals remains indispensable to ensuring that these technologies are applied judiciously and that their outputs are validated in context.

CONCLUSION AND RECAP

From this chapter, it's clear that DevSecOps is not an aspirational concept reserved for technology-forward organizations, it is a business-critical necessity in the modern enterprise. The fusion of software development, IT operations, and security into a cohesive delivery pipeline is no longer optional. In a world where software defines operational value, customer engagement, and strategic agility, embedding security into the software lifecycle is the only path to sustainable innovation.

Traditional models that isolate security as a final step or treat it as a gating mechanism are incompatible with the speed and complexity of modern development practices. DevSecOps offers a new paradigm, one that integrates security principles from the earliest stages of software design and sustains them throughout the build, deployment, and operational lifecycle. This model does not slow down innovation; rather, it supports innovation by ensuring the outcomes are trustworthy, resilient, and compliant from inception to operation.

The early sections of this chapter emphasized the evolving role of software within government, industry, and critical infrastructure. Software has become more than just a support tool, it is the backbone of digital strategy, economic competitiveness, and service delivery. In this context, security cannot be peripheral. It must be engineered into systems from the ground up. DevSecOps enables that level of integration, fostering a software development culture that sees risk as something to address continuously and programmatically.

Adopting DevSecOps requires more than just new tools or testing protocols. It demands a fundamental rethinking of how teams collaborate. Security, development, and operations cannot remain siloed disciplines; they must converge around shared goals, common platforms, and aligned incentives. This cultural shift is critical. When security becomes everyone's responsibility, it transitions from a bottleneck to a force multiplier, accelerating delivery while strengthening assurance.

In this chapter we explored the distinction between DevOps and DevSecOps in depth. DevOps gave organizations the blueprint for agile, high-velocity delivery, but often lacked embedded mechanisms to govern security at speed. DevSecOps takes that blueprint and reinforces it with architectural rigor, governance enforcement, and risk-aware engineering. The result is not only a faster pipeline, but a safer and more resilient one.

We discussed how security by design is not merely a best practice, it's a strategic requirement. Vulnerabilities introduced during planning and coding are significantly harder and more expensive to address later in the lifecycle. By embedding threat modeling, secure coding patterns, and architectural validation early, enterprises reduce exposure and increase system integrity. This is essential in a world where adversaries are exploiting weaknesses in the software supply chain with increasing sophistication.

The role of automation was examined as a core enabler of scale and consistency. Static and dynamic testing, IaC validation, and continuous compliance mechanisms all contribute to the repeatable enforcement of security policy without manual intervention. Yet automation alone is not enough. These systems must be context-aware and integrated into developer workflows to be truly effective. Otherwise, they risk becoming noise generators or operational dead weight.

Developer enablement emerged as a recurring theme. Secure development cannot succeed unless developers are empowered to make informed, secure decisions in real time. This includes integrating security feedback into integrated development environments, establishing security champions within teams, and offering practical training on real-world threat scenarios. When developers are treated as partners in security and not adversaries, organizations build stronger systems and more resilient teams.

As enterprises shift toward programmable infrastructure and containerized deployments, the need to secure IaC becomes paramount. Misconfigurations, privilege escalation paths, and shadow infrastructure can propagate rapidly in cloud-native environments. We discussed how declarative policy frameworks, continuous scanning, and configuration drift detection can provide guardrails that reduce risk without slowing down provisioning.

Security toolchain fragmentation was identified as a systemic challenge. Without integration, even the most capable tools become operational liabilities. A unified approach to DevSecOps requires tight integration across code repositories, CI/CD orchestrators, orchestration platforms, telemetry feeds, and compliance systems. When these tools work together, they produce not just data, but actionable insight and operational coherence.

The maturation of observability and monitoring was highlighted as a critical milestone in the DevSecOps journey. Real-time telemetry, runtime behavioral analysis, and automated incident response workflows are transforming security operations from reactive responders to proactive defenders. These capabilities reduce MTTD and respond, ensuring that enterprises are not just catching threats, they are staying ahead of them.

Compliance, long viewed as a constraint on innovation, is evolving into a continuous assurance model. When policies are codified and audit trails are automated, compliance becomes a natural byproduct of secure engineering. This shift reduces overhead while increasing visibility and transparency, positioning organizations to meet regulatory demands with confidence and agility.

Security culture, more than any individual control or capability, was shown to be the most important determinant of DevSecOps success. Technology alone cannot solve systemic challenges. Leadership engagement, team alignment, and a culture that rewards secure behavior are necessary to sustain long-term transformation. Without cultural reinforcement, even the most elegant architectures will fail under pressure.

Emerging technologies are poised to take DevSecOps to the next level. From AI-assisted code analysis to intelligent fuzzing, from replayable system state testing to predictive vulnerability modeling, the future of secure development is increasingly data-driven and adaptive. These technologies will help teams find previously hidden flaws and act preemptively. However, their successful application requires governance, validation, and ethical oversight.

The DevSecOps model represents the convergence of innovation, speed, and trust. It is a model that recognizes that secure software delivery is not an obstacle to business, it is the foundation of digital success. As security architects, our mission is to ensure that this convergence is deliberate, robust, and future-proofed, supporting not just the needs of today's systems, but the evolving demands of tomorrow's enterprise.

NOTES

1 Atlassian. n.d. *DevOps Best Practices.* Accessed June 16, 2025. www.atlassian.com/devops/what-is-devops/devops-best-practices.

2 Beck, Kent, Mike Beedle, Arie van Bennekum, Alistair Cockburn, Ward Cunningham, Martin Fowler, et al. *Manifesto for Agile Software Development.* 2001. https://agilemanifesto.org.

3 Patrick Debois, "DevOps Days Ghent 2009," *DevOpsDays*, 2009. https://devopsdays.org/events/2009-ghent/.

11 IT Operations, Cybersecurity and Governance, Risk, and Compliance

LEARNING OBJECTIVES

- Understand how aligning IT and Cybersecurity improves GRC maturity, enabling better risk management, governance, and compliance
- Discover the cultural and organizational silos which must be broken down to achieve effective alignment, requiring unified leadership and collaboration
- Learn that shared visibility, unified metrics, and automation are essential for streamlining governance and enabling continuous compliance
- Understand how measuring business outcomes like reduced risk and improved audit performance helps demonstrate the value of alignment and secure executive buy-in

The convergence of IT Operations and Cybersecurity is not merely a tactical necessity but a strategic imperative for organizations seeking to mature their Governance, Risk, and Compliance (GRC) posture. The integration of these disciplines forms the backbone of a resilient enterprise security architecture, one that aligns operational efficiency with robust risk management and regulatory accountability.

From a governance perspective, this integration brings structure, transparency, and accountability to how technology and security decisions are made and executed. When IT and security operate in alignment, governance bodies, such as executive leadership, risk committees, and boards of directors, gain clearer visibility into enterprise risk exposure, security controls, and operational dependencies. This facilitates informed decision-making, drives consistency in policy enforcement, and embeds security into the organization's strategic roadmap. Moreover, aligning IT Operations and Cybersecurity fosters unified reporting, metrics standardization, and executive dashboards that enable proactive oversight and governance at scale.

In the realm of risk management, a tightly coupled IT Operations and Cybersecurity ecosystem enables the organization to shift from reactive firefighting to proactive risk mitigation. Integrated processes allow for real-time threat intelligence sharing, unified incident response frameworks, and coordinated Business Continuity and Disaster Recovery (BC/DR) planning. This ensures that operational disruptions and security incidents are addressed holistically, minimizing downtime and reputational damage. Risk-based prioritization, anchored in business context, enables IT and security teams to collaboratively identify, assess, and safeguard mission-critical systems and data assets. Additionally, the adoption of automation, AI-driven threat detection, and adaptive response mechanisms further enhances the organization's ability to withstand and recover from sophisticated cyber threats.

From a compliance standpoint, the fusion of IT Operations and Cybersecurity creates an environment where regulatory requirements are operationalized through embedded controls, continuous

DOI: 10.1201/9781003562153-14

monitoring, and automated policy enforcement. Rather than treating compliance as a checkbox exercise, organizations can operationalize frameworks within day-to-day workflows, ensuring audit readiness and minimizing the risk of noncompliance. Centralized control repositories, evidence collection pipelines, and integrated GRC platforms allow for streamlined audits, enhanced traceability, and accelerated remediation of gaps. This proactive posture not only reduces the likelihood of fines and reputational harm, but also demonstrates to regulators, partners, and customers a steadfast commitment to secure and ethical operations.

Ultimately, the strategic integration of IT Operations and Cybersecurity within the GRC framework enables organizations to achieve secure digital transformation with confidence. It ensures that security is not an afterthought, but an embedded, measurable, and continually evolving component of IT governance. By harmonizing these functions, enterprises can enhance operational resilience, ensure regulatory alignment, and elevate their risk posture, creating a defensible and adaptive architecture capable of thriving in an increasingly complex threat and compliance landscape. However, there are many challenges to achieving this convergence. In this chapter we will highlight the many GRC obstacles the IT Operations and Cybersecurity face.

WHAT IS GRC

GRC is a foundational discipline that brings cohesion to how organizations manage their strategic objectives, operational risks, and regulatory responsibilities. It is not a tool or a single process, but an integrated approach that connects executive oversight with frontline execution. In a complex digital ecosystem, GRC serves as the backbone of responsible and secure enterprise operation.

Governance defines the decision-making structure within an organization. It sets the tone from the top by establishing policies, assigning accountability, and enabling transparent oversight. Strong governance ensures that security and IT operations are not operating in silos but are aligned with corporate values, business goals, and ethical expectations. It also provides the framework by which roles, responsibilities, and escalation paths are clearly defined across technical and nontechnical domains.

Risk management is the engine that drives informed decision-making. It focuses on identifying threats, assessing vulnerabilities, estimating impact, and prioritizing mitigation efforts based on business context. In the digital age, risk is fluid, it extends beyond cyber incidents to include third-party failures, regulatory shifts, and supply chain disruptions. The ability to continuously monitor and adapt to this evolving threat landscape is a hallmark of mature enterprise security architecture.

Compliance, meanwhile, is the mechanism through which organizations ensure they meet the legal, regulatory, and contractual obligations imposed on them. These may include industry-specific mandates such as Health Insurance Portability and Accountability Act (HIPAA), or General Data Protection Regulation (GDPR), as well as broader frameworks like ISO 27001 or NIST CSF. Compliance is a demonstration of operational discipline and accountability and not merely a checkbox to satisfy basic audit controls. It also builds trust with customers, partners, and regulators.

The true power of GRC lies in its integration. When GRC are approached as interconnected disciplines rather than isolated functions, organizations can break down silos and align around a common understanding of priorities, threats, and responsibilities. This synergy allows for faster decision-making, more efficient resource allocation, and a consistent approach to security and control implementation.

From the perspective of an enterprise security architect, GRC provides the structural integrity that allows security programs to scale. It translates abstract policies into operational requirements and embeds controls directly into IT workflows. Whether it's defining security requirements for a new application, assessing third-party risks, or responding to a regulatory inquiry, GRC ensures that these activities are coordinated, repeatable, and measurable.

Modern organizations rely on GRC platforms to orchestrate this complexity. These systems aggregate data from across the enterprise from ticketing systems, asset inventories, vulnerability scanners, and cloud configurations in order to provide real-time insight into risk posture and compliance status. Automation plays a critical role here, enabling continuous control validation, automated evidence collection, and real-time alerts when deviations from policy occur. However, tools alone are not enough. Effective GRC is rooted in culture. It requires cross-functional collaboration and leadership buy-in. Governance must be lived, not just documented. Risk awareness must permeate daily operations, and compliance must be seen as a shared responsibility rather than a burdensome obligation. Without cultural alignment, even the most sophisticated GRC strategies will falter.

Metrics bring clarity to GRC execution. Without measurement, governance becomes aspirational, risk becomes subjective, and compliance becomes reactive. By tracking metrics such as risk remediation timelines, policy adherence rates, control effectiveness, and audit outcomes, organizations can identify gaps, optimize processes, and communicate progress to stakeholders in meaningful terms.

Ultimately, GRC enables organizations to operate with confidence in an unpredictable environment. It provides the scaffolding for secure innovation, resilient operations, and sustained regulatory alignment. In a world where digital velocity often outpaces control, GRC is the architectural discipline that allows organizations to move fast—without losing sight of trust, accountability, and security.

Component	**Definition**	**Purpose**	**Key Elements**
Governance	The set of rules, policies, and processes that guide an organization's operations to achieve its objectives ethically and effectively.	Ensures accountability, ethical behavior, and alignment of organizational activities with strategic goals.	– Ethical management – Transparent decision-making – Clear roles and responsibilities – Resource management.
Risk	The process of identifying, assessing, and managing potential threats to an organization's operations or objectives.	Minimizes adverse effects of risks while enabling informed decision-making and resilience against uncertainties.	– Risk identification – Risk assessment (likelihood and impact) – Risk mitigation strategies – Continuous monitoring.
Compliance	Adherence to laws, regulations, standards, and internal policies applicable to the organization's operations.	Ensures legal and regulatory adherence to avoid penalties, protect reputation, and build trust with stakeholders.	– Regulatory compliance – Internal policy adherence – Monitoring and reporting compliance status – Alignment with standards like GDPR or HIPAA.
Integrated GRC	A unified approach combining governance, risk management, and compliance to enhance efficiency, reduce redundancies, and align organizational objectives with ethical practices.	Promotes principled performance by addressing uncertainty, achieving objectives reliably, and acting with integrity.	– Centralized processes – Cross-functional collaboration – Use of GRC tools for automation and efficiency – Continuous improvement through monitoring and feedback loops.

CHALLENGES IN ALIGNING IT OPERATIONS AND CYBERSECURITY WITH GRC

Aligning IT Operations and Cybersecurity under a unified governance model is essential for organizations seeking to manage risk, ensure compliance, and maintain operational resilience in an increasingly complex digital environment. While the value of integration is well understood, enhancing transparency, consistency, and accountability, the path to achieving it is fraught with practical and organizational challenges. These range from cultural resistance and siloed tools to conflicting objectives and fragmented data flows. As enterprise environments evolve toward hybrid infrastructures, agile development, and regulatory scrutiny, bridging the gap between IT Operations and Cybersecurity becomes both more urgent and more difficult. The following sections explore the key challenges enterprises face in aligning these critical functions to support effective governance.

Fragmented Objectives between Functions

One of the core challenges in aligning IT Operations and Cybersecurity for governance lies in the divergence of objectives. IT operations are typically measured by performance, availability, and uptime, goals that prioritize speed, efficiency, and service continuity. In contrast, cybersecurity focuses on confidentiality, integrity, and risk reduction. These different lenses can create friction. For example, a security team may recommend strict access controls or downtime for patching, which the IT team might view as disruptive. Without a shared set of priorities and integrated governance oversight, these misalignments can manifest as operational inefficiencies or even policy violations.

Disjointed Organizational Structures

In many enterprises, IT and security teams report to different executives, reinforcing siloed decision-making. IT may report to a CIO focused on digital transformation and cost optimization, while security reports to a CISO with a mandate to reduce cyber risk. The lack of a unified leadership chain complicates the development of cohesive policies. It also dilutes accountability for governance outcomes. When escalation paths are unclear and cross-functional governance is weak, initiatives stall. Worse, gaps emerge in coverage, especially where responsibilities overlap or fall between departments.

Inconsistent Policy Enforcement

Even when governance frameworks exist, inconsistent enforcement across IT and cybersecurity domains undermines effectiveness. IT operations might implement automated workflows that bypass critical security checks. Conversely, security teams may deploy controls that inadvertently affect IT services without adequate change management. This results in fragmented policy adherence. Governance thrives on predictability and standardization, two qualities that suffer when enforcement varies by team, tool, or process. The challenge is not only technical but cultural; aligning both functions requires a shared commitment to unified policy execution.

Visibility Gaps and Data Silos

Governance depends on accurate, real-time visibility into systems, risks, and performance. Yet, IT and security often operate with different telemetry, tools, and data models. IT teams may focus on system logs, performance dashboards, and incident tickets, while security operates in the realm of Security Information and Event Management (SIEM), threat intelligence feeds, and compliance checklists. The result? Blind spots. When data is siloed, governance bodies lack a single source of truth. Decision-makers are forced to rely on incomplete or conflicting reports, which erodes confidence in oversight mechanisms and leads to suboptimal risk posture.

Tool and Platform Fragmentation

Modern enterprises rely on a sprawling ecosystem of tools across both IT operations and security domains. Configuration Management Databases (CMDB), IT Service Management (ITSM) platforms, monitoring suites, SIEMs, vulnerability scanners, the list is extensive. Unfortunately, these tools often lack integration. This leads to duplicated effort, disconnected workflows, and governance drift. Tool fragmentation complicates the implementation of cross-functional controls such as incident response, configuration management, and change tracking. Governance frameworks like COBIT and NIST expect integrated control environments but achieving that integration across a fractured tool landscape remains an operational and architectural hurdle.

Cultural Resistance and Legacy Mindsets

Culture is often the most stubborn barrier to alignment. IT teams accustomed to prioritizing uptime may view security requirements as unnecessary friction. Conversely, security teams may harbor distrust toward operations for pushing rapid changes without sufficient testing. This tension is exacerbated in organizations with legacy infrastructure or entrenched silos. Change can feel threatening. Governance initiatives that aim to unify IT and security efforts may be met with passive resistance or slow adoption. Without cultural alignment, governance is reduced to documentation rather than practice.

Ambiguous Metrics and Key Performance Indicators (KPIs)

Governance thrives on measurement, but aligning metrics between IT Operations and Cybersecurity is challenging. IT may track mean time to resolution (MTTR), system uptime, or ticket closure rates. Security may report on vulnerabilities, policy violations, or threat indicators. These metrics speak different languages. For governance to be meaningful, organizations must establish shared KPIs that reflect both performance and protection. Creating these unified metrics requires effort such as defining risk tolerance thresholds, mapping controls to business outcomes, and ensuring that reporting systems are aligned across functions.

Regulatory Complexity and Overlap

Modern governance is deeply influenced by external compliance mandates such as HIPAA, GDPR, and others. These frameworks impose requirements that touch both IT Operations and Cybersecurity. However, without clear ownership and alignment, responsibilities may be duplicated or neglected. For example, a compliance control around data encryption may be enforced by IT through storage configurations and by security through Data Loss Prevention (DLP) tools, leading to confusion or redundant audits. Governance programs must address this complexity by defining roles, avoiding overlap, and ensuring that compliance activities are orchestrated rather than fragmented.

Lack of Adaptive Governance Models

Static governance models are ill-suited for today's dynamic IT environments. With the adoption of cloud services, containerization, and infrastructure-as-code, both IT and security functions must adapt to continuous change. Traditional governance structures, based on periodic audits and fixed control sets, struggle to keep up. Aligning IT Operations and Cybersecurity requires a governance model that is adaptive, risk-aware, and embedded into agile workflows. Unfortunately, many organizations still rely on outdated GRC tools and models that do not reflect the speed or complexity of modern digital operations.

Absence of a Unified Strategic Vision

Perhaps the most critical challenge is the lack of a unified strategic vision that encompasses both IT Operations and Cybersecurity within the governance framework. Too often, governance is seen as a compliance obligation rather than a driver of resilience and trust. Without executive sponsorship and strategic alignment, integration efforts remain tactical and short-lived. Enterprise security architects must work with CIOs, CISOs, and governance leaders to craft a shared vision, one that positions governance not as a constraint, but as an enabler of secure, efficient, and compliant operations across the enterprise.

Challenges and Negative Impacts for GRC

The challenges of aligning IT Operations and Cybersecurity within a GRC framework are significant but cannot be ignored. Siloed operations, evolving threats, regulatory complexities, resource constraints, integration issues, and misaligned priorities collectively create vulnerabilities that increase security breaches, compliance failures, inefficiencies, reputational damage, and stifled growth. Addressing these challenges requires a unified approach that integrates risk management across all functions while balancing operational efficiency with robust security practices.

Challenges	**Description**
Siloed operations	IT, cybersecurity, and compliance teams often operate in isolation, using separate tools and processes. This lack of integration leads to fragmented risk management efforts and inconsistent compliance practices.
Evolving cyber threats	Cybercriminals increasingly use advanced technologies like AI to exploit vulnerabilities. Organizations struggle to keep pace with these sophisticated threats, leaving critical gaps in their defenses.
Fragmented regulatory landscape	The proliferation of overlapping and inconsistent regulations creates compliance bottlenecks. Organizations must navigate multiple reporting requirements for a single incident, leading to delays and errors.
Resource constraints	Limited budgets and staffing shortages hinder the ability to implement robust GRC programs. Organizations often misallocate resources by focusing on less critical vulnerabilities while neglecting high-risk areas.
Integration issues	Disparate GRC tools make it difficult to centralize data management and reporting. This fragmentation prevents organizations from gaining a holistic view of their risk profile, leading to missed vulnerabilities and compliance gaps.
Misaligned priorities	IT operations prioritize system performance and uptime, while cybersecurity focuses on threat mitigation. This misalignment results in conflicting objectives that delay decision-making and impede business agility.
Negative impacts	Description
Increased security breaches	Organizations with siloed or ad-hoc risk management approaches are significantly more likely to experience breaches. A lack of coordination between IT Operations and Cybersecurity increases exposure to threats like ransomware attacks and data theft.
Compliance failures	Misaligned GRC efforts lead to noncompliance with regulatory requirements such as GDPR or PCI DSS, resulting in penalties, legal actions, and reputational harm.
Operational inefficiencies	Fragmented tools and manual processes waste resources and slow down response times during incidents or audits. For example, organizations spend an average of one-third of their time on repetitive administrative tasks due to siloed systems.

Challenges	Description
Reputational damage	High-profile breaches or regulatory violations erode customer trust. Mismanagement of sensitive data can lead to long-term damage to brand reputation, especially if customers perceive the organization as failing to safeguard their information adequately.
Delayed business growth	Misaligned cybersecurity strategies can hinder innovation by imposing overly restrictive measures that conflict with business goals. This can delay product launches or technological rollouts, reducing competitiveness in the market.

OPPORTUNITIES RESULTING FROM GRC ALIGNMENT

The strategic alignment of IT Operations and Cybersecurity within a GRC framework unlocks transformative value across the enterprise. When these functions operate in unison, organizations gain the ability to manage risk holistically, embed governance into daily operations, and foster a security-first culture that supports business objectives rather than impeding them. This integration strengthens enterprise resilience, increases agility, and ensures regulatory confidence across increasingly complex digital ecosystems.

One of the most immediate benefits is the harmonization of operational and security objectives. IT operations drive service availability and efficiency, while cybersecurity ensures those services remain protected. When aligned, these functions can co-engineer secure solutions from the outset. Security no longer feels like a constraint; rather, it becomes a proactive design principle. This integration supports faster innovation cycles while ensuring systems are resilient and compliant by default.

Shared visibility is another major gain. Unifying telemetry across IT and security platforms enables real-time monitoring of system health, performance, and threat activity. Centralized dashboards provide leadership with a single source of truth. This clarity improves situational awareness and shortens decision cycles, empowering teams to detect issues early and respond with precision. Unified observability bridges gaps that traditionally allowed risks to go unnoticed.

Clear governance structures emerge naturally through this alignment. When IT and security teams operate under shared governance models, accountability is well defined. Ownership of controls, policies, and processes becomes transparent. This clarity reduces delays in issue remediation, accelerates project delivery timelines, and ensures that security policies are consistently enforced across the IT landscape. It also fosters trust between teams and promotes responsible risk-taking in support of innovation.

The integration also enables intelligent automation. By embedding security controls into IT workflows organizations can automate policy enforcement and reduce manual overhead. Infrastructure-as-code policies, automated patch deployment, and continuous compliance scans improve efficiency while ensuring consistent adherence to regulatory and internal standards. This enhances scalability and supports lean operations.

Risk management improves exponentially when IT and cybersecurity collaborate. IT provides critical insights into system interdependencies, service availability, and operational impact. Security contributes threat intelligence, vulnerability data, and risk analytics. When combined, these insights enable targeted risk mitigation strategies focused on the systems and assets that matter most. This risk-based approach optimizes resource allocation and minimizes business exposure.

A major positive impact is the acceleration of BC/DR planning. With aligned playbooks, integrated incident response procedures, and shared tooling, organizations can detect, contain, and recover from disruptions much faster. Whether facing a cyber incident or infrastructure failure, the enterprise benefits from cohesive response efforts that minimize downtime and protect critical services. Business continuity becomes a built-in function, not a separate effort.

Regulatory compliance is streamlined. When controls are embedded across IT and security processes, compliance becomes continuous and demonstrable. Audit evidence is generated automatically, policies are consistently enforced, and exceptions are tracked in real time. This reduces the burden of audit preparation and accelerates response to regulatory inquiries. Organizations can confidently meet evolving requirements from frameworks and others with minimal disruption.

This convergence also boosts stakeholder confidence. Executives, boards, and regulators gain clearer insight into how operational risk is managed and how compliance is maintained. Instead of receiving siloed metrics, they are presented with integrated risk narratives that tie business priorities to control performance. This transparency fosters credibility and strengthens trust while demonstrating a mature, defensible security posture.

Another powerful benefit is cultural transformation. As IT and security teams engage in joint planning, cross-functional problem-solving, and shared accountability, a collaborative culture emerges. Silos are replaced with partnerships. Shared wins, whether meeting uptime targets or passing audits, build mutual respect and alignment. This cultural shift is foundational to sustaining GRC success and fostering innovation in a secure environment. Moreover, organizations gain agility in adapting to the evolving threat and regulatory landscape. Integrated governance models and shared risk intelligence allow businesses to pivot quickly when new threats or compliance requirements arise. Whether it's responding to a zero-day exploit or adapting to new privacy legislation, the enterprise is better positioned to respond with speed and strategic clarity.

Ultimately, aligning IT Operations and Cybersecurity under a unified GRC framework delivers more than just technical efficiency, it delivers strategic advantage. Organizations become more resilient, audit-ready, and innovation-capable. Security is a value enabler and not just a control layer. This alignment turns risk into a managed function, compliance into a continuous process, and operations into a secure, agile foundation for future growth.

MEASURING THE GRC IMPACT OF ALIGNMENT

Evaluating the alignment of IT Operations and Cybersecurity within the GRC framework demands a mature, metrics-driven approach. This evaluation must span beyond technical outputs and address the strategic effectiveness of risk mitigation, regulatory adherence, and governance maturity. Both quantitative indicators and qualitative insights play critical roles in capturing the full scope of impact. For enterprise leaders, the ability to measure and communicate the tangible outcomes of IT–security alignment becomes essential for driving continuous improvement, securing executive sponsorship, and justifying investments.

Enhancing Strategic Oversight and Policy Integration

Governance efficacy is best assessed by the level of executive awareness and strategic oversight that cybersecurity and IT risks receive. Metrics such as the frequency and quality of board-level risk briefings, the use of integrated IT–security dashboards, and the consistency of reporting cadence reveal how visible and actionable cyber and operational risks are to leadership. If risk reports are buried under layers of technical jargon or presented infrequently, governance suffers.

Equally important is policy adherence across business units. Measuring compliance with IT-security policies, such as access control standards, change management procedures, and secure development protocols, helps quantify whether governance mandates are enforced operationally. Cross-functional collaboration audits, governance maturity assessments, and structured interviews can identify gaps between policy and execution. Strong alignment often manifests in fewer policy exceptions, clearer escalation protocols, and more efficient decision-making cycles.

Quantifying Threat Mitigation and Operational Resilience

Risk is dynamic. As such, any assessment of alignment must include real-time, risk-centric performance metrics that reflect the organization's ability to detect, contain, and respond to threats. Core indicators such as Mean Time to Detect (MTTD) and MTTR provide insight into how well IT and security teams are working together. Improvements in these areas often signify greater threat intelligence integration, clearer incident escalation paths, and more efficient response coordination.

Organizations should also monitor the volume and severity of incidents over time, especially before and after alignment initiatives. Reductions in breach impact, containment delays, or system downtime indicate risk posture improvements. Further, evaluating business continuity metrics such as Recovery Time Objectives and Recovery Point Objectives reveals how well aligned teams can ensure operational resilience in the face of disruptions. A drop in downtime or faster service restoration is a direct indicator of alignment efficacy.

Validating Regulatory Readiness and Control Effectiveness

Compliance metrics offer a structured lens through which alignment can be evaluated. Organizations must track audit outcomes, pass rates, and regulatory issue remediation times across relevant frameworks. An upward trend in successful audits and a downward trend in corrective actions required reflect improved alignment between IT workflows and security controls. Furthermore, automation maturity in compliance enforcement should be assessed. Are configuration management and security monitoring tools integrated to automatically enforce compliance baselines? Metrics such as automated policy enforcement coverage, compliance deviation detection rates, and response time to violations help determine if alignment is producing operationalized compliance. Over time, reduced manual oversight, fewer policy breaches, and faster remediation windows demonstrate a resilient, compliant control environment.

Optimizing Resources and Reducing Redundancy

Alignment should also drive efficiency gains and cost rationalization. One key performance indicator is the elimination of redundant tools and duplicated processes between IT and security. Consolidating endpoint agents, reducing alert fatigue, and unifying service management platforms can generate measurable savings and simplify operations. Evaluating the speed and security of system deployments also reveals the effectiveness of collaboration. Are changes being pushed to production faster without increasing risk? Is security validation embedded in deployment pipelines? Improvements in deployment velocity, change failure rates, and rollback frequencies serve as tangible indicators of streamlined operations. Efficient alignment is further evidenced by faster ticket resolution times, especially where operational and security teams must jointly triage and remediate incidents.

Strengthening Resilience and Stakeholder Confidence

Metrics must extend beyond internal efficiencies to measure the external impact of IT–security alignment on customer trust, brand reputation, and business continuity. Organizations can leverage stakeholder sentiment surveys, customer trust indexes, and incident impact analyses to measure how alignment influences business perception and performance. From a financial perspective, organizations should track cost avoidance associated with breach prevention, reduced regulatory penalties, and minimized downtime. Calculating the Return on Investment (ROI) of security investments based on reduced risk exposure and improved operational continuity helps reinforce the business value of alignment. In some cases, favorable cyber insurance premiums may reflect the insurer's recognition of reduced organizational risk, further quantifying the financial impact of alignment.

Embedding Shared Metrics and Ownership

For alignment to take root, performance measurement must reflect shared accountability. Establishing joint KPIs for IT and cybersecurity teams, such as joint incident resolution Service-Level Agreements (SLAs), compliance health scores, and shared availability metrics, ensures alignment is operationalized and owned by all parties. Misaligned KPIs can result in fragmented execution even when governance intentions are sound. Leadership must embed these shared metrics into performance reviews, project evaluations, and strategic scorecards, reinforcing that GRC alignment is a cross-functional mandate, not a siloed initiative. Over time, these integrated metrics help break down organizational barriers and drive a culture of cooperation around shared risk objectives.

Adapting to an Evolving Threat and Regulatory Landscape

The threat landscape does not remain static, nor should GRC measurement practices. Organizations must adopt a continuous monitoring strategy that includes real-time dashboards, automated compliance alerts, and evolving threat intelligence feeds. These enable leadership to make informed, timely decisions and respond proactively to emerging risks. Periodic metric reviews should inform strategic adjustments to controls, processes, and governance structures. Lagging indicators and leading indicators must be evaluated in tandem to identify trends, bottlenecks, and areas for improvement. A resilient organization uses these insights to recalibrate alignment strategies before small misalignments turn into systemic vulnerabilities.

Mapping Progression and Benchmarking Outcomes

To ensure ongoing improvement, organizations should integrate GRC impact measurements into a maturity model. This model should map progress across dimensions such as visibility, integration, automation, and risk responsiveness. Using established frameworks, like NIST Tiers, CMMI, COBIT maturity levels, or custom models, enables teams to benchmark progress over time and against peers in the industry. Maturity assessments help identify strategic gaps, such as low integration between ITSM and security tools, underutilized GRC platforms, or ineffective incident collaboration. They also support targeted investments, focusing budget and resources on the capabilities that will yield the highest improvement in alignment and risk posture.

Aligning Metrics to Business Objectives

Ultimately, GRC impact metrics must align with broader business objectives such as digital transformation, market expansion, or merger and acquisition readiness. The goal is not just secure operations but secure, agile business enablement. By demonstrating how alignment improves scalability, accelerates innovation, and safeguards brand value, enterprise security leaders can elevate cybersecurity and IT operations from tactical functions to strategic enablers. This requires telling a clear, metrics-backed story that connects alignment efforts with reduced risk exposure, stronger compliance posture, and improved operational efficiency. When IT Operations and Cybersecurity are measured not just on what they do but on how they contribute to enterprise outcomes, alignment becomes a boardroom imperative and not just a backend initiative.

USE CASE: ALIGNING IT–CYBERSECURITY GRC IN FINANCIAL SERVICES

Scenario

A multinational bank faces increasing cyber threats and regulatory scrutiny. Its IT and cybersecurity teams operate in silos, leading to inefficiencies in risk reporting and delayed compliance audits. The organization aims to integrate GRC metrics into its operations to improve decision-making and demonstrate ROI.

Key Objectives

- Governance alignment: Establish unified policies for IT and cybersecurity risk oversight.
- Risk reduction: Quantify cyber risk exposure and prioritize mitigation efforts.
- Compliance efficiency: Streamline adherence to regulations like GDPR.
- Strategic reporting: Provide actionable insights to the board and stakeholders.

Implementation Steps

1. Cross-functional collaboration
   - Form a GRC committee with IT, cybersecurity, legal, and compliance leaders to define shared objectives.
   - Conduct workshops to map IT infrastructure risks to compliance requirements.
2. Adopt a GRC–Cybersecurity framework
   - Track risk exposure rate: Monitor unpatched vulnerabilities in critical systems.
   - Track control effectiveness: Measure the percentage of security controls operating as intended.
   - Track incident response time: Track mean-time-to-detect and respond to breaches.
3. Continuous monitoring and reporting
   - Compliance audit success rate: Percentage of audits passed without findings.
   - Third-party risk exposure: Vendor risk ratings and mitigation progress.
   - Report quarterly to the board using Key Risk Indicators (KRIs) and KPIs.

Conclusion

Integrating GRC metrics into IT and cybersecurity operations enables organizations to quantify risks, streamline compliance, and align cyber initiatives with business goals. This use case highlights how cross-departmental collaboration, automated reporting, and financial risk quantification transform GRC from a cost center to a strategic asset.

CONCLUSION AND RECAP

The convergence of IT Operations and Cybersecurity within the GRC ecosystem is no longer a theoretical ideal, it is a foundational necessity. As enterprises face escalating cyber threats, tightening regulatory scrutiny, and rising expectations for operational resilience, the strategic alignment of these functions becomes a critical differentiator. This chapter has explored the structural, operational, and cultural dimensions that shape both the challenges and the significant benefits of such alignment.

We began by recognizing that this integration redefines governance itself. No longer confined to policy enforcement or audit preparation, modern GRC becomes a dynamic control plane for risk-informed decision-making. By aligning IT and cybersecurity strategies, governance gains clarity, accountability, and executive visibility. Risk oversight evolves from static reporting to real-time operational intelligence, enabling leadership to act decisively and confidently in the face of complexity.

In the risk management domain, alignment transforms fragmented efforts into unified resilience. Shared telemetry, integrated threat response, and coordinated business continuity planning all contribute to a proactive security posture. This shift enables organizations to anticipate, mitigate, and recover from disruption with speed and precision. Crucially, it ensures that risk prioritization is based not just on technical vulnerability, but on business impact and operational criticality.

From a compliance perspective, the benefits are equally pronounced. Embedding controls into both IT workflows and security policies automates compliance and reduces manual overhead. The alignment simplifies audits, accelerates remediation, and provides ongoing assurance to regulators, partners, and customers. Organizations can confidently demonstrate compliance posture through continuous evidence collection, policy enforcement, and control effectiveness metrics. While there may be potential benefits, this chapter highlighted the practical obstacles that must be addressed to realize this vision. Divergent objectives between IT and cybersecurity teams often lead to misaligned priorities. Performance-driven metrics in IT can clash with risk-averse security controls. Without shared KPIs and unified leadership, these tensions become structural barriers to governance effectiveness. Successful alignment requires that both functions operate under a common set of objectives linked to enterprise risk and performance outcomes.

Organizational structures further complicate the picture. Separate reporting chains, siloed tools, and inconsistent data flows undermine visibility and create confusion around accountability. Without integration, governance efforts remain fragmented and reactive. We discussed how tool and telemetry fragmentation erodes the ability to create unified risk narratives or respond cohesively to incidents. To overcome this, enterprises must rationalize tools, normalize data, and adopt shared operational platforms.

Cultural transformation emerged as one of the most critical enablers of alignment. Trust, collaboration, and shared ownership are required to replace legacy mindsets and institutional inertia. Change does not happen through policy alone, it requires deliberate leadership, joint planning sessions, cross-functional incentives, and a unified narrative around shared goals. Culture is the operating system of transformation, and without it, alignment efforts will stall regardless of tooling or process maturity.

The chapter also examined how adaptive governance models are essential for alignment at scale. Legacy governance constructs that are anchored in static controls and periodic audits are ill-suited for modern, dynamic IT environments. Cloud-native architectures, continuous delivery pipelines, and evolving threat vectors demand real-time, risk-aware, and embedded governance. Adaptive GRC models that are integrated directly into IT and DevSecOps pipelines are not just innovative but they are now table stakes.

The latter sections of the chapter pivoted toward the positive impacts and opportunities that alignment unlocks. These include accelerated incident response, improved uptime, and strategic automation of compliance and risk management functions. Aligned organizations are able to operate faster, safer, and with greater strategic clarity. Governance becomes embedded in business-as-usual operations, not a reactive overlay.

This chapter also emphasized the strategic value of shared metrics and performance measurement. Establishing joint KPIs that reflect both system availability and security control efficacy ensures that alignment is not conceptual, it's operationalized. Integrated reporting enables leadership to understand tradeoffs, justify investments, and course-correct in real time. Over time, these metrics support benchmarking, maturity modeling, and continuous improvement initiatives that strengthen the entire enterprise.

Looking forward, enterprises must invest in platforms, playbooks, and partnerships that support this alignment. This includes not only technical integration across ITSM, SIEM, and compliance platforms but also organizational constructs such as integrated risk committees, security champions within operations teams, and unified escalation paths. Governance must be designed for velocity that's capable of guiding decisions at the pace of change.

Aligning IT Operations and Cybersecurity under a unified GRC framework is a strategic enabler of enterprise resilience, trust, and agility. It transforms governance from a compliance checkpoint into a mechanism for secure innovation. It ensures that risk management is not a series of isolated events, but a continuous function aligned to business priorities. And it positions organizations to not only survive but lead in an era defined by digital complexity and relentless change. The path forward requires intention, collaboration, and sustained executive sponsorship, but the payoff is a secure, compliant, and adaptive enterprise built for the future.

12 Aligning IT Operations and Cybersecurity with Business Objectives

LEARNING OBJECTIVES

- Understand how risk and architectural frameworks align IT and cybersecurity with business goals by integrating security into enterprise architecture and focusing on business-driven decision-making
- Learn how to incorporate risk management and requirements gathering into security architecture to prioritize security efforts based on real business impact
- Explore how The Open Group Architecture Framework (TOGAF), Sherwood Applied Business Security Architecture (SABSA), and ERSM complement other IT and cybersecurity frameworks to create a unified, flexible, and standards-aligned security strategy
- Gain insight into building and managing a comprehensive, adaptable enterprise security architecture that supports regulatory compliance, stakeholder engagement, and continuous improvement

Architectural frameworks provide a structured way to align IT and cybersecurity efforts with an organization's business objectives. By using well-established frameworks companies can bring together different standards under one umbrella, creating a more cohesive strategy. This integration supports a unified approach where both IT and security efforts are driven by business goals. A key element of this alignment is adopting a business-focused approach that emphasizes treating security as an enabler rather than just a series of restrictions. This means that security is developed to support the business, not hinder it.

Risk management is another essential part of these frameworks. They incorporate risk analysis in a way that ties back to business priorities. This ensures cybersecurity efforts are focused on what matters most to the company, helping decision-makers prioritize based on real business impact. These frameworks also emphasize the importance of managing requirements effectively. They address gaps in traditional IT architecture approaches by helping businesses engage stakeholders and ensure security measures meet their operational needs. This ensures that IT, security, and business objectives remain aligned at all stages of development.

Architectural frameworks promote a more holistic view of security. Instead of treating cybersecurity as a separate area, they integrate it into overall enterprise architecture. This unified perspective helps organizations ensure that security measures are aligned with business processes and IT systems, creating a seamless flow between these elements. Flexibility is a significant advantage of using these frameworks. They can be tailored to suit an organization's unique needs while still aligning with industry standards. This adaptability allows businesses to remain compliant with regulations while evolving to meet new business goals and security challenges. By engaging various

DOI: 10.1201/9781003562153-15

stakeholders and establishing clear metrics, organizations can continuously align their cybersecurity strategies with their broader objectives.

ARCHITECTURAL AND RISK MANAGEMENT FRAMEWORKS DRIVING BUSINESS ALIGNMENT

In this chapter, we will examine three of the most prominent architectural and risk management frameworks that enterprise organizations leverage to establish alignment between business strategy, IT, cybersecurity, and other critical functions. These frameworks include TOGAF, the SABSA, and Enterprise Security Risk Management (ESRM), which serve as foundational tools for designing integrated architectures that support both operational performance and risk governance. Each offers a distinct perspective on how to structure and manage the complex interplay between business drivers, technology systems, and security requirements.

TOGAF provides a comprehensive methodology for developing enterprise architecture that ensures IT investments are aligned with business objectives, with built-in guidance for lifecycle management and governance. SABSA, on the other hand, approaches architecture from a security-first perspective, embedding security considerations directly into the business architecture through its layered, attribute-driven methodology. ESRM offers a risk-based governance model that integrates security functions across the enterprise by aligning risk ownership with business leadership and enabling continuous risk-informed decision-making. Together, these frameworks represent a multidimensional strategy for managing enterprise complexity while safeguarding critical assets.

While TOGAF, SABSA, and ESRM are the most widely referenced and implemented, they do not operate in isolation. Organizations often complement these frameworks with others discussed in earlier chapters, such as COBIT for governance, ITIL for service management, and the NIST Cybersecurity Framework for control implementation. By combining these models, enterprises can build a tailored, integrated architecture that supports scalability, agility, and resilience across all business domains.

TOGAF

TOGAF[1] is a globally recognized standard for enterprise architecture that offers a structured, methodical approach to designing, planning, implementing, and governing an organization's IT landscape. Its core purpose is to ensure that IT architecture is not only technically sound but also tightly aligned with the strategic goals and operational needs of the business. By providing a comprehensive blueprint for enterprise architecture, TOGAF enables organizations to drive efficiency, scalability, interoperability, and security across complex IT ecosystems.

TOGAF organizes enterprise architecture into four primary domains, each representing a critical pillar of business–IT alignment. Business Architecture defines the organization's strategy, governance structures, and operational processes, ensuring that all IT decisions are rooted in business intent. Data Architecture governs the structure, storage, and lifecycle of information assets, with an emphasis on integrity, accessibility, and regulatory compliance. Applications Architecture focuses on the software systems that support business functions, addressing their interactions, dependencies, and performance. Lastly, Technology Architecture encompasses the foundational infrastructure that enables reliable and secure delivery of services.

At the heart of TOGAF lies the architecture development method, a repeatable and iterative process that guides organizations through the complete lifecycle of enterprise architecture, from initial vision and capability assessment to implementation and ongoing governance. The architecture development method supports modularization, standardization, and reuse, promoting architectural consistency and agility while minimizing duplication of effort.

From a security architecture perspective, TOGAF is especially powerful when applied to enterprise cybersecurity and IT operations. It facilitates the integration of security into every phase of architectural development, ensuring that protective controls are not bolted on as afterthoughts but designed as intrinsic elements of the enterprise architecture. TOGAF enables alignment between cybersecurity strategies and business objectives, allowing organizations to embed risk-aware decision-making throughout the IT environment. It also supports the incorporation of complementary security frameworks such as NIST, SABSA, or ISO 27001, strengthening the overall risk management posture.

In IT operations, TOGAF helps streamline processes by reducing redundancies and improving operational efficiency. It promotes the design of scalable, interoperable IT systems while supporting structured change management, essential for guiding the organization through transitions from current-state architectures to future-state models. Whether the objective is cloud migration, digital transformation, or enterprise-wide security modernization, TOGAF provides a roadmap to manage complexity and drive sustainable outcomes.

The benefits of adopting TOGAF are substantial. It ensures that IT investments are strategically aligned with business goals, enabling leadership to make informed, risk-aware decisions. Its standardized methodology fosters transparency and accountability, improving both governance and execution. Organizations also gain cost efficiency by identifying reusable architecture assets and eliminating redundant systems or services. Moreover, TOGAF's modular and adaptable nature makes it suitable for organizations of all sizes and sectors, from global enterprises to midmarket firms undergoing digital growth.

To effectively align IT and cybersecurity processes, policies, and controls with business objectives using the TOGAF, a structured and phased approach is recommended. This method not only ensures alignment with overarching business goals but also integrates security considerations throughout the entire enterprise architecture lifecycle.

TOGAF Phase	Security Focus	Alignment with Business Objectives
Architecture vision	– Define security principles aligned with architecture principles – Involve key security stakeholders	– Ensures security direction supports business goals from the outset – Encourages stakeholder buy-in and clarity
Business architecture	– Identify security-related business requirements – Develop Security Domain Model – Define KPIs	– Maps security to business domains – Ensures measurable alignment between security and business performance
Information systems architecture	– Create Security Services Catalog – Map services to application/data architecture	– Embeds security into core IT systems – Ensures security capabilities directly support business system integrity
Technology architecture	– Select integrated security technologies aligned with enterprise architecture	– Enhances protection while supporting operational efficiency – Avoids siloed or redundant security investments
Opportunities and solutions	– Prioritize security projects based on business impact and risk reduction	– Optimizes resource allocation for security – Aligns security investments with risk appetite and business outcomes
Migration planning	– Develop roadmap for security implementation aligned with IT transition plans	– Minimizes disruption during change – Synchronizes security with broader transformation initiatives
Implementation governance	– Establish governance structures linking policies to objectives – Monitor security control execution	– Maintains strategic alignment post-deployment – Ensures ongoing business relevance of security measures

TOGAF Phase	Security Focus	Alignment with Business Objectives
Architecture change management	– Continuously assess and adapt security based on business change – Apply risk management practices	– Keeps security posture responsive and value-driven – Prevents obsolescence and overengineering

Throughout the entire process, TOGAF's concept of artifacts should be used to document security-related deliverables at each phase. These artifacts serve as important references and ensure that all stakeholders have a clear understanding of the security measures in place. TOGAF's architecture development method provides a systematic approach that guides the integration of security into the overall architecture.

SABSA

SABSA[2] is a robust, business-aligned framework and methodology designed to build security architectures that are both risk-aware and strategically integrated with organizational objectives. Unlike traditional, technology-driven approaches, SABSA ensures that security is embedded as a value-adding function, enabling business operations rather than restricting them. It establishes a direct and traceable connection between security controls and the business drivers they support, making it particularly valuable for organizations that view security as a strategic asset.

At the heart of SABSA is its business-driven approach. It begins by thoroughly analyzing business requirements, objectives, and constraints, ensuring that every security measure implemented is designed to directly support those needs. This top-down methodology initiates at the highest level of business context and flows systematically through each phase of the architecture lifecycle. By doing so, it guarantees that security architecture is not built in isolation but instead reflects and reinforces the business strategy.

SABSA's structure is based on a layered architecture model, composed of six distinct but interconnected layers: Contextual, Conceptual, Logical, Physical, Component, and Operational. Each layer addresses a different level of abstraction, from defining business imperatives down to implementing specific technologies and operational controls. To ensure comprehensive analysis across all layers, SABSA utilizes its matrix that poses six critical questions: What, Why, How, Who, Where, and When. This matrix-driven analysis ensures multidimensional coverage of security considerations and provides traceability across business, technical, and operational domains.

A core strength of SABSA lies in its risk-driven methodology. It places strong emphasis on identifying and managing business risks, recognizing that security is fundamentally about uncertainty management. The SABSA Risk Model enables organizations to assess threats and opportunities in a structured manner, supporting informed decisions that optimize both security and business performance. This risk-centric approach supports a balanced view that avoids overengineering while ensuring appropriate levels of protection.

SABSA is also designed for full lifecycle integration, encompassing phases such as strategy development, architectural design, technical implementation, and ongoing operational management. This ensures that security remains aligned with evolving business needs, regulatory requirements, and the dynamic threat landscape. Throughout this lifecycle, SABSA provides essential tools, such as the SABSA Matrix and the Business Attributes Profile, which support the definition, mapping, and continuous validation of security requirements against architectural elements. These tools are critical for maintaining architectural traceability and ensuring that business value remains the guiding principle.

Importantly, SABSA does not operate in isolation. It is well suited for integration with other enterprise frameworks such as TOGAF, ITIL, COBIT, and ISO 27001. SABSA complements these models by adding a rigorous, business-focused method for embedding security into broader enterprise and IT governance processes. This makes it an ideal choice for organizations seeking coherence across compliance, risk, and security disciplines.

SABSA proves especially effective in several key scenarios. It is valuable for organizations aiming to align security strategies with business objectives, ensuring that security investments are business-justified and outcome-driven. For those needing to develop enterprise-wide security architectures, SABSA offers a repeatable structure that is scalable across IT and OT environments. Organizations seeking to enhance their risk management posture will benefit from its ability to assess both threats and opportunities within a business context. Additionally, SABSA's flexibility allows it to integrate diverse frameworks into a unified model, streamlining compliance and governance. Its scalability makes it suitable for both targeted projects and large-scale enterprise implementations.

To align IT and cybersecurity processes, policies, and controls with business objectives using the SABSA framework, it's essential to follow a structured approach.

SABSA Phases	Description	Business Alignment Focus
Understand the business context	Analyze the business goals, assets, stakeholders, and operational environment via the Contextual Architecture.	Ensures security priorities are directly tied to core business needs and objectives.
Translate business requirements into security concepts	Create a Business Attributes Profile and define control objectives in the Conceptual Architecture.	Converts business drivers into specific security attributes (e.g., confidentiality, integrity, availability).
Define security policies and services (logical architecture)	Design policies and security services that support business processes and control objectives.	Ensures security is embedded without disrupting business workflows.
Transform logical designs into physical solutions	Specify actionable controls, mechanisms, and infrastructure in the Physical Architecture.	Ensures technical implementation is practical and directly supports business operations.
Select and deploy security components	Choose tools and technologies that align with architectural requirements and business standards.	Aligns solution procurement with technical fit and business needs, avoiding unnecessary complexity or cost.
Develop operational management processes	Build procedures for ongoing management and support of security operations.	Maintains security performance in line with business risk tolerance and operational demands.
Utilize the SABSA matrix for comprehensive coverage	Apply SABSA's Matrix (What, Why, How, Who, Where, When) across all architecture layers.	Provides traceability and comprehensive coverage of business and technical dimensions.
Directly align security with business drivers	Map security services to specific business goals using the Business Attributes Profile.	Ensures every control contributes measurable business value (e.g., customer trust, compliance).
Balance security controls with business opportunities	Use SABSA's Risk and Opportunity Management Framework to assess risk without limiting growth.	Supports innovation by balancing risk mitigation with opportunity enablement.
Develop a policy architecture	Create a hierarchical, adaptable set of security policies aligned with business strategy.	Ensures flexibility and responsiveness to evolving business needs.
Implement a strong governance framework	Establish metrics, KPIs, and governance bodies to oversee ongoing alignment.	Maintains accountability and measures both security effectiveness and business contribution.

SABSA Phases	Description	Business Alignment Focus
Ensure continuous alignment with changing objectives	Use Through-Life Security Service Management for ongoing updates and alignment.	Keeps security architecture adaptive to business growth and evolving threat landscapes.

By following these steps and leveraging the comprehensive SABSA framework, organizations can build a security architecture that is both robust and flexible, ensuring that IT and cybersecurity efforts directly support and drive business success.

ESRM

ESRM[3] is a risk-centric framework designed to align security functions with organizational objectives, integrating them directly into the business decision-making process. Unlike traditional security models that operate in silos or react to threats in isolation, ESRM treats security as an enterprise-wide responsibility. It promotes a strategic approach in which risk is not merely controlled but understood, evaluated, and managed in the context of business priorities. Through this alignment, ESRM ensures that security enables the business rather than obstructing it, positioning security professionals as trusted advisors who provide actionable insight into the organization's threat landscape.

At its core, ESRM operates on five foundational principles. First, it is grounded in a risk-based approach that prioritizes security efforts according to the severity and likelihood of potential threats. This ensures that finite resources, such as personnel, time, technology, and budget, are allocated to the areas of greatest risk to enterprise assets. Second, ESRM is intentionally aligned with business strategy, ensuring that security decisions support the organization's mission, vision, and operational objectives. This principle reframes security from a compliance-driven activity into a strategic enabler of innovation, resilience, and growth.

Third, ESRM reinforces delegated risk ownership, where business unit leaders retain responsibility for the security of their assets. Security professionals serve in an advisory capacity, offering expertise, analysis, and recommended treatments, but final decisions rest with those who own the risk. This approach empowers stakeholders and fosters a culture of shared responsibility. Fourth, ESRM maintains a holistic risk perspective, integrating physical, cyber, information, operational, and reputational risk domains into a single cohesive view. It acknowledges that modern threats often cross these boundaries and must be addressed with unified strategies. Finally, ESRM emphasizes continuous improvement, requiring organizations to consistently reassess controls, adapt to emerging threats, and measure effectiveness through performance metrics and feedback loops.

The ESRM lifecycle is a repeatable process that guides the identification, evaluation, and treatment of risks across the organization. It begins with a thorough understanding of business context, including the organization's mission, values, operational model, digital ecosystem, and regulatory obligations. This foundational knowledge ensures that all security initiatives are properly aligned with enterprise goals and constraints. Next, the process moves to asset identification and prioritization, cataloging critical resources such as data, personnel, intellectual property, facilities, and supply chain components. These assets are evaluated based on their business value, sensitivity, and impact on operations if compromised.

ESRM Lifecycle Phase	Description
Understand the business context	Develop a deep understanding of the organization's mission, strategic goals, operating environment, stakeholder landscape, and regulatory obligations. This context ensures all security efforts are aligned with business priorities and constraints.

ESRM Lifecycle Phase	Description
Identify and prioritize assets	Catalog critical tangible and intangible assets such as data, personnel, infrastructure, intellectual property, and brand reputation. Prioritize them based on their business value, sensitivity, and role in enabling strategic objectives.
Identify and assess risks	Identify potential threats (e.g., cyberattacks, insider threats, natural disasters) and analyze vulnerabilities. Use risk assessment methodologies like CASE (Consequence, Asset, Source, Event) or FAIR to evaluate both the likelihood and impact of each risk to inform mitigation strategies.
Develop risk treatment strategies	– Avoidance: Eliminate high-risk activities. – Mitigation: Apply technical, administrative, or physical controls. – Transfer: Shift risk via insurance or outsourcing. – Acceptance: Acknowledge residual risk within tolerance.
Implement and monitor controls	Deploy the selected mitigation strategies and establish controls. Monitor control performance through KPIs and continuous oversight to detect inefficiencies, emerging risks, or compliance issues. Ensure security remains responsive and effective.
Governance, communication, and reporting	Establish a governance structure comprising cross-functional stakeholders (e.g., security, IT, risk, compliance, legal, operations). Facilitate consistent oversight, transparent communication, and reporting on ESRM performance, risk posture, and program maturity to senior leadership.

Several operational domains fall within the scope of ESRM, each contributing to the broader objective of enterprise protection. Physical security safeguards people, facilities, and physical assets through measures such as access control systems, surveillance technologies, and emergency response protocols. Cybersecurity addresses digital risk, protecting systems and networks through firewalls, threat detection, vulnerability management, and incident response automation. Information security focuses on data confidentiality, integrity, and availability, leveraging encryption, identity and access management (IAM), and data loss prevention (DLP) technologies. A robust incident response capability ensures the organization can rapidly detect, contain, and recover from security events, minimizing impact and preserving operational continuity.

Underlying all these domains is the need for structured governance. ESRM governance requires clearly defined roles, accountability matrices, and escalation paths. Responsibilities must be distributed across leadership, security teams, and business units in a way that promotes risk transparency and rapid decision-making. Routine audits, maturity assessments, and control effectiveness evaluations are essential to ensure alignment with policy, legal obligations, and strategic intent.

ESRM represents a transformational shift from fragmented, reactive security toward an integrated, forward-looking risk governance model. It equips organizations to navigate an increasingly complex threat landscape by aligning protection strategies with business goals, embedding risk ownership within the enterprise, and fostering a culture of resilience and informed decision-making. When executed effectively, ESRM transforms security from a tactical concern into a strategic pillar of sustainable enterprise value.

ARCHITECTURAL FRAMEWORK COMPARISON

Organizations require frameworks that not only support enterprise architecture but also align security practices with business goals. TOGAF, SABSA, and ESRM are three prominent frameworks that provide distinct approaches to achieving these objectives. While TOGAF focuses on comprehensive enterprise-wide architecture with a strong integration foundation, SABSA offers a security-driven approach that ensures risk management is tightly aligned with business needs. ESRM, on the other hand, takes a holistic view of security risk management, ensuring that security measures are seamlessly integrated with overall business strategies. Each framework brings unique strengths to the table, allowing organizations to choose the most suitable approach based on their specific needs and objectives.

TOGAF is the preferred framework for organizations seeking a comprehensive, enterprise-wide architecture. Its strength lies in its robust integration capabilities, making it an ideal choice for enterprises aiming to align IT infrastructure with broader business objectives. By providing a flexible and scalable methodology, TOGAF supports organizations in navigating the complexities of evolving business landscapes while ensuring the alignment of IT with business strategies.

SABSA, on the other hand, stands out as a framework tailored specifically for security-driven architectures. It offers a well-defined and comprehensive methodology that emphasizes risk management, security architecture, and alignment with business needs. SABSA ensures that security is deeply embedded within the enterprise architecture, providing organizations with a structured approach to managing security risks while maintaining a strong connection to business goals.

ESRM is focused on the strategic management of security risks, offering a holistic approach to security governance. With its emphasis on comprehensive risk assessments, threat management, and vulnerability mitigation, ESRM excels in integrating security into business processes. Its strength lies in its ability to provide a clear alignment between security and business objectives, ensuring that organizations can effectively manage their security posture while supporting overall business resilience.

Category	TOGAF	SABSA	ESRM
Core components	Architecture Development Method (ADM), Enterprise Continuum, Architecture Repository, TOGAF Resource Base	Risk Management Framework, Security Architecture, Business Requirements, Security Governance	ESRM Process, Security Risk Management Strategies, Threat and Vulnerability Assessments
Key benefits	Comprehensive framework for aligning enterprise architecture with business strategy; promotes flexibility, scalability, communication, and risk management	Strong security focus aligned with business goals; facilitates structured risk management	Enhances resilience and asset protection; improves decision-making through structured assessments
Primary focus	Enterprise architecture design and implementation aligned with business goals	Security architecture and governance with a risk-driven, business-aligned methodology	Enterprise-wide risk management with an emphasis on security posture and resilience
Risk management integration	Embedded in ADM phases and supported by the Architecture Repository	Central to the framework; risk is a foundational design principle	Core function; risk identification, mitigation, and strategy are the main pillars
Business alignment	Strong—ADM and tools promote IT alignment with business objectives	Directly aligns security requirements with business drivers	Security decisions are based on business impact and risk to assets

ALIGNING ARCHITECTURAL AND RISK MANAGEMENT FRAMEWORKS WITH IT AND CYBERSECURITY FRAMEWORKS

Aligning TOGAF, SABSA, and ESRM frameworks establishes a comprehensive, business-aligned strategy that fuses enterprise architecture with proactive cybersecurity and risk governance. This integrated approach enables organizations to translate business objectives into secure, resilient, and agile IT systems. It ensures that security is not treated as an isolated function but embedded throughout the enterprise architecture lifecycle, supporting regulatory compliance, operational efficiency, and digital innovation.

At the foundation of this integration lies TOGAF's ADM, which provides a structured, phased methodology for developing enterprise architecture. TOGAF's ADM is highly adaptable and allows for security and risk considerations to be infused throughout all stages of the architectural lifecycle. In the architecture vision stage, security objectives are defined in direct alignment with business outcomes. Here, SABSA's business attributes profiling becomes a powerful tool, translating strategic business drivers, such as market trust, data privacy, and regulatory obligations, into security requirements. By applying SABSA early in the ADM cycle, security becomes an enabler of business strategy rather than a reactive constraint.

In the business, data, application, and technology architecture phases, ESRM principles are integrated to assess and manage risk across the entire architecture stack. This includes identifying security risks tied to business processes, data flows, and infrastructure components, and aligning mitigations with recognized standards such as the NIST CSF or ISO 27001. This ensures consistency in how risks are identified, prioritized, and treated across the enterprise. As organizations progress to the Opportunities & Solutions, Migration Planning, Implementation Governance, and Architecture Change Management phases, SABSA's risk-driven design approach provides a rigorous model for validating security controls, ensuring they align with the organization's evolving risk appetite and compliance posture. This phase also serves as the governance checkpoint, where architecture compliance reviews are conducted, and deviations are formally addressed.

The SABSA framework, with its layered architecture model, from Contextual to Component, ensures full traceability between strategic business objectives and technical security controls. At the Contextual Layer, business-driven outcomes such as confidentiality of customer data or regulatory audit readiness are defined using the business attributes profile. These outcomes drive downstream security design choices and become measurable objectives within the security architecture. SABSA's risk and opportunity management model complements TOGAF's ADM by providing a structured mechanism to weigh potential threats against business opportunities, reinforcing risk-informed decision-making. At the operational level, SABSA's Security Services-Oriented Architecture (SSOA) can be mapped directly into TOGAF's Technology Architecture phase. This mapping ensures that specific security services, such as encryption, IAM, or network segmentation, are implemented as reusable, scalable components within the IT architecture.

ESRM, as a governance-focused framework, plays an essential role in sustaining alignment between business risk tolerance and the technical controls implemented through TOGAF and SABSA. ESRM brings clarity to risk ownership, allowing business leaders to make informed decisions about acceptable risk levels while enabling security architects to support those decisions with robust technical and procedural safeguards. Tools such as ISO 27001 can be employed within this ecosystem to quantify risks identified through TOGAF/SABSA integration. These risk metrics are then fed back into TOGAF's Architecture Compliance Reviews, creating a unified reporting structure that ensures all stakeholders, from business executives to operational security teams, have visibility into the organization's risk posture.

To further strengthen this integrated model, it is essential to align with established IT governance and cybersecurity frameworks. The NIST CSF aligns naturally with TOGAF's architectural domains. For instance, the Identify and Protect functions map closely to the Business and Technology

Architectures, while Detect, Respond, and Recover functions are addressed within TOGAF's implementation and change management phases. Similarly, COBIT offers governance and management objectives that complement TOGAF's Preliminary and Governance Phases. Specific objectives, such as Manage Security and Ensure Risk Optimization, can be woven into the architecture governance framework to reinforce accountability and continuous improvement. Finally, ISO 27001 can be operationalized using SABSA, which provides the logical scaffolding to embed ISMS requirements into TOGAF's implementation, monitoring, and optimization phases.

Aspect	Outcome
Holistic risk management	Combines ESRM's business-centric risk analysis with SABSA's threat modeling and TOGAF's governance.
Business alignment	SABSA's business attributes profiling ensures security controls directly support strategic goals.
Proactive security	Security-by-design via TOGAF ADM phases reduces vulnerabilities early.
Streamlined compliance	Unified view of controls across frameworks (e.g., ISO 27001, NIST) simplifies audits.
Collaborative governance	Breaks silos between EA, security,

Integrating TOGAF, SABSA, and ESRM frameworks creates a unified, traceable, and scalable approach to enterprise security architecture. It enables organizations to link business strategy, risk appetite, and technical implementation through a common language of architecture and governance. This synergy not only improves the effectiveness of cybersecurity programs but also elevates security as a strategic business enabler, capable of supporting transformation, innovation, and sustained resilience in an ever-evolving threat landscape.

THE POTENTIAL FROM ALIGNING WITH BUSINESS OBJECTIVES

Aligning IT and cybersecurity frameworks with business objectives through TOGAF and SABSA brings multiple advantages. SABSA offers a unified structure that integrates existing standards like ISO 27001 and ITIL, creating a streamlined approach. When combined with TOGAF, security considerations become a core part of enterprise architecture, ensuring that security is integrated, not just an afterthought. This approach shifts the focus to security as a business enabler, rather than a restriction. SABSA helps align security needs with business goals, enhancing TOGAF's architecture development by incorporating a business-driven security perspective. This ensures that risks are managed more effectively while still supporting broader business objectives. SABSA also strengthens requirements management, filling gaps in previous versions of TOGAF. By applying its business attributes profiling method, organizations can engage stakeholders more thoroughly and manage business needs across the enterprise. The result is better alignment between IT and business functions, breaking down silos and improving productivity.

The holistic integration of security and enterprise architecture fosters improved communication between architects and business leaders. This reduces costs, increases efficiency, and helps meet regulatory requirements. Ultimately, aligning these frameworks supports a more cohesive strategy, where IT and security directly contribute to business success.

CONCLUSION AND RECAP

Aligning IT and cybersecurity efforts with business objectives is critical for organizations striving for long-term resilience, innovation, and operational excellence. Through frameworks such as TOGAF, SABSA, and ESRM, organizations can establish a structured approach that ensures security is not merely a compliance-driven function but a core enabler of business success. By adopting these frameworks, companies can integrate security measures directly into the architecture and decision-making processes, ensuring that security aligns with both operational goals and strategic business objectives. Each framework brings a unique value proposition that contributes to the development of a robust, flexible, and adaptable enterprise security posture.

TOGAF's comprehensive approach to enterprise architecture provides the blueprint necessary for aligning IT strategies with business goals. Its ADM ensures that security is integrated at every stage of the architectural lifecycle, supporting seamless transitions and the continuous alignment of business and IT strategies. TOGAF's flexibility allows it to adapt to a wide range of industries and organizational needs, making it an ideal framework for enterprises of all sizes. Its integration capabilities are especially critical for organizations navigating complex, multilayered IT ecosystems, ensuring that security considerations are embedded in every layer, from business processes to technology infrastructure.

SABSA, with its security-first methodology, addresses the need for a risk-driven approach to enterprise security. By focusing on business objectives and aligning security measures directly with these goals, SABSA ensures that security investments are not just reactive but proactive and business justified. This framework's layered architecture model allows for detailed, multidimensional analysis of security, ensuring that risks are managed in a structured, traceable way. SABSA's emphasis on business alignment guarantees that security supports, rather than hinders, business operations. Its integration with other frameworks such as TOGAF and ISO 27001 further strengthens its ability to embed security into the broader organizational fabric, creating a cohesive strategy across both IT and business domains.

ESRM takes a holistic approach to managing security risks, positioning security as an enterprise-wide responsibility. By integrating risk management into the decision-making process, ESRM ensures that security strategies are aligned with business priorities. Its focus on risk ownership and continuous improvement fosters a culture of shared responsibility, where business leaders and security professionals collaborate to manage risk effectively. ESRM's comprehensive view of risk spans physical, cyber, information, operational, and reputational domains, ensuring that organizations can respond to a wide range of threats. This holistic perspective is essential for managing today's complex threat landscape, where risks often cross multiple boundaries.

When combined, TOGAF, SABSA, and ESRM offer a powerful, integrated approach to enterprise security architecture. These frameworks complement each other by addressing different aspects of enterprise architecture and security management. TOGAF provides the structural foundation for aligning IT systems with business strategies, SABSA embeds security at the heart of the architecture, and ESRM ensures that risk is continuously managed across the enterprise. Together, they create a cohesive and adaptive security strategy that is aligned with business goals and capable of evolving in response to changing threats and business needs.

The integration of these frameworks into the enterprise architecture lifecycle facilitates smoother governance, clearer communication, and more efficient decision-making. By adopting TOGAF, organizations can ensure that their IT infrastructure is strategically aligned with business objectives, while SABSA ensures that security is an integral part of the business strategy. ESRM adds a risk-centric layer to this approach, ensuring that security measures are continuously evaluated and adjusted based on emerging threats and business priorities.

Furthermore, these frameworks provide significant cost-saving benefits by reducing redundancies and eliminating siloed efforts. Through TOGAF's architecture development methods and SABSA's structured methodology, organizations can streamline their architecture development, ensuring that security measures are built into systems from the outset rather than bolted on later. This not only reduces the risk of vulnerabilities but also enhances operational efficiency by eliminating unnecessary complexity.

The adoption of these frameworks also promotes a culture of accountability and transparency within organizations. By clearly defining roles and responsibilities through ESRM's risk ownership model, business leaders are empowered to make informed decisions about acceptable risk levels, while security teams provide the necessary expertise and guidance. This shared ownership of security ensures that security risks are understood and managed at every level of the organization.

Incorporating these frameworks into the organization's governance structure also strengthens compliance with regulatory requirements. TOGAF and SABSA both emphasize the importance of documentation, traceability, and governance, ensuring that security measures meet legal and regulatory standards. ESRM's continuous improvement cycle ensures that security practices remain up-to-date with evolving threats and regulations, minimizing the risk of noncompliance.

The integration of TOGAF, SABSA, and ESRM with other IT and cybersecurity frameworks, such as COBIT, ITIL, and NIST, further enhances their effectiveness. By combining these frameworks, organizations can create a comprehensive and cohesive strategy that supports both operational efficiency and risk management. This integrated approach ensures that all aspects of enterprise architecture, from governance to security, work together seamlessly to drive business success.

Ultimately, aligning architectural and risk management frameworks with IT and cybersecurity strategies ensures that security is embedded into the organization's DNA. Rather than being treated as an afterthought or a barrier to innovation, security becomes an enabler of business resilience, growth, and agility. By adopting TOGAF, SABSA, and ESRM, organizations can build a strong foundation for managing risk, protecting critical assets, and supporting the achievement of strategic business objectives.

This approach also fosters a more collaborative environment between IT, security, and business leaders. By working together to define security requirements and align them with business priorities, organizations can create more effective and adaptive security strategies. This collaborative model ensures that security is not a siloed function but an integrated, strategic component of the overall business architecture.

The integration of TOGAF, SABSA, and ESRM represents a best practice for organizations seeking to align their IT and cybersecurity efforts with their broader business objectives. These frameworks provide the structure, methodology, and tools necessary to ensure that security is embedded throughout the enterprise architecture lifecycle, supporting both operational needs and long-term business goals. By adopting a holistic, business-focused approach to security, organizations can enhance their resilience, drive innovation, and ensure that their security practices are always aligned with the evolving business landscape. These frameworks provide a clear and structured path forward, ensuring that security remains a strategic enabler, not just a risk mitigation function. By embracing TOGAF, SABSA, and ESRM, organizations can navigate the complexities of modern business and security challenges, positioning themselves for long-term success and resilience.

NOTES

1 The Open Group, *The TOGAF® Standard, Version 9.2* (2018). www.opengroup.org/togaf.

2 John Sherwood, Andrew Clark, and David Lynas, *Enterprise Security Architecture: A Business-Driven Approach*, Boca Raton, FL: CRC Press, 2005.

3 ASIS International, *Enterprise Security Risk Management (ESRM): Concepts and Strategies*, Alexandria, VA: ASIS International, 2020.

Part IV

Integrated Assurance Unified Risk Strategy

13 Integrated Assurance

Unifying Cybersecurity and IT Operations for the Enterprise

LEARNING OBJECTIVES

- Understand that Integrated Assurance embeds security into operational workflows, turning protection and performance into shared responsibilities
- Learn how Integrated Assurance emphasizes interoperable architecture, cross-functional governance, and strategy-driven integration over tactical tooling
- Explore how Integrated Assurance makes assurance a real-time, active function embedded into backlog planning, change control, incident response, and architectural design
- Gain awareness of how Integrated Assurance recognizes that cybersecurity is an organizational responsibility that scales by aligning all domains to a shared risk posture, enabling unity without forcing uniformity

Let's start with the core question presented in this book, "What is Integrated Assurance?"

Integrated Assurance is not a prescriptive framework or a set of control checklists. It's a strategic mindset born out of necessity, one that acknowledges the deep interdependence between cybersecurity and IT operations in the modern enterprise. While governance structures and technical baselines serve a purpose, they are insufficient on their own to manage the complexity of today's interconnected systems and global business environments.

RETHINKING THE NARRATIVE

In almost all enterprises, the disconnect between security and operations is not malicious, it's inherited. Security is tasked with reducing risk, often by limiting change. Operations is tasked with maintaining uptime, often by avoiding friction. Left unmanaged, this creates a persistent undercurrent of misalignment where both functions work hard but rarely work together. Integrated Assurance aims to correct that course. It's not about reassigning blame or centralizing control. It's about creating connective tissue between teams that, for too long, have operated in parallel rather than in sync. When implemented properly, Integrated Assurance doesn't force uniformity, it enables collaboration without compromising autonomy.

At its core, this model embeds security directly into operational workflows. It insists that resilience and availability are not separate from security as they are extensions of it. This is a departure from the conventional bolt-on approach, where security is introduced late in the development or deployment lifecycle, often as a compliance gate. Instead, security becomes a design principle from the outset. The practical implications are significant. A system cannot be considered resilient if its security posture is an afterthought. Likewise, security controls that are not operationally viable only

DOI: 10.1201/9781003562153-17

serve to increase friction and resistance. Integrated Assurance eliminates this dichotomy by framing protection and performance as co-requisites, not competitors.

Integrated Assurance also thrives on intentional design. It encourages security architects, infrastructure engineers, and business leaders to codevelop strategies that acknowledge constraints, whether they be legacy dependencies, resource limitations, or regulatory obligations. This is not about building utopian systems; it's about building safe, sustainable ones within the constraints of the enterprise's reality.

In the traditional model, compensating controls are reactive by nature. They're added as patches to mitigate risks that cannot be fully addressed due to cost, complexity, or practicality. Integrated Assurance treats compensating controls differently. It brings them into the light, gives them purpose, and folds them into the strategic architecture of the enterprise. They become known quantities that are governed, measured, and revisited as systems evolve. This, in turn, demands an evolution in governance. Periodic review boards and quarterly audits aren't sufficient. Assurance needs to be embedded in the daily rhythm of the enterprise. It should influence backlog grooming, infrastructure provisioning, incident retrospectives, and architectural review processes. Assurance must become a verb, not a noun, rather it's an active function that's practiced continually, not examined occasionally.

From an architectural standpoint, Integrated Assurance aligns naturally with capability-based planning. Security is no longer a vertical silo or an overlay; it becomes a horizontal layer that permeates infrastructure, applications, data, and user experience. It influences design patterns, controls provisioning, and lifecycle decisions at every tier of the enterprise stack. But this model isn't purely technical. Culture is its real linchpin. The most sophisticated architecture will fail if the people operating within it lack shared goals and mutual trust. Integrated Assurance depends on a shift in mindset across the organization, from executives and architects to engineers and analysts. It requires a recognition that success is measured not by functional isolation but by collective effectiveness.

Metrics, too, must evolve. Traditional indicators like patch compliance or intrusion attempts are useful, but they don't tell the whole story. Integrated Assurance demands metrics that reflect convergence: control drift rates, remediation velocity, risk-adjusted uptime, and the time it takes to move from detection to coordinated action. These metrics tell us whether we're operating as one or as many. What makes these metrics powerful is their alignment to business value. They don't just speak to the health of technical controls, metrics also they tell a story about operational readiness, organizational maturity, and strategic posture. When the CFO or COO can understand a security metric in the context of business risk or continuity, it ceases to be abstract and becomes actionable.

Integrated Assurance should also transform how we prioritize work. In a world of finite resources and infinite risk, prioritization is everything. Security initiatives must be weighed not just by their severity but by their potential to enable core business functions. The assurance lens helps organizations make smarter tradeoffs without losing sight of long-term resilience. The model demands new cadences for collaboration. One-off crisis meetings won't suffice. Integrated Assurance institutionalizes collaboration through recurring engagement and cross-domain incident simulations, architecture councils, and shared tooling that enables transparency. These are not add-ons to the workflow; they are the workflow.

Technology, while undeniably critical, is not the centerpiece of Integrated Assurance. It is the enabler and never the strategy. One of the most common missteps in enterprise security and IT operations is the overreliance on tooling as a substitute for clarity, coordination, or capability maturity. A new platform might address a visible symptom, but it rarely addresses the structural causes of risk fragmentation. The assumption that buying a better tool will fix a broken process or a misaligned team dynamic is not just misguided, it's dangerous. It creates a false sense of security, one where investment is mistaken for improvement.

In reality, most enterprises already have more tools than they know what to do with. Endpoint protection suites, vulnerability scanners, SIEMs, CMDBs, configuration management platforms and most organizations are drowning in dashboards. But visibility without integration is just noise. And when those tools are operated in isolation, maintained by siloed teams with little cross-functional insight, they create duplication, drift, and operational drag. Integrated Assurance challenges the impulse to solve strategic problems with tactical purchases. It shifts the focus from what a tool can do to how it fits into a broader architectural vision. Interoperability becomes the priority. Can the system exchange data cleanly? Can workflows span tool boundaries without friction? Can context move fluidly between detection, analysis, and response without requiring three meetings and a custom API?

Architecture, not tools, becomes the organizing principle. A well-designed architecture defines how systems interconnect, how controls are enforced across environments, and how assurance is delivered as a function of design. It enables the business to scale and secure itself simultaneously. Tools may be swapped in and out over time, but the architecture holds the blueprint for how the organization thinks about risk, availability, and performance.

Underlying all of this is a commitment to principles over products. Tools change, vendors shift, and technologies evolve, but foundational principles endure. When decisions are anchored in principle, the organization is less vulnerable to market hype and more capable of assessing tools on their operational merit and architectural fit. This doesn't mean tools are irrelevant. Far from it. But in the context of Integrated Assurance, their role is subordinated to strategy. They serve the architecture, not define it. They automate what has already been architected, governed, and agreed upon. The right tool, in the right place, in service of the right outcome, that is the essence of technology's role in the Integrated Assurance model.

Incident response provides one of the clearest illustrations of this philosophy. In the old world, security owned the breach, operations owned the outage. In the world of Integrated Assurance, there is no breach without a system, no system without a business outcome. Integrated Assurance redefines incident response as a shared responsibility. It collapses the artificial boundary between the security incident and the operational disruption. In this model, response is not an escalation from one team to another.

Response becomes a joint function which is coordinated, practiced, and measured. Response playbooks are no longer crafted in isolation by the security team. They are codeveloped with input from infrastructure leads, application owners, compliance officers, and business unit stakeholders. The goal is to build response protocols that reflect the full lifecycle of an incident, from detection to containment, recovery, communication, and postmortem analysis. Communication becomes structured, hierarchical, and purposeful. Integrated Assurance introduces escalation tiers, communication bridges, and decision rights that are prenegotiated. No more scrambling for approvals during a crisis. No more guesswork on who speaks to legal, PR, or the board. Everyone knows their role before the fire starts.

This Integrated Assurance mindset also demonstrates remarkable scalability, which is essential in today's global enterprises. Large organizations rarely operate as a single, cohesive unit. They are complex and often federated across business lines, geographies, and regulatory jurisdictions. Each division may have its own operational tempo, technology stack, and localized risk posture. In such an environment, enforcing rigid, centralized control frameworks often results in friction, resistance, or superficial compliance. Integrated Assurance offers an alternative, one that doesn't sacrifice consistency for flexibility. It provides a scalable approach that accommodates local variance without undermining enterprise-wide risk visibility or governance objectives.

Rather than dictate uniform implementation, Integrated Assurance establishes a flexible scaffolding. It defines core principles and strategic intent at its core while allowing the edge to execute in context. This means that a business unit operating under GDPR in Europe can adapt its assurance activities differently than a unit dealing with HIPAA in the United States, yet both remain

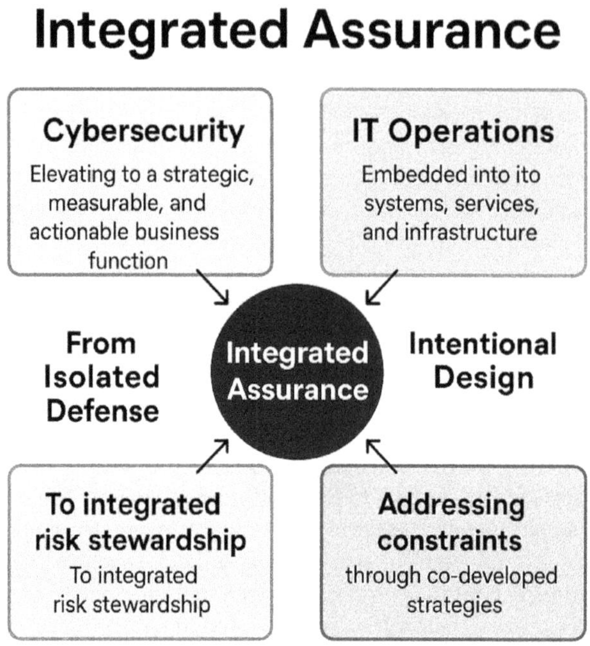

FIGURE 13.1 Integrated Assurance.

tethered to the same enterprise-wide security posture. Operational autonomy is preserved, but it operates within a shared governance envelope. This model respects the nuanced realities of global operations while ensuring that risk management is neither fragmented nor reactive.

What makes the Integrated Assurance approach powerful is its ability to enable unity without imposing uniformity. Integrated Assurance becomes the binding agent across divergent teams and operating models. Whether it's a logistics subsidiary in Southeast Asia or a digital R&D hub in North America, Integrated Assurance ensures that all parts of the organization understand their role in the broader security ecosystem. It cultivates alignment through shared purpose, common language, and interoperable processes as shown in Figure 13.1.

Resilience, in this model, is the North Star. Not just the ability to bounce back from failure, but the ability to adapt in the face of uncertainty. Integrated Assurance doesn't guarantee that nothing will go wrong, yet it guarantees that when things do, the organization will know what to do, how to do it, and who to do it with. Ultimately, Integrated Assurance is about synchronizing the enterprise. When cybersecurity and IT operations stop competing for resources and begin collaborating toward shared objectives, the organization becomes more than just defended. It becomes adaptable. It becomes efficient. It becomes capable of evolving at the pace of both threat and opportunity.

THE CASE FOR INTEGRATED ASSURANCE

Most enterprises don't fail at cybersecurity because of a lack of frameworks. They fail because those frameworks never touch the operational core. The disconnect isn't in the policy; it's in the execution. It's the chasm between what's written in a governance document and what actually happens across infrastructure, applications, and business processes on a daily basis. Frameworks like NIST, ISO, and COBIT provide valuable scaffolding, but they don't build the house. That requires organizational alignment and that's where most security programs fall short.

Fragmentation is the real threat. Not just technical fragmentation, although that's part of it, but structural fragmentation. When IT operations, cybersecurity, compliance, procurement, and business units all act independently, using different tools, pursuing different goals, reporting to different leadership chains it creates fragmented silos. In that environment, no amount of technical control will create resilience. At best, it creates the illusion of control. At worst, it amplifies risk through conflicting actions and uncoordinated response.

Disconnected operations and security functions create blind spots. A security team flags a misconfigured workload, but IT operations doesn't see it as a priority because it's not impacting uptime. A development team deploys a new feature with hard-coded secrets, and security learns about it two months later during a post-incident review. These aren't hypothetical scenarios; these are the daily reality in most large organizations. This disconnection isn't just operational, it's also financial. Fragmented tooling leads to duplicated spend. Fragmented reporting drives poor decision-making at the executive level. Fragmented ownership results in overlapping roles with unclear accountability. When functions operate in silos, the organization bleeds value in terms of risk exposure and wasted investment.

Integrated Assurance may not be a silver bullet, but it is a mindset and cultural blueprint. It shifts the center of gravity away from siloed controls and toward unified operations. It asks a different question: not "Do we have a policy for this?" but "Are our systems, teams, and processes aligned to act on this risk consistently and deliberately?" Integrated Assurance focuses on real, actionable integration across functional domains. That means embedding security into IT service management, platform engineering, identity governance, change management, and asset lifecycle. It means using shared telemetry, common taxonomies, and harmonized workflows, not just between security and IT, but across business units and supporting functions.

The result isn't just better security. It's better enterprise performance. Fewer delays in product releases due to last-minute security concerns. More accurate risk reporting for the board. Faster resolution times during incidents. Greater trust between teams and a culture where security is no longer perceived as the team that says no, but as a partner that helps the organization move forward safely.

Integrated Assurance is the future of enterprise security. Not another framework to layer on top, but a fundamental shift in how security is embedded, operationalized, and sustained across the business. Integrated Assurance is how we move from fragmented control to unified resilience, from reactive compliance to proactive enablement. And it's how we finally begin to close the gap between what security intends and what the enterprise actually delivers.

Integrated Assurance recognizes that every function in the organization has a role to play in managing risk and delivering assurance. In large-scale enterprises, where complexity and fragmentation are persistent, alignment across domains becomes essential for both security and resilience. Below, we examine how Integrated Assurance maps into the core functional areas of the enterprise, transforming isolated controls into cohesive, enterprise-wide capabilities.

ELEVATING CYBERSECURITY TO A STRATEGIC, MEASURABLE, AND ACTIONABLE BUSINESS FUNCTION

In large-scale enterprises, the effectiveness of cybersecurity is inextricably tied to the clarity of executive leadership and the maturity of governance structures. Without executive sponsorship and strategic alignment, even the most well-architected security program will struggle to achieve lasting impact. Integrated Assurance begins at the top not by dictating controls, but by framing security as a driver of enterprise resilience, business continuity, and stakeholder trust.

At its core, executive leadership must shift its perception of cybersecurity from a technical function to a strategic enabler. This requires embedding cyber risk into enterprise risk management processes, treating it as a top-tier concern on par with financial, operational, and reputational risks. Doing so reframes security conversations from "how secure are we?" to "how well are we managing the risk that could derail our business objectives?" It ensures that cybersecurity is not relegated to a line item in the IT budget, but elevated to a board-level priority with meaningful accountability.

This elevation demands new metrics. Traditional security KPIs like the number of vulnerabilities closed or phishing emails detected have little meaning in the boardroom. Instead, performance metrics must be translated into business-relevant terms: financial exposure from cyber risk, dwell time reduction in critical business systems, time-to-containment of high-impact incidents, or assurance levels in regulated business units. Integrated Assurance helps security leaders craft a narrative that resonates and one that connects technical realities with operational consequences.

Equally important is clarity around risk appetite. Executive leaders must define the thresholds of acceptable risk across the enterprise, differentiated by business unit, geography, and function. A blanket zero-tolerance policy is both unrealistic and counterproductive. Instead, Integrated Assurance encourages nuanced discussions about risk tradeoffs. Decisions must be made at the leadership level, not pushed down to operational teams who lack the authority to act holistically.

Governance structures must also evolve. Security governance cannot remain static or siloed within IT. Instead, Integrated Assurance promotes the creation of cross-functional risk and assurance committees that bring together cybersecurity, enterprise architecture, compliance, legal, HR, and operations. These bodies should meet regularly to review posture, prioritize investments, track remediation progress, and reconcile risk decisions against business goals. The goal is to shift from reactive governance to proactive steering while building a cadence of decision-making that integrates security into the rhythm of the enterprise.

Board engagement is another critical component. Boards must be educated not just on cybersecurity trends, but on the specific risk posture of the enterprise, the assumptions behind that posture, and the dependencies that could change it. This requires regular, transparent assurance reporting that avoids technical jargon and focuses on enterprise impact. Integrated Assurance drives the development of reporting frameworks that communicate risk in terms of probability, consequence, and preparedness which empowers the board to make informed decisions rather than rubber-stamping annual budgets.

Leadership sets the tone for culture. If cybersecurity is viewed as a barrier or an afterthought, that perception will cascade through the enterprise. If it is treated as a strategic pillar, it becomes a shared value. Executive leaders must model this mindset, speak about cybersecurity in business terms, and sponsor initiatives that make secure practices accessible and expected at every level of the organization. Furthermore, executive governance must include accountability structures. Who owns security risk for a business unit? How are CISOs evaluated? How are tradeoffs between speed and assurance escalated and resolved? Integrated Assurance promotes clear lines of ownership, defined escalation paths, and a documented decision-making framework that ensures security risk is not left in ambiguity.

The strategic influence of leadership also extends into budget planning. Security is often underfunded not because the need isn't recognized, but because its value isn't clearly articulated in financial terms. Integrated Assurance provides a model for aligning security investments to risk reduction outcomes, allowing CFOs and CIOs to make informed decisions based on return on security investment. This alignment helps avoid both overspend and underprotection and creates financial discipline without compromising resilience.

Visibility is one of the most impactful outcomes of Integrated Assurance. When security controls, risk decisions, and operational activities are aligned under a unified assurance model, leadership gains a holistic view of enterprise readiness. This allows them to anticipate regulatory impact, respond confidently to incidents, and demonstrate defensibility to shareholders, regulators, and customers alike. Executive leadership and governance are the central point of authority in the security journey and not merely passive stakeholders. Integrated Assurance empowers them to lead with confidence, align with purpose, and govern with foresight. In doing so, they enable cybersecurity to evolve from a technical hurdle into a strategic lever for growth, trust, and competitive advantage.

USE CASE: EMBEDDING CYBERSECURITY INTO ENTERPRISE RISK GOVERNANCE AT A MULTINATIONAL FINANCIAL SERVICES FIRM

Background

A global financial services firm with operations in 18 countries was struggling to effectively communicate cybersecurity priorities to the executive board. Despite heavy investment in tools and talent, cyber risk remained siloed within the IT function, and board-level discussions rarely included meaningful metrics on cybersecurity posture. The disconnect resulted in fragmented governance, misaligned risk appetite across regions, and underfunded security initiatives that failed to keep pace with evolving threats.

Challenge

- Cybersecurity was seen as a technical burden, not a business enabler.
- KPIs were and failed to influence strategic decisions.
- Security risk acceptance decisions were frequently made by technical leads without input from business stakeholders.
- Annual budgets lacked a defensible ROI model for cybersecurity investment.
- The board lacked visibility into enterprise-wide cyber risk exposure and preparedness.

Integrated Assurance Solution

The firm adopted the Integrated Assurance model with a specific focus on elevating cybersecurity to a strategic business function. The program was jointly sponsored by the CIO, CRO (Chief Risk Officer), and CISO, with board oversight.

Implementation Steps

Implementation Steps	Details
Strategic reframing	– Cybersecurity was integrated into the enterprise risk management framework. – Risk appetite thresholds for cybersecurity were defined by business unit and region, accounting for criticality, regulatory exposure, and threat profile.
Governance transformation	– A Cross-Functional Assurance Committee was established, including representatives from cybersecurity, IT operations, compliance, enterprise architecture, legal, HR, and finance. – Quarterly assurance reviews were introduced to prioritize risk remediation and align investments with business goals.
Business-relevant metrics	– New KPIs were developed: time-to-containment for critical business systems, cyber risk-adjusted exposure per business unit, and assurance level scores for regulated functions. – Assurance reports were tailored for the board using risk-based dashboards and financial impact visualizations.
Budget alignment	– Cybersecurity investments were mapped to risk reduction outcomes. – ROI models showed projected cost avoidance, compliance savings, and risk mitigation tied to each major initiative.

Implementation Steps	Details
Cultural change	– Executive leadership began openly communicating the role of cybersecurity in enabling business continuity and stakeholder trust. – Security performance was linked to business outcomes in leadership evaluations and operational KPIs.

Outcomes

- The board approved a 30% increase in the cybersecurity budget, justified by a defensible ROI tied to reduced regulatory exposure and improved resilience.
- Incident response time for high-impact events decreased by 42% due to better cross-functional coordination.
- The firm passed two consecutive audits with zero critical findings and achieved early compliance with upcoming EU data protection mandates.
- Cybersecurity became a standard agenda item in quarterly board meetings, with scenario planning and readiness scoring included in executive risk reviews.

Key Takeaway

Integrated Assurance enabled the firm to shift from reactive, siloed security operations to a board-aligned, risk-informed cybersecurity strategy. This transformation empowered executives to treat cybersecurity not as an IT function, but as a strategic lever for protecting business value, enabling innovation, and sustaining enterprise resilience.

INTEGRATED ASSURANCE ACROSS SYSTEMS, SERVICES, AND INFRASTRUCTURE

In most enterprises, IT operations is the nervous system of the business that is responsible for delivering and maintaining the systems that enable every function, from HR and Finance to Manufacturing and Customer Service. Yet in many organizations, IT and cybersecurity still operate in parallel, not in concert. This disconnect isn't due to negligence or lack of effort, it's systemic, born from historical separation of responsibilities, divergent performance metrics, and competing priorities. Integrated Assurance aims to dissolve those silos by embedding security directly into the operational fabric of IT, turning service delivery into a continuous assurance process.

Security cannot be bolted onto IT operations; it must be designed into it. That begins with service management. Whether you follow ITIL, or a custom operations model, security must be a first-class citizen in incident management, problem resolution, change control, and service delivery. Integrated Assurance ensures that when services are defined, risks are identified; when changes are proposed, controls are reviewed; and when incidents are resolved, lessons are fed back into the system to reduce future exposure as shown in Figure 13.2.

One of the key benefits of Integrated Assurance is aligning change and configuration management with security expectations. Enterprises often struggle to maintain configuration baselines, enforce hardened templates, or track changes across hybrid environments. These gaps aren't just operational liabilities; they are security vulnerabilities in disguise. By embedding control validation

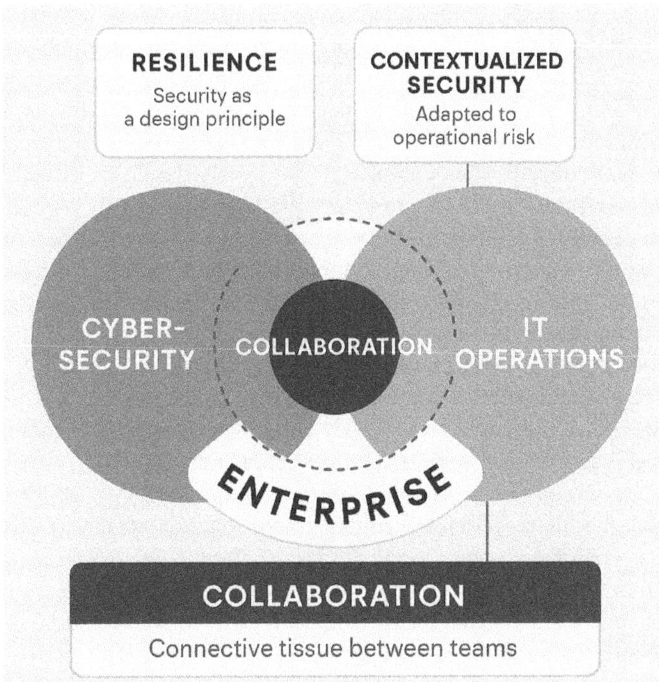

FIGURE 13.2 Integrated Assurance the connective tissue.

into change approval workflows and using configuration drift detection as both an operational and assurance signal, organizations can reduce risk without slowing delivery velocity.

Infrastructure delivery is another area where alignment is critical. In hybrid environments maintaining consistent control coverage is inherently difficult. IT operations owns much of this complexity, from virtualization platforms to container orchestration, from IAM systems to API gateways. Integrated Assurance enables IT teams to apply consistent security baselines, enforce policy as code, and implement observability strategies that detect anomalies across environments, not just within them.

Observability, in fact, becomes a cornerstone of operational assurance. Telemetry is focused on integrity and is no longer just about uptime. Are systems behaving as expected? Are workloads executing only what they should? Are privileged accounts accessing systems during odd hours or in abnormal ways? Integrated Assurance promotes the use of shared telemetry across IT and security, combining logs, traces, and metrics with contextual business data to detect not just failures, but malicious or risky behavior. This convergence supports faster detection, better diagnostics, and more informed response.

Integrated Assurance also addresses the historical friction between availability and security. IT operations are often measured on uptime, performance, and user satisfaction. Security, conversely, is measured on risk reduction, control effectiveness, and compliance. These goals don't have to be in conflict, yet in most organizations they are due to fragmentation. Integrated Assurance reframes the relationship from that of security versus uptime to security as a prerequisite for sustainable uptime. A system that is frequently compromised, misconfigured, or subject to hidden failure modes is not truly available because it is vulnerable.

This shift also changes how incidents are managed. Under Integrated Assurance, incident response becomes a joint operational function and not a purely cybersecurity function. IT owns the systems, security owns the threat model, and both own the response. Response playbooks should be codeveloped, runbooks should include both technical and business context, and post-incident reviews should be multidisciplinary. This collaboration ensures that remediations are operationally sound, and that root causes are addressed across control layers rather than just patched superficially.

Capacity planning and platform lifecycle management are additional dimensions of operational performance. IT operations must work with architecture and security teams to evaluate when legacy platforms should be modernized, when compensating controls should be extended, and how infrastructure investments are prioritized. For example, a platform that is fully depreciated but mission-critical may warrant continued operation, but only under a rigorously defined assurance model that includes isolation, access restrictions, enhanced monitoring, and predefined recovery strategies.

Cloud operations also present unique challenges. Platform teams are often given autonomy to deploy infrastructure on demand, sometimes without centralized oversight. Integrated Assurance introduces governance frameworks that enable agility without sacrificing control. That means enforcing guardrails through infrastructure-as-code templates, implementing centralized identity and access management, and using tagging and policy enforcement engines to maintain visibility and compliance. The goal is to empower delivery teams without compromising the assurance posture of the organization.

Finally, Integrated Assurance promotes cultural transformation within IT operations. Security becomes part of the operational vocabulary and not just an afterthought or external audit requirement. This means shifting from reactive ticket resolution to proactive risk identification, from manual processes to policy automation, and from isolated teams to cross-functional collaboration. Security champions within operations teams, just-in-time knowledge sharing, and shared KPIs between IT and security are all tactics that accelerate this convergence. In the Integrated Assurance model, IT operations are no longer simply responsible for "keeping the lights on." It becomes a guardian of business continuity, a steward of secure infrastructure, and a frontline actor in enterprise risk management. The outcome is not just more secure systems, but a more resilient, reliable, and aligned enterprise.

USE CASE: EMBEDDING INTEGRATED ASSURANCE INTO HYBRID IT OPERATIONS

Overview

A global manufacturing enterprise with a hybrid IT environment is facing increasing regulatory pressure, operational incidents, and fragmented IT/security coordination. Historically, IT operations and cybersecurity have operated in silos, leading to reactive security practices, inconsistent controls, and friction during audits. The organization initiates an Integrated Assurance program to embed security into operational workflows, align change control with risk visibility, and transform incident response into a coordinated enterprise function.

Actors

- IT Operations Teams—Responsible for infrastructure, cloud services, and application uptime
- Cybersecurity Teams—Accountable for risk management, threat detection, and compliance
- Enterprise Architects—Define patterns, standards, and security baselines
- Service Owners—Oversee critical business systems and ensure delivery outcomes
- Change Advisory Board (CAB)—Reviews proposed changes and evaluates risk
- Security Governance Committee—Ensures cross-functional alignment and oversight

Trigger

A series of post-incident reviews reveal recurring misconfigurations in production systems due to poor visibility between operations and security. A failed patch leads to system downtime and an SLA breach, resulting in lost revenue and reputational damage.

Preconditions

- IT operates across hybrid infrastructure (on-prem, cloud, containers)
- Configuration drift is common due to inconsistent change control
- Security incidents are managed post-facto with limited coordination
- Operational KPIs focus on uptime, while security KPIs focus on control status

Integrated Assurance Approach

Activity	Details
Joint service management redesign	• Embed security checkpoints into ITIL-aligned service management processes. • All service definitions must include risk profiles and associated controls. • Change requests must include pre-assurance validation from security tools.
Configuration drift detection	• Implement drift detection mechanisms with real-time telemetry and alerting. • Use a shared configuration baseline catalog managed by operations and security. • Drift metrics contribute to both operational and assurance dashboards.
Federated incident response playbooks	• Codevelop incident response playbooks across IT, Security, and Business Continuity. • Include both threat containment and system recovery in runbooks. • Conduct quarterly joint tabletop exercises and postmortems with both teams.
Policy-as-code guardrails	• Adopt infrastructure-as-code with embedded policy-as-code enforcement. • Validate every deployment against control standards using CI/CD pipelines. • Apply tagging and policy engines to enforce cloud security posture management.
Shared observability framework	• Build a centralized observability layer with unified logging, metrics, and traceability. • Integrate behavioral anomaly detection into both IT and security monitoring tools. • Map telemetry to service criticality and user impact to guide prioritization.
Assurance-driven change control	• Change Advisory Board includes risk ratings from the security team. • CAB decisions based on control coverage, operational readiness, and business impact. • All emergency changes are followed by accelerated assurance reviews.

Outcomes

Outcome	Description
Reduced incidents	Misconfigurations caught earlier due to policy automation and drift detection.

Outcome	Description
Improved Mean Time to Repair (MTTR)	MTTR reduced through coordinated incident response and better telemetry.
Audit readiness	Real-time compliance posture dashboards aligned with service configurations.
Cross-functional trust	Security and IT Operations collaborate continuously instead of episodically.
Business resilience	Systems are not just available, but provably secure and recoverable.

KPIs and Metrics

- Configuration drift rate by service tier
- Change success rate with control validation
- Mean time to containment for incidents
- SLA adherence rate post-assurance integration
- Number of codeveloped playbooks and exercises completed
- Risk-adjusted uptime for critical services

FROM ISOLATED DEFENSE TO INTEGRATED RISK STEWARDSHIP

In many enterprises, cybersecurity has matured into a distinct, well-resourced discipline with specialized teams, tools, and mandates. However, maturity doesn't always translate to integration. Too often, cybersecurity functions operate in isolation, focused on threat detection, control implementation, and compliance enforcement, while the rest of the enterprise moves at a different pace, driven by uptime, innovation, and business expansion. Integrated Assurance reshapes the role of cybersecurity from a standalone defensive function into a strategic enabler of trust, resilience, and operational excellence.

Traditional cybersecurity thinking centers on protecting assets through a layered defense model. This model still has value, but in the enterprise, the threat landscape is far more complex. Risk doesn't reside solely in technology; it lives in organizational seams that can be found in the space between IT and OT, between DevOps and Compliance, between Product and Procurement. These seams are where assumptions fail, controls break down, and adversaries thrive.

Integrated Assurance reframes cybersecurity as a connective tissue across these domains. It aligns defensive capabilities not just to infrastructure, but to enterprise workflows, business processes, and real-world interdependencies. Security becomes operational and woven into the day-to-day decisions of product teams, service owners, and executives. This is not just "shifting left", it's about expanding laterally. Security is no longer the final checkpoint, as it becomes part of every operational touchpoint, from code deployment to vendor onboarding to customer interaction.

One of the defining challenges of enterprise-scale security is the variability of control maturity across business units. Some domains operate with modern cloud-native architectures, robust identity governance, and continuous monitoring. Others are still dependent on legacy systems, manual processes, and minimal oversight. Trying to apply uniform policies across such a diverse landscape leads to two outcomes: overengineering in low-risk areas and underprotection where it's needed most. Integrated Assurance introduces contextualized security that focuses on adapting controls based on operational risk, business impact, and system criticality.

This approach requires security teams to evolve from control enforcers to risk partners. That means collaborating with the business to identify compensating controls when modernization isn't feasible, working with architecture to prioritize transformation roadmaps based on risk exposure, and supporting IT operations with practical, maintainable security practices. The focus shifts from ideal-state security to what can be consistently implemented, monitored, and improved over time without disrupting business continuity.

Cybersecurity also becomes more threat-informed under the Integrated Assurance model. Threat intelligence is not just consumed by SOC analysts; it's operationalized across the enterprise. This includes using threat modeling in application design, mapping detection use cases to real adversary behaviors and aligning incident response strategies to current attack trends. The cybersecurity team becomes the intelligence hub that translates external threat data into internal relevance and helps business leaders understand not just what the threats are, but where the enterprise is most exposed.

Incident response, likewise, is no longer a standalone function. Integrated Assurance transforms incident response into a federated model where responsibilities are distributed but coordinated. Cybersecurity teams lead detection and containment, but resolution involves IT operations, business continuity, legal, HR, and communications. Every incident becomes a systemic event requiring both technical remediation and organizational alignment. This model reduces resolution time, improves root cause analysis, and enhances the quality of lessons learned.

Metrics and reporting also evolve under Integrated Assurance. Cybersecurity performance is not measured solely by volume of alerts processed, vulnerabilities patched, incidents closed, but by outcomes. Are the organization's critical business processes protected? Are the right risks being prioritized? Are the investments made in security reducing exposure where it matters most? Cybersecurity leaders must be able to answer these questions in terms the business understands and Integrated Assurance provides the cross-domain visibility and governance structure to do so.

Cybersecurity's relationship with other functions also matures. With enterprise architecture, the focus is on building secure foundations. With compliance, it's about translating control requirements into operational behavior. With procurement, it's about ensuring that third-party risk is evaluated consistently and managed continuously. With HR, it's about managing insider threats and securing the workforce lifecycle. Integrated Assurance turns cybersecurity into a horizontal enabler and a partner to every domain, not just a stakeholder in a few.

Perhaps most critically, Integrated Assurance enables cybersecurity to become proactive. In traditional models, security spends too much time responding to alerts, chasing patch deadlines, or preparing for audits. With assurance embedded across functions, the security team gains the time and insight to focus on architecture, strategy, and resilience. This shift allows for more mature security architecture, investment in automation, and deeper engagement with transformation initiatives—all while maintaining visibility and control. Cybersecurity in the Integrated Assurance model is not simply about defending the enterprise. It's about enabling it by supporting faster decision-making, more resilient operations, smarter investments, and sustained business confidence in the face of uncertainty. It is the evolution from reactive control to strategic stewardship of risk and a transformation that is not just necessary, but overdue.

USE CASE: TRANSFORMING CYBERSECURITY INTO STRATEGIC RISK STEWARDSHIP AT A GLOBAL MANUFACTURING ENTERPRISE

Scenario

A global manufacturing company with 60,000 employees across 20 countries faces growing cybersecurity challenges due to a fragmented security model. Cybersecurity is siloed from IT operations and business units. Each region has adopted different security tools, practices, and policies, creating uneven control maturity and inconsistent risk postures across the enterprise. Despite a well-funded cybersecurity team and extensive tooling, breaches still occur due to gaps between detection and response, slow remediation timelines, and misaligned priorities between security, operations, and business leadership.

Problem Statement

Security is treated as an isolated defensive function, rather than a business enabler. Operations teams prioritize uptime and productivity; security teams prioritize threat prevention and compliance. This cultural and structural divide leads to:

- Delayed patching of critical systems due to production concerns.
- Missed threats in legacy systems with limited visibility.
- Inconsistent third-party risk management across procurement teams.
- Confusion during incident response due to unclear roles and fragmented communications.

Integrated Assurance Intervention

Implementation Steps	Activities
Establish executive sponsorship and governance realignment	– Create a cross-functional Risk and Assurance Steering Committee led by the CIO and CRO, with participation from cybersecurity, IT operations, enterprise architecture, compliance, HR, and business leaders. – Redefine cybersecurity KPIs to reflect business outcomes: risk-adjusted uptime, mean time to containment, and financial exposure reduction. – Translate cybersecurity strategy into board-level reporting frameworks, focused on enterprise resilience and business continuity.
Integrate cybersecurity into operational workflows	– Embed control validation and threat modeling into DevOps, change management, and service delivery processes. – Align configuration baselines and drift detection with operational SLAs to ensure that control hygiene and uptime are not in conflict. – Integrate security telemetry into IT observability platforms to enable shared visibility and joint response.
Contextualize and prioritize controls	– Classify business units by operational risk and control maturity using a heatmap. – Apply contextual security controls based on criticality and operational feasibility, avoiding uniform policies that cause friction or noncompliance. – Develop compensating controls for legacy platforms and enforce enhanced monitoring and access restrictions.
Operationalize threat intelligence	– Integrate real-world adversary tactics into detection engineering and threat modeling. – Use threat-informed defense strategies to shape investments and guide proactive hardening efforts.
Federate and coordinate incident response	– Design a federated incident response model where cybersecurity leads detection and containment, while IT, legal, communications, and business continuity functions collaborate on remediation and communication. – Develop joint playbooks and run tabletop simulations with all stakeholders. – Implement tiered escalation protocols with predefined decision rights.

Implementation Steps	Activities
Embed assurance across domains	– Collaborate with procurement to embed third-party risk scoring into vendor onboarding. – Work with HR to align insider threat detection with employee lifecycle events (e.g., terminations, job dissatisfaction). – Partner with enterprise architecture to ensure security is considered in platform selection and lifecycle management.

Outcomes

Metric	Before	After Integrated Assurance Implementation
Average time to contain a high-priority incident	72 hours	18 hours
% of systems with configuration drift exceeding SLA	40%	10%
Alignment score between IT and Security priorities (survey-based)	52%	91%
Time from threat identification to executive briefing	7 days	<24 hours
Third-party risk assessment completion before contract signing	55%	96%

Conclusion

This use case illustrates how a large enterprise can move beyond reactive, siloed cybersecurity practices to a model of Integrated Risk Stewardship. By embedding assurance into architecture, operations, and business governance, the organization improves not just its security posture, but also its agility, trust, and ability to respond to disruption. Integrated Assurance doesn't just protect the business. It empowers it.

CONCLUSION AND RECAP

This book began with a simple question: What is Integrated Assurance? After exploring the architecture, operational implications, organizational enablers, and domain-level execution strategies, the answer should now be clear. Integrated Assurance is not a framework in the traditional sense, it is a strategic model, a mindset, and a method for weaving cybersecurity and IT operations into a single, resilient fabric.

Integrated Assurance is a response to the reality of enterprise complexity. A reality where silos persist, tools multiply, and operational friction creates blind spots that no amount of traditional control layering can fully mitigate. Integrated Assurance doesn't discard the governance structures, standards, or frameworks we've built, rather it orchestrates them, ensuring they are lived, not just referenced. At the heart of Integrated Assurance is the recognition that alignment is security. Not alignment in the form of top-down mandates, but operational alignment where infrastructure, applications, and teams all move with shared context and coordinated purpose. This is not theoretical. It's practical. It's measurable. And it's achievable.

We've examined how executive leadership must champion security not as a cost but as a value-creating enabler. We've seen how IT operations, once focused solely on uptime, now bear a shared responsibility for assurance. And we've explored how cybersecurity must shed its isolation and become a horizontal layer of enablement, embedded in the architecture and rhythm of the enterprise. Throughout, one truth remains consistent: fragmentation is the enemy. Whether it's tool sprawl, siloed metrics, or duplicated controls, fragmentation breeds inefficiency and vulnerability. Integrated Assurance counters this by introducing interoperability by design, in systems, in processes, and in relationships.

The power of Integrated Assurance lies in its scalability. Whether you're operating in a centralized model or a federated multinational, this approach accommodates both global consistency and local autonomy. It provides scaffolding where it's needed, flexibility where it's justified, and a common language to bridge divergent business lines, technical domains, and risk postures. It also elevates assurance from an episodic task to a continuous function. No longer confined to audits, reviews, or post-incident retrospectives, assurance becomes a daily operational behavior that is practiced through backlog prioritization, architectural decision-making, incident response, and service delivery. It becomes something the organization does, not just something it documents.

With Integrated Assurance the role of technology shifts as well. Technologies and tools matter, but not as silver bullets. Their value is unlocked only when they are part of a coherent architectural vision and governed by principle. Tools don't create assurance; systems do. And systems are shaped by people, processes, and clarity of intent. The same holds true for metrics. Integrated Assurance requires new measurements and not just of control effectiveness, but of organizational convergence. Metrics must reflect shared outcomes, operational confidence, and business value. These are the indicators that tell us whether assurance is functioning and not just as a technical discipline, but as a cultural and operational norm.

Culture, ultimately, is the linchpin. Integrated Assurance demands collaboration, mutual trust, and shared accountability. It rewards transparency, encourages cross-functional dialogue, and promotes continuous improvement. Without cultural alignment, even the best-architected models will fail. With it, even imperfect systems can become remarkably resilient. What we are building here is not a static model. Integrated Assurance is adaptive by design. It evolves with the threat landscape, with technology shifts, and with the business itself. It supports transformation without compromising control. It enables innovation without increasing chaos. It's a security posture built not just for today's challenges, but for tomorrow's volatility.

14 Integrated Assurance as an Organizational Competency

LEARNING OBJECTIVE

- Gain insights how Integrated Assurance embeds security into all enterprise functions, making assurance a shared responsibility
- Learn that Enterprise Architecture becomes a strategic enabler of resilience through secure-by-design principles
- Understand that Assurance shifts from periodic audits to continuous, data-driven, and operationalized control
- Explore how culture, people, and partnerships are essential to sustaining security and building enterprise trust

As we introduced in Chapter 13, Integrated Assurance isn't simply a framework, it's an operational model that embeds security into the way an enterprise runs. It recognizes that every function in the organization has a role to play in managing risk and delivering assurance. In large-scale enterprises, where complexity and fragmentation are persistent, alignment across domains becomes essential for both security and resilience. Below, we examine how Integrated Assurance maps into the core functional areas of the enterprise, transforming isolated controls into cohesive, enterprise-wide capabilities.

DESIGNING RESILIENCE, ENABLING CONTROL, AND BRIDGING STRATEGIC INTENT WITH OPERATIONAL REALITY

Enterprise Architecture (EA) is often perceived as a governance function, focused on maintaining technology standards, managing system lifecycles, and ensuring alignment between IT investments and business goals. But in today's enterprise, where transformation is constant and complexity is endemic, EA has an even more critical role to play: enabling security and resilience by design. Integrated Assurance expands the traditional scope of EA, embedding cybersecurity principles into architectural planning, system design, and technology decision-making and not as constraints, but as intrinsic attributes of enterprise success.

Security is architecture. That is the fundamental shift Integrated Assurance brings. Instead of treating cybersecurity as a downstream concern and something to be reviewed after systems are deployed or solutions are selected. EA under this model positions assurance as a foundational design principle. It drives intentional decision-making around technology choices, interoperability, and risk tolerance across the portfolio. Secure-by-design becomes more than a slogan; it becomes a standard embedded in reference architectures, design patterns, and technology roadmaps.

DOI: 10.1201/9781003562153-18

One of the most strategic contributions EA makes under Integrated Assurance is the promotion of resilience and recoverability as first-class architectural qualities. While functional requirements typically dominate project planning, assurance requires equal weight to be given to how systems behave under stress, how quickly they can be restored, and how gracefully they degrade when compromised. Enterprise architects, working in tandem with security architects, can define service-level objectives not just for availability, but for incident response readiness, containment thresholds, and post-incident recovery timelines.

Legacy systems are where architecture and assurance frequently collide. These platforms, many of which are critical to core operations, often lack modern security controls, have limited vendor support, or are deeply integrated with upstream and downstream processes. Rather than forcing premature replacement or applying generic controls, Integrated Assurance guides EA to embed compensating controls into modernization roadmaps. This includes architectural isolation, stricter identity and access policies, network segmentation, runtime monitoring, and predefined rollback mechanisms. These controls must be designed intentionally and not as stopgaps, but as enduring risk management strategies that extend the safe life of legacy platforms.

EA also plays a pivotal role in governing technology sprawl. In large enterprises, the proliferation of applications, platforms, APIs, and integration layers introduces an attack surface that is both expansive and opaque. Integrated Assurance positions EA to take an active role in rationalizing this sprawl through cataloging assets, mapping interdependencies, and establishing control points at architectural junctures. By maintaining an authoritative system-of-record for enterprise applications and services, EA enables more effective control implementation, threat modeling, and compliance mapping across environments.

Architecture review boards, which are a common mechanism in mature enterprise organizations, become more powerful under the Integrated Assurance model. These boards are not simply gatekeepers; they evolve into cross-functional forums for risk negotiation, bringing together cybersecurity, IT operations, compliance, legal, and business representatives. Decisions are made not solely on technical merit, but on a shared understanding of business impact, control feasibility, and acceptable risk. This governance integration ensures that security concerns are addressed early, and that solutions are both secure and sustainable.

Another area of impact is cloud and hybrid architecture. As enterprises expand into multicloud environments, EA must ensure consistent security policies, visibility, and control enforcement across providers. Integrated Assurance helps architecture teams define cloud adoption frameworks that include embedded identity management, encryption standards, monitoring capabilities, and shared responsibility models. This minimizes the variance in control maturity between cloud-native and on-premises systems and supports a unified approach to infrastructure governance.

Data architecture also intersects with Integrated Assurance. EA must account for how data flows through the enterprise, where it resides, and how it is protected, especially in an environment where regulatory requirements around privacy, residency, and sovereignty are growing more complex. Working with data governance teams, enterprise architects can define assurance zones based on data classification, ensure encryption and tokenization are enforced at key transit and storage points, and validate that data architectures support both operational needs and compliance requirements.

Furthermore, EA provides a bridge between strategy and execution. It translates high-level governance and security policy into actionable designs that solution architects, engineers, and product teams can implement. This translation includes the codification of security principles into architecture artifacts that are reusable templates, policy-as-code definitions, design blueprints, which ultimately accelerate secure adoption and reduce interpretation errors. Integrated Assurance relies on this architectural rigor to maintain consistency without stifling agility.

EA also helps define the boundaries of responsibility and ownership. In large organizations, ambiguity over who owns what leads to control failures and delayed remediation. Through clearly defined architectural domains and ownership models, EA supports Integrated Assurance by ensuring that security responsibilities are distributed appropriately and embedded within the teams closest to the risk. This decentralization is managed, not chaotic, because it is grounded in a common architectural language and governance model. Under the Integrated Assurance model, EA becomes the linchpin that connects intent to implementation, strategy to security, and vision to viable execution. By designing for assurance as an operational imperative EA enables the enterprise to grow securely, modernize responsibly, and withstand the pressures of transformation and threat alike. It is not only a discipline of control, but one of coherence and in a complex, high-stakes environment, coherence is the foundation of enterprise resilience.

Use Case	Example	EA Contributions
Designing for resilience	Cloud-native redesign for logistics systems with geo-redundancy and immutable backups.	Defined RTO/RPO, resilient architecture patterns, integrated chaos engineering for failure validation.
Enabling control	Securing a legacy banking platform through segmentation and API gateway enforcement.	Zero Trust architecture, Runtime Application Self-Protection (RASP), and network isolation zones.
Bridging strategy with operations	Multi-cloud governance for a retail enterprise with embedded policy enforcement.	Policy-as-code, standardized accountability models, regulatory control mapping.
System-of-record rationalization	Centralization of application portfolio for a media organization to reduce redundant controls.	Dependency mapping, retirement of legacy apps, implementation of assurance zones.
Governance by design	Cross-functional Architecture Review Board (ARB) at a manufacturing firm using risk scoring.	Integrated DevSecOps gates, traceable control decisions, risk impact scoring embedded in lifecycle.
Secure data architecture	Healthcare data infrastructure segmented to enforce HIPAA and GDPR compliance.	Data residency enforcement, privacy-by-design principles, tokenization and encryption zones.
Cyber risk metrics alignment	Executive dashboards tracking uptime, risk thresholds, and containment metrics.	Role-specific dashboards, telemetry-based risk alignment, and business-centric risk indicators.

TRANSLATING CONTROL FRAMEWORKS INTO ACTIONABLE ASSURANCE ACROSS THE ENTERPRISE

In today's enterprise environment, compliance and risk management functions are under increasing pressure to do more than maintain regulatory alignment, they must deliver continuous, demonstrable assurance that the organization is actively managing risk in an increasingly complex operating environment. The traditional approach of periodic audits, static risk registers, and framework-level control mapping is no longer sufficient. Integrated Assurance redefines the compliance and risk management function as a dynamic, operationally integrated capability and one that connects governance intent with day-to-day execution and informs decision-making across every function of the enterprise.

At its most foundational level, Integrated Assurance brings clarity and coherence to control frameworks. Large enterprises often operate under multiple regulatory regimes such as GDPR and PCI-DSS, or sector-specific mandates like NERC Critical Infrastructure Protection, or HIPAA. Add to those internal corporate policies, contractual obligations, and voluntary framework such as NIST CSF, ISO/IEC 27001, and COBIT, and the result is a tangled web of overlapping and sometimes conflicting controls. Integrated Assurance helps harmonize these requirements into a single unified control model that eliminates redundancy, reduces audit fatigue, and enables focused, risk-aligned execution. However, harmonization alone isn't enough. Compliance often breaks down at the operational level because mapped controls lack operational context. A control might exist in theory, but how is it enforced? Who owns it? How is its effectiveness measured over time? Integrated Assurance closes this gap by ensuring that control objectives are tied to actual processes, systems, and behaviors and that those mappings are validated through live control testing, not just documentation. This makes assurance evidence-based and continuous, rather than reactive and event-driven.

Risk quantification is another critical challenge. Traditional risk assessments tend to be qualitative, subjective, and point-in-time. They rarely reflect the real-time posture of the organization or the interconnected nature of modern threats. Integrated Assurance modernizes risk analysis by incorporating data-driven, dynamic inputs from control telemetry, vulnerability intelligence, incident trends, and business impact models. This allows for quantitative risk scoring that is both defensible and actionable, helping leadership prioritize investment, remediation, and strategic decision-making. This approach also supports the transition from risk documentation to risk ownership. Many enterprises suffer from distributed responsibility, centralized accountability, where control failures are tracked by risk teams but remediation is expected from operational units without clear handoff, context, or authority. Integrated Assurance formalizes risk handoffs and accountability structures, ensuring that identified risks are assigned to the appropriate business or technical owner, with clarity around remediation timelines, escalation paths, and required artifacts. This drives real ownership of risk, rather than passive acknowledgment.

Another core tenet of Integrated Assurance is the shift toward continuous assurance and adaptive compliance. Rather than preparing for audits as isolated events, assurance activities are embedded into normal operations. This includes automated control testing, configuration validation, access reviews, data retention enforcement, and other indicators that can be monitored at scale. Feedback loops ensure that failures are detected early, and that control deficiencies are not only remediated, but learned from enabling iterative improvement in both design and execution.

Compliance reporting also transforms under this model. Reports are no longer static checklists but interactive dashboards that reflect current posture, trends, and risk exposure. These outputs are tailored to different audiences are detailed evidence for auditors, risk summaries for executives, and operational metrics for line managers. Integrated Assurance enables compliance teams to provide real-time visibility into assurance status across domains, supporting better governance, faster decision-making, and reduced surprises during audits or incidents. Integrated Assurance strengthens the relationship between compliance, cybersecurity, IT operations, and legal. Compliance is no longer an island, interpreting control requirements in a vacuum. Instead, it becomes a facilitator of coordinated assurance, working alongside these functions to interpret regulations in context, align them with operational constraints, and design enforcement mechanisms that are both practical and durable. This collaboration ensures that controls are not just compliant on paper, but effective in reality.

In global enterprises, regulatory complexity is amplified by geographic variation. Data sovereignty laws, sectoral regulations, and local privacy mandates often require differentiated approaches to control implementation. Integrated Assurance provides the scaffolding for a federated compliance model, where global policy is centrally defined but locally adapted which ensures that control objectives are met without imposing uniformity where it's infeasible. This balance between consistency and flexibility is essential for sustainable compliance at scale.

Third-party risk management is another area where compliance and risk teams play a central role. With expanding reliance on cloud providers, SaaS platforms, BPOs, and strategic vendors, control boundaries increasingly extend beyond the organization. Integrated Assurance embeds third-party risk assessments, contractual control requirements, and continuous validation into the vendor lifecycle. Risk teams move beyond initial due diligence and into lifecycle-based assurance that reflects the evolving nature of vendor relationships.

Ultimately, Integrated Assurance elevates compliance and risk management from oversight functions to strategic enablers of trust. They provide the connective tissue between board-level risk expectations and frontline execution. They ensure that risks are not just identified, but owned, managed, and reduced. They create the mechanisms for the enterprise to demonstrate defensibility and not just to regulators, but to customers, shareholders, and internal stakeholders.

Assurance Practice	Example	Outcome
Unified control model	Map PCI-DSS, ISO/IEC 27001, GDPR, and SOX controls into a centralized repository using a unified control framework (UCF).	Reduces audit duplication, aligns controls across frameworks, enables traceable ownership and telemetry-based validation.
Operationalized control objectives	Automated privileged access reviews conducted quarterly via IAM platform, with evidence linked to ticketing system.	Provides live assurance data, ensures accountability, and reduces manual audit prep.
Continuous risk quantification	Dynamic risk scores calculated using real-time control telemetry and mapped to system criticality.	Enables business-aligned prioritization of remediation and investment decisions.
Formal risk ownership	Kubernetes misconfigurations are assigned with SLA, escalation path, and owner mapped via Integrated Assurance Platform.	Improves accountability and timely remediation with audit traceability.
Federated compliance	Centralized data retention policy with EU-specific automation for GDPR and US exceptions for litigation holds.	Enables localization without compromising global compliance objectives.
Real-time reporting	Dashboards showing control drift, remediation velocity, and risk-adjusted uptime by unit and function.	Supports decision-making for executives, line managers, and auditors with real-time insights.
Third-party continuous assurance	Vendors monitored post-onboarding via external threat feeds, SLA ticket checks, and contract enforcement.	Transforms point-in-time reviews into continuous third-party risk governance.

EMBEDDING INTEGRATED ASSURANCE INTO HIGH-VELOCITY ENGINEERING AND THE SOFTWARE SUPPLY CHAIN

As enterprises accelerate digital transformation, software development becomes one of the most essential functions in the organization. DevOps and platform engineering teams are tasked with delivering features quickly, automating infrastructure, and enabling scale. But with speed comes exposure: insecure code, misconfigured cloud resources, hardcoded secrets, vulnerable third-party libraries, and inadequate access controls. Traditional security models can't keep pace. Integrated Assurance meets this challenge by embedding security into the entire software delivery lifecycle and enabling agility without compromising control.

The essence of DevSecOps is shifting security left, but Integrated Assurance takes it further. It's not just about embedding security in code but aligning assurance practices with the rhythm and architecture of high-velocity delivery. This means rethinking the role of cybersecurity from an external validator to an integrated design and delivery partner. In this model, security is part of the engineering process from backlog grooming and threat modeling, through CI/CD execution, to monitoring and response in production. One of the foundational capabilities in this model is Security as Code. Infrastructure, policies, identity configurations, and controls are all codified, versioned, peer-reviewed, and tested like any other software artifact. This ensures that security practices are repeatable, testable, and auditable. With policy-as-code frameworks such as Open Policy Agent, or native tooling in cloud platforms, organizations can enforce access rules, network configurations, encryption standards, and deployment guardrails automatically and consistently.

Integrated Assurance also demands a robust Secure Software Development Lifecycle that is actually lived, not just documented. This includes the automation of Static Application Security Testing, Dynamic Application Security Testing, Software Composition Analysis, and secrets scanning, all within the CI/CD pipeline. The results of these scans shouldn't create operational drag or noise; they must be triaged in real time, with severity contextualized based on the system's criticality and threat model. Development and security teams must collaborate to define risk-based thresholds for blocking deployments or creating exceptions.

Another critical dimension is software supply chain security. Modern applications are built from hundreds of dependencies including open-source libraries, container images, APIs, and infrastructure modules, many of which are sourced from unvetted or unverifiable origins. Integrated Assurance embeds controls to manage this sprawl: verified Software Bills of Materials, signed artifacts, trusted registries, and runtime validation. These are essential for resilience against upstream compromise, dependency confusion attacks, and zero-day vulnerabilities in widely adopted libraries.

Secrets management is another area where Integrated Assurance plays a vital role. Hardcoded secrets, API keys in source code, and unmanaged credentials are still common in enterprise codebases. With automated secrets scanning and integration of secrets managers, development teams can automate secret injection and rotation, reducing the risk of exposure without adding friction to development workflows. This ensures that sensitive data is handled with the same rigor as critical infrastructure.

In high-velocity environments, observability becomes assurance. Integrated Assurance encourages development and platform teams to integrate logging, tracing, and anomaly detection directly into their build and deployment patterns. If a container behaves differently in production than it did in staging, or if an internal API suddenly starts receiving large volumes of traffic from unusual sources, these are signals of risk that must be captured, correlated, and actioned. DevOps teams, alongside security operations center and incident response teams, must share this telemetry to detect and contain threats faster.

Integrated Assurance also demands a shift in culture which means training developers on secure coding principles, threat modeling techniques, and common misconfiguration patterns in cloud-native environments. But more than training, it means building feedback loops into tools developers already use: code editors, pull request workflows, issue trackers, and CI dashboards. Developers should receive real-time, contextual guidance and not generalized policy documents after the fact.

It is important to note metrics also evolve and success cannot be measured solely by the number of vulnerabilities closed or compliance passed. Under Integrated Assurance, metrics must capture the security health of the engineering process itself, such as time to remediate critical findings, policy violation frequency, secure coding adherence, and drift from secure configurations. These metrics must be fed into broader enterprise assurance reporting so that leadership sees a full picture, not just operational risk, but development risk as well.

Governance structures must adapt too. Integrated Assurance recommends embedding security architects within engineering teams as individuals who understand both development workflows and enterprise security policies. These embedded roles act as accelerators, not gatekeepers. They provide just-in-time guidance, help developers navigate architectural reviews, and ensure security is part of design thinking, not a late-stage audit.

Integrated Assurance helps balance innovation with control. Enterprises often fear that embedding security into DevOps will slow delivery. The opposite is true when done right. Automated controls, preapproved secure templates, reusable policy modules, and preintegrated observability remove uncertainty and reduce rework. Security becomes a feature of the delivery pipeline, not a friction point. It empowers teams to move faster, because they're moving with confidence, not guesswork.

In total, Integrated Assurance enables DevSecOps to scale across the enterprise by aligning tooling, culture, and governance. It transforms security from a series of disconnected checks into a continuous, embedded quality that travels with the code from ideation to production. And in doing so, it ensures that speed and safety are not at odds, but mutually reinforcing capabilities in the enterprise software delivery machine.

OPERATIONALIZING INTEGRATED ASSURANCE IN THE AGE OF DATA-DRIVEN ENTERPRISES

Data is no longer a byproduct of enterprise operations, it is the fuel that powers every strategic decision, customer interaction, and innovation initiative. From real-time analytics and AI model training to customer personalization and compliance reporting, data underpins business value. But with great data comes great risk. The volume, variety, and velocity of enterprise data has grown beyond traditional controls, and the exposure of sensitive data, whether through misconfiguration, misuse, or compromise, now constitutes one of the most material risks to an organization. Integrated Assurance brings structure, visibility, and enforceability to data governance and security, enabling enterprises to manage data not just as an asset, but as a sustained assurance responsibility.

At the heart of this challenge is information governance and the policies, processes, and technologies that ensure data is accurate, secure, and used ethically. Integrated Assurance operationalizes governance by linking data policies directly to business processes and systems. This goes beyond defining data owners and stewards; it means mapping data flows across the enterprise, enforcing controls at ingestion, transit, and storage, and ensuring that data governance policies are actually implemented and not just documented.

A critical enabler of this model is data lineage visibility. Enterprises must understand not only where data resides, but how it moves, from source to transformation to output and who touches it along the way. Integrated Assurance embeds lineage tracking into data platforms, extract transform and load pipelines, and analytical tooling, enabling the organization to trace data back to origin and forward to consumption. This capability is essential not just for compliance, but for validating the integrity of analytical outputs and AI models.

Data classification is another foundational pillar, because without understanding the sensitivity of data, it's impossible to apply controls proportionally. Integrated Assurance drives automated classification at scale using pattern recognition, machine learning, and metadata tagging in order to categorize data based on regulatory requirements, business sensitivity, and lifecycle stage. These classifications then inform access controls, encryption policies, retention schedules, and logging requirements. The result is a risk-aligned control model where protections scale with sensitivity.

Integrated Assurance also strengthens data retention and lifecycle management. In many enterprises, data persists long past its useful life and is often spread across shadow IT systems, old backups, and forgotten databases. This persistence not only increases storage costs but significantly amplifies risk. Through automated retention enforcement, scheduled purging, and immutable audit logs, Integrated Assurance ensures that data is retained only as long as it is needed, and that its disposition is both verifiable and policy driven. In regulated environments, data sovereignty and localization are increasingly complex concerns. Integrated Assurance helps organizations build a data architecture that respects jurisdictional boundaries through isolating datasets by geography, tagging assets by regulatory domain, and ensuring that residency requirements are not just policy intentions but operational realities. This is especially critical for multinational enterprises navigating conflicting laws across the several jurisdictions.

Access governance is another area where Integrated Assurance delivers value. Traditional identity and access management systems often struggle to keep pace with dynamic, data-centric environments where users and applications require fine-grained access to data subsets. Integrated Assurance extends identity and access management into the data layer by implementing attribute-based access control, role-based policies, and just-in-time data entitlements. This enables contextual, least-privilege access enforcement that scales with both data volume and user complexity.

Real-time monitoring and anomaly detection are vital for maintaining trust in data environments. Integrated Assurance integrates data activity monitoring, database audit logging, and end user behavior analytics to detect anomalous access patterns, exfiltration attempts, or policy violations in progress. This telemetry is shared with security operations center and analytics teams to support unified response and forensics. Rather than relying solely on static permissions, enterprises gain dynamic awareness of how data is actually being used.

The rise of AI and ML introduces new data assurance challenges. Model drift, training data contamination, and unintended bias are risks not captured by traditional controls. Integrated Assurance extends into AI governance and ensures that models are trained on properly classified and curated datasets, that model decisions can be explained and traced, and that privacy risks are mitigated through techniques such as differential privacy, anonymization, and federated learning. This enables the secure and ethical deployment of AI at enterprise scale.

Data analytics platforms also must support multitenant, multiuse environments. Business users, analysts, data scientists, and external partners often share access to centralized data lakes or warehouse environments. Integrated Assurance ensures that platform-level controls, such as row-level security, masking, encryption at rest and in transit, and sandbox isolation, are enforced consistently, regardless of use case. These controls must be transparent, automated, and auditable, so that assurance doesn't rely on manual intervention or point-in-time reviews.

Finally, Integrated Assurance around data requires a cross-functional governance model. Data owners, platform engineers, security architects, compliance officers, and business analysts must work from a shared understanding of data value, risk, and control expectations. Integrated Assurance formalizes this collaboration through data governance councils, data classification working groups, and integrated audit-readiness reviews that ensure continuous alignment between data strategy and operational control.

EXTENDING INTEGRATED ASSURANCE THROUGH TRUSTED PARTNERSHIPS AND THIRD-PARTY RELATIONSHIPS

Organizations operate within vast ecosystems of third-party providers, managed service partners, cloud platforms, SaaS vendors, offshore development teams, logistics firms, and supply chain intermediaries. While each plays a critical role in delivering business outcomes, every external relationship expands the enterprise's risk surface. Procurement and vendor management functions are no longer just responsible for cost control and contract execution; they are also the front lines of cybersecurity and operational assurance. Integrated Assurance embeds security into the entire vendor lifecycle, transforming these functions into strategic enablers of resilience, trust, and defensibility.

The first principle of Integrated Assurance in procurement is recognizing third-party risk as first-party risk. Enterprises are frequently blindsided by breaches, disruptions, or regulatory violations originating from vendors. These aren't edge cases anymore, rather they are systemic vulnerabilities, especially when sensitive data, critical infrastructure, or customer trust is handled by partners. Whether it's a SaaS provider managing HR data, a logistics vendor accessing internal APIs, or a business process outsourcing provider operating on shared systems, the blast radius of third-party compromise often extends deep into core business functions. To address this, Integrated Assurance embeds security and risk criteria into the procurement process itself. Security isn't introduced after vendor selection or during onboarding, it is a selection criterion, right alongside cost, capability, and delivery timelines. This includes security questionnaires, control self-assessments, compliance attestations, and risk scoring based on industry reputation, prior incidents, or geopolitical exposure.

Procurement teams must be trained and empowered to evaluate these inputs with rigor and consult with security and risk teams as part of their standard due diligence workflow.

Contractual controls are another critical component. Integrated Assurance requires that security obligations are codified into contracts and not as vague statements of intent, but as enforceable clauses. This includes requirements for encryption, incident notification timelines, access restrictions, data handling practices, subcontractor vetting, audit rights, and termination protocols. Where feasible, security service-level agreements should be included, setting measurable expectations for response times, system availability, and compliance with agreed-upon controls. Contracts become a vehicle for assurance, not just a legal formality.

Onboarding is only the beginning. Integrated Assurance extends assurance throughout the vendor lifecycle, emphasizing ongoing validation over one-time assessments. This means periodic reassessments based on criticality, continuous monitoring for changes in posture, and automated integration of third-party risk intelligence. High-risk vendors may require technical validation through penetration tests, API scanning, cloud security reviews, or secure configuration audits. Integrated Assurance isn't static as it evolves with the relationship and with the changing risk landscape.

Vendor segmentation is essential to scale this model as not every vendor requires the same level of scrutiny. Integrated Assurance introduces a tiered risk model, categorizing vendors based on access level, data sensitivity, system integration, and business criticality. Low-risk vendors may undergo streamlined assessments, while high-risk providers, such as those hosting regulated data or embedded in critical infrastructure, are subject to deeper evaluation, enhanced monitoring, and executive oversight. This tiering ensures that assurance efforts are proportional and sustainable. Supply chain security requires special focus. Enterprises must not only evaluate their direct suppliers but also gain visibility into subtier relationships. This includes verifying that vendors follow secure development practices, do not rely on unvetted third parties, and have continuity plans in place. Integrated Assurance supports transitive risk modeling, enabling organizations to map dependency chains and identify concentration risks, single points of failure, or potential geopolitical conflicts that could affect operational continuity.

Vendor offboarding is another critical, yet often overlooked, phase of assurance. When a relationship ends, whether due to contract expiration, strategic shift, or risk concern, the offboarding process must ensure that access is revoked, data is returned or destroyed, and integrations are dismantled. Integrated Assurance formalizes offboarding procedures, ensuring that off-cycle departures do not result in lingering access, data leakage, or operational gaps. These procedures should be rehearsed, auditable, and documented with input from security, IT, legal, and business stakeholders.

Integrated Assurance also enables shared responsibility modeling with vendors. In cloud services and managed platforms, security responsibilities are often split between provider and customer, but the boundaries can be ambiguous. Who's responsible for patching? For monitoring? For identity and access management? Through collaborative assurance exercises, joint incident response plans, and clearly defined roles and responsibilities, enterprises can eliminate gaps and minimize misunderstandings before they become failures. To drive all of this, procurement and vendor management teams must be empowered with the right tools and governance to provide visibility, workflow automation, and documentation necessary to manage assurance at scale. Just as importantly, assurance governance bodies must include representation from procurement, ensuring that third-party risks are reviewed and prioritized alongside internal threats.

Finally, the culture must shift. Procurement cannot be seen as a transactional gatekeeper, and security cannot treat vendors as liabilities by default. Integrated Assurance fosters a collaborative model, where vendors are viewed as strategic partners in risk management. This includes regular security reviews, mutual knowledge sharing, participation in security exercises, and aligned incentives around compliance, uptime, and data protection. High-trust relationships, underpinned by strong assurance structures, yield better outcomes for both parties.

BUILDING A CULTURE OF SECURITY, TRUST, AND BEHAVIORAL ASSURANCE ACROSS THE HUMAN LAYER

People remain the most complex and variable element of any enterprise risk model. Employees, contractors, vendors, interns, each individual represents a unique combination of access, intent, behavior, and potential vulnerability. Over the past several years digital transformation has accelerated and hybrid work has become much more of the norm, with traditional boundaries of the enterprise workforce dissolving. HR teams are no longer peripheral to cybersecurity; they are essential stakeholders in shaping enterprise security posture. Integrated Assurance embeds security into the entire employee lifecycle, ensuring that security is not just a technical concern but a lived, organizational value.

The foundation begins with security-aligned onboarding. HR plays a pivotal role in defining what access is granted, how roles are provisioned, and what behavioral expectations are communicated on day one. Integrated Assurance ensures that identity and access controls are embedded into onboarding workflows, with role-based access assigned through automated provisioning tied to job functions, not manual approvals. Employees should receive not just policies to read, but contextual, scenario-based security training aligned to their function such as different modules for finance personnel handling wire transfers versus developers deploying to production.

One of the most impactful areas of collaboration is in insider risk management. Whether through negligence, burnout, coercion, or malice, insiders are often involved in the most damaging breaches and the signs are rarely technical at first. Behavioral changes, HR grievances, offboarding anomalies, or access requests inconsistent with job roles can all be early indicators. Integrated Assurance formalizes communication channels between HR, legal, and security, enabling behavioral threat intelligence to be incorporated into risk models, and ensuring that appropriate action can be taken discreetly, ethically, and lawfully.

Offboarding is just as critical as onboarding. The sudden departure of a privileged user, contractor, or remote employee must trigger a coordinated workflow that includes immediate deprovisioning, asset recovery, revocation of credentials, and audit logging. Integrated Assurance ensures these processes are well documented, automated where possible, and tested regularly. HR, IT, and Security must share ownership of offboarding workflows, reducing the time between employee exit and access removal to minutes, not days.

HR is also instrumental in managing role changes and organizational restructuring. As employees are promoted, reassigned, or change departments, their access needs change, yet many enterprises lack the automation and governance to adjust entitlements accordingly. Integrated Assurance promotes dynamic access governance, where HR systems of record feed identity management systems in real time. This ensures that access is right-sized continuously and that unnecessary or excessive privileges are detected and remediated promptly.

The integration of HR into incident response and crisis management is another dimension of Integrated Assurance. During breaches involving personnel, whether as victims, sources, or collateral, HR must coordinate with security, legal, and communications teams to manage the human impact. This includes communication plans, disciplinary processes, legal consultation, and support services. Integrated Assurance ensures that playbooks include HR involvement and that HR staff are trained in their role during cyber incidents, especially in cases involving privacy violations, harassment, or reputational damage.

Culture is the throughline that ties it all together. HR is the steward of organizational culture and culture is where security succeeds or fails. Integrated Assurance empowers HR to partner with executive leadership and cybersecurity teams to shape a culture where secure behavior is expected, supported, and recognized. This includes incentivizing secure practices, celebrating security champions, and embedding security values into leadership training, performance reviews, and company-wide messaging.

As hybrid and remote work persist, so too must the assurance of workforce identity, location, and activity. HR teams are increasingly involved in defining remote work policies, trusted locations, travel scenarios, and flexible work arrangements. Integrated Assurance enables these policies to be reflected in conditional access controls, geofencing, time-based restrictions, and enhanced authentication for high-risk roles or regions. The model emphasizes that security in remote environments is not a workaround and it must be architected into the employee experience from the start.

Finally, HR plays a governance role in ethical oversight. As security technologies become more powerful, questions of employee privacy, fairness, and transparency become central. Integrated Assurance requires that privacy, ethics, and security be cogoverned, with HR representing the voice of the workforce in ensuring that surveillance does not become invasive, and that monitoring aligns with organizational values and legal obligations. In a truly resilient enterprise, security should be embraced and not imposed on the workforce. HR, when aligned under Integrated Assurance, become active contributors to security outcomes. They operationalize trust, accountability, and behavior in ways no technology alone can. This partnership ensures that the human element, long seen as the weakest link, becomes a source of strength, alignment, and assurance.

CONVERGING THE PHYSICAL AND CYBER DOMAINS TO BUILD ENTERPRISE-SCALE RESILIENCE

Cybersecurity does not begin and end in the digital realm. Data centers, control rooms, office buildings, distribution hubs, and operational sites all present physical access points that, if compromised, can lead to cascading digital failures. Facilities and Physical Security teams, therefore, are essential partners in Integrated Assurance, responsible not just for traditional safety and access, but for securing the physical perimeter of digital trust. Integrated Assurance recognizes the convergence of physical and cyber domains as a critical shift in enterprise security thinking. In many breach scenarios, especially in critical infrastructure, manufacturing, or hybrid IT/OT environments, the initial compromise is physical. A misplaced badge, an unsecured terminal, an unmonitored delivery entrance, or an improperly decommissioned device can create entry points into networked systems. By embedding physical security into the broader enterprise assurance model, organizations can reduce risk at the root.

At the core of this integration is identity and access control. Facilities teams manage physical access often using badge systems, biometric readers, or keypads. However, these systems are frequently managed independently of digital identity platforms. Integrated Assurance mandates a unified identity governance model, where physical and logical access are correlated. A terminated employee's badge should deactivate with the same immediacy as their user account. Access logs should feed into security operations tools, enabling correlation between physical presence and digital activity.

Surveillance and monitoring systems also play an important role as organizations deploy extensive video surveillance, motion detection, intrusion alarms, and environmental sensors across facilities. Integrated Assurance promotes the convergence of these telemetry sources with cyber-monitoring platforms. Similarly, environmental sensors detecting overheating or humidity can be linked to data center monitoring tools, triggering preemptive risk mitigation workflows.

Data centers and on-premises server rooms remain high-risk areas. Even as cloud adoption increases, many enterprises still operate hybrid environments with colocation facilities, regional compute nodes, and legacy systems that cannot be easily virtualized. These assets require robust physical protections beyond locks and guards, but layered controls such as access zones, dual-authentication entry, logging, mantraps, video analytics, and tamper-evident protections. Integrated Assurance ensures that physical control frameworks are documented, regularly tested, and audited alongside digital controls.

In OT environments, such as manufacturing plants, energy grids, utilities, and logistics centers, the interdependency of physical systems and digital controls is especially acute. Programmable Logic Controllers (PLCs), Supervisory Control and Data Acquisition (SCADA) systems, and industrial sensors often reside in physically accessible locations. A threat actor doesn't need to exploit a vulnerability in code if they can walk up and plug into a control system directly. Integrated Assurance addresses this by aligning physical security postures with industrial systems control cybersecurity frameworks, applying zoning strategies, asset isolation, and incident escalation paths specific to OT environments.

Facilities security also extends to remote and hybrid work models. As employees increasingly operate from home offices, coworking spaces, and on-the-go locations, the physical security perimeter becomes amorphous. Integrated Assurance requires organizations to define policies for remote physical security, such as approved workspace configurations, secure storage for company assets, webcam and microphone restrictions, and guidelines for securing printed materials and mobile devices. HR, IT, and Facilities must work together to enable a secure yet flexible work environment.

Visitor management is another often-overlooked assurance layer. In many enterprise facilities, visitors, contractors, and service providers are granted temporary access that is sometimes unsupervised. Integrated Assurance introduces structured, auditable workflows for visitor vetting, badging, time-limited access provisioning, and escorting policies. These processes should be digitally logged and correlated with access control and surveillance systems, ensuring a full chain of custody for all individuals entering sensitive areas.

During incidents, Facilities and Physical Security teams play a key role in crisis response and business continuity. Whether it's a data breach, fire, flood, civil unrest, or coordinated cyber-physical attack, they are responsible for evacuation procedures, lockdown protocols, safe zones, and continuity of operations planning. Integrated Assurance ensures these responsibilities are integrated into enterprise-wide incident response playbooks, with clearly defined roles for facilities personnel and rehearsed coordination with cybersecurity, IT, and executive leadership.

Integrated Assurance also brings a governance dimension to physical security. Access policies must be documented, regularly reviewed, and aligned with enterprise security objectives. Surveillance retention policies must comply with privacy regulations. Facility audits should include not only safety and maintenance checks but also security control validations, such as door audits, access revocation reviews, and incident scenario simulations. Physical security must no longer be siloed under facilities management and it must be represented in risk councils, assurance forums, and architecture boards.

Finally, the cultural component of physical assurance is essential. Facilities teams are often the first point of contact for new employees, visitors, or third-party contractors. Their awareness of social engineering threats, tailgating, badge misuse, and suspicious behavior can serve as an early warning system for broader security concerns. Integrated Assurance encourages cross-training and collaboration between physical and cybersecurity teams, building a shared understanding of threat scenarios and a common vocabulary for risk.

EMBEDDING DEFENSIBILITY, COMPLIANCE READINESS, AND ETHICAL RISK GOVERNANCE INTO THE ENTERPRISE

In a global business environment shaped by escalating regulatory complexity, evolving legal precedents, and heightened public scrutiny, Legal and Regulatory Affairs functions have become enablers of enterprise resilience. Security incidents today are not just technical failures; they are legal events, often with far-reaching implications for compliance, liability, reputation, and regulatory standing. Integrated Assurance positions Legal and Regulatory Affairs as essential collaborators in designing, governing, and enforcing enterprise risk posture and ensuring the business is not just secure, but defensible, ethical, and prepared. At its foundation, Integrated Assurance recognizes that legal risk and cybersecurity risk are deeply interconnected. Every control failure, whether a data breach, policy violation, unauthorized disclosure, or improper surveillance, carries potential legal consequences. These can include regulatory investigations, class-action lawsuits, breach of contract claims, and even criminal exposure. By embedding Legal early in assurance design, enterprises ensure that security measures are not only effective but aligned with evolving legal standards and enforceable under law.

One of the most immediate areas of impact is data protection and privacy law. Regulations such as GDPR, CCPA, CPRA, HIPAA and a growing number of global equivalents impose strict requirements on how personal and sensitive data is collected, stored, processed, shared, and deleted. Legal teams must work closely with cybersecurity, data governance, and business units to ensure that privacy-by-design and privacy-by-default principles are embedded into systems and workflows. This includes evaluating data minimization practices, managing data subject rights, ensuring lawful consent mechanisms, and defining jurisdiction-specific data handling practices. Integrated Assurance ensures that these privacy requirements are operationalized. Legal interpretations of obligations are translated into technical controls, such as retention enforcement, encryption, access restrictions, and data localization. Policies are codified into procedures and workflows that can be monitored, audited, and adapted as regulations evolve. Legal becomes not just a reviewer of privacy controls, but an active participant in their design and validation.

Contractual risk is another critical domain. Enterprises increasingly operate through ecosystems of cloud service providers, SaaS platforms, outsourced IT operations, and global suppliers. Each of these relationships is governed by contracts that define security obligations, liability limits, indemnity clauses, breach notification requirements, and audit rights. Integrated Assurance ensures that Legal is involved in contract negotiation and review from the outset, embedding security expectations as enforceable terms and not just vague boilerplate language.

When security events do occur Legal and Regulatory Affairs should be at the center of incident response and crisis governance. Data breaches, ransomware attacks, insider threats, and third-party compromises all require a coordinated legal response. Integrated Assurance integrates Legal directly into the enterprise incident response plan, ensuring that notification obligations are clearly understood, evidence is properly preserved, attorney-client privilege is maintained where applicable, and communications are coordinated to reduce liability and preserve reputation. In many cases, regulatory obligations extend beyond just reporting. They may include impact assessments, remediation plans, follow-up audits, and attestation of control improvements. Legal teams must ensure these responses are complete, accurate, and timely and that the business is not inadvertently creating new legal exposures through inconsistent or premature disclosures. Integrated Assurance formalizes these workflows, ensuring Legal is looped in early, rather than after key technical decisions have been made.

In multinational organizations, Legal must also guide the enterprise through cross-border regulatory compliance. Data residency laws, export controls, embargo restrictions, and sector-specific mandates require careful interpretation and alignment. Integrated Assurance facilitates federated policy enforcement and allows global policies to be adapted locally while maintaining overall governance cohesion. Legal's insights ensure that this balance is maintained without triggering unnecessary exposure or noncompliance. Furthermore, Legal and Regulatory Affairs contribute to the enterprise's governance architecture. Legal representatives should sit on risk committees, assurance councils, and architecture review boards. Their role is not to slow down innovation but to ensure that emerging initiatives are legally viable, ethically sound, and defensible under regulatory scrutiny. This involvement turns Legal from a reactive gatekeeper into a proactive partner that enables growth and innovation.

ENABLING STRATEGIC INVESTMENT, RISK-BASED PRIORITIZATION, AND MEASURABLE OUTCOMES

Security, while essential to enterprise sustainability, is often perceived as a cost center and a necessary, but nonproductive, function that consumes resources without directly contributing to revenue. This perception is not only outdated, it's dangerous. In the context of Integrated Assurance, Finance and Budget Planning functions are pivotal in transforming cybersecurity from a reactive, compliance-driven cost into a strategic investment in risk reduction, operational continuity, and enterprise trust. When aligned with security, finance enables intentional funding, performance transparency, and business-aligned risk decisions that support both protection and progress. At the core of this alignment is the concept of risk-based investment. Security initiatives cannot be funded in isolation from enterprise priorities. Integrated Assurance introduces a financial planning model where cybersecurity budgets are justified by quantifiable risk reduction, alignment to critical business capabilities, and defensible returns. Finance leaders, in partnership with CISOs, risk officers, and business unit heads, evaluate security investments based on how effectively they mitigate top risks, support regulatory compliance, and enable secure transformation efforts.

To support this, organizations must adopt risk quantification and financial modeling frameworks. Strategies such as total cost of control, and expected loss modeling, enabling finance teams to understand the economic impact of risk and prioritize spend accordingly. So rather than debating whether to implement a new identity management system based on vendor features, the discussion shifts to whether it can reduce account compromise risk by a defined dollar amount over a given time horizon. This approach also enables scenario-based budgeting, where finance teams can evaluate multiple levels of investment against projected security outcomes. What does the "minimum viable security" posture look like, and what are its tradeoffs? What does a "best-in-class" program cost, and what incremental risks does it mitigate? Integrated Assurance supports this kind of modeling by tying security capabilities to risk domains and enabling tiered funding strategies that align to the organization's risk appetite and maturity goals.

Integrated Assurance also helps shift the cybersecurity budgeting conversation from project-based funding to program-based investment. Rather than treating security as a series of isolated initiatives it supports the development of multiyear, cross-functional roadmaps tied to architectural and business transformation plans. Finance becomes a partner in building out multiyear investment horizons, enabling the enterprise to evolve its security posture alongside growth, modernization, and digital acceleration efforts. Cross-functional alignment is essential to this model. Security teams must work closely with Finance to forecast operating expenses and capital expenditures based on actual platform needs, tool life cycles, resource growth, and control coverage gaps. Integrated Assurance supports this collaboration by providing visibility into security tool utilization, identifying redundant capabilities, overlapping licenses, or underperforming investments. This financial hygiene improves budget efficiency and ensures that spending is not just sustained but optimized.

Another important area is value realization and performance tracking. Finance must be able to assess whether cybersecurity investments are delivering the intended outcomes. Integrated Assurance facilitates this by defining measurable KPIs and KRIs linked to risk domains, such as reduced dwell time, faster access revocation, lower policy violations, or improved audit scores. These metrics should be reported alongside financial summaries, enabling CFOs and boards to evaluate both financial ROI and risk-adjusted performance which is a necessary evolution in how cybersecurity success is communicated and governed. Finance also plays a critical role in third-party risk modeling and contract management. As organizations depend more on external vendors for infrastructure, data processing, and software delivery, finance leaders must ensure that security risk is factored into procurement decisions, pricing models, and contract negotiation.

This includes accounting for cyber insurance premiums, liability exposure in vendor contracts, and the long-term costs of poor vendor assurance practices. Integrated Assurance enables this by embedding financial modeling into third-party risk assessments, allowing for better cost–risk tradeoffs.

Cyber insurance is another domain where Finance must partner with security. Premiums, deductibles, and exclusions are directly tied to the organization's control environment and incident history. Integrated Assurance helps security teams provide structured evidence of controls, maturity levels, and assurance testing that can be used to negotiate better terms. Finance teams can, in turn, evaluate whether the cost of premiums aligns with the potential coverage and whether certain risks are better self-insured or mitigated directly. Finance is also responsible for ensuring funding agility and the ability to redirect or augment cybersecurity resources in response to emerging threats or incidents. Integrated Assurance promotes the establishment of contingency reserves or adaptive funding models that allow for rapid response investments, such as emergency licenses, consulting support, breach response, or accelerated remediation.

Finally, Finance plays a governance role in ensuring cybersecurity investments align with ethical, legal, and strategic enterprise values. Funding surveillance technologies, monitoring systems, or AI-driven threat detection requires careful consideration of data privacy, labor laws, and employee rights. Finance leaders, working with Legal and HR, must ensure that cost-saving measures or rapid deployments do not introduce unintended ethical or compliance liabilities.

In total, Finance and Budget Planning, when integrated into the broader assurance model, become force multipliers for effective cybersecurity. They provide the financial discipline, analytical rigor, and strategic foresight needed to scale assurance sustainably. Integrated Assurance transforms Finance from a funding gatekeeper into a strategic partner in enterprise resilience and enables smarter investment, faster response, and measurable, business-aligned security outcomes.

USE CASE: STRATEGIC INVESTMENT AND RISK-BASED PRIORITIZATION THROUGH INTEGRATED ASSURANCE

Scenario

A global financial services company is undergoing digital transformation, expanding its cloud footprint, adopting AI-driven tools, and integrating third-party vendors into its core systems. Despite growing security investments, the CFO and board question the ROI of cybersecurity spending, especially given continued operational disruptions and fragmented reporting across business units.

Challenge

Cybersecurity is treated as a reactive, compliance-driven cost center, with limited visibility into how investments reduce risk or support business objectives. Budgeting is project-based, siloed from enterprise risk discussions, and disconnected from IT and business transformation priorities.

Integrated Assurance Solution

The organization adopts an Integrated Assurance model to realign security, finance, and risk functions around shared goals, business value, and measurable performance.

Implementation Steps	Details
Establish risk-based budgeting framework	– Finance and Security teams collaborate to develop a risk quantification model, mapping security initiatives to critical business capabilities and loss scenarios. – Projects are prioritized based on expected risk reduction per dollar spent, not vendor marketing claims. – Example: An identity access management platform is justified by a projected 60% reduction in account compromise losses, valued at $4.5 million over three years.
Scenario-based investment modeling	– Multiple investment tiers are modeled: o *Minimum viable posture*: Meets compliance, mitigates high-impact risks. o *Target posture*: Aligns with enterprise growth plans and transformation initiatives. o *Best-in-class*: Maximizes automation, real-time assurance, and market reputation. – Boards and executives make funding decisions based on tradeoffs between cost, coverage, and resilience.
Transition to program-based funding	– Cybersecurity is embedded into multiyear transformation roadmaps, not isolated yearly projects. – Finance supports forecasting of operational and capital expenses tied to lifecycle plans for platforms, cloud migration, and regulatory changes.
Financial hygiene and efficiency optimization	– Integrated Assurance reveals tool overlaps, underutilized licenses, and control redundancies. – Finance reclaims $2 million annually by rationalizing toolsets and shifting to platform-based capabilities.
KPI/KRI tracking and executive reporting	– Measurable outcomes like remediation velocity, policy violation reductions, and audit readiness scores are reported alongside budget utilization. – CFO gains a clear risk-adjusted ROI on cybersecurity investments, enhancing budget defensibility at the board level.
Cyber insurance optimization	– With structured evidence of control maturity and Integrated Assurance test results, Finance negotiates a 15% reduction in cyber insurance premiums. – Risk modeling also helps determine when self-insurance or direct mitigation is more cost-effective.

Outcomes

- Strategic alignment: Security is no longer a budget line item but a driver of business continuity and transformation.
- Measurable ROI: Security spending is tied to reduced risk exposure, faster incident response, and higher audit scores.
- Informed decision-making: Executives can clearly weigh cost versus risk, enabling smarter investment and governance.
- Budget efficiency: Redundancies are eliminated, underperforming tools replaced, and overlapping investments consolidated.
- Organizational trust: With shared metrics and transparent planning, trust between security, finance, and business units improves significantly

CONCLUSION AND RECAP

Integrated Assurance is a philosophy that redefines how organizations think about risk, resilience, and control in the face of accelerating complexity. Across every domain we've explored in this chapter, architecture, compliance, engineering, data, vendor management, human capital, physical security, legal governance, and finance, the message is consistent: assurance is no longer a peripheral function. It is now a core competency, inseparable from enterprise performance and strategic agility.

EA becomes the blueprint for resilience. No longer relegated to standards enforcement or system lifecycle management, EA emerges as a connective tissue between security intent and operational execution. Whether it's embedding secure-by-design principles or rationalizing legacy platforms, architecture under Integrated Assurance ensures that security isn't bolted on, it's baked in, and when risk changes, the architecture adapts with it, not after it.

Compliance and risk functions are elevated from administrative oversight to active operational enablers. The era of checklists and static controls is over. Integrated Assurance demands continuous validation, dynamic telemetry, and risk ownership at the edge of execution. Through harmonized control models and automated testing, enterprises can demonstrate not just compliance, but defensibility in real time, across functions, and under scrutiny.

High-velocity engineering presents both the challenge and opportunity of scale. Speed, when unmanaged, becomes exposure. But when assurance is embedded through policy-as-code, secure templates, and supply chain validation, speed becomes strength. DevSecOps under Integrated Assurance isn't slower, it's smarter. Secure code isn't just an aspiration, it's a baseline. Software delivery becomes both fast and safe by default, not exception.

Data has become the lifeblood of modern enterprises, but it is also one of the most volatile risk vectors. Integrated Assurance operationalizes data protection by aligning governance, lineage, access, and retention with evolving business and regulatory demands. Privacy, sovereignty, and AI trustworthiness are not left to chance or policy documents. They are validated, enforced, and embedded with data owners, architects, and compliance officers all accountable to the same real-world outcomes.

Third-party ecosystems have multiplied the enterprise's blast radius. Vendors are not just support functions they are embedded actors in the operational fabric. Integrated Assurance repositions procurement and vendor governance as assurance-critical functions, using lifecycle-based risk models, contractual enforcements, continuous validation, and collaborative response frameworks. Supply chain security moves past reactive and punitive and becomes proactive and strategic.

Perhaps most critically, Integrated Assurance addresses the human layer with deliberate care. HR is repositioned from background actor to active co-owner of risk posture. From behavioral threat detection to offboarding precision, cultural alignment to remote work governance, people are no longer treated as risk vectors to be constrained, but as active contributors to assurance outcomes. Trust, after all, is built at the human level and trust is security's foundation.

Integrated Assurance redefines what enterprise security means. It is no longer a siloed function, a late-stage reviewer, or a compliance checkbox. It is a strategic, embedded, and continuous practice that links leadership vision with frontline execution. It connects the technical, the human, and the legal into a coherent model of resilience. And above all, Integrated Assurance transforms security from a defensive posture into a generative force, one that enables the enterprise not just to survive disruption, but to lead through it.

15 Operationalizing Integrated Assurance

LEARNING OBJECTIVES

- Understand the five-phase methodology for embedding Integrated Assurance across enterprise architecture, operations, and governance
- Learn how to translate Integrated Assurance from strategic vision to daily execution using real-world best practices and use cases
- Gain the ability to assess organizational maturity using the Integrated Assurance Maturity Model (IAMM) and prioritize targeted improvements
- Discover practical strategies for accelerating adoption, overcoming resistance, and aligning assurance with strategic business outcomes

As we have discussed in previous chapters, Integrated Assurance is a design principle, an operational philosophy, a mindset, and a strategic enabler. To realize its full value, it must be embedded into the enterprise's systems, structures, and behaviors. Implementation cannot be superficial or isolated. It must be holistic, crossing organizational boundaries and weaving assurance into the rhythm of day-to-day operations. This chapter translates the Integrated Assurance model into actionable steps. We focus on pragmatic execution: how to integrate assurance into architecture, operations, engineering, compliance, and governance. We detail best practices grounded in real-world enterprise constraints and present use cases that demonstrate how assurance moves from aspiration to action.

APPROACH AND METHODOLOGY FOR IMPLEMENTING INTEGRATED ASSURANCE

Integrated Assurance is not introduced through a singular initiative or a technology deployment. It is established through a methodical transformation that advances organizational capability, governance maturity, and cultural alignment in parallel. The methodology is designed to scale across federated enterprises while remaining grounded in operational realism and strategic value. It follows five progressive phases, (as seen in Figure 15.1) each representing a critical step toward embedding assurance as a sustainable enterprise competency.

The journey begins with establishing strategic intent and securing alignment across the organization. Executive leadership must be unified in its vision, and a named Integrated Assurance Lead should be appointed to guide execution. An enterprise-wide council is formed to include representation from cybersecurity, IT operations, enterprise architecture, compliance, legal, finance, HR, and business risk. Together, these stakeholders define the core mission of Integrated Assurance, ratify a shared language for risk and control, and identify the business drivers that demand unified risk

DOI: 10.1201/9781003562153-19

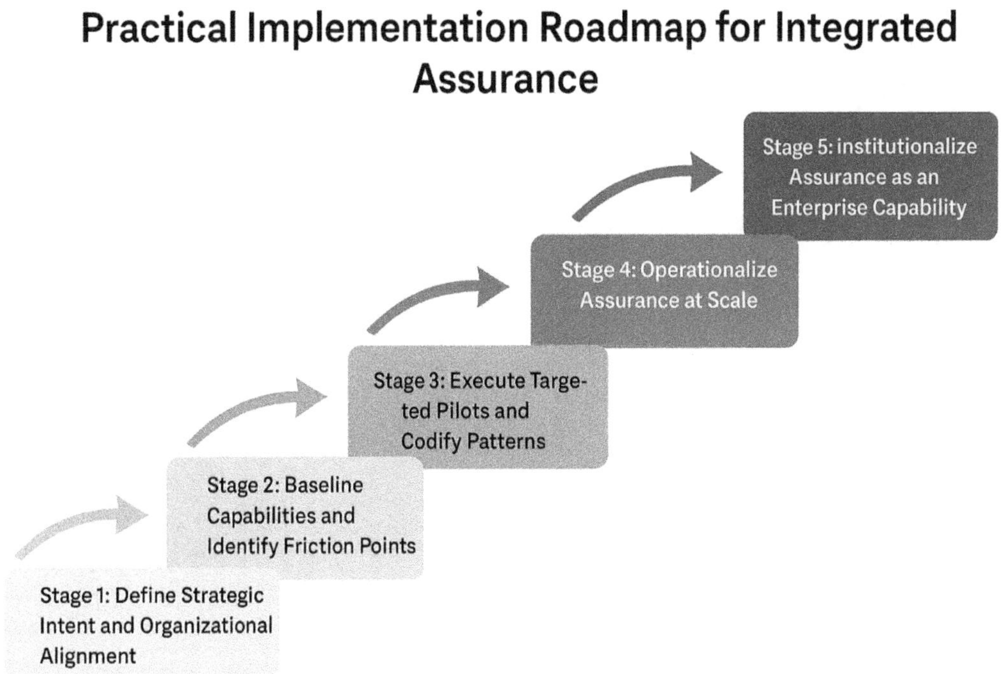

FIGURE 15.1 Practical implementation for Integrated Assurance.

governance. The outcome of this phase is a fully aligned mandate, backed by executive sponsorship, and informed by a clearly articulated vision of what Integrated Assurance will look like when it is functioning effectively.

Following alignment, the organization must establish a baseline understanding of its current maturity. This is achieved through a detailed capability inventory, examining the presence and effectiveness of control frameworks, governance structures, toolsets, and operational practices. A parallel assessment is conducted to identify where control ownership is unclear, where tool redundancy or overlap occurs, and where key friction points exist, such as delayed software releases due to security exceptions, or lack of alignment between uptime metrics and risk thresholds. These insights form the foundation for identifying tactical wins and systemic blockers that must be addressed to move forward.

With the baseline in place, targeted pilots are launched to validate value and build momentum. These pilots are chosen for their visibility and impact. Ideal domains for early implementation include secure software delivery pipelines, high-risk third-party vendor management, and identity governance for sensitive access groups. Each pilot establishes traceability from defined control objectives to real-world execution. Enterprise artifacts are codified during this phase, including secure design patterns, control validation procedures, policy templates, and incident response playbooks. Shared dashboards are developed to reflect operational assurance metrics. As these patterns demonstrate measurable improvements in clarity, collaboration, and efficiency, they become the scaffolding for broader deployment.

Once validated, the methodology advances toward operational scale. Assurance becomes embedded into daily workflows through federated execution and centralized oversight. Local teams adopt standardized patterns and operate within defined governance guardrails, while central functions manage shared telemetry, metrics, and escalation protocols. Assurance is integrated

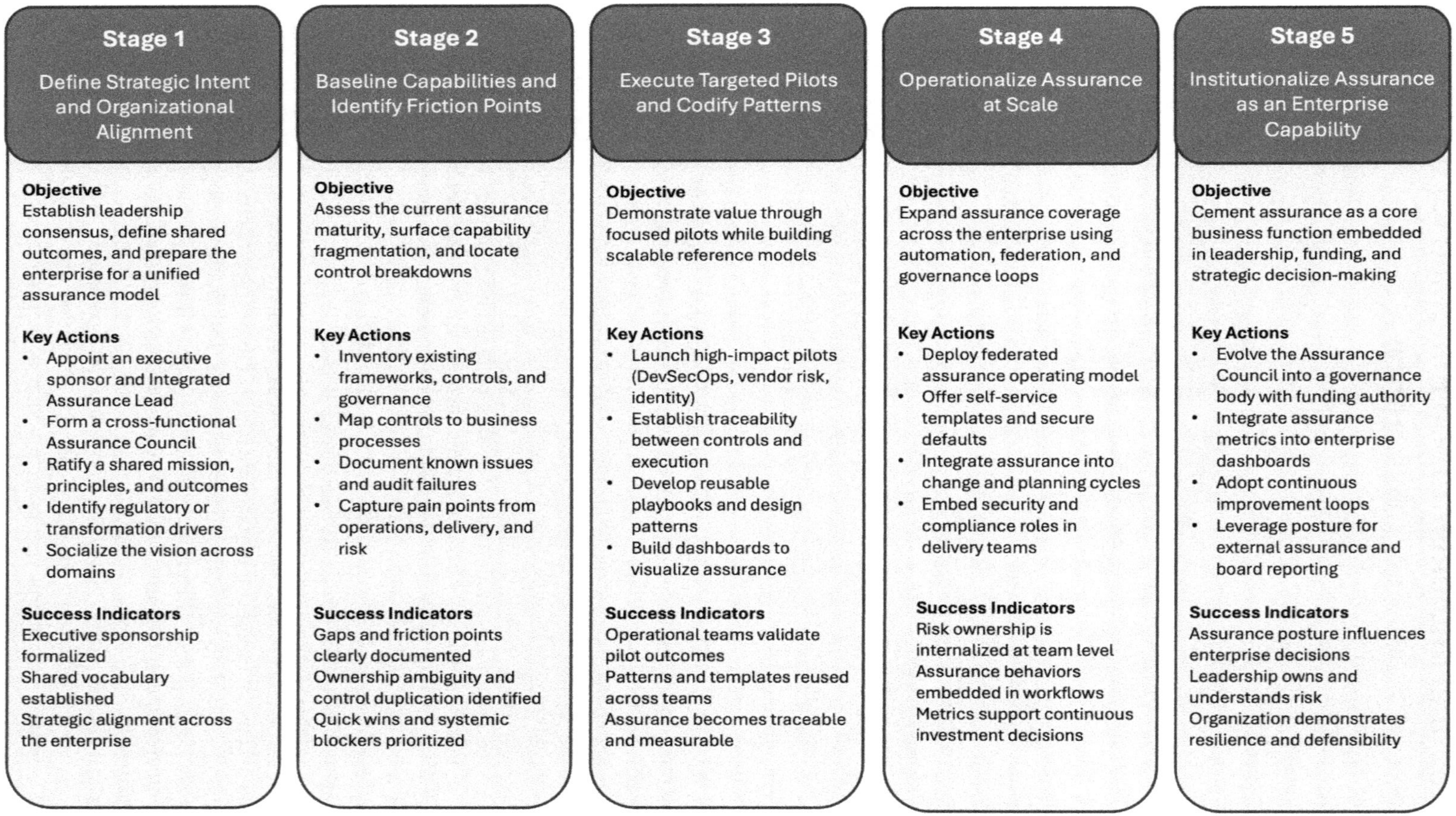

FIGURE 15.2 Integrated Assurance approach and methodology.

into change management workflows, resilience planning exercises, and quarterly performance reviews. Self-service capabilities are expanded through preapproved templates and infrastructure modules. Key roles such as security architects, compliance officers, and risk analysts are rotated into embedded partnerships with delivery teams, reinforcing shared accountability and accelerating cultural convergence.

In the final phase, assurance is institutionalized as a strategic enterprise capability. The Assurance Council evolves into a decision-making authority with influence over funding, prioritization, and long-term transformation planning. Assurance becomes a lens through which the organization views digital transformation initiatives, platform modernization efforts, and strategic planning cycles. Metrics are continuously refined to reflect shifts in threat landscapes, regulatory expectations, and business needs. Assurance outcomes become central to board-level discussions, investor communications, and customer trust-building. The enterprise not only demonstrates compliance but achieves operational resilience and strategic defensibility at scale.

This methodology does not prescribe uniformity. Instead, it establishes a unifying framework that aligns diverse business units, technology teams, and governance functions under a common objective. Integrated Assurance is not delivered, it is earned through disciplined execution, cultural adoption, and a relentless focus on outcomes that matter to the business. Figure 15.2 demonstrates how IAMM can be used to assess the current maturity of an organization.

IAMM SELF-ASSESSMENT QUESTIONNAIRE

INSTRUCTIONS

Rate the current state in each area on a scale of 1–5, where:

1—Not Present / Fragmented
2—Defined but Siloed
3—Coordinated and Aligned
4—Embedded and Operationalized
5—Institutionalized and Strategic

Add comments or examples where applicable to support context and future planning.

Section	Category	Subcategory	Rating (1–5)	Comments/Evidence
Governance	Are there formal cross-functional forums that govern assurance-related decisions?	How often do these forums meet and what is their mandate?		
		Are decisions documented and followed through operationally?		
		Do representatives from all key business and technical units participate?		
	Do security, IT, compliance, and business teams jointly prioritize risks and manage exceptions?	Is there a shared risk taxonomy across teams?		
		Are exception processes transparent and time-bound?		
		Do all teams contribute data to the risk prioritization process?		

Section	Category	Subcategory	Rating (1–5)	Comments/Evidence
	Is there a federated model for assigning and managing risk ownership across the enterprise?	Are roles and responsibilities clearly defined and documented?		
		Is there accountability for residual risks at the line-of-business level?		
		Are federated decisions escalated appropriately when needed?		
	Does executive leadership visibly sponsor and engage in assurance initiatives?	Do executives receive regular briefings on assurance posture?		
		Are leaders involved in incident response or control failures?		
		Are sponsorships linked to strategic investments?		
	Are assurance principles integrated into enterprise strategy and business planning?	Is assurance discussed during annual planning and budget cycles?		
		Are strategic programs assessed for assurance risks?		
		Are business leaders evaluated on assurance-related objectives?		
Architecture and engineering	Are "secure by design" and "resilient by default" principles embedded into enterprise architecture?	Are threat models used during early architecture phases?		
		Is resilience part of capacity and availability planning?		
		Are these principles codified in architecture governance?		
	Do reference architectures and templates include standardized security controls?	Are templates routinely updated to reflect new threats or tech stacks?		
		Are they used consistently across projects and platforms?		
		Are control requirements traceable to policy?		
	Are policy-as-code and infrastructure-as-code practices used to enforce controls in development pipelines?	Are these controls version-controlled and peer-reviewed?		
		Are code changes tested against policy gates automatically?		
		Are deviations logged and escalated?		

Section	Category	Subcategory	Rating (1–5)	Comments/Evidence
	Are security architects engaged early during solution design and modernization planning?	Are security reviews part of the solution intake process?		
		Do architects participate in backlog grooming or epic and user story reviews?		
		Are nonfunctional requirements for security enforced?		
	Is architectural risk regularly assessed and tracked throughout implementation?	Are architectural risks documented as part of project risk logs?		
		Are risk mitigations embedded in design choices?		
		Is risk reassessed when solutions pivot?		
IT and engineering operations	Are assurance controls embedded in daily operational workflows?	Are change, incident, and problem workflows mapped to controls?		
		Are control failures logged as operational incidents?		
		Are approvals gated by assurance criteria?		
	Are systems validated against hardened baselines with drift detection in place?	Are baselines reviewed and updated periodically?		
		Is deviation automatically detected and alerted?		
		Are exceptions managed through a formal process?		
	Is telemetry from IT and security systems shared for unified risk monitoring?	Are logging formats standardized across domains?		
		Are SIEMs, NMS, or observability platforms used by both IT and SecOps?		
		Is telemetry used for performance and security equally?		
	Are resilience and recovery practices documented and operationally tested?	Are backup and recovery tests automated and scheduled?		
		Are recovery time objectives (RTO) validated?		
		Are lessons learned from tests used to improve runbooks?		
	Do delivery teams contribute to risk remediation and mitigation planning?	Are developers and engineers involved in root cause reviews?		
		Is risk mitigation logged as part of the user story backlog?		
		Do teams have KPIs tied to reduced exposure?		

Section	Category	Subcategory	Rating (1–5)	Comments/Evidence
Risk, compliance, and audit	Are control frameworks aligned to avoid duplication and audit fatigue?	Is there a single source of truth for control mapping?		
		Are frameworks rationalized (e.g., NIST to ISO crosswalks)?		
		Is audit scheduling coordinated across teams?		
	Are controls continuously monitored and validated in operational settings?	Are automated control checks part of daily operations?		
		Are failures triaged and resolved quickly?		
		Is validation evidence stored centrally?		
	Is operational risk ownership clearly defined and assigned?	Are risks mapped to the responsible department head?		
		Are risk acceptances logged and justified?		
		Is there a process to reassess ownership when teams shift?		
	Are risk registers actively maintained and tied to business priorities?	Are registers updated in real time or periodically?		
		Are risks categorized by business function and impact?		
		Do leaders use these registers to drive prioritization?		
	Are audit findings resolved through root cause analysis and cross-team collaboration?	Is RCA documented and linked to the finding?		
		Are systemic gaps tracked and remediated beyond symptoms?		
		Are findings presented to and reviewed by multidisciplinary teams?		
Metrics and reporting	Do assurance metrics measure control effectiveness and business impact—not just coverage?	Are metrics based on real events, not just compliance checkboxes?		
		Are outcomes based on reduced fraud, or downtime included?		
		Are metrics periodically challenged for relevance?		
	Are dashboards tailored for executive, operational, and technical audiences?	Are different levels of abstraction used per audience?		
		Are visuals actionable or just informational?		
		Are dashboards used in regular reporting cadences?		

Section	Category	Subcategory	Rating (1–5)	Comments/Evidence
	Do KPIs and KRIs influence strategic decisions like funding and risk acceptance?	Are performance indicators tied to budget cycles?		
		Are risk thresholds formally defined?		
		Are these indicators referenced in investment cases?		
	Are metrics used to track convergence and collaboration across functions?	Are shared metrics used across departments?		
		Are friction points flagged through trend analysis?		
		Are cross-functional remediations tracked over time?		
	Is assurance performance reviewed regularly by leadership teams?	Are metrics part of board or C-level reviews?		
		Are corrective actions owned and tracked by leadership?		
		Is assurance maturity discussed as a KPI?		
Culture and collaboration	Is assurance widely understood as a shared organizational responsibility?	Are there awareness campaigns or leadership messaging?		
		Are responsibilities reflected in team charters?		
		Are shared failures and successes debriefed together?		
	Are assurance roles embedded within both business and technical teams?	Are business units accountable for specific controls?		
		Are security champions or liaisons designated?		
		Are embedded roles part of org charts or job descriptions?		
	Do employees receive role-specific training on assurance expectations?	Is training targeted (e.g., DevSecOps for engineers)?		
		Is onboarding mapped to assurance role requirements?		
		Are there refresher or just-in-time learning modules?		
	Are assurance behaviors encouraged through incentives or performance reviews?	Are positive behaviors recognized informally and formally?		
		Are control failures addressed in performance feedback?		
		Are there gamified or competitive assurance initiatives?		

Section	Category	Subcategory	Rating (1–5)	Comments/Evidence
	Are working groups established to address cross-functional control, risk, or security concerns?	Are these groups empowered with decision rights?		
		Are their charters aligned to risk strategy?		
		Do they report out to leadership or governance boards?		

Scoring and Interpretation

Total score range	Maturity level
30–59	Levels 1–2: Fragmented/Defined
60–89	Level 3: Aligned
90–114	Level 4: Embedded
115–150	Level 5: Institutionalized

INTEGRATED ASSURANCE IN ACTION

While the principles of Integrated Assurance are clear, their value is proven only when translated into day-to-day enterprise outcomes. The following expanded use cases illustrate how large organizations are embedding Integrated Assurance into critical functions, demonstrating not only increased resilience but also improved agility, trust, and operational alignment.

Here are several real-world use cases to underscore the versatility and strategic depth of the Integrated Assurance model. These use cases demonstrate how assurance is no longer confined to audit prep or risk registers, it is a living capability embedded into architecture, automation, collaboration, and culture. Whether the challenge is aging infrastructure, decentralized DevOps, AI ethics, or vendor governance, Integrated Assurance provides the operational scaffolding to manage risk at scale, with agility, accountability, and confidence.

USE CASE: ALIGNING CYBERSECURITY INVESTMENTS WITH RISK AND BUSINESS STRATEGY

Enterprise Context

A multinational manufacturing company's CISO struggles to justify annual budget increases as the board views cybersecurity as a reactive cost center.

Challenges

1. Budgets built on technical justifications, not business outcomes.
2. Minimal understanding of risk exposure by business unit.
3. CFO resists nonquantified security investments.

Integrated Assurance Approach

- Quantitative risk modeling: Developed threat-to-impact maps to quantify business risk in dollar terms.
- Business-aligned risk register: Tied control gaps to specific business lines (e.g., factory operations, supply chain, IP protection).
- Investment impact scenarios: Presented options (minimum viable, baseline, aspirational) with modeled impact reduction per funding level.
- Assurance dashboards: Shared metrics on reduction in critical vulnerabilities, improved RTO/RPO alignment, and decreased third-party risk index per dollar invested.
- Finance co-ownership: Finance and Risk jointly reviewed funding proposals in the Assurance Council and tracked quarterly performance against expected ROI.

Outcome

Cybersecurity is repositioned as a strategic enabler. Funding is not just approved but prioritized and aligned to quantified risk reduction, resilience enhancement, and long-term cost avoidance.

USE CASE: MODERNIZING LEGACY SYSTEMS WITH BUILT-IN ASSURANCE

Enterprise Context

A Fortune 100 insurance provider continues to rely on a 20-year-old mainframe platform for core claims processing. The system lacks native encryption, modern authentication mechanisms, and logging integrations—but its business logic is irreplaceable in the short term.

Challenges

1. No native support for MFA or federated identity.
2. Regulatory requirements for auditability and data protection.
3. Organizational pressure to defer system replacement.

Integrated Assurance Approach

- Architectural isolation: Network segmentation and firewall zoning to isolate the mainframe from east–west traffic and reduce lateral movement risk.
- Identity brokerage: Introduced an identity abstraction layer via a secure API gateway, enabling integration with the enterprise IAM system.
- Compensating controls: Implemented host-based intrusion detection, session monitoring, and outbound traffic whitelisting.
- Resilience blueprint: Defined incident response playbooks and recovery RTO/RPO targets for this legacy environment.
- Federated governance: Control deviations documented and reviewed quarterly by a cross-functional risk committee with Legal, Compliance, Architecture, and Business Ops.

Outcome

Assurance is maintained despite technical limitations. The platform remains operational and auditable, with risk owned and mitigated through a documented and monitored control plan, rather than deferred replacement or ignored exposure.

USE CASE: SCALING DEVSECOPS WITH FEDERATED CONTROL ENFORCEMENT

Enterprise Context

A multinational consumer goods company has adopted DevOps across five regional product lines, each with different toolchains, hosting platforms, and regulatory obligations.

Challenges

1. No consistent CI/CD controls or security gates.
2. Variance in cloud security maturity between business units.
3. Fragmented ownership of application risk.

Integrated Assurance Approach

- Central DevSecOps platform team: Formed a global enablement group to develop reusable pipeline templates, policy modules, and onboarding automation.
- Baseline controls: Defined enterprise-wide minimum viable controls (e.g., Software Composition Analysis (SCA), secrets scanning, image validation) required across all pipelines.
- Policy-as-Code framework: Implemented OPA-based policies embedded into CI/CD pipelines, enabling regional teams to customize without violating baseline assurance.
- Embedded security architects: Assigned to high-risk or strategic delivery teams to coach, not police—focused on enablement, not gatekeeping.
- Continuous feedback loops: Metrics like vulnerability mean-time-to-remediate (MTTR), policy bypass frequency, and build-time security exceptions tracked and shared in DevSecOps scorecards.

Outcome

Security becomes a design constraint, not a delivery bottleneck. Regional teams retain autonomy, while enterprise risk teams maintain assurance through transparent, code-enforced controls. Speed and compliance coexist.

USE CASE: THIRD-PARTY RISK OPERATIONALIZED ACROSS THE VENDOR LIFECYCLE

Enterprise Context

A healthcare network depends on 300+ third-party SaaS vendors, BPO providers, and technology partners, many of whom handle Protected Health Information (PHI).

Challenges

1. Limited visibility into vendor control effectiveness post-onboarding.
2. Inconsistent contract language and enforcement across departments.
3. Manual and ad hoc vendor reassessments, leading to high audit risk.

Integrated Assurance Approach

- Risk-tiered vendor framework: Vendors classified into four tiers based on system access, data sensitivity, and business criticality.
- Embedded security in procurement: Security questionnaires, certifications, breach history, and geopolitical requirements incorporated into RFPs and contract scoring.
- Contractual assurance clauses: Standardized language for breach notification timelines, encryption expectations, audit rights, and SLAs.
- Lifecycle monitoring: Implemented continuous assurance monitoring tools to track posture drift, threat intelligence hits, and public breach indicators.
- Joint escalation protocols: Defined shared incident response protocols for critical vendors, with regular tabletops and joint remediation drills.

Outcome

Vendor relationships are no longer compliance time bombs. Procurement, Legal, and Security are aligned from selection through offboarding, reducing onboarding friction and enabling continuous defensibility across the third-party ecosystem.

USE CASE: EMBEDDING DATA ASSURANCE INTO AI/ML WORKFLOWS

Enterprise Context

A global bank is building ML models to detect fraudulent transactions and automate credit risk scoring. The models are trained on customer behavior data from multiple jurisdictions.

Challenges

1. Inconsistent data lineage and unclear model training provenance.
2. Risk of bias, drift, or unexplainable outcomes in regulated environments.
3. No formal controls for privacy compliance or model governance.

Integrated Assurance Approach

- Data classification pipeline: Automated metadata tagging and sensitivity labeling during ingestion, feeding access and retention policies.
- Lineage and provenance mapping: Embedded data lineage tracking into ETL workflows and ML pipelines to trace model training inputs.
- Model risk framework: Defined thresholds for explainability, fairness, and drift detection that is auditable by compliance and risk teams.
- Federated privacy enforcement: Applied jurisdiction-specific privacy constraints (e.g., GDPR, CCPA) based on data residency and subject origin.
- Integrated governance council: Cross-functional AI Assurance Board (Legal, Data Science, Risk, Compliance, Ethics) reviews all high-risk models prior to deployment.

Outcome

The AI program becomes auditable, defensible, and resilient to future regulatory scrutiny. Confidence in data integrity and ethical model outcomes supports business scaling and customer trust.

OPERATIONALIZING INTEGRATED ASSURANCE

Bringing Integrated Assurance to life requires more than adoption, it demands operationalization. The model must be translated into policies, platforms, workflows, and relationships that shape daily behavior across the enterprise. This section outlines foundational best practices that enable this transition from theory to practice.

ANCHOR ASSURANCE IN GOVERNANCE, NOT TECHNOLOGY

Too many assurance initiatives begin with tooling and end with dashboards that nobody owns. Technology without governance is noise. Integrated Assurance demands governance structures that are durable, cross-functional, and accountable.

Key Practices

- Establish an Enterprise Assurance Council composed of senior representatives from cybersecurity, enterprise architecture, IT operations, compliance, legal, data governance, HR, and business units. This council should define the strategic objectives of assurance and own the integrated risk posture.
- Define shared decision rights for risk acceptance, control exceptions, investment prioritization, and incident response escalation. Document who makes the call, with what authority, and under what conditions.
- Institutionalize federated governance, allowing global principles to be executed locally with contextual adaptations. This enables consistency in outcomes without demanding uniformity in implementation.

- Empower domain-specific working groups (e.g., for software delivery, data assurance, third-party risk) to translate enterprise strategy into operational execution, with clear feedback loops to governance bodies.

Architect for Assurance from the Start

Architecture is where strategy meets execution. Assurance must be encoded into the architecture itself and not layered on later.

Key Practices

- Embed secure-by-design and resilient-by-default principles into architectural standards, including reference models, blueprints, and platform designs.
- Incorporate policy-as-code into infrastructure-as-code pipelines, enforcing identity, network, encryption, and logging controls at build time—not runtime.
- Use architectural review boards as risk negotiation forums, where business, compliance, security, and technology stakeholders converge to make risk-informed, sustainable decisions.
- Treat compensating controls as architectural artifacts, governed and revisited as part of lifecycle management, especially in legacy or hybrid environments.
- Maintain an authoritative system-of-record for applications, data flows, dependencies, and control ownership to support threat modeling, compliance mapping, and incident forensics.

Integrate Assurance across the Software Lifecycle

Integrated Assurance cannot be bolted onto the end of the SDLC. It must be woven into every phase, from planning to deployment to production monitoring.

Key Practices

- Define a secure software delivery reference model, including minimum viable controls for CI/CD pipelines, code quality gates, and artifact validation.
- Codify security controls using infrastructure-as-code and policy-as-code tools to ensure enforceability, repeatability, and auditability.
- Automate security testing at multiple points:
- Static Analysis (SAST) in the commit stage.
- SCA in dependency resolution.
- Dynamic Analysis (DAST) during pre-prod testing.
- Secrets scanning and artifact signing in the release phase.
- Shift from security sign-off to risk-informed deployment gates, where high-severity issues block release and lower-severity issues are accepted with traceable business rationale.
- Provide developers with real-time, contextual security feedback and not just quarterly training or policy documents.

Enable Continuous, Evidence-Based Control Validation

Assurance must be active, not archival. Controls that exist only in documentation are not truly controls, they are just theater and ultimately liabilities. Integrated Assurance demands live, tested, and traceable controls.

Key Practices

- Implement automated control testing across infrastructure, identity, configuration, and access layers using telemetry from security tools and platform APIs.
- Leverage drift detection tools to identify deviation from approved baselines in real time, whether due to intentional changes, human error, or malicious tampering.
- Develop a control effectiveness framework that aligns each control to business impact, expected outcome, testing method, and ownership.
- Feed control telemetry into enterprise dashboards for real-time visibility and reporting, including compliance status, control health, and remediation SLAs.
- Use assurance evidence to support audits, board reporting, cyber insurance negotiations, and third-party attestations, turning control maturity into measurable business value.

Rethink Metrics to Reflect Convergence and Actionability

Traditional cybersecurity and IT metrics are siloed, lagging, and often unaligned to business priorities. Integrated Assurance requires metrics that are actionable, converged, and strategic.

Key Practices

- Define shared KPIs and KRIs across security and IT operations, such as:
  - Time-to-remediate high-risk vulnerabilities.
  - Policy drift frequency across cloud and on-prem systems.
  - Control effectiveness scores by platform and business unit.
  - Risk-adjusted uptime for critical business services.
  - Risk-adjusted performance and throughput.
- Measure assurance as a function of collaboration and convergence, not just control volume:
  - Number of cross-functional risk decisions made.
  - Frequency of architecture boards with business representation.
  - Mean time from detection to joint remediation.
- Link security outcomes to business enablement:
  - Reduction in delivery delays due to late-stage security issues.
  - Improved audit readiness time.
  - Percentage of secure-by-default deployments without manual override.
- Present metrics in audience-specific formats:
  - Technical KPIs for engineers and SOC teams.
  - Business-aligned risk heatmaps for executives.
  - Control confidence levels for regulators and auditors.

PRACTICAL RECOMMENDATIONS FOR ACCELERATING ADOPTION

Implementing Integrated Assurance across a large enterprise is a sustained transformation and not singular initiative. Integrated Assurance requires coordinated shifts in process, culture, tooling, governance, and mindset. Adoption must be intentional, iterative, and supported by both executive vision and frontline enablement. This section offers practical guidance for accelerating adoption, change management, overcoming resistance, and embedding Integrated Assurance as a sustainable capability in your organization.

Strategy	Tactics	Outcome
Start small, scale strategically	Start with high-impact pilots (e.g., software delivery, identity governance), measure outcomes (e.g., fewer outages, faster fixes), formalize lessons into repeatable frameworks, and scale adoption using a low-effort franchise model.	Builds credibility, reduces resistance, creates enterprise momentum with minimal disruption, and plants the seeds for the right cultural mindset.
Operationalize compensating controls	Compensating controls should be formally governed, integrated into architectural plans with clear timelines, continuously monitored for effectiveness using drift detection tools, and reassessed quarterly by cross-functional teams.	Maintains defensibility in legacy or constrained environments without introducing unmanaged risk.
Build feedback loops into workflows	Embed assurance throughout the development lifecycle by integrating it into planning, change management, and review processes. Use existing tools to provide contextual risk visibility, adopt both proactive and reactive approaches to manage risk, and emphasize continuous learning rather than strict enforcement.	Assurance becomes embedded in delivery culture, increasing responsiveness and reducing friction.
Shift security from gatekeeper to accelerator	Integrate security into delivery workflows by embedding architects in teams, providing preapproved templates, establishing secure-by-design development paths, and measuring gains in speed and compliance.	Security enables innovation, reduces rework, and earns trust by aligning with business velocity.
Align incentives and recognition	Embed assurance into culture by integrating metrics into performance evaluations, recognizing cross-functional achievements, creating visible champion programs, and highlighting outcomes with dashboards and reviews.	Assurance becomes part of team identity and is recognized as a contributor to business success.
Create a common risk vocabulary	Establish a unified approach to risk by standardizing terminology, control classifications, and accountability models across the enterprise, and reinforce alignment through cross-functional simulations.	Shared understanding improves communication, decision speed, and accountability across domains.
Integrate assurance into strategy and continuity	Integrate assurance with enterprise priorities by linking it to major initiatives, embedding it in crisis response planning, and aligning assurance roadmaps with broader enterprise planning cycles.	Assurance supports agility and resilience, making risk posture a factor in strategic decision-making.
Use metrics to drive accountability	Establish domain-specific KPIs and KRIs, create role-based dashboards, and measure key trends like convergence, remediation speed, and control maturity. Use these metrics to inform planning, governance, and investment decisions.	Metrics influence behavior, drive investment, and reinforce assurance as a continuous enterprise function.

IAMM

The IAMM provides a structured approach for assessing and improving how assurance is embedded across a large enterprise. It spans five maturity levels including Fragmented, Defined, Aligned, Embedded, and Institutionalized, capturing the evolution from siloed, reactive control to proactive, continuous risk stewardship. Organized across six core domains including Governance, Architecture & Engineering, IT & Engineering Operations, Risk & Compliance, Metrics & Reporting, and Culture & Collaboration, the model offers a holistic view of how assurance manifests in policy, practice, and behavior.

At lower maturity levels of 1 and 2, assurance functions are disconnected, driven primarily by compliance needs, and reactive to incidents. Risk is centralized, ownership is ambiguous, and tooling is often redundant or underutilized. Controls exist on paper but are not operationalized. Security is frequently seen as a blocker, and assurance is managed as an event rather than an ongoing responsibility. Metrics are technical, siloed, and fail to communicate business value or risk posture effectively and response to actual incidents are surprisingly slow to executive leadership.

As organizations progress to levels 3 and 4, assurance becomes a shared responsibility. Cross-functional governance bodies are established, risk decisions are made collaboratively, and compensating controls are documented and governed. Security shifts from bolted-on to built-in through reference architectures and policy-as-code. Assurance becomes part of daily workflows, embedded in CI/CD pipelines, change control processes, and service delivery models. Shared telemetry and feedback loops begin to support real-time control validation, and assurance behaviors are recognized and rewarded.

At the highest maturity level of 5, Integrated Assurance is institutionalized. It influences enterprise strategy, funding decisions, and operational planning. Assurance metrics are converged, role-specific, and actionable. Governance structures are fully federated, enabling local execution within global guardrails. Business leaders, developers, and operators understand their assurance responsibilities, and cultural alignment drives proactive risk management. The organization achieves continuous audit readiness, measurable resilience, and stakeholder confidence.

Using the model begins with assessing the current state of maturity across each domain. This involves reviewing artifacts, conducting interviews, and mapping control effectiveness and ownership. Organizations should prioritize domains where risk exposure is highest or where friction is undermining velocity and defensibility. The maturity gaps identified become the foundation for a roadmap, guiding where to invest in architecture, automation, governance, or cultural enablement.

The model should be revisited at minimum annually, or as part of transformation milestones, to track progress and recalibrate goals. It's not necessary to achieve level 5 everywhere. What matters is intentional, risk-aligned maturity that supports business objectives while reducing complexity, improving agility, and enabling defensible security outcomes. In short, the maturity model is both a mirror and a compass, revealing where assurance stands today and guiding where it must go to sustain trust, performance, and resilience.

COMPARATIVE ANALYSIS OF THE IAMM

The IAMM represents a new generation of operational maturity modeling, one that is explicitly engineered to bridge gaps across cybersecurity, IT operations, business resilience, and enterprise governance. In contrast to legacy models like CMMI, NIST Cybersecurity Framework Tiers, and governance-centric models like COBIT, SABSA, COSO ERM, ESRM, and ISO, IAMM is purpose-built for federated, digital-first enterprises that require actionable, evidence-based assurance across complex ecosystems.

IAMM Comparative Analysis

Framework	Purpose and Orientation	Maturity Levels and Progression	Domains of Focus	Use Case Applicability	Measurement and Metrics
IAMM	Operationalize assurance by embedding it into architecture, tooling, workflows, and culture across cybersecurity, IT operations, and business functions.	Offers a five-level progression: Fragmented → Defined → Aligned → Embedded → Institutionalized. It emphasizes operational integration, cross-domain collaboration, and cultural adoption.	Domains include, Architecture & Engineering, IT & Engineering Operations, Metrics & Reporting, Culture & Collaboration	Ideal for federated, highly regulated, or digitally transforming enterprises that require convergence of assurance disciplines.	Provides domain-specific, real-time metrics such as time-to-remediate, policy drift rate, and control coverage by domain. It supports both qualitative maturity and quantitative telemetry.
CMMI	Focuses on process improvement and reducing variability across organizational functions, particularly in engineering and service delivery.	Defines maturity from Initial (1) to Optimizing (5) and is focused on repeatable and controlled processes.	Domain-agnostic, with strength in engineering, service, and support processes, but lacks native cybersecurity or risk integration.	Best suited for process improvement initiatives across engineering-heavy or contract-driven organizations.	Uses formal assessments tied to model compliance.
NIST Tiers	Provide a high-level view of cybersecurity risk management maturity and its integration with enterprise risk governance.	Not maturity levels but describe cybersecurity risk management integration: Partial → Risk-Informed → Repeatable → Adaptive.	Emphasize governance, external engagement, and risk awareness, but stop short of implementation guidance.	Valuable for executive communication and establishing a risk-informed narrative.	Rely on self-assessment with qualitative descriptors.
COBIT	Top-down governance design methodology that emphasizes stakeholder needs, value creation, and governance system tailoring for enterprise IT.	Uses capability levels (0–5) tied to process performance and governance objectives, tailored via design factors.	Organizes its domains under Governance and Management Objectives but requires mapping to security architecture and operational realities.	Excels in governance system design, particularly when oversight, regulatory compliance, or board-level alignment is critical.	Links goals to metrics via performance management but often lacks operational data granularity.
SABSA	A security architecture methodology focused on aligning security services with business drivers through attribute-based design, ensuring traceability from business requirements to controls.	Is layered (Contextual to Component), enabling traceability but not prescribing linear maturity.	Provides a role-based architectural framework that encompasses risk, trust, assurance, and control, but assumes that implementation patterns will be derived at lower levels.	Essential in security architecture planning, especially when traceability and control rationalization are key.	Promotes control traceability but leaves metric implementation open.

Framework	Purpose and Orientation	Maturity Levels and Progression	Domains of Focus	Use Case Applicability	Measurement and Metrics
COSO ERM	Provides a structured, principles-based approach for managing enterprise risk in alignment with strategic objectives.	Does not define discrete maturity levels but support principle-based or capability-based progression, which must be adapted into operational models.	Domains include Governance, Strategy, Risk, Performance, Culture	Suited for strategic risk alignment at the board level, embedding risk into enterprise decision-making.	Guide risk evaluation and performance tracking, but not at a control/system level.
ESRM	Aligns traditional security risk management with business priorities, emphasizing risk ownership and strategic contribution.	Does not define discrete maturity levels but support principle-based or capability-based progression, which must be adapted into operational models.	Domains include Physical & Cybersecurity, Business Risk Alignment, Communication, Stakeholder Responsibility	Works well for physical and security teams integrating with business risk discussions.	Includes risk exposure alignment but relies on external measurement systems for implementation.
ISO	Established international best practices for designing and implementing enterprise-wide risk management frameworks.	Do not define discrete maturity levels but support principle-based or capability-based progression, which must be adapted into operational models.	Organizes its domains under Principles, Framework, and Process for enterprise risk	Used when organizations need a globally recognized standard for enterprise risk processes.	Guide risk evaluation and performance tracking, but not at a control/system level.
IAMM commentary	IAMM uniquely translates these high-level constructs into executable patterns, enabling real-time governance, enforcement, and reporting that spans business and technical domains.	IAMM complements these by defining maturity not only as a governance state but as a measurable, enforceable, and cultural transformation journey.	IAMM is more operationally granular and its domains enable assurance integration into systems, platforms, teams, and behavior, rather than staying at the policy or framework level.	IAMM serves as the connective tissue between these models and turns governance, risk, and architecture principles into measurable, continuous execution.	IAMM excels by operationalizing performance indicators, offering evidence-backed metrics that inform both technical execution and strategic decision-making.

Domain	Level 1 Fragmented	Level 2 Defined	Level 3 Aligned	Level 4 Embedded	Level 5 Institutionalized
Governance	Security and IT operate in silos with no shared governance mechanisms.	Policies exist but lack cross-functional enforcement or integration.	Cross-functional risk forums and workflows are emerging.	An Integrated Assurance Council oversees risk, investment, and policy decisions.	Assurance is integral to strategic planning and enterprise governance.
Architecture & Engineering	Security is applied after-the-fact with little design integration.	Reference architectures exist but are inconsistently applied.	Secure-by-design principles adopted in review cycles.	Reusable secure patterns and policy-as-code are integrated into engineering pipelines.	Assurance is a foundational design constraint; artifacts are governed and auto-validated.
IT & Engineering Operations	Availability is prioritized over security; controls are ad hoc or absent.	Basic security checks incorporated into change control processes.	Shared telemetry and partial control ownership across teams.	Policies and recovery standards are automatically enforced across systems.	Operations are accountable for assurance KPIs; assurance is embedded in every lifecycle phase.
Risk, Compliance & Audit	Risk registers are static; audits are limited and event-driven.	Compliance frameworks are adopted inconsistently, contributing to audit fatigue.	Control harmonization is in progress; ownership is being clarified.	Control testing is automated; compliance is federated across domains.	Assurance is adaptive, continuous, and audit-ready by default.
Metrics & Reporting	Isolated, technical metrics lacking context or strategic use.	Output-driven dashboards in place.	Risk and remediation timelines are tracked collaboratively.	Metrics drive prioritization, governance, and resource allocation.	Metrics demonstrate convergence, impact, and cultural adoption of assurance.
Culture & Collaboration	Security is seen as obstructive; no shared responsibility.	Awareness is basic and engagement reactive.	Assurance champions emerge; inter-team collaboration begins.	Security roles are embedded; cross-functional collaboration formalized.	Security and assurance are core cultural values reinforced by leadership behavior.

FIGURE 15.3 IAMM.

Strategic Alignment and Integration

The IAMM operates at the convergence point of governance (COBIT, COSO), architecture (SABSA), risk (ISO 31000, ESRM), and operations (CMMI, NIST). Rather than competing with these frameworks, IAMM activates their strategic intent—bridging silos and enabling continuous, integrated, and evidence-based assurance across federated environments.

- *Governance:* IAMM aligns with COBIT's governance system principles, embedding assurance into value delivery and risk optimization.
- *Risk:* IAMM operationalizes COSO and ISO 31000 by translating risk principles into actionable, real-time IT and cybersecurity controls.
- *Architecture:* IAMM enhances SABSA's traceability model with dynamic maturity indicators and control enforcement telemetry.
- *Operations:* IAMM transforms NIST Cybersecurity Framework tiers and CMMI practices into executable models driven by live operational telemetry.
- *Stakeholder alignment:* IAMM integrates ESRM's focus on stakeholder responsibility with collaborative assurance domains that foster ownership and accountability across business units.

IAMM does not replace established frameworks, rather it integrates and extends them to make their strategic objectives measurable, adaptable, and operationally effective.

Original Contributions and Necessity of Integrated Assurance

Integrated Assurance brings forward a set of original constructs that depart meaningfully from the limitations of legacy frameworks. Unlike traditional models that focus on runtime enforcement, Integrated Assurance introduces control-as-code and policy enforcement at design time, embedding security and compliance considerations directly into the architecture and engineering lifecycle. It establishes cross-functional ownership models that move beyond merely assigning risk; instead, they operationalize accountability across the enterprise, ensuring that responsibilities are both actionable and measurable.

A key differentiator is the integration of risk handoff and escalation paths within core business workflows such as CI/CD pipelines, vendor onboarding, and identity provisioning. This alignment ensures that security becomes a native part of enterprise operations rather than an external checkpoint. Assurance zones are defined based on the criticality of data, workloads, and business processes and not solely compliance boundaries, enabling a more precise, risk-aligned approach to governance. The model also supports adaptive governance through hybrid centralized and federated structures, allowing for flexibility across diverse business units and geographies. Moreover, Integrated Assurance recognizes culture as a measurable domain of control, framing assurance as a behavior rather than merely a set of technical or procedural requirements.

The necessity for Integrated Assurance stems from the fact that most existing frameworks were conceived in a fundamentally different era, before the cloud, before pervasive digitization, and during a time when IT and security operated in silos under a perimeter-based security mindset. Today's operating environment demands a framework purpose-built for cloud-native and hybrid ecosystems, DevOps-driven delivery models, distributed teams, and the growing complexity of insider and third-party risk. In a climate of continuous regulatory evolution and heightened board-level scrutiny, Integrated Assurance is not a derivative of past frameworks, it is an intentional response to the operational, architectural, and cultural fragmentation that legacy approaches failed to address.

Traditional Framework Limitations	IAMM Enhancement
Risk ownership unclear beyond executive layer	Federated ownership at domain and control level, documented and measurable
Static risk registers and periodic assessments	Continuous, telemetry-based control validation with automated drift detection
Controls often decoupled from operations	Embedded controls in CI/CD pipelines, cloud governance, and infrastructure workflows
Metrics are abstract and disconnected from actionable decisions	Metrics focused on convergence, remediation velocity, and cross-functional collaboration
Compliance-driven culture	Culture of shared accountability and assurance enablement across roles and functions

CONCLUSION AND RECAP

Integrated Assurance is not a framework you deploy. It is a transformation you lead. This chapter has taken the concept from its strategic intent and translated it into operational reality, showing how assurance becomes not only embedded but lived across the enterprise. From boardrooms to pipelines, from compliance teams to product squads, assurance must operate as an enterprise-wide function that scales with the business and adapts with the environment.

We began by establishing a practical methodology for implementation. The model is deliberate in its structure, progressing from strategic alignment to operational scale, culminating in institutionalized resilience. This is not a linear journey, nor is it uniform across all business units. It requires clarity of purpose, sponsorship at the top, and a recognition that assurance cannot remain the responsibility of any one team. It must belong to the enterprise.

The methodology is anchored in realism. At its foundation is an enterprise-wide council that aligns executive intent with operational capability. A current-state baseline identifies the maturity gaps, and pilots validate approaches before they are scaled and provides a natural progression to guide cultural change management. This is not about overhauling the enterprise overnight. It is about surfacing the right patterns, proving them in context, and scaling responsibly. Federated execution enables local innovation within shared guardrails, ensuring consistency without suppressing autonomy.

What distinguishes Integrated Assurance is its operational approach and methodology. It is not theoretical. We showed how Integrated Assurance becomes tangible and embedded in code, enforced through templates, surfaced in dashboards, and validated continuously. This transformation touches architectural design, service delivery, identity management, vendor governance, and software pipelines. Assurance becomes part of how work gets done, not something assessed after the fact.

Use cases bring these ideas to life. They show that Integrated Assurance is not bound to a particular domain or control set. It applies as much to legacy system protection as it does to AI governance. Whether you are managing cloud adoption, securing third-party ecosystems, or modernizing operational technology, the same principles hold. Assurance is contextual. It is cross-functional. And when implemented correctly, it aligns resilience with business velocity. But principles are not enough. Execution demands structure. The IAMM offers a way to measure where you are and define where you need to go. It spans six enterprise domains and five maturity levels. It is role-aware, action-oriented, and focused on convergence. Organizations can use the model to prioritize investment, align stakeholders, and track progress in operational and cultural terms.

At the lower levels of maturity, assurance is fragmented. It is driven by audit cycles, supported by incomplete telemetry, and undermined by tool sprawl and ownership ambiguity. But as maturity grows, assurance becomes built-in. It is no longer viewed as overhead, but as a strategic enabler.

Controls are enforced by design. Metrics are actionable. Governance becomes a living system. And security is a shared responsibility, not a siloed constraint. The final level of maturity institutionalizes assurance as an enterprise capability. Here, assurance is visible in board-level discussions and embedded in strategic planning. It informs digital transformation, supports investment planning, and builds trust with regulators, customers, and internal stakeholders alike. The value of assurance is no longer theoretical, it is measurable, defendable, and aligned to outcomes that matter.

Practical adoption requires more than maturity models. It demands leadership. This chapter provided pragmatic recommendations for how to drive change from within. We explored how to start small, operationalize compensating controls, embed feedback loops, and position security as a productivity enabler. We emphasized the role of incentives, recognition, and shared language. These are the cultural levers that sustain change.

Integrated Assurance thrives on clarity. That clarity comes through metrics. Not the vanity numbers of the past, but metrics that reflect convergence, collaboration, and business alignment. Metrics that drive funding decisions, shape planning conversations, and inform executive decisions. When assurance metrics are aligned to business outcomes, they become not only indicators of health but levers for transformation. As the organization matures, so must the cadence of governance. Assurance must be reviewed continuously, not quarterly. The model must be recalibrated against emerging threats, shifting regulations, and evolving business priorities. Risk is dynamic. Assurance must be too. What matters is not perfection across all domains, but intentional progress where the business needs it most.

Comparing IAMM to NIST Tiers and CMMI illustrates the distinct value of this model. Where NIST Tiers emphasizes governance and CMMI emphasizes process, IAMM emphasizes execution. It is operational by design. It fills the gap between strategy and implementation, uniting architecture, engineering, compliance, and security in pursuit of shared outcomes. It does not compete with other models, it activates them. IAMM is built for complexity. It scales in federated environments and respects operational realities. It acknowledges that transformation is not uniform, but it provides the scaffolding needed to make progress coherent, measurable, and aligned. For global enterprises dealing with hybrid infrastructure, regulatory fragmentation, and cultural divergence, IAMM it is necessary.

The chapter concludes where it began. Integrated Assurance is not a one-time project. It is a living capability. One that must be cultivated, governed, and continuously improved. It is the connective tissue between protection and performance, between compliance and innovation. When assurance becomes a way of operating, when it is embedded in architecture, culture, and daily decisions, the enterprise becomes more than secure. It becomes resilient by design.

16 Future Trends and Considerations for Integrated Assurance

LEARNING OBJECTIVES

- Learn how Integrated Assurance enables scalable and consistent risk management by embedding controls into architecture, platforms, and development workflows
- Understand how real-time monitoring and AI transform assurance from static assessments into continuous, intelligent, and proactive control validation
- Gain an appreciation for how assurance includes governance for AI systems, human behavior, and federated operations across global environments
- Explore how Integrated Assurance becomes strategic, enabling business agility, trust, and resilience while supporting innovation and growth

As organizations embrace Integrated Assurance as an operational model the question turns from "how do we implement it?" to "how do we sustain and evolve it in a dynamic enterprise landscape?" Assurance, by its very nature, is not static. It must respond to shifting regulatory environments, emerging technologies, changing threat vectors, and evolving business models. This chapter explores the future of Integrated Assurance, what trends will shape its trajectory, what strategic considerations enterprises must account for, and how the model itself will mature to remain a source of competitive advantage.

INTEGRATED ASSURANCE-BY-DESIGN: FROM PATTERNS TO PLATFORMS

As Integrated Assurance matures, the next frontier lies in shifting from reactive compliance and fragmented tooling to fully embedded architectural capabilities. This transition marks a deliberate movement toward assurance-by-design, where security, control, and resilience are not layered on after the fact, but intentionally built into the foundational systems, services, and delivery mechanisms of the enterprise. In the near future, Integrated Assurance will be realized not as a set of scattered controls or disconnected assessments, but as a unified enterprise capability delivered through shared platforms. These platforms will expose key assurance functions as reusable services available to all domains of the organization. This includes control validation, policy enforcement, telemetry ingestion, identity orchestration, exception handling, and compliance evidence generation. Rather than requiring each business unit or engineering team to build these capabilities independently, the organization will centralize and abstract them into composable services that integrate seamlessly into development pipelines, infrastructure automation, and operational workflows.

This evolution will also see the rise of reusable assurance design patterns. These patterns will not only define how technical systems should be secured, but also how entire business and

DOI: 10.1201/9781003562153-20

technology scenarios can be executed with built-in assurance. For example, patterns for secure cloud onboarding, third-party data sharing, AI model deployment, or zero trust network segmentation will become standardized. Each pattern will include architectural guidance, control mappings, policy-as-code modules, and operational metrics. These patterns will be cataloged, version-controlled, and continuously updated by cross-functional teams responsible for enabling and governing assurance across the enterprise.

Organizations that successfully adopt this model will treat assurance capabilities as products. These internal products will be designed, maintained, and supported like any other enterprise platform, with user experience, documentation, onboarding support, and service level objectives. Security, risk, and compliance teams will no longer be viewed merely as policy enforcers, but as product owners responsible for delivering usable, scalable, and value-aligned assurance services to the rest of the business.

Architecture will become the primary delivery vehicle for assurance. Secure-by-design becomes a measurable outcome tied to architecture review boards, infrastructure blueprints, and platform engineering practices. Development and operations teams will build solutions using preapproved templates and components that embed controls from the outset. This reduces the burden on individual teams to interpret complex security requirements and minimizes the risk of noncompliance due to inconsistent implementation.

Governance structures must also evolve to support this model. Architecture councils, platform teams, and assurance leaders will work together to define and maintain the reusable patterns and platform services that enable this scalable model. Rather than forcing teams to comply with static policies, governance bodies will empower teams to adopt pre-integrated assurance capabilities as part of their normal workflows. This shift creates a federated model of governance where control is distributed but coordinated. By moving to assurance-by-design, organizations eliminate the gap between intent and implementation. Security is no longer something that is "checked later" but becomes intrinsic to how systems are conceived, built, and operated. This results in reduced audit fatigue, faster delivery velocity, higher confidence in production environments, and more predictable risk management outcomes.

The value of this model lies in its scalability and sustainability. In a global enterprise with hundreds of applications, dozens of business units, and multiple regulatory regimes, it is no longer feasible to manage assurance manually or individually. Only through the combination of architectural coherence, platform-based delivery, and reusable assurance patterns can organizations meet the demands of speed, scale, and defensibility simultaneously. In the assurance-by-design model, security becomes a fabric woven through every function, rather than a separate thread added afterward. It empowers teams to move faster, with greater confidence, and aligns the enterprise to a shared vision of trusted operations. This model represents the future of Integrated Assurance which is operationally embedded, architecturally grounded, and natively scalable across the digital enterprise.

EXAMPLE: SECURE CLOUD ONBOARDING PATTERN VIA PLATFORM-BASED ASSURANCE

SCENARIO

A global financial services enterprise is expanding its digital services and needs to onboard new applications across multiple public cloud providers. Historically, each business unit managed its own cloud setup, leading to inconsistent configurations, control gaps, and audit failures. Security reviews were manual and occurred after deployment, creating delivery delays and compliance risks.

INTEGRATED ASSURANCE-BY-DESIGN IMPLEMENTATION

1. *Platform-based assurance capabilities:* The organization creates a Cloud Onboarding Assurance Platform, exposing reusable assurance capabilities as APIs and modules, including:
   - Control Validation Engine: Automatically checks configurations (e.g., IAM, encryption, logging) against approved baselines.
   - Policy-as-Code Service: Embeds security, regulatory, and architecture policies as code, integrated into CI/CD pipelines.
   - Telemetry Ingestion Layer: Collects cloud activity logs and configuration states in real time for continuous assurance.
   - Identity Orchestration: Ensures role-based access control (RBAC) is enforced and federated across cloud providers.
   - Exception Handling API: Allows teams to request, document, and autoexpire justified control exceptions.
2. *Reusable assurance pattern:* The architecture team publishes a "Secure Cloud Onboarding Pattern", which includes:
   - Architectural diagrams showing approved cloud reference architecture.
   - Mappings to NIST, ISO, and internal controls.
   - Terraform modules for preconfigured secure landing zones.
   - GitOps integration scripts for autodeployment into monitored environments.
   - Prebuilt dashboards for assurance posture and control drift.
3. *Governance as enablement:* Rather than issuing static policy documents, governance is enforced through:
   - Architecture review boards approving only pattern-compliant projects, or providing for, and monitoring, exception projects.
   - Shared platform metrics driving maturity discussions.
   - Developer experience teams providing onboarding support, documentation, and sandbox environments for rapid prototyping.
4. Operational outcomes
   - Security-by-default: Developers use a CLI tool to generate new projects with prewired assurance modules.
   - No audit surprises: Compliance evidence is generated automatically and linked to real-time control telemetry.
   - Scalability: Over 70 application teams adopt the pattern, reducing time-to-deploy securely.
   - Resilience: Incidents tied to misconfigured cloud resources drop by 80% due to proactive control validation.

SUMMARY

This example shows how Integrated Assurance-by-Design transforms security from a reactive gatekeeper to a proactive enabler. By providing shared assurance platforms and reusable patterns, the organization aligns risk management with delivery velocity, achieving consistency, agility, and defensibility at scale.

REAL-TIME INTEGRATED ASSURANCE THROUGH CONTINUOUS CONTROL MONITORING AND AI

As the speed of business accelerates and digital ecosystems grow more complex, enterprises must move beyond periodic audits and manual control attestations. The future of Integrated Assurance demands a shift toward real-time validation of controls, risks, and security posture. This evolution is enabled by continuous control monitoring and augmented by artificial intelligence. In this model, Integrated Assurance becomes an always-on capability. Control effectiveness is no longer inferred from documentation or quarterly assessments but measured continuously through real-time telemetry. Systems are instrumented to validate whether controls are present, correctly configured, and functioning as intended. When misconfigurations, deviations, or anomalies arise, they are flagged immediately, enabling corrective actions before risk materializes into impact.

AI plays a pivotal role in this transformation. Machine learning models can baseline normal behavior across systems, applications, and user activities. Once these baselines are established, the AI engine can detect drift, anomalous patterns, or subtle indicators of control decay. For example, it might identify that a previously stable access control policy is being overridden more frequently or that network traffic patterns are shifting in a way that suggests exfiltration risk. These insights would be nearly impossible to detect with manual processes or static rules.

Real-time assurance also changes how risk is owned and managed. Instead of routing every decision through centralized security teams, business units are empowered with live dashboards that show their current assurance posture. They can see which controls are failing, which compensating mechanisms are active, and how their systems compare against expected baselines. This transparency enables distributed risk ownership and faster decision-making, aligned to both technical and business context.

Control telemetry will increasingly be aggregated into enterprise assurance engines. These engines serve as a system of record for risk and compliance state across the organization. They integrate with CI/CD pipelines, IT service management platforms, cloud infrastructure, endpoint agents, and identity providers, pulling in evidence of control implementation and effectiveness. Assurance leaders can query these engines to support audits, measure progress, or evaluate readiness in near real time.

This model also introduces a more dynamic approach to exception handling. Instead of manually submitted risk exceptions reviewed weeks later, exceptions can be contextually granted, time-bound, and autoexpiring. AI can evaluate whether a proposed control bypass presents an acceptable risk based on similar scenarios, existing compensating controls, and the sensitivity of the system involved. Exceptions become measurable and governed, rather than ad hoc and forgotten. By adopting real-time assurance and AI augmentation, organizations will reduce the lag between detection and response, eliminate blind spots, and support a more agile governance model. Controls will be treated as living assets, constantly validated and improved. Risk will become a dynamic signal, not a static label. This evolution transforms assurance from a retrospective reporting function into a forward-looking operational capability that drives resilience and trust across the enterprise.

EXAMPLE: REAL-TIME INTEGRATED ASSURANCE IN A GLOBAL FINANCIAL INSTITUTION

SCENARIO

A global financial institution manages highly sensitive customer data, operates critical transaction systems, and is subject to intense regulatory scrutiny. Historically, control validations were done quarterly via manual assessments, leading to audit fatigue and delayed risk detection.

INTEGRATED ASSURANCE IN ACTION

1. *Control telemetry and continuous monitoring:* All critical systems, such as transaction processing platforms, identity services, and cloud infrastructure, are instrumented with telemetry agents. These agents continuously report on:
   - Encryption status of databases
   - Firewall rule configurations
   - Endpoint detection and response (EDR) coverage
   - Privileged access activity
   - Patch levels and configuration baselines

   This telemetry is streamed into a centralized Assurance Engine that aggregates and visualizes the real-time control state across the enterprise.
2. *AI-augmented baselines and drift detection:* A machine learning model was trained over six months on typical access patterns, system configurations, and user behavior. The model now continuously monitors for:
   - Access control drift: AI detects a 35% increase in access overrides to critical customer databases over the past two weeks.
   - Network anomaly: Lateral traffic between two subsidiary regions that historically don't communicate begins to spike, which indicates possible data exfiltration.

   These anomalies are flagged immediately and routed to both the cybersecurity and IT operations teams for real-time investigation.
3. *Distributed risk ownership via dashboards:* Each business unit has access to live dashboards that reflect their assurance posture:
   - Red flags for failing controls
   - Active compensating controls
   - Comparisons against risk baselines
   - Time-to-remediation and risk impact scores

   The marketing team notices they're the only business unit with expired certificates on public-facing APIs. With this visibility, they remediate the issue within hours and no central escalation needed.
4. *Dynamic, AI-assisted exception handling:* A data science team needs to deploy a new ML model using an unsupported cloud service. An exception is requested for bypassing part of the identity federation policy. The AI engine evaluates the exception request in context:
   - Confirms enhanced network segmentation and compensating DLP controls are in place
   - Tags the request as "low residual risk"
   - Grants a ten-day time-bound exception with automated revocation and notification workflow

   No manual approvals. No delays. Fully governed and auditable.
5. *Real-time metrics and assurance outcomes:* Instead of quarterly checklists, executives see:
   - Control drift rate: down quarter-over-quarter
   - Time-to-detection: reduced from days to minutes

- Risk-adjusted uptime: 99.995% across critical systems
- Exception lifecycle metrics: 87% autoexpired within policy window

These metrics are used in board reports, regulatory filings, and even insurance negotiations, showcasing Integrated Assurance as both a risk reducer and business enabler.

RESULT

What once took weeks to uncover, now takes minutes. Risk decisions are made where they happen. Security and operations no longer work in silos, instead they operate in synchronicity. Integrated Assurance, powered by real-time telemetry and AI, enables this financial institution to move fast, stay secure, and maintain stakeholder trust at scale.

ASSURANCE FOR AI AND AUTONOMOUS SYSTEMS

As AI becomes increasingly embedded into core enterprise workflows, the need for transparent, governable, and secure AI systems has become a defining challenge for Integrated Assurance. AI no longer resides solely in innovation labs. It is actively used to automate decisions, personalize customer experiences, manage supply chains, and even detect fraud. As these systems take on more consequential roles, organizations must develop new methods to ensure their integrity, accountability, and resilience.

The first pillar of AI assurance is data governance. Machine learning models are only as reliable as the data they consume. This means the provenance, integrity, and representativeness of training data must be verifiable. Integrated Assurance requires enterprises to track how datasets are collected, labeled, stored, and transformed. Data lineage must be auditable end-to-end to ensure that AI outputs can be explained, validated, and trusted. This includes maintaining a clear record of which systems contributed data, how that data was preprocessed, and under what assumptions it was used.

Integrated Assurance Maturity Model (IAMM) introduces an additional layer of complexity. Integrated Assurance must account for model drift, bias, and explainability. Models evolve over time as data changes, which can introduce unintended behavior or amplify systemic bias. Assurance frameworks must monitor model performance continuously, flag degradation, and enforce retraining thresholds. They must also mandate explainable AI practices, where model decisions are interpretable by humans, especially in regulated or high-risk domains such as healthcare, finance, or criminal justice.

As AI systems begin to act autonomously, particularly in operational or physical environments, new risks emerge. Autonomous vehicles, robotic process automation, and intelligent agents introduce potential harm that spans both cyber and physical domains. Integrated Assurance must ensure that these systems have defined escalation protocols, safe operating parameters, override mechanisms, and incident response procedures that mirror traditional IT risk protocols.

Ultimately, AI assurance is not about constraining innovation. It is about creating a sustainable, transparent, and resilient foundation for AI adoption at scale. By embedding assurance into AI architecture and lifecycle management, enterprises can accelerate adoption while protecting against algorithmic failures, regulatory scrutiny, and reputational harm. Integrated Assurance ensures that organizations do not just use AI, but use it safely, responsibly, and with measurable trustworthiness.

EXAMPLE: AI-POWERED LOAN APPROVAL SYSTEM IN A FINANCIAL INSTITUTION

CONTEXT

A global bank has implemented an AI-powered system to automate loan approvals. The system uses a machine learning model trained on historical credit data to assess risk and approve or deny applications in real time. It integrates with customer databases, credit bureaus, and internal risk scoring platforms.

HOW INTEGRATED ASSURANCE IS APPLIED

1. Data governance
   - Action: The bank establishes a data lineage framework to track every dataset used for model training—from source systems to preprocessing logic.
   - Control: All training data is version-controlled, and metadata includes data origin, transformation logic, and timestamps.
   - Outcome: If the model outputs a questionable decision, the institution can trace back exactly what data influenced it, ensuring explainability and defensibility.
2. Model drift and bias monitoring
   - Action: The assurance team integrates model drift detection pipelines into the AI lifecycle. Weekly retraining thresholds are enforced based on monitored drift metrics.
   - Control: A bias detection tool regularly analyzes model outputs for disparities across protected attributes like race, gender, age, or geography.
   - Outcome: When performance degradation is detected, a human-in-the-loop review is triggered, and the model is automatically rolled back or retrained.
3. Explainability and compliance
   - Action: All decisions made by the AI are accompanied by explainability modules (e.g., SHAP values) that describe the key factors influencing the approval or denial.
   - Control: Regulatory compliance is ensured by mapping model behavior against fair lending laws, with audit trails available for external review.
   - Outcome: Customers receive meaningful reasons for decisions, satisfying legal transparency requirements and building trust.
4. Escalation and override mechanisms
   - Action: A dual-control mechanism is built where high-risk or borderline applications are flagged for human analyst intervention.
   - Control: Analysts have override capabilities and escalation protocols for cases that do not fit standard decision criteria.
   - Outcome: The system ensures that edge cases are reviewed, reducing false rejections and reputational damage.
5. Incident response integration
   - Action: AI incident scenarios (e.g., unexpected decision spikes, service disruption, data poisoning attacks) are included in enterprise-wide incident response playbooks.
   - Control: These playbooks define roles for the AI development team, IT ops, compliance, and communications.
   - Outcome: AI-related incidents are responded to with the same coordination and governance as any cyber or IT failure.

RESULT

By embedding assurance into the AI system's design, monitoring, and operations, the financial institution doesn't just comply with regulations, it enhances customer trust, reduces business risk, and increases operational reliability.

FEDERATED GOVERNANCE AT GLOBAL SCALE

As enterprises expand across geographies, jurisdictions, and markets, the complexity of managing risk and compliance multiplies. Each region may be governed by different regulations, privacy laws, data residency requirements, and cultural expectations around trust and security. A single, monolithic assurance model is no longer practical, nor is it effective. The future of Integrated Assurance will be shaped by federated governance, where central principles guide distributed execution, and control enforcement adapts to local context without sacrificing enterprise consistency.

Federated governance acknowledges that different parts of the enterprise move at different speeds. Some business units operate in high-regulation industries such as financial services or pharmaceuticals, where strict control enforcement and audit readiness are required. Others may focus on innovation, research, or digital experimentation, where agility, speed, and rapid iteration are critical. Integrated Assurance provides a framework that allows both to coexist under a common governance model. IAMM begins by establishing core assurance principles at the enterprise level. These principles define the organization's baseline expectations for identity, access, data protection, monitoring, and risk ownership. They do not prescribe implementation detail but instead serve as the foundation for locally tailored execution. Each business unit, region, or function is then empowered to implement controls that meet or exceed the baseline, adapting to their specific regulatory, operational, and cultural realities.

Technology plays a key role in enabling this federation. Policy engines must support dynamic, context-aware enforcement. Identity governance platforms must be able to apply different policies based on geography, user role, or risk profile. Control libraries must allow for modular adaptation, where local teams can extend global patterns with regional specificity. Governance platforms must aggregate telemetry and control evidence across diverse environments into a unified view that supports audit, compliance, and executive oversight.

Federated governance also demands new operating structures. Cross-functional working groups, embedded assurance leads, and regional security councils provide the connective tissue between central strategy and local execution. These bodies meet regularly to align on risk posture, share lessons learned, and escalate systemic issues. They also serve as two-way channels of communication, enabling feedback from the front lines to shape enterprise policy and investment decisions. Reporting under this model must be role and region aware. Local teams need detailed dashboards that reflect their control health, exception volumes, and remediation timelines. Executives need aggregated views that show how assurance posture varies across regions, which controls are degrading, and where investment is needed. Compliance teams need jurisdictional traceability to demonstrate adherence to specific legal frameworks. Integrated Assurance enables all three by standardizing telemetry and control metadata while preserving local context.

The IAMM approach also facilitates scalable audit readiness. Rather than preparing separate control narratives and evidence sets for each jurisdiction, organizations define a unified control framework that maps to multiple regulations. Local implementations demonstrate how enterprise controls are realized in practice. This dramatically reduces audit fatigue, eliminates duplication, and improves defensibility. Federated governance represents a maturation of Integrated Assurance. It shifts the enterprise from enforcing control through top-down mandates to enabling control through shared platforms, adaptable tooling, and role-specific ownership. It balances consistency with flexibility and ensures that assurance is embedded in both the structure and the rhythm of global operations. In a world of rising regulatory scrutiny and geopolitical volatility, this model becomes essential for maintaining trust, demonstrating compliance, and supporting growth at scale.

EXAMPLE: MULTINATIONAL HEALTHCARE AND RESEARCH ORGANIZATION

OVERVIEW

A global healthcare and pharmaceutical company operates across North America, Europe, Asia, and Latin America. Its business spans highly regulated pharmaceutical manufacturing, R&D labs, cloud-based digital health services, and regional sales and marketing teams. The company adopts Integrated Assurance through a federated governance model to align cybersecurity, risk, and compliance across diverse regulatory, operational, and cultural environments.

ENTERPRISE-LEVEL CORE (CENTRAL GOVERNANCE)

- Global assurance charter: Defines enterprise-wide principles for identity governance, data protection, monitoring, and control ownership.
- IAMM baseline: Establishes minimum expectations such as encryption at rest, privileged access management, and continuous telemetry across all systems.
- Control mapping engine: Central governance team maintains a unified control framework mapped to GDPR, HIPAA, ISO 27001, and local standards.

REGIONAL EXECUTION EXAMPLES

1. European Business Unit (subject to GDPR)
    - Implements enterprise identity and access policies using region-specific tagging for data residency.
    - Enhances baseline with stricter privacy impact assessments and local consent management tools.
    - Collaborates with the central team via a Regional Assurance Council to localize policies while maintaining global visibility.
2. U.S. R&D Division (subject to HIPAA and High-Speed DevOps)
    - Uses the same IAMM principles but integrates them into DevSecOps pipelines for speed.
    - Implements runtime security and behavior analytics in containerized environments.
    - Executes continuous assurance via integrated CI/CD controls that map to centralized telemetry.
3. Latin American Commercial Unit (low regulatory burden, high agility needs)
    - Adopts the global baseline but applies lightweight control implementations (e.g., secure SaaS with central SSO).
    - Focuses on awareness, device posture checks, and exception-based risk approvals to maintain pace.
    - Participates in regional working groups to align emerging risks with global policy evolution.

TECHNOLOGY ENABLEMENT

- Policy-as-Code Platform: Enforces baseline security requirements through reusable templates.
- Federated Dashboards: Local teams access tailored views of their control posture, while executives see aggregate assurance health.
- Unified Telemetry Bus: Integrates data from CMDBs, SIEMs, and endpoint agents across all regions into one analytics platform.

ORGANIZATIONAL STRUCTURES AND COMMUNICATION

- Embedded Assurance Leads in each region act as liaisons between the global strategy office and local teams.
- Quarterly Risk and Assurance Committees coordinate cross-domain assurance, surface systemic issues, and track remediation.
- Feedback loops: Lessons learned from regional incidents inform global policy updates, improving overall resilience.

AUDIT AND COMPLIANCE

- The company passes multiple global audits using a single control framework mapped to local implementations.
- Avoids duplicated effort by showing how the same foundational controls satisfy diverse requirements.
- Achieves reduction in audit prep time and drop in compliance exceptions year over year.

OUTCOME

The federated governance model enabled the organization to scale Integrated Assurance globally while preserving local autonomy. This approach reduced regulatory risk, improved incident response times, and increased trust with regulators, partners, and customers and all without slowing down innovation.

HUMAN-CENTRIC ASSURANCE AND BEHAVIORAL INTELLIGENCE

While technology provides the infrastructure for assurance, people remain the most dynamic and influential element of enterprise risk. The behaviors, decisions, and intent of individuals, whether executives, engineers, contractors, or partners, can either reinforce or undermine the strongest control frameworks. As enterprises mature in their adoption of Integrated Assurance, the focus must expand to include the human layer as both a source of strength and a potential point of failure. Human-centric assurance in IAMM begins with behavioral context. Traditional identity and access management systems confirm who a user is and what they are permitted to do. However, they often fail to detect why a user is acting a certain way or whether their behavior aligns with historical patterns or organizational norms. Integrated Assurance must incorporate behavioral analytics to build richer user risk profiles, identifying anomalies such as excessive data downloads, unusual access times, repeated policy violations, or geographic inconsistencies.

This intelligence enables adaptive risk-based controls. For example, a user accessing financial data from an approved device in a typical location may proceed with minimal friction. However, if that same user suddenly accesses sensitive intellectual property from an unrecognized network at an unusual time, additional controls can be triggered. These may include multifactor authentication, temporary session quarantine, or escalation to a human analyst. In this model, assurance becomes not just conditional, but contextual.

Behavioral assurance also applies to organizational patterns. Teams that consistently delay remediation, bypass controls, or fail to participate in incident response exercises may reflect a breakdown in culture or alignment. Integrated Assurance introduces team-level assurance metrics, tracking engagement with security practices, frequency of exception requests, response times to risks, and collaboration with governance functions. These metrics are not punitive, but diagnostic. They help leadership understand where additional training, enablement, or support is needed. The role of culture is foundational. Security awareness programs that rely on generic training modules are insufficient. Instead, Integrated Assurance supports function-specific enablement, where employees receive contextual training based on their roles and the risks they face. Developers learn about secure coding and CI/CD risks. Finance teams learn about wire fraud and social engineering. Executives learn about strategic risks, regulatory implications, and decision-based exposure. This customization ensures that assurance is embedded in daily behaviors, not just policy documentation.

Partnership with human resources is essential. Onboarding workflows must integrate identity provisioning, role-based access controls, and behavioral expectation setting. Offboarding must ensure timely deprovisioning, audit logging, and access revocation. Insider risk management must incorporate signals from HR, such as changes in job satisfaction, unusual time-off patterns, or recent performance issues. These signals, when used ethically and lawfully, enable early identification of potential threats and support proactive intervention.

Privacy and ethics are critical dimensions of this evolution. As User Entity Behavior Analytics (UEBA) becomes richer, enterprises must ensure that data collection is transparent, proportionate, and aligned with organizational values. Integrated Assurance requires collaboration between security, legal, ethics, and HR teams to define what is monitored, how it is governed, and how privacy is preserved. Surveillance must never erode trust. It must support a culture of accountability, where the workforce understands not only what is expected but why it matters.

Ultimately, human-centric assurance reframes people not as the weakest link, but as active contributors to enterprise resilience. It recognizes that culture, intent, and behavior shape the effectiveness of every control. By investing in behavioral intelligence, contextual awareness, and cultural alignment, organizations create an environment where security is not enforced from the outside but sustained from within. This transformation will become a defining feature of Integrated Assurance in the years ahead.

USE CASE: ENHANCING INSIDER THREAT DETECTION AND CULTURAL ALIGNMENT IN A FINANCIAL SERVICES ENTERPRISE

Background

GlobalBank, a multinational financial services provider, has adopted the IAMM to unify cybersecurity, IT operations, and governance. After successfully embedding technical controls across infrastructure and applications, GlobalBank shifts focus to the human layer, recognizing it as both a critical control point and a potential vulnerability.

Challenge

Recent internal audits reveal two areas of concern:

1. Behavioral anomalies among privileged users are not being flagged by traditional IAM tools.
2. Team-level cultural disengagement from security practices—such as delayed patching, poor incident participation, and policy exceptions—are increasing enterprise risk without formal visibility.

Integrated Assurance Solution

1. Behavioral Intelligence Implementation

GlobalBank deploys a UEBA platform integrated into its IAMM framework. Key integrations include:

- Identity and access logs
- Endpoint telemetry
- HR metadata (role, tenure, performance flags)
- Geolocation and network access patterns

The system builds a behavioral baseline for each user. One detection includes:

- A senior financial analyst, typically active 9 a.m.–6 p.m. EST from NYC, begins accessing M&A deal data at 2 a.m. from an overseas IP, using a personal device.

Adaptive Assurance Response

- The session is quarantined in real time.
- The analyst is prompted for step-up MFA and verification of location.
- A case is created in the Integrated Assurance dashboard and routed to insider risk analysts and HR for review.
- HR flags recent dissatisfaction from the employee's 360° review and missed promotion.

Outcome

A potential data exfiltration incident is mitigated without user lockout or disruption of critical operations and an example of contextual control enabled by behavioral telemetry.

2. Team-Level Cultural Metrics

IAMM introduces Assurance Engagement Scores across business units:

- Patching timelines
- Participation in red team exercises
- Number of exception requests
- Frequency of policy violations
- Collaboration with security and governance teams

The trading team scores low. Analysis shows:

- Frequent control exceptions
- Poor response to phishing simulations
- Minimal engagement in training

Action Taken

- Leadership receives a dashboard summary highlighting gaps.
- Custom training is deployed for the trading team focusing on fraud, phishing, and real-world financial sector breaches.
- Security champions are embedded within the team.
- HR and Risk collaborate to align performance reviews with assurance behaviors.

Outcome

- Within one quarter, phishing clickthrough rates drop by 75%.
- Engagement in tabletop exercises improves.
- The team begins submitting proactive security improvement suggestions, reflecting cultural change.

3. Privacy and Ethical Governance

To ensure ethical oversight:

- A joint task force (Security, HR, Legal, Ethics) defines acceptable telemetry scope and usage.
- Employees are transparently informed about data types collected and the purpose.
- Behavioral data is anonymized when used for team-level metrics.
- A privacy impact assessment is conducted and reviewed quarterly.

Value Delivered

- Proactive risk detection through behavioral insights
- Reduced insider threat exposure without harming user experience
- Improved security culture through function-specific enablement
- Sustainable assurance embedded in daily work behaviors
- Ethical governance of human telemetry aligned with trust and privacy

ASSURANCE AS STRATEGIC LEVERAGE

As the business landscape becomes more volatile, digital, and interconnected, organizations are rethinking how they compete, how they grow, and how they manage risk. In this context, assurance is evolving from a defensive necessity into a strategic asset, one that enables trust, unlocks opportunity, creates organizational transparency, and differentiates resilient enterprises from their peers. Integrated Assurance, when fully operationalized, becomes more than a governance function. It becomes a lever of competitive advantage.

At its core, assurance provides confidence. It assures customers that their data is protected, regulators that obligations are being met, investors that risk is being managed, and employees that their workplace is trustworthy. This confidence translates into tangible outcomes: faster time to market, fewer disruptions, improved audit performance, stronger customer retention, and more favorable terms with insurers, partners, and acquirers.

Integrated Assurance also enables strategic agility. Transformation initiatives, such as cloud adoption, M&A, AI scaling, and digital platform consolidation, are often slowed or constrained by security and compliance concerns. By embedding assurance into architecture, development, and operations, organizations can move quickly and confidently, knowing that controls are already in place, that risks are understood, and that governance is continuous. Assurance becomes a foundation for safe innovation, where speed and safety reinforce rather than compete with each other.

This strategic view of assurance also changes how cybersecurity and compliance teams are perceived within the organization. Instead of being seen as cost centers or blockers, they are recognized as enablers of growth and protectors of enterprise value. Boards and executives begin to allocate investment not based on fear or obligation, but based on alignment with growth, differentiation, and brand trust. Metrics shift from technical volume to business impact, with assurance tied directly to outcomes such as downtime avoided, breaches prevented, contracts won, or compliance costs reduced. To reach this level of influence, assurance leaders must speak the language of the business. They must translate control performance into operational resilience, link risk trends to financial exposure, and demonstrate how assurance enables strategic decisions such as entering new markets, launching new products, or responding to crises. This requires collaboration with finance, operations, legal, and product leaders, as well as an enterprise-wide approach to measuring and communicating the value of assurance.

The future enterprise will not be judged solely on its profitability, scalability, or innovation. It will be judged on its defensibility, transparency, and resilience too. Integrated Assurance provides the operating system for achieving these qualities. When elevated to a strategic capability, it becomes not just a shield against risk, but a driver of trust and an amplifier of value.

USE CASE: INTEGRATED ASSURANCE AS A STRATEGIC ENABLER IN A GLOBAL CLOUD TRANSFORMATION

Company Profile

A global pharmaceutical firm, NovaCura Health, operating in 35 countries, with an extensive research and manufacturing footprint, embarks on a major digital transformation initiative. The strategy involves migrating core business platforms to a multicloud environment while integrating AI for drug discovery and improving patient engagement through digital health platforms.

Challenge

Despite executive support, the transformation roadmap faced resistance from internal risk, compliance, and IT security teams due to concerns about regulatory compliance, third-party risk, and data sovereignty. Business leaders were also concerned about potential delays, operational disruptions, and negative regulatory scrutiny.

Solution—Operationalizing Integrated Assurance

The CISO and Chief Risk Officer partnered with enterprise architects and transformation leads to embed Integrated Assurance as a foundational strategy. They established a cross-functional Assurance Enablement Office tasked with aligning cybersecurity, risk management, legal, and IT governance with business objectives.

Key actions included:

- Real-time control telemetry: Deployed automated telemetry for continuous monitoring of critical controls across cloud workloads, linked to a centralized risk dashboard consumable by business executives.
- Assurance-by-design: Embedded assurance requirements into cloud architecture patterns, agile development pipelines, and third-party onboarding processes.
- Risk-to-value translation: Introduced business-centric assurance KPIs, such as compliance acceleration rate, breach probability delta, and time-to-recovery per business unit, tied directly to transformation milestones.
- Board-level storytelling: Assurance leaders began presenting not just security risks, but how assurance reduced project delays, secured patient data, and protected IP pipelines, framing assurance as a business enabler.

Outcomes

- The transformation program maintained an on-time launch across 90% of migration waves.
- Audit exceptions dropped due to early control integration and continuous monitoring.
- Third-party onboarding time reduced through prevalidated assurance profiles.
- The company secured cyber insurance premium reductions due to real-time risk transparency.
- Investor confidence rose, with public disclosures emphasizing defensibility and resilience, contributing to an increase in market cap post-migration.

Strategic Leverage Realized

- NovaCura's assurance capabilities became a competitive differentiator when pursuing data-intensive partnerships in the biotech space.
- The company entered two new geographic markets with faster regulatory clearance due to pre-established assurance frameworks.
- Internal perception of cybersecurity shifted from blocker to business accelerator, leading to increased funding for assurance automation initiatives.

CONCLUSION AND RECAP

Integrated Assurance moves governance and compliance well beyond the policing and auditing roles that they have traditionally held. Integrated Assurance is the framework that allows them to break out of those roles and become true business partners and enablers for the business strategically. It is now recognized as a foundational capability for enterprises navigating complexity, risk, and constant transformation. This chapter has examined the future of assurance not in abstract terms but as a series of practical evolutions that align security, operations, and strategy in the face of accelerating change.

The shift toward assurance by design marks a pivotal moment. Assurance must be built into the core of enterprise architecture, not applied as an afterthought. Reusable design patterns, standardized control sets, and embedded policy engines are now critical components of any secure and scalable platform. The organizations that embrace this model will operate with greater confidence and deliver with fewer disruptions.

Continuous control monitoring represents the next necessary advancement. Periodic assessments are no longer sufficient in a landscape where systems change daily and threats evolve hourly. Enterprises must adopt real-time telemetry, automated control validation, and dynamic exception handling. These capabilities make assurance proactive rather than reactive and ensure that control failures are detected and corrected before they impact the business.

Artificial intelligence will play an increasingly important role. By learning patterns of normal behavior across systems and users, AI can help surface risks that would otherwise go unnoticed. These insights empower teams to act faster and with more precision. They also enable a more nuanced understanding of assurance posture across business units, allowing for timely and informed decision-making.

AI and autonomous systems themselves will require robust governance. As machine learning becomes more deeply integrated into customer experience, operations, and decision-making, organizations must be able to assure these systems with the same rigor applied to traditional infrastructure. That means validating training data, tracking model drift, enforcing explainability, and defining escalation paths for AI-driven processes.

To support these capabilities at scale, governance must evolve. The federated model allows central principles to be executed locally, enabling flexibility without compromising consistency. This approach respects the regulatory, cultural, and operational diversity across global enterprises. It also supports innovation by giving teams the freedom to adapt assurance frameworks to the realities of their environments.

Technology will support this shift through adaptable policy engines, modular control libraries, and role-aware reporting. Governance teams will no longer rely solely on policy documents and manual reviews. Instead, they will govern through platforms that aggregate evidence, highlight deviations, and promote accountability. This model also reduces audit fatigue and improves readiness through standardized yet flexible implementations.

Assurance cannot be sustained through technology alone. People are central to every outcome. Human-centric assurance begins by understanding user behavior and aligning controls to intent. Identity and access management must evolve from verifying who someone is to understanding why they act. Behavioral analytics can detect risks early, while adaptive controls respond in context, ensuring that security enhances rather than obstructs the user experience.

Cultural alignment is equally important. Assurance is not just a technical construct. It is a shared responsibility shaped by leadership, communication, and incentive structures. Contextual training, cross-functional collaboration, and role-specific enablement create the foundation for a security-aware workforce. These elements must be embedded into hiring, onboarding, performance management, and leadership development.

This convergence of systems, data, and people transforms assurance into a source of strategic value. Organizations that can prove their resilience, demonstrate compliance, and maintain operational continuity in the face of disruption will gain the trust of customers, regulators, partners, and investors. Trust becomes an asset. Assurance becomes the capability that protects and amplifies that asset.

The enterprises that thrive in the future will not be defined solely by how fast they grow or how many customers they reach. They will be recognized for their transparency, accountability, and ability to manage complexity without losing control. Integrated Assurance is the operating model that supports this kind of maturity. It enables organizations to take bold steps without exposing themselves to unnecessary risk.

Let this chapter serve as both a summary and a starting point. Integrated Assurance is not a project to be completed. It is a continuous journey toward greater clarity, confidence, and convergence. With the right architecture, culture, and operational discipline, it becomes a lasting source of trust and strategic resilience. The future of assurance is here. It is adaptive. It is embedded. And it is ready to be led by those who are willing to architect it into every layer of the enterprise.

Glossary

Access Control Mechanisms that restrict user access to IT systems, ensuring only authorized personnel can access sensitive data.

Adaptive Threat Modelling A dynamic approach to continuously assessing and evolving threat models based on changing attack patterns and system architectures.

Administrative Controls Management-driven security controls such as security policies, training programs, and access control measures that define user permissions and security responsibilities.

Advanced Persistent Threats (APTs) Sophisticated, long-term cyberattacks often conducted by nation state actors or organized cybercriminal groups.

Adversarial AI The use of AI by cybercriminals to bypass security defenses, such as AI-generated phishing attacks or deepfake-based fraud.

Agile Decision-Making The ability to make rapid, informed decisions based on real-time security and IT operational data to enhance response times and adaptability.

Application Performance Management (APM) The practice of monitoring and optimizing software applications to ensure reliability and efficiency.

Application Programming Interface (API) A set of rules and protocols that allow different software applications to communicate and exchange data. APIs are essential for integrating cloud services, enterprise applications, and third-party solutions.

Artificial Intelligence (AI) The simulation of human intelligence in machines that can analyze data, recognize patterns, and make decisions with minimal human intervention. AI is widely used in enterprise IT for automation, predictive analytics, and cybersecurity.

Attack Surface The total number of potential entry points or vulnerabilities that attackers can exploit to gain unauthorized access to a system or network. Reducing the attack surface minimizes security risks.

Attack Surface Management (ASM) The process of identifying and reducing potential entry points that attackers can exploit within an application or infrastructure.

Audit Readiness The process of preparing for security and compliance audits by maintaining accurate documentation and evidence of adherence to regulations.

Automated Incident Response The use of predefined workflows, scripts, and AI-driven tools to detect and respond to cybersecurity incidents without manual intervention.

Automated Patch Management The use of automation tools to detect, test, and apply security patches to IT systems, reducing vulnerabilities and minimizing manual effort.

Behavioral Analytics The use of AI and machine learning to analyze user behavior and detect anomalies that may indicate a security threat.

Big Data Analytics The process of examining large and complex datasets to uncover insights, trends, and patterns that can inform business decisions. Enterprises use big data analytics to optimize operations, enhance customer experiences, and drive innovation.

Blameless Postmortems A cultural practice in DevOps and DevSecOps that analyzes security incidents and system failures without assigning blame, fostering a learning-oriented environment.

Blockchain A decentralized and tamper-proof digital ledger technology used for secure and transparent transactions. In enterprise IT, blockchain is employed for supply chain tracking, identity management, and cybersecurity applications.

Breach Notification Requirements Legal mandates that require organizations to inform authorities and affected individuals when a data breach occurs.

Business Continuity Plan (BCP) A strategic plan outlining procedures that ensure critical business functions continue during and after a security incident or IT disruption.

Business-Driven Methodology A strategic approach that aligns security practices with overall business objectives, ensuring cybersecurity supports operational resilience and growth.

Business Email Compromise (BEC) A cybercrime technique where attackers impersonate executives or employees to trick individuals into transferring funds or disclosing sensitive information.

Business Impact Analysis (BIA) A process that evaluates the potential effects of disruptions on business operations and identifies critical dependencies.

Capacity Planning The practice of forecasting future IT resource needs to ensure adequate infrastructure and prevent downtime.

CIA Triad The three foundational principles of cybersecurity: Confidentiality, Integrity, and Availability.

Cloud Computing A model for delivering computing resources, such as storage, processing power, and applications, over the internet on demand. Cloud computing enables enterprises to scale IT infrastructure efficiently while reducing costs.

Cloud Orchestration Tools Software that automates the management and coordination of cloud-based resources and services.

Cloud Security The implementation of security measures designed to protect cloud-based applications, data, and infrastructure. Cloud Access Security Brokers (CASB) and Secure Web Gateways (SWG) are common cloud security compensating controls.

Cloud Security Posture Management (CSPM) Tools and practices designed to continuously monitor cloud environments for security risks and misconfigurations.

COBIT An IT governance framework that ensures IT aligns with business objectives and regulatory requirements.

Code Repositories Centralized storage locations where source code is managed, versioned, and controlled, often with access restrictions to enhance security.

Compensating Control A security measure implemented as an alternative when a primary control cannot be fully deployed. It must provide equivalent or comparable protection against security risks.

Compliance Adherence to industry regulations and standards such as GDPR, HIPAA, and PCI DSS, ensuring legal and ethical handling of data security.

Compliance Audits Formal assessments to evaluate an organization's adherence to cybersecurity policies, industry regulations, and legal requirements.

Compliance Automation The use of technology to streamline compliance monitoring, reporting, and enforcement, reducing reliance on manual administrative compensating controls.

Compliance Management The process of ensuring that an organization adheres to industry regulations, legal requirements, and internal security policies.

Configuration Management Database (CMDB) A centralized repository that stores information about IT assets, configurations, and their relationships.

Container Security A set of security measures applied to containerized applications, including image scanning, runtime monitoring, and access control to prevent container-based attacks.

Containerization The process of packaging applications and their dependencies into lightweight, portable containers.

Continuous Assessment and Adaptation The process of regularly evaluating and refining cybersecurity measures to respond to evolving threats and regulatory requirements.

Continuous Deployment (CD) An extension of Continuous Integration that automates the release of validated code into production, reducing the time between writing code and deploying it.

Continuous Integration (CI) A DevOps practice where developers frequently merge their code into a shared repository, triggering automated builds and tests to detect defects early.

Continuous Security Monitoring The process of continuously tracking and analyzing security events and system behavior to detect and respond to threats in real time.

Controls The specific tools, measures, and mechanisms used to enforce policies and manage risks. Controls can be classified into administrative, technical, and physical categories.

Crisis Management The coordination of resources and responses to mitigate and recover from major security incidents or operational failures.

Cyber Insurance A type of insurance coverage that helps organizations recover financially from cyberattacks, data breaches, and other security incidents.

Cyber Resilience The ability of an organization to prepare for, respond to, and recover from cyber threats. A cyber-resilient enterprise implements proactive security measures, continuous monitoring, and robust incident response strategies.

Cyber Threat Any malicious activity that targets an enterprise's IT environment, such as ransomware, phishing, DDoS attacks, and insider threats.

Cyber Threat Intelligence (CTI) Data and insights collected to understand and anticipate cyber threats, allowing for proactive risk mitigation.

Cybercrime Syndicates Organized groups that engage in cyber-enabled crimes such as fraud, ransomware, and data theft.

Cybersecurity Automation The use of AI and machine learning to enhance threat detection, streamline security operations, and reduce manual workload.

Cybersecurity Awareness Training Programs designed to educate employees on security best practices and threat recognition.

Cybersecurity Governance Framework A structured approach that organizations use to manage cybersecurity risks, ensuring alignment with business objectives, executive oversight, and regulatory requirements.

Cybersecurity Posture The overall strength and preparedness of an organization's cybersecurity defenses.

Cybersecurity Resilience The ability of an organization to withstand, recover from, and adapt to cyber threats and attacks.

Data Analytics The use of statistical and computational techniques to analyze large volumes of data for detecting security threats, operational inefficiencies, and business insights.

Data Breach An incident in which sensitive, protected, or confidential data is accessed, disclosed, or stolen without authorization. Breaches can lead to financial, legal, and reputational damage for organizations.

Data Loss Prevention (DLP) Tools and strategies designed to prevent sensitive data from being lost, stolen, or accidentally shared outside the organization.

Data Security Policy A policy that outlines how an organization classifies, stores, and protects data, ensuring confidentiality, integrity, and availability.

Decentralized Architecture A computing framework that distributes data processing across multiple nodes rather than relying on centralized data centers. Decentralized systems improve security, scalability, and fault tolerance.

Defense Strategies Security frameworks and methodologies used to anticipate, prevent, and mitigate cyber threats.

DevOps An organizational approach that fosters collaboration between software development, operations, and quality assurance teams to enable continuous software delivery through automation and iterative development.

DevSecOps A methodology that integrates security practices within the DevOps framework to ensure security is embedded in software development and deployment processes.

Digital Transformation The strategic adoption of digital technologies to enhance business processes, improve customer experiences, and drive operational efficiency. This transformation often includes cloud computing, AI, automation, and IoT.

Disaster Recovery (DR) A plan and set of processes designed to restore IT systems and data after a cybersecurity breach, system failure, or disaster.

Disaster Recovery Plan (DRP) A structured document outlining an organization's procedures to restore IT systems and data after a cyberattack, system failure, or natural disaster.

Edge Computing A distributed computing model that processes data closer to its source rather than relying solely on cloud data centers. Edge computing reduces latency and enhances real-time analytics.

Encryption A security method that converts data into a coded format to prevent unauthorized access. Only users with the correct decryption key can read the encrypted information.

Endpoint Detection and Response (EDR) A security solution that monitors and analyzes endpoint activity to detect and respond to threats.

Endpoint Security Protection for devices such as computers, mobile phones, and IoT systems that connect to an organization's network.

Enterprise Applications Large-scale software solutions designed to support business processes, such as Enterprise Resource Planning (ERP), Customer Relationship Management (CRM), and Supply Chain Management (SCM).

Enterprise IT Operations Management (ITOM) The processes and activities involved in ensuring a company's IT infrastructure functions properly, including monitoring, maintenance, and performance optimization.

Enterprise Resource Planning (ERP) A suite of integrated applications that help organizations manage business functions, including finance, HR, procurement, and operations. Modern ERP systems leverage AI and cloud computing for greater efficiency.

Enterprise Risk Management (ERM) A comprehensive approach to identifying, assessing, and mitigating risks across an organization, including IT and cybersecurity risks.

Extended Detection and Response (XDR) A security solution that integrates and correlates data across multiple security layers (e.g., endpoints, networks, cloud) to improve threat detection and response.

Firewall A network security system that monitors and controls incoming and outgoing network traffic based on predetermined security rules. Firewalls prevent unauthorized access and protect systems from cyber threats.

Forecasting Future Demand The process of predicting IT resource requirements based on past usage patterns and expected growth.

Global IT Compliance Ensuring IT operations across multiple countries adhere to regional laws and industry regulations.

Governance The framework of rules, practices, and policies that ensure an organization meets its business objectives while maintaining compliance with security and regulatory standards.

Governance Framework A set of policies, roles, responsibilities, and controls that ensure IT operations and cybersecurity align with organizational objectives.

Governance, Risk, and Compliance (GRC) The framework used by organizations to align IT and security with business objectives and regulatory requirements.

Help Desk A centralized IT support function that handles technical issues and service requests from users.

Hybrid Cloud An IT environment that combines on-premises infrastructure with cloud-based services, offering flexibility in data storage and application deployment.

Identity and Access Management (IAM) A framework for ensuring that the right individuals have appropriate access to enterprise resources. IAM solutions include multifactor authentication, role-based access control, and biometric verification.

Incident Management The process of identifying, assessing, and resolving IT issues to restore normal operations as quickly as possible.

Incident Response A structured approach to identifying, containing, and mitigating cybersecurity incidents. An Incident Response Plan (IRP) outlines procedures for handling breaches and minimizing damage.

Incident Response Playbook A predefined set of steps and best practices for handling different types of security incidents efficiently.

Industrial Internet of Things (IIoT) The use of IoT technology in industrial environments to enhance automation, predictive maintenance, and operational efficiency. IIoT devices collect real-time data from machinery, sensors, and production lines.

Information Security Standards Guidelines and best practices designed to help organizations protect their information assets, such as NIST, ISO 27001, and CIS.

Information Technology Infrastructure Library (ITIL) A widely used framework for IT service management that focuses on aligning IT services with business needs.

Infrastructure as Code (IaC) The practice of managing and provisioning IT infrastructure through machine-readable configuration files rather than manual processes.

Infrastructure as a Service (IaaS) A cloud computing model where enterprises rent virtualized computing resources such as servers, storage, and networking from a cloud provider. IaaS enables scalability without the need for physical hardware.

Insider Threat A security risk originating from employees, contractors, or other trusted insiders who may intentionally or unintentionally compromise security.

Integrated Assurance A strategic framework that aligns IT operations and cybersecurity to create a unified approach to risk management, compliance, and business resilience.

Intellectual Property Theft The unauthorized access or theft of proprietary business information, patents, or trade secrets.

Internet of Things (IoT) A network of connected devices, such as smart sensors and industrial control systems, that communicate and exchange data over the internet.

Intrusion Detection System (IDS) A security tool that monitors network traffic and system activities to detect suspicious behavior or security breaches. It provides alerts when potential threats are identified.

ISO 27001 An international standard for managing information security through a structured Information Security Management System (ISMS).

ISO/IEC 20000 An international standard for IT service management that ensures consistency and continuous improvement.

IT Infrastructure The combination of hardware, software, network resources, and services that support an organization's IT operations.

IT Lifecycle The entire process of planning, designing, deploying, managing, and retiring IT systems and infrastructure.

IT Service Management (ITSM) The practice of designing, delivering, managing, and improving IT services to meet the needs of a business.

Kernel-Based Virtual Machines (KVMs) A virtualization technology that allows multiple virtual machines to run on a single physical server with improved security isolation.

Key Performance Indicator (KPI) A measurable metric used to evaluate the effectiveness of security controls, including compensating controls, in mitigating risks and maintaining compliance.

Kubernetes Security The implementation of security best practices in Kubernetes environments, including network segmentation, admission controls, and runtime threat detection.

Least Privilege Principle A security best practice where users and systems are granted the minimum level of access required to perform their functions, reducing potential attack surfaces.

Legacy System An outdated IT system or application that may lack modern security features, often requiring compensating controls to maintain compliance.

Machine Learning (ML) A subset of AI that enables systems to learn from data and improve performance without explicit programming. ML is used in IT operations, cybersecurity, predictive maintenance, and business analytics.

Malware Malicious software designed to damage, disrupt, or gain unauthorized access to systems. Common types of malware include viruses, worms, trojans, ransomware, and spyware.

Managed Security Service Providers (MSSPs) Third-party organizations that provide outsourced security services, including threat monitoring, incident response, and compliance management.
Microsegmentation A security technique that divides networks into smaller segments to limit an attacker's ability to move laterally if they gain access.
Microservices Architecture A software development approach that structures applications as a collection of loosely coupled services. Microservices improve scalability, flexibility, and resilience in enterprise applications.
Multifactor Authentication (MFA) A security mechanism that requires users to verify their identity using multiple authentication factors (e.g., password, security token, fingerprint) before gaining access to a system.
Multilayered Security Approach A defense strategy that uses multiple security controls to protect IT infrastructure.
Network Monitoring The continuous tracking of network performance to detect, diagnose, and resolve issues.
Network Security A cybersecurity discipline that focuses on protecting an organization's digital infrastructure from unauthorized access, breaches, and cyber threats through tools like firewalls, IDS, and encryption.
Network Uptime The amount of time a network remains operational and accessible.
NIST Cybersecurity Framework (CSF) A framework developed by the National Institute of Standards and Technology to help organizations manage cybersecurity risks.
Operational Efficiency The ability to optimize IT resources, reduce redundancies, and enhance security without compromising performance or business continuity.
Orchestration The automated coordination of IT services, applications, and infrastructure to ensure seamless functionality.
Organizational Assurance The confidence that an organization's systems, processes, and security measures are effective and resilient against threats.
Patch Management The process of identifying, testing, and deploying security updates to software and operating systems to mitigate vulnerabilities.
Penetration Testing A controlled security assessment conducted by ethical hackers to identify vulnerabilities in IT systems and evaluate the effectiveness of security controls, including compensating controls.
Perimeter-Based Security A traditional security model that focuses on defending a network's outer boundaries rather than protecting individual assets and data.
Phishing A social engineering attack in which cybercriminals use fraudulent emails, messages, or websites to trick individuals into providing sensitive information such as login credentials or financial details.
Phishing Simulation A security awareness training technique that tests employees' ability to recognize and report phishing emails.
Physical Controls Security measures that protect the physical environment of an organization, such as access control systems, surveillance cameras, and secured data centers.
Policies High-level guidelines that provide direction for IT operations and security. Policies define expectations, help meet regulatory requirements, and establish the foundation for risk management.
Policy Enforcement The implementation of security and IT policies to ensure compliance and risk mitigation across an organization.
Primary Control The original security measure designed to mitigate specific risks within an IT environment. It is typically proactive and aligned with security best practices and compliance requirements.

Privileged Access Management (PAM) A security strategy that controls and monitors access to privileged accounts with high levels of system permissions. It helps reduce the risk of insider threats and unauthorized access.

Problem Management The process of identifying and eliminating the root causes of recurring IT issues.

Processes Step-by-step procedures that define how tasks should be completed in a standardized manner. In IT and cybersecurity, processes ensure consistency, efficiency, and structured responses to security incidents.

Quantum Computing An emerging computing paradigm that leverages quantum mechanics to solve complex problems exponentially faster than classical computers. Quantum computing has applications in cryptography, AI, and scientific research.

Ransomware A type of malware that encrypts a victim's data and demands payment (usually in cryptocurrency) in exchange for the decryption key. Ransomware attacks often target businesses, hospitals, and government institutions.

Real-Time Monitoring The use of automated tools to continuously track security threats, system performance, and network activity for immediate response.

Red Teaming The use of automated tools to continuously track security threats, system performance, and network activity for immediate response.

Regulatory Compliance The adherence to legal and industry-specific security requirements, such as GDPR, HIPAA, and PCI DSS.

Regulatory Compliance Frameworks Industry-specific regulations, such as NIST, ISO 27001, and SOX, that define best practices for cybersecurity governance.

Resiliency The ability of an organization to recover quickly from disruptions, including cyber incidents and IT failures.

Resource Allocation The strategic distribution of personnel, budgets, and technology across cybersecurity and IT operations to optimize security and performance.

Resource Optimization The process of strategically allocating IT and security resources to maximize efficiency, reduce redundancies, and improve protection.

Risk Acceptance The conscious decision by an organization to accept a specific level of security risk, due to either operational constraints or strategic business reasons.

Risk-Based Authentication (RBA) An adaptive security approach that dynamically adjusts authentication requirements based on real-time risk assessments, user behavior, and device posture.

Risk Management The process of identifying, assessing, and mitigating risks that could impact an organization's cybersecurity posture, business operations, and regulatory compliance.

Risk Mitigation The process of reducing security risks to an acceptable level through security controls, policies, and compensating controls when necessary.

Risk Transfer The process by which an organization shifts the responsibility for mitigating a security risk from one area to another, often as a consequence of implementing compensating controls.

Role-Based Access Control (RBAC) A security model that restricts system access based on predefined user roles, ensuring that users have only the permissions necessary for their tasks.

Scalability The ability of an IT system, application, or infrastructure to expand or contract resources dynamically based on demand. Cloud computing and microservices architectures improve scalability in enterprise IT.

Secrets Management The process of securely storing and managing sensitive data such as API keys, encryption keys, and credentials to prevent unauthorized access.

Secure Access Service Edge (SASE) A security model that integrates cloud-based networking and security services to protect remote workforces and cloud environments.

Secure Coding Practices A set of development guidelines and techniques that help prevent common security vulnerabilities, such as SQL injection and cross-site scripting (XSS).

Security Architecture A structured approach to integrating security measures into IT and business processes to protect critical assets.

Security Awareness Training Educational programs designed to teach employees about cybersecurity threats, best practices, and how to recognize and respond to cyber risks.

Security as Code (SaC) A security strategy that treats security configurations, policies, and compliance controls as code to ensure consistency and automation.

Security Controls Technical and administrative measures implemented to protect IT systems and data from security risks.

Security Controls Mapping The process of aligning security controls from different frameworks (e.g., NIST CSF, ISO 27001) to ensure comprehensive cybersecurity compliance.

Security Culture An organizational mindset that prioritizes cybersecurity best practices across all departments and employees.

Security Framework A structured set of policies and controls used to manage cybersecurity risks, such as the Risk Management Framework (RMF), Zero Trust Architecture (ZTA), and NIST Cybersecurity Framework (CSF).

Security Framework Integration The process of combining multiple cybersecurity and IT governance frameworks to create a unified and efficient security strategy.

Security Gap Analysis The process of identifying weaknesses in an organization's security framework and determining whether compensating controls are required to address those gaps.

Security Governance The policies, processes, and frameworks used to ensure that cybersecurity aligns with business goals and regulatory requirements.

Security Incident Dwell Time The amount of time an attacker remains undetected within a system or network after gaining unauthorized access.

Security Information and Event Management (SIEM) A centralized system that aggregates and analyzes security data from multiple sources to detect and respond to potential threats.

Security Observability The ability to monitor and analyze security-related data across an application and infrastructure stack to detect anomalies and potential threats.

Security Operations Center (SOC) A centralized unit responsible for continuous monitoring, threat detection, and incident response in an organization.

Security Orchestration, Automation, and Response (SOAR) A set of tools that automates security processes, helping organizations respond to threats efficiently while maintaining compliance

Security Policy Framework A structured set of guidelines, procedures, and controls that define how security is implemented and enforced in an organization.

Security Posture The overall security strength of an organization, based on the effectiveness of its security policies, controls, and risk management strategies.

Service Catalog A structured list of IT services offered by an organization, helping to manage IT resources and set clear expectations.

Service Design The phase in IT service management where IT services are planned to ensure security, scalability, and reliability.

Service-Level Agreement (SLA) A contractual agreement between an organization and a third-party service provider that outlines security expectations, responsibilities, and performance metrics.

Service Uptime The percentage of time that IT services and applications remain operational and accessible without disruptions.

Shadow IT The use of unauthorized applications and devices within an organization, increasing security risks.

Shared Responsibility Model A security framework in cloud computing that defines the responsibilities of cloud service providers and customers in securing cloud environments.

Shared Risk Management A collaborative approach where IT and cybersecurity teams jointly assess and mitigate security and operational risks.

Sherwood Applied Business Security Architecture (SABSA) A risk-driven enterprise security architecture framework that aligns IT security with business objectives.

Shift-Left Security A security strategy that incorporates security measures early in the SDLC, allowing vulnerabilities to be identified and mitigated before they reach production.

Siloed Approach A traditional IT and security structure where departments operate independently, leading to inefficiencies and security gaps.

Siloed Operations The separation of IT and cybersecurity functions into independent teams, which can create inefficiencies and security gaps.

Software Composition Analysis (SCA) An automated process that scans application dependencies to detect known vulnerabilities in third-party and open-source components.

Software-Defined Networking (SDN) A networking approach that separates the control plane from the data plane, enabling centralized management, automation, and improved network efficiency.

Software as a Service (SaaS) A cloud computing model where software applications are delivered over the internet on a subscription basis. SaaS solutions reduce the need for on-premises installations and maintenance.

Stakeholder Engagement The process of involving key personnel, including executives and department heads, in cybersecurity and IT operations decision-making.

State Sponsored Cyber Attacks Cyberattacks conducted or backed by national governments to achieve strategic objectives.

Static Application Security Testing (SAST) A security testing method that analyzes source code, bytecode, or binary code for vulnerabilities without executing the application.

Supply Chain Management (SCM) The use of technology to optimize the flow of goods, services, and information across a supply chain. AI and blockchain are increasingly integrated into SCM for enhanced visibility and efficiency.

Supply Chain Security Measures taken to secure third-party vendors, contractors, and service providers to prevent security breaches originating from external sources.

Tactics, Techniques, and Procedures (TTPs) Methods used by threat actors to carry out cyberattacks, including reconnaissance, exploitation, and persistence mechanisms.

Technical Controls Technology-based security measures such as firewalls, IDS, encryption, and MFA.

Technology Optimization The practice of streamlining and integrating security tools to improve efficiency, reduce redundancy, and enhance threat detection capabilities.

Threat Actors Individuals or groups that engage in cyberattacks, including hackers, nation-states, and insider threats.

Threat Detection The process of identifying potential security risks, malicious activities, or system vulnerabilities through monitoring and analysis.

Threat Hunting The proactive search for cyber threats that have bypassed traditional security defenses.

Threat Intelligence The process of collecting, analyzing, and applying information about cyber threats to improve an organization's security posture. It enables proactive threat mitigation.

Threat Landscape The overall cybersecurity risks faced by an organization, influenced by evolving attack methods and vulnerabilities.

Threat Modeling A proactive approach to identifying potential security threats, attack vectors, and vulnerabilities to mitigate risks before software deployment.

The Open Group Architecture Framework (TOGAF) A framework for enterprise architecture development that integrates IT processes with business goals.

Tool Sprawl The excessive accumulation of security tools that leads to inefficiencies, operational complexity, and reduced visibility into security threats.

Version Control Systems (VCS) Tools such as Git that track and manage changes to source code over time, enabling collaboration and rollback capabilities.

Virtual Private Network (VPN) A secure communication method that encrypts internet traffic, ensuring safe and private online activity over public or untrusted networks.

Virtualization The process of selecting, evaluating, and maintaining relationships with third-party IT service providers.

Visibility Gaps Blind spots in an organization's IT infrastructure where security teams lack sufficient insight into system activity, increasing vulnerability to threats.

Vulnerability A weakness in software, hardware, or security controls that can be exploited by attackers to gain unauthorized access to a system or network.

Vulnerability Assessment A systematic evaluation of an organization's IT infrastructure to identify, prioritize, and remediate security weaknesses.

Workforce Development The process of training and equipping cybersecurity professionals with the necessary skills to manage cyber threats effectively.

Zero-Day Vulnerability A security flaw that is unknown to the software vendor and has no available patch. Cybercriminals often exploit zero-day vulnerabilities before they are detected and fixed.

Zero Trust Architecture A security framework that requires strict identity verification and continuous monitoring, assuming no system is inherently trusted.

Zero Trust Security Model A security approach where every access request is verified, regardless of whether it originates from inside or outside the organization.

Index

Q

R

S

T

U

V

W

Z

For Product Safety Concerns and Information please contact our EU
representative GPSR@taylorandfrancis.com
Taylor & Francis Verlag GmbH, Kaufingerstraße 24, 80331 München, Germany

www.ingramcontent.com/pod-product-compliance
Ingram Content Group UK Ltd.
Pitfield, Milton Keynes, MK11 3LW, UK
UKHW052219190926
475702UK00006B/1110
9781032910734